Wendar-Shuban

CHANGING PARTY COALITIONS

CHANGING PARTY COALITIONS:

THE MYSTERY OF THE
RED STATE-BLUE STATE ALIGNMENT

Jerry F. Hough

Agathon
New York

Library of Congress Cataloging-in-Publication Data —

Hough, Jerry F., 1935-
    Changing party coalitions: the mystery of the red state-blue state
alignment / Jerry F. Hough.
        p. cm.
    Includes bibliographical references and index.
    ISBN-13: 978-0-87586-407-5 (trade paper : alk. paper)
    ISBN-10: 0-87586-407-4 (trade paper : alk. paper)
    ISBN-13: 978-0-87586-408-2 (hard cover : alk. paper)
    ISBN-10: 0-87586-408-2 (hard cover : alk. paper)
    [etc.]
    1. Party affiliation—United States. I. Title.

JK2271.H68 2006
324.273'11—dc22

                            2005032549

Printed in the United States

PREFACE

The book is not a distillation of the conventional wisdom on American politics and history. I have a very unusual perspective for a scholar writing about the evolution of the American political system. From the mid-1950s until the mid-1990s I was known as a specialist on comparative government, first of all, on the Soviet Union. I abandoned teaching and research on Russia in the late 1990s, and I have only taught the courses on the US Presidency at Duke University since then. This book essentially expands on what I have been teaching.

The change in the focus of my research and teaching did not, however, change the basic questions that I have worked on since the mid-1950s: the relationship of long term economic development and political institutions. This was the central question about the Soviet Union at the time of Joseph Stalin's death in 1953 when I was a college undergraduate, and it was always the focus of my work on the Soviet Union and post-Soviet Russia.

The goal of my recent work has been to look at the American experience in order better to understand the way that states, markets, and democracies develop and the way in which effective and stable ones can be created and maintained. The American experience is not incorporated in the theories of comparative politics and nation-building because it has been too encased in mythology. The taboos were created to help solve the North-South conflict and the antagonistic relationship of European-American "races." Now that these problems have been solved, it is time to break the taboos.

My interest in American politics and history did not begin in the 1990s. My first memory of public events was hearing the news of the bombing of Pearl Harbor, when I was a six-year-old in Bremerton, Washington, the great naval port on the West Coast. I saw the submarine nets on the ferry trips to Seattle, and I saw the ships come in from the Pacific wars for repairs. My father, a machinist foreman, moved to an experimental rocket base in the California desert where he remained until his retirement.

My parents came from Asheville, North Carolina, and we often drove across the country to visit relatives. The opening pages of this book on the old South do not come primarily from research. My parents were also typical representatives of the ethnic groups found in western North Carolina, my father coming from German-American roots and my mother Scotch-Irish ones. All of this combined to give me an intense interest in American history.

The courses I currently teach at Duke on the US Presidency are not the first that I have taught on the United States. At the University of Illinois, I taught in freshman courses that centered on the US in comparative perspective. At the University of Toronto, all my courses dealt with the Soviet-American-Canadian comparison. At Duke University in the 1970s I taught courses on American political participation, as well as the Soviet Union.

In addition, however, I was a very active participant in the American debates on Soviet-American relations beginning in the 1960s and continuing through the 1990s. As such, I developed a very keen sense of which aspects of the American foreign policy process could not be discussed at the time. Republican Presidents, after all, always improved relations with the Soviet Union, and Democratic Presidents always had severe conflict with that country. Even though the rhetoric of the two parties made this seem almost a chance occurrence, this was not the case.

It became clear that the conflicts between Britain and Germany affected the two largest ethnic groups in America — my ethnic groups, the British-Americans and the German-Americans — as deeply as policy toward Cuba affects the Cuban-Americans in recent decades. I came to understand the crucial role of European-American ethnicity in US policy toward Europe. I came to understand that the consistent pro-détente position of the Republican Party, the party of the Northern British-American and German-American Protestants, came from the party's need to hold its coalition together. This all led me to look at earlier stages of American history to see where and how this coalition originated.

This short biographical survey is important for two reasons. First, it helps to explain why, besides my comparative background and political experience, this book has a very atypical different perspective. My ethnicity and Southern roots not only created a sensitivity to the conflicts between the North and the South and those between the British-Americans and German-Americans in the 20th century, but also removed any of the psychological awkwardness that those of different backgrounds might have in breaking the taboos on these subjects. I have no desire to offend the memory of my father and mother or their traditions. I firmly believe that I have not done so.

The second reason for the biographical introduction is to make clear that I would have a hopeless task in trying to acknowledge the debts I have incurred. There are too many crucial ones over too long a period.

I do have confident memories about certain early debts. They obviously include my parents, but also my key early professors. Those in my first American history course in the 1951-1952 academic year were the great specialist on the Western movement, Frederick Merk, and Arthur Schlesinger, Sr. (I may be the only person alive who still thinks of Arthur Schlesinger, Jr., now 88 years old, as a young whippersnapper.) Stalin died during my first class on the Soviet Union. It was taught by Merle Fainsod, a great Americanist and a great specialist on the Soviet Union who became the supervisor of my doctoral dissertation.

Perhaps my greatest debt at Harvard is to William Yandell Elliott, who was given the task of being my tutor in my junior and senior year and who supervised my honors thesis on American policy toward the Soviet Union from 1940 to 1946. At that time Elliott was a close adviser to Vice President Richard Nixon and the dissertation supervisor of Henry Kissinger — and, as such, had a key unrecognized role in bringing the two together. I learned about the problems of nuclear deterrence from Elliott five years before Kissinger was to make the arguments in public. But most of all Elliott delighted in teaching a young boy from the California desert the insider's perspective on how Washington politics really worked.

Others also come to mind. Talcott Parsons and Barrington Moore infused Soviet studies at Harvard with a developmental perspective. I took courses from Zbigniew Brzezinski, Jimmy Carter's National Security Adviser, and was the teaching assistant for Marshall Shulman, who was to become the adviser on the Soviet Union to Cyrus Vance, Carter's Secretary of State. Never was I a more confident — or accurate — forecaster than on the problems Carter would have in his foreign policy when he gave both of my former professors a key role in his Administration. Yet, I learned an enormous amount from the conflicting perspectives of the two. There are many others from whom I have, no doubt, stolen many ideas, but without remembering which ones.

It seems to me wrong to mention any of the thousands and thousands of scholars, government officials, and students with whom I have had contact both directly and through their writing in subsequent years. The network of influences has simply been too great and too complex for me to trust memories. To mention some whom I absolutely know deserve thanks would be to fail to mention others whose impact has faded in my memory and who rightly would be offended. Perhaps other students will forgive me, however, if I do express my thanks to the large number of Duke students who took my courses on the presidency, served as guinea pigs while I learned, and gave me ideas and corrected mistakes in ways they never knew.

I also would like to mention several persons who had an enormous impact through their institutional as well as intellectual position: H. Gordon Skilling, who brought me to Toronto; James David Barber, who brought me to Duke and whose courses on the presidency I now teach; John Steinbruner, who was responsible for my 20 extremely fruitful years at the Brookings Institution.

Personal debts are also too numerous to mention. It would, however, be wrong not to thank Jean Marshall Crawford, who has taught me much about politics and especially the women's movement over nearly twenty years. Similarly, the sociologist Susan Goodrich Lehmann was my chief collaborator on public opinion surveys in the Soviet Union in the 1990s and greatly broadened my perspective on a number of issues. She also was extremely kind in giving the manuscript a close editorial review and in helping with the tables.

The archive work that underlies this book is more extensive than indicated in the footnotes and bibliography, and it would not have been possible without countless archivists. I have never met a uniformly more helpful group of people.

Finally, I would like to thank Andrea Sengstacken for her patience as she edited the manuscript at Algora Publishing.

It is customary to absolve any whose help is acknowledged from any mistakes. That is probably wrong, for some people who were either mentioned or thanked generally undoubtedly contributed to my errors as well as my insights. But, of course, it is my poor judgment that led me to retain erroneous analyses and to fail to respond properly to those who had it right and tried to correct me.

TABLE OF CONTENTS

CHAPTER 1. INTRODUCTION

The 1950s through the 1970s were a period of great political turmoil in the United States. The media directed its attention at the dramatic events of the black revolution, the anti-Vietnam demonstrations, and the women's liberation movement, but some of the most fundamental changes were less visible. The relations between North and South were highly confrontational, but the period actually led to the end of the historic North–South conflict that had defined the America political system since the Revolution. This required a fundamental change in party alignment.

The two parties have been groping for three decades to find a satisfactory new set of coalitions, but they have thus far failed. The red state–blue state alignment produces narrow and polarized electoral results in a society that is not polarized. Both parties have structured their economic policy so as to try to maximize their support in the upper class of the population — the 25% of the population that makes above $75,000 a year in family income. Without any meaningful choice on economic questions, voters have been forced to choose between the parties on the basis of cultural issues alone. Those of middle income are highly alienated because neither party focuses on their economic interests, and the result may be explosive if major economic difficulties develop.

In essence, the two parties have gone back to the period prior to 1933 when they did not compete on economic issues. The Constitution had been designed to guarantee autonomy for the South, and this was restored after the Civil War. The Democrats formed an alliance between the conservative Southern elite and the conservatives of New York and New Jersey, while the Republicans united well-to-do Easterners with populist Midwesterners. This pushed the Republican Party just marginally to the left of the Democratic Party on both economic and social issues, and Theodore Roosevelt correctly called the Democrats a party of "rural toryism."[1] Today the middle income whites vote as if they believe that the Democrats are once again to the right of the Republicans on economic questions.

In 1933, however, Franklin Roosevelt moved the Democratic Party from the right side of the economic spectrum to the left side, and he took measures that clearly were unconstitutional by existing Supreme Court interpretations and by the rules of the game that the Founding Fathers had established. Then in 1937 the President proposed an expansion in the number of Supreme Court Justices to force a change in its interpretation of the Constitution. The highly credible nature of the threat induced the old Court to reinterpret some of the powers of the federal government. Roosevelt's intention was to legalize his New Deal economic policy, but in the process he inevitably ended the historic guarantee of autonomy to the South.

The redefinition of the powers of the federal government made a party realignment inevitable. Yet the actual realignment was to take over three decades. It only began when Truman proposed civil rights legislation in 1948 and when Dwight Eisenhower and Lyndon Johnson then enacted it. It was not completed until the 1980s. Indeed, the current alignment seems very unlikely to survive for any length of time in its present form.

In part, the process of party realignment took so long because the old alignment itself had lasted for almost two centuries. But, in addition, ancient antagonisms greatly complicated the formation of new party alliances. Those between Northern and Southern white Protestants dated back to the British civil wars and probably earlier. If the South were to feature party competition, Southern Protestants would have to ally with at least some Northern Protestants and/or with different Northern non-Protestants. A new sense of community had to be created between North and South — and at a time when the North was forcing the South to change its behavior toward blacks.

The attitude of many Northern and Southern Protestants toward non-Protestants was even more hostile. The European-Americans outside the South had called each other "races" prior to World War II, and the word connoted the kind of emotion we attribute to it today. Indeed, the phrase "race, creed, and color" was not redundant, and "race" referred primarily to white "races." A firm in the 1930s could answer a survey on its hiring practices by saying "no colored hired in office [and] no discrimination as of race."[2]

The greatest problem for European-Americans in the North in the 20th century resulted from World Wars I and II. Since almost all their homelands were at war, the European-Americans naturally reacted to US policy in Europe as the Cuban-Americans have reacted to policy toward Cuba. Yet the two main protagonists, the British-Americans and German-Americans, were not tiny minorities like the Cubans; each constituted a quarter of the white population. The conflict among European-Americans over European policy remained so intense after World War II that it produced McCarthyism from 1946 to 1954.

---

1. Patricia O'Toole, *When Trumpets Call: Theodore Roosevelt After the White House* (New York: Simon & Schuster, 2005), p. 142.
2. Claudia D. Goldin, *Understanding the Gender Gap: An Economic History of American Women* (New York: Oxford University Press, 1990), pp. 147 and 249, n14.

In addition, while new coalitions and programs would be part of the new party alignments, their nature was not foreordained. As late as the 1950s and 1960s, politicians and political observers usually foresaw a continuation of the old party strategies. The Republicans had been the culturally liberal party of the middle class in the mainline Protestant churches of the North, and the party was building its Southern base among like-minded voters. It seemed likely to continue to do so.

Franklin Roosevelt and Harry Truman had added Northern Protestants to the Democratic non-Protestant base with a New Deal economic policy and a moderately conservative cultural policy associated with the Catholic Church. This policy should have been attractive to many of the poor Evangelicals of the South who were suspicious of the mainline Protestant churches. The spectacular failure both of Barry Goldwater's "red state" strategy in 1964 and then of George McGovern's "blue state" cultural strategy in 1972 strengthened the expectation that old party programs would continue.

Yet, in practice, the Evangelicals came to define the cultural face of the mainstream-Protestant Republican Party, and the McGovern supporters came to define the cultural face of the Catholic Democratic Party. The Democrats abandoned the New Deal economic strategy, and the two parties essentially ceased to compete on economic issues. The result was a highly unnatural and polarized party alignment based on cultural issues in a country that was not culturally polarized. The result was the neglect of economic issues in a country deeply worried about the economic situation and alienated from both parties because of it.

The main purpose of this book is to analyze the unexpected change in party strategy since 1975 and to explain how such an unnatural new party alignment occurred. In addition, however, the book deals with the future. The stability of the present party alignments seems to depend on a high level of personal consumption based on personal debt, on the use of housing equity for consumption, on a foreign trade deficit, and on a low saving rate. If, as most economists agree, this is not sustainable, then the present party strategies and the strange red state–blue state alignment will be very difficult to maintain. If so, the political stratum needs to be thinking about new party strategies. This book is intended to help in that process.

THE FORGOTTEN POLITICAL WORLD OF THE PAST

In the two elections of the 1990s, the Democratic presidential and vice presidential candidates both came from Confederate states, and that Democratic ticket won each election comfortably. In 1994, the son of a prominent Connecticut Yankee family was elected governor of Confederate Texas as the candidate of Abraham Lincoln's party. He then won reelection in 1998 in a landslide. In the 2000 presidential election, both major-party candidates came from states of the Confederacy. The Republican Texan swept all the states of the Confederacy and also the three most southern slave states that had stayed with the Union. White Southerners voted overwhelmingly for this Republican. The only exception was Florida south of Orlando, an area that was settled largely by Northerners.

When the National Cathedral in Washington, DC held a memorial service for the victims of the terrorist attacks of September 11, 2001, President George W. Bush approved every detail of the program. The closing number was the battle song of the Union Army in the Civil War, *The Battle Hymn of the Republic*. No one thought that this was strange. Instead, the service was universally hailed as a healing event that brought the country together.

None of this would have been remotely possible as recently as the early 1970s. The Republicans had no chance in the South until 1952 and made no effort to compete. The Democrats had not nominated a presidential candidate from a Confederate or even a border state between 1848 and 1948.[3] Indeed, no candidate from a former slave state was nominated until 1976 except for two vice presidents, Harry Truman and Lyndon Johnson, each of whom had become President when their predecessors died. A person driving through the United States in the 1940s and 1950s might hear *The Battle Hymn of the Republic* on the radio in the North, but never in the South. Instead, Southern radio played *Dixie*, the battle song of the Confederate Army.

In other respects, too, the American political scene today would be unrecognizable to a sophisticated observer from the 1930s. The Democratic Party had primarily been the party of the South, and it had been on the right side of the political spectrum prior to 1933. It was truly revolutionary when Franklin Roosevelt shifted it to the left side of the spectrum during the Great Depression. Conservatives worried that Roosevelt, like the first moderate revolutionaries of the French or Russian Revolution, was unintentionally preparing the way for a more violent revolution and for dictatorship.

The quite responsible Robert Taft, the son of President William Howard Taft, thought in 1936 that Roosevelt was introducing a socialist policy and worried that "no democracy has ever succeeded in operating a socialistic state." He added, "I do not say, and no Republicans have said, that President Roosevelt is a Communist, but his policy of planned economy, if persisted in, will make democracy impossible.... Every radical party feels that four years more of Roosevelt will put it in a position seriously to enter the contest in 1940."[4]

Racial concerns and issues were crucial in politics in the 1930s, but they were totally different from those we take for granted today. When top New Deal reformers were later interviewed, they asserted that no one gave any thought to blacks at the start of the Roosevelt Administration because the issue had no political importance.[5]

---

3. A partial exception was Woodrow Wilson, who was born and raised in the South but moved to the North in his twenties. He became president of Princeton University and then governor of New Jersey, the post he held at the time of his nomination as President.
4. Speech of Robert A. Taft, Ardmore, Pennsylvania, October 21, 1936, pp. 7–8. Robert A. Taft papers, Box 1291, Library of Congress. (The full reference to this archive collection and those cited later will be found in the bibliography.)
5. Nancy J. Weiss, *Farewell to the Party of Lincoln: Black Politics in the Age of FDR* (Princeton: Princeton University Press, 1983), p. 350.

The crucial "racial" conflicts of the 1930s involved European-Americans, and they seriously distorted American foreign policy both in the 1930s and the 1940s.

Everyone knew the mistreatment of blacks in the South was a festering sore and eventually would have to be addressed.[6] Yet Northerners knew little about the South. Except for Southern border areas, Northerners seldom visited the South or vacationed there. The Disney World area did not exist as an entertainment center. Orange County, which contains Orlando and the surrounding amusement centers, reflected its name in 1940 and had only 70,000 people. It had a population of 965,000 in 2003.[7]

James Byrnes of South Carolina, Roosevelt's real majority leader in the Senate in the 1930s, accurately caught the ignorance of the North in a story he told local audiences in the 1930s. In this story, a Northern couple was driving through South Carolina and noticed Spanish moss hanging from the trees. When the wife asked what it was, her husband answered, "That must be the Mardi Grass we've heard so much about." Television did not exist to show the South to Northerners, and only Eleanor Roosevelt's visits to the Southern poor resulted in some brief images on the newsreels that were shown in movie houses at the time. People knew that President Roosevelt went to Warm Springs, Georgia, to swim to strengthen his legs, but few understood that this was his privately-owned and segregated farm, not a spa.

The South was, indeed, almost a strange foreign country, especially outside the major cities. Statues of rebel leaders were everywhere, leaders who would have been hanged in many countries after such a rebellion. Southern schools taught a history of "the war between the states" that was very different from that taught in Northern schools. The sermons of Evangelical ministers filled the Southern radio airways.

In 1930, 74% of American blacks (the polite word used at the time, "Negro," was Spanish for "black") lived in the rural South where they received virtually no education. Most "urban" blacks were living in small towns such as Selma, Alabama, having recently come from rural areas. Since blacks were so poorly educated, it was natural that most urban and rural blacks would lead a life that was racially segregated on an informal basis. Yet all "blacks," even the most educated and those whose ancestry was largely European "white," were subject to the same legally-enforced segregation.

Unlike the attitude in India about Untouchables in the past, however, white Southerners welcomed close contact with blacks in many settings. Blacks served as maids and cooks in white homes and sometimes even nursed white babies. Adlai Stevenson was criticized in 1952 when he introduced his black nursemaid to a crowd in Kentucky during his presidential campaign, apparently to show his contact with blacks. A black critic complained that "Nurse Maids and Black Mammas are symbols of a system which we would like to forget forever."[8] Blacks could not normally enter

---

6. The classic statement of this thesis which was universally known among the educated population was Gunner Myrdal, *An American Dilemma: The Negro Problem and Modern Democracy* (New York: Harper & Brothers, 1944).

7. *Sixteenth Census of the United States: 1940 — Population*, Vol. 2, Part 1, p. 45 (Washington, D.C.: US Government Printing Office, 1943); *2005 County and City Extra: Annual Metro, City, and County Data Book* (Lanham, Md: Bernan Press, 2005), p. 142.

white movie theaters, but black women were readily sold tickets to such theaters as babysitters if they had white children with them.

As the reforming Southern humorist Harry Golden pointed out, the requirements of trade and business had led to nearly universal voluntary "vertical desegregation" in the South. So long as people were standing, there was little segregation. This was true of grocery store lines, lines for bank tellers, stand-up places at lunch counters. But the law that permitted blacks and whites to stand together in the pickup line at a restaurant would not allow them to sit at the lunch counter in the same restaurant. Political rallies in which people stood to hear a candidate could be integrated, but not a rally in an auditorium. This posed a growing problem for Democratic presidential campaigns in the South.

Golden advised those involved in a desegregation controversy on public libraries in Charlotte, North Carolina, to follow Southern mores and to remove the reading tables. That way everyone would stand at a counter or lectern. This idea actually was adopted, and it achieved desegregation peacefully. Golden then went on a flight of fancy. He wrote that the obvious solution to school segregation was to take away the seats to school desks. No one could object to students standing at their desks, he said. And think of the money that could be saved. He also had a "White Baby Plan" in which blacks would borrow white children when they wanted to see a movie at a white theater.[9]

John Dollard seems right that the main issue was relative status.[10] Educated Southerners were pleasing "the crackers," as they called the poor whites. The poor whites were being told that they were inherently equal to educated whites and superior to educated non-whites. The Southern practice of calling all black men "boy" was highly revealing. "Boy" basically is a friendly and even affectionate word, but it denotes a person not ready to make adult decisions. A boy, of course, is also not ready to vote, and the denial of the vote to most blacks removed a large number of poor people from the electorate.

The political alignment chosen by the South in the Democratic Party also led in a conservative direction. The South was the poorest and most rural area in the country, and as it exported commodities, it had an economic interest in low tariffs. Its natural partner in the Democratic Party was the rural Midwestern and Prairie region that exported grain and that also had an interest in low tariffs and in regulation of Eastern industry and railroads. From the 1870s onward, the South often actually did cooperate with the West and Midwest in the Congress, at least on issues

---

8. The letter was quoted in a letter of Max M. Kampelman (legislative counsel to Senator Hubert Humphrey) to Arthur Schlesinger, Jr., September 25, 1952, Adlai Stevenson Papers, Box 215, Folder 8, Princeton University. For the discussion of the Mammy in Southern culture and literature, see Grace Elizabeth Hale, *Making Whiteness: The Culture of Segregation in the South, 1890–1940* (New York: Pantheon Press, 1998), pp. 85–119.
9. "The Vertical Negro Plan," Harry Golden, *Only in America* (Cleveland, Ohio: World Pub. Co., 1958), pp. 21.
10. John Dollard, *Caste and Class in a Southern Town* (New Haven: Yale University Press, 1937); John Dollard, Neal E. Miller, Leonard W. Doob, O. H. Mowrer, and Robert R. Sears, *Frustrations and Aggression.* (New Haven: Yale Univ. Press, 1939).

that dealt with monetary policy and regulation of railroads and large corporations. The Congressmen of the Midwest and South tended to vote together on the soft-money, pro-regulation side, while the Democratic Congressmen of the East voted conservatively.[11] In large part, this pattern was to continue well into the New Deal period.

The South's alliances in presidential politics were very different. After the Civil War, the South did not ally with the Midwestern Democrats to nominate candidates and write a platform, but allied with New York, New Jersey, and Connecticut — relatively industrialized and well-to-do states that had an economic interest in high tariffs. In cultural politics, the anti-Catholic South was allied with the Northern Catholic immigrants. This unnatural alliance within the Democratic Party created a similar anomaly in the Republican coalition, an alliance of the industrial and affluent of the East with the populists of the Midwest. Prior to 1932, the Republicans were a moderately liberal party on cultural issues, and they continued to be so on all cultural issues except anti-Communism. In the first decades of the 20th century, the Republicans were the party of women's rights and environmentalism (conservation, as it then was called) and the party for which blacks voted.

In the North, the Democrats were highly responsive to the Catholic Church, and the Church was less tolerant on cultural issues than it is today. Massachusetts and Connecticut legalized the sale of contraceptives to married couples only in the postwar period — and Connecticut only after the Supreme Court forced it to do so in 1965. The Democratic Woodrow Wilson was the President who segregated government buildings in Washington, DC and conducted the "Red Scare" in 1919 against socialists.[12] The Catholic Church seemed a natural ally for the Evangelicals and represented the main opposition to abortion in the 1976 campaign. Indeed, Samuel Alito's confirmation as a Supreme Court Justice created a Catholic majority for the first time, and they are the Court conservatives. The Evangelicals are the strongest supporters of these Catholic Justices.

Marin County north of San Francisco in California is the archetypical liberal county in the early 21st century, but it illustrates the nature of the old Republican Party. Marin County consistently voted Republican in the postwar world: Dwight Eisenhower over Adlai Stevenson 66% to 34% in 1956, Richard Nixon over John Kennedy 57% to 42% in 1960, Richard Nixon over Hubert Humphrey 50% to 44% in 1968, Nixon over George McGovern 52% to 46% in 1972, Gerald Ford over Jimmy Carter 53% to 43% in 1976, and Ronald Reagan over Carter by 46% to 36% in 1980. (In 1980, Marin County gave many votes to the third party candidate, John Anderson.)

Only in 1964 did Marin County vote for the Democrat Lyndon Johnson over Barry Goldwater. The county divided its vote evenly between Reagan and Walter

---

11. Carl V. Harris, "Right Fork or Left Fork: The Section–Party Alignment of Southern Democrats in Congress, 1873–1897," *The Journal of Southern History*, vol. XLII, no. 4 (November 1976), pp. 471–508.
12. One of best discussions of the politics of the Red Scare is a biography of the attorney general who was in charge of it. Stanley Coben, *A. Mitchell Palmer: Politician* (New York: Columbia University Press, 1963), pp. 196–216, 235–245, and 265–267.

Mondale in 1984 and moved decisively to the Democratic column only in 1988. It supported Michael Dukakis over George H.W. Bush by 59% to 40% in that year. Bill Clinton defeated Robert Dole 58% to 28% in the county in 1996, and Gore won 64% to 28% in 2000.[13] The character of Marin County did not change that much. Instead, it was responding to a change in the two parties. As Table 1 shows, Marin County was typical of many affluent counties in the North.

Table 1: Voting Percentages in Presidential Elections in Well-To-Do Northern Counties, 1952–2000

COUNTY	1952 R	1952 D	1960 R	1960 D	1976 R	1976 D	1980 R	1980 D	1984 R	1984 D	1988 R	1988 D	1992 R	1992 D	1992 P	2000 R	2000 D
Marin, CA	67	32	57	42	54	43	46	36	49	50	40	59	23	58	18	28	64
Fairfield, CT	61	39	53	47	58	41	55	28	66	34	59	40	43	39	19	43	52
DuPage, IL	76	24	69	30	69	28	64	34	76	24	69	30	48	31	21	55	42
Lake, IL	63	37	59	41	60	38	58	29	68	31	64	36	44	36	19	50	48
Kane, IL	68	32	64	36	62	36	62	28	69	30	64	35	44	35	21	55	43
Montgomery, MD	62	37	49	51	48	51	47	40	50	50	48	51	33	55	12	34	63
Norfolk, MA	65	34	47	53	45	51	45	39	54	46	48	51	32	46	21	34	59
Oakland, MI	72	27	54	45	58	39	55	35	67	33	61	38	44	39	17	48	49
Washtenaw, MI	67	33	61	39	51	46	42	44	51	48	47	52	30	53	16	36	60
Hennepin, MN	53	46	51	48	44	53	39	47	48	51	44	54	31	48	21	39	54
Bergen, NJ	69	30	59	41	56	43	56	34	63	36	58	41	44	42	13	42	55
Morris, NJ	72	27	64	36	61	37	61	28	72	29	68	31	52	32	16	54	43
Somerset, NJ	63	36	56	44	57	40	57	32	67	32	64	35	46	35	17	50	47
Monroe, NY	59	41	51	49	55	44	42	46	58	42	50	49	39	42	19	45	51
Nassau, NY	70	30	55	45	52	48	56	35	62	38	57	42	40	46	13	39	58
Rockland, NY	64	35	55	45	51	48	56	34	61	39	57	42	41	47	12	40	57
Westchester, NY	67	32	57	43	54	45	54	35	59	41	63	46	40	49	11	38	59
Geauga, OH	68	32	59	41	57	40	59	32	68	30	64	34	45	28	26	60	36
Lake, OH	60	40	49	51	51	47	50	41	59	40	57	42	39	36	25	50	45
Lorain, OH	56	44	47	52	55	43	50	40	51	47	47	52	31	43	26	43	53
Multnomah, OR	55	44	50	49	44	51	39	46	45	54	37	62	24	55	20	28	63
Washington, OR	64	35	59	41	58	39	51	34	63	47	52	46	34	40	25	46	49
Bucks, PA	63	38	54	46	51	47	56	33	63	36	60	39	38	39	22	46	50
Montgomery, PA	67	33	61	39	58	42	58	31	64	35	60	39	40	43	17	44	54
Fairfax, VA	61	39	52	48	54	45	57	31	63	37	61	38	44	42	14	49	48
Falls Church, VA	60	40	48	51	51	48	52	36	53	47	50	50	35	53	11	38	56
Benton, WA	57	42	52	47	64	33	65	26	69	30	65	34	43	31	25	64	33
King, WA	54	45	51	47	51	45	45	39	52	47	45	54	27	50	22	34	60

Source: The county-by-county voting for President, governor, and Senator in every election since 1953 is recorded in the biennial *America Votes*, published by CQ Press, Washington, DC. The co-editors varied, but the main editor until 2000 was Richard Scammon.

As the Republicans began to make inroads in the South, their first major support naturally came from members of the middle class who lived in the suburban ("blue") areas of the South. The South was beginning to industrialize and urbanize, and the growing middle class was the most willing to support desegregation. This class tended to vote Republican. A detailed examination of Thomas Dewey's support in the South in 1948 shows that he did best in the most urbanized states, in the larger

---

13. For the source of this information, see Table 1.

cities within them, and in the more affluent residential districts and precincts within these cities.[14]

An identical pattern was found in 1952 when Eisenhower won 45% of the Electoral College vote of the Confederate states and in 1956 when he won 53% of their votes.[15] He carried the Outer South — Florida, North Carolina, Tennessee, and Texas — but also the urban areas in the Deep South as well. As Kevin Phillips, an aide to Nixon's chief political adviser John Mitchell, expressed it, "the list of the General's victories and near victories reads like a gazetteer of the Confederacy — Charleston, Savannah, Mobile, Montgomery, Jackson, Natchez, Vicksburg, and New Orleans."[16]

It was natural that Eisenhower, as head of the first Republican Administration in twenty years, launched the first serious attack on segregation in the South. Truman's Chief Justice, Fred Vinson, had repeatedly tried to find ways to avoid the "Dread School" decision that people knew would eventually be coming.[17] His successor, the Republican Earl Warren, quickly led the Supreme Court in destroying the legal basis of segregation. Eisenhower was later to say that Warren's appointment was a mistake; he surely was not referring to the key desegregation decision, but to others. Warren had been the Republican governor of the second most populous state in 1953, a year when eight of the governors of the ten most populous Northern states were Republicans. All would have acted in a similar manner as Warren on segregation.

Dwight Eisenhower also was the first President to send troops to enforce desegregation at the Little Rock High School in Arkansas, and his administration was the first to pass voting rights legislation to protect black voting rights in the South — the Civil Rights Laws of 1957 and 1960. The Justice Department drafted the civil rights legislation, and all Republican Senators and 90% of Republican House members supported the 1957 law, but only 61% of the Democrats both in the Senate and in the House of Representatives.[18]

---

14. Samuel Lubell, *The Future of American Politics* (New York: Harper, 1952), pp. 113–114, 120–125, and 135.
15. Here and elsewhere in this book, statistics on the percentage of the popular vote and Electoral College vote by region and state are taken from or calculated from *The Congressional Quarterly's Guide to U.S. Elections*, 4th ed. (Washington: CQ Press, 2001), vol. 1, pp. 644–688 and 718–771.
16. Kevin P. Phillips, *The Emerging Republican Majority* (New Rochelle, NY: Arlington House, 1969), p. 199. For testimony by another high political adviser that Mitchell was "Nixon's closest political associate in government," see H. R. Haldeman, *The Ends of Power* (New York: Times Book, 1978), p. 217.
17. Lubell, *The Future of American Politics*, pp. 131–134.
18. William S. White, "House Passes Rights Bill; Senators Rule Out a Delay," and William S. White, "Senate Votes Rights Bill and Sends It to the President; Thurmond Talks 24 Hours," *The New York Times*, August 28, 1957, pp. 1 and 55, and August 30, 1957, pp. 1 and 20. See J. W. Anderson, *Eisenhower, Brownell, and the Congress: The Tangled Origins of the Civil Rights Bill of 1956-1957* (Tuscaloosa: University of Alabama Press, 1964).

THE STRANGE POLITICAL WORLD OF THE EARLY 21ST CENTURY

Obviously those living in 2075 will find political life in 2005 as strange as we find that in 1935. Unfortunately, of course, we can have no idea what people in the future will see as the most peculiar feature of the way we act and think. That almost surely will be something that we consider totally natural and take absolutely for granted.

Nevertheless, one aspect of American mentality and politics in the early 21st century that will seem strange is the widespread failure to realize that the very success of American efforts abroad will turn it into a middle-rank power in the 21st century. The only real alternative will be the political merger of the United States with Europe. The United States today has a population of 300 million people, while the world has 6.3 billion people. The ratio in 2075 is not likely to be much different, and a country with as few people as the United States simply will not be able to dominate such a populous world when most countries have become economically strong. Those in the future may wonder if an unconscious sense of this future (conscious to some extent in the case of China) lay at the base of the immense insecurity found in the United States at the turn of the century. The process of adjusting to the new national situation is likely to be turbulent.

As observers in the future look at the politics of the early 21st century, they are not likely to focus on the reasons for a party alignment that probably will be short lived. Or, at least, they will not focus on it unless it is seen as producing disastrous results. They will be interested in broader questions about the way in which both Democratic and Republican Presidents maximized short-term consumption instead of taking long-term considerations into account. They may well give far more attention than we do to the problem of the political institutional incentives that reward near-term behavior detrimental to the achievement of long-term goals. It is conceivable that institutional changes will have occurred that we consider unthinkable and undesirable.

To the extent that people in the future look at the red state–blue state party alignment, they will find the symbolic nature of early 21st-century politics most puzzling. The population overwhelmingly rejected political interference in the case of the brain-damaged Terri Schiavo, and surely the public was right. But what is one to say about hopeless constitutional amendments on gay marriage, about fierce battles to prevent oil drilling in protected areas in Alaska that are so remote that they will never be visited, about a politics that centers on an abortion issue that was decided 30 years ago, or about a polity in which "red" sections of the country almost totally immune from foreign terrorism were the most concerned about security measures against foreign terrorism?

The scholars of the future who will look closely at the politics of the early 21st century almost surely will wonder about the narrow focus on cultural issues at the time. Indeed, that is a question to which we already have reason to give more attention. Since the presidential election maps were virtually identical in 2000 and 2004, the "blue states" of the Democrats, the "red states" of the Republicans, and a few "battleground states" with a mixture of red and blue areas now seem permanent features of American political life. Yet the present alignment would have been thought a most improbable prediction in the mid-1970s.

Richard Nixon was a classic Republican moderate who followed the long-time cultural and economic policies of the party. His so-called "Southern strategy" focused on the more-educated voters in the South, and he was deeply suspicious of the religious right in the South and elsewhere. His victory in 1968 and especially his landslide victory in 1972 seemed to reaffirm the wisdom of the old Republican posture. The key development in the Republican Party's adoption of a red state strategy was the movement of the Evangelical Christians of the South from the Democratic Party to the Republican Party.

In the early 1970s, however, the old Democratic coalition seemed more attractive to the Evangelicals than the old Republican one. The Catholics seemed a more natural ally for the Evangelicals than the mainline Protestant churches. Church allegiance in America had always been strongly correlated both with income and values. Other than Unitarians, the Episcopalian Church always was the wealthiest of the Protestant sects and also culturally liberal. It naturally had also been heavily Republican. The next most affluent and culturally liberal Protestant denominations were the Presbyterians and Lutherans, and then came the Methodists. They too were usually Republican. The Baptists and especially the newer Evangelical churches were composed of the poorest and most culturally conservative elements of society.

The mainline Northern Protestant churches that were the base of the Republican Party had also been a leading force pushing black civil rights and women's rights. By contrast, the Catholic Church, a key part of the Northern Democratic base, had very conservative cultural values. During the 1976 presidential election, the Catholic Church was the center of opposition to abortion and *Roe v. Wade*, not the Evangelical Protestants. As a result, it was the major concern of those high in the campaign of Jimmy Carter.[19]

Economic factors also seemed to push the Evangelical Christians into alliance with the Catholics in the Democratic Party. The average income of Evangelical Christians was below that of the members of the mainline Protestant churches. The Catholics were relatively recent immigrants, and their average income was below that of the old-time Northern Protestants. The Evangelicals needed to overcome their old anti-Catholic prejudices, but they did this quite easily with the Democratic Jews as the two formed a coalition based on a common policy toward Israel. The common views of the Catholic and Evangelical Churches about abortion and *Roe v. Wade* should have made their cooperation even easier.

In fact, the Evangelical Christians *did* give their support in the mid-1970s to the Democrats. As a political adviser to Jimmy Carter, Peter Bourne, noted casually, southern Evangelical Christians were "Carter's most bedrock constituency."[20] The

---

19. The Jimmy Carter papers on the 1976 election in the Jimmy Carter Presidential Library show a continuous concern of all Carter political advisers with the Catholic Church and the "urban ethnics," as descendants of Catholic immigrants were called.
20. Peter G. Bourne, *Jimmy Carter: A Comprehensive Biography from Plains to Postpresidency* (New York: Scribners, 1997), pp. 347.

head of Carter's public opinion firm reported after the election that Carter had won because of the South and that his success in the South was especially great in the rural areas and small counties. Similarly, the secret to Carter's success in Pennsylvania, Ohio, Wisconsin, and other states was his ability to cut into traditional Republican margins in rural areas and small-town communities, and to some extent, in the suburbs. Had he not been able to better traditional showings in these areas, he would have lost.[21]

Even if the Evangelical Christians came to support the Republican Party in substantial numbers, nothing seemed more unlikely than that they would determine the cultural face of the party. Ronald Reagan carried almost all the blue states in 1980 and 1984, and his policy was far more nuanced than is remembered either by his most ardent supporters or his opponents. His hard-line Director of Management and the Budget, David Stockman, lamented that Reagan was "a consensus politician, not an ideologue.... He had no business trying to make a revolution because it wasn't in his bones." Similarly, Reagan's wife probably spoke for her husband when she told his chief of staff, "I don't give a damn about the right-to-lifers."[22] Reagan's successor, George H.W. Bush, won eight of the ten most populous non-slave states (California, Illinois, Indiana, Michigan, Missouri, New Jersey, Ohio, and Pennsylvania) and lost only Massachusetts and New York.

The only future political development that would have seemed as improbable in the mid-1970s as the role of the Evangelicals in the mainline-Protestant Republican Party was the similar victory of the white cultural radicals of the late 1960s in the Catholic Democratic Party. These radicals seemingly had been decisively discredited by McGovern's landslide defeat. The Democrats had won overwhelmingly in 1964 with Johnson's New Deal Policy and, despite the black revolution, alienation among the population was relatively low.[23] The Democrats had almost won with Hubert Humphrey in 1968 even in the face of the Vietnam War and the chaos at the Democratic Convention in Chicago. Yet the party barely won the 1976 election with Carter's more conservative economic policy even with the advantage of the Watergate scandal, the economic and foreign policy disaster of the 1975 oil crisis, and the fall of Saigon. The Democrats then lost heavily in 1980.

Surely the experience of the Democratic Party from 1964 to 1980 would lead it to return to its New Deal strategy. Yet, instead of moving to consolidate an alliance between the Catholics and the Evangelicals on the basis of common economic interests and cultural values, Carter deeply offended the leading Catholic politician in the country, Speaker of the House Tip O'Neill, and fired the leading Catholic in the cabinet, Secretary of Health, Education, and Welfare Joseph Califano. Both conflicts

---

21. Patrick H. Caddell, "Initial Working Paper on Political Strategy," December 10, 1976, Presidential Papers; Staff Offices — Press: Powell," pp. 8–9 and 14–15, Box 4, Jimmy Carter Presidential Library.

22. David A. Stockman, *The Triumph of Politics: How the Reagan Revolution Failed* (New York: Harper & Row, 1986), p. 9; Donald T. Regan, *For the Record: From Wall Street to Washington* (San Diego: Harcourt Brace Jovanovich, 1988), p. 77.

23. Paul R. Abramson, John H. Aldrich, and David W. Rohde, *Change and Continuities in the 1992 Election* (Washington, DC: CQ Press, 1994), p. 122.

were extremely well publicized and centered on Carter's unwillingness to continue New Deal policies in the health realm.[24]

When the low-income Evangelicals began shifting to the Republican Party on values issues, the Democrats still did not put them under cross pressure by appealing to their economic interests. Instead, the Democrats not only adopted the cultural values favored by the affluent suburbanites, but also the economic policy. The memoirs of the Clinton era, be they written by the conservative Robert Rubin, the liberal Robert Reich, or the President himself, agree that the guiding principle of economic policy in the Administration was to take measures to keep interest rates down. For better or for worse, the Democrats basically returned to the gold standard of Grover Cleveland. Although Clinton had campaigned for a middle class tax cut and a comprehensive health care plan, Bob Woodward reported that he was to declare to his economic team, "I hope you're all aware we're all Eisenhower Republicans.... We're Eisenhower Republicans. And we are fighting the Reagan Republicans. We stand for lower deficits and free trade and the bond market." Woodward said Clinton spoke with sarcasm but another liberal economist, Gene Sperling, confirms the statements and remembers taking them seriously and "recoiling." [25] He certainly was accurate.

Hence the polarized red-state/blue-state dichotomy of the 2000 and 2004 elections would have seemed a bizarre prediction in the early and mid-1970s, perhaps even in the early 1980s. This is particularly true if it had been foreseen that American society itself would not be deeply polarized in 2000 and 2004. After all, the great majority of American conservatives in 2005 are tolerant of gays, although not, of course, gay marriage. Liberal support for gay marriage is weak at best. President George W. Bush, like John Kerry, supported gay civil unions in the 2004 campaign. Abortion remains divisive, but most Americans accept it during the first five months of pregnancy. Most support parental notification for minors. In the economic sphere, there is broad public support in both parties for a government prescription drug policy and for greater regulation when scandals such as Enron occur.[26]

What changed the bizarre into the seemingly inevitable? Indeed, what turned cultural values into the main issue of the electoral struggle? Cultural issues, most recently Prohibition, had been most important prior to 1933 when neither party really competed for the vote of the lower and middle income with economic policies. During Roosevelt's four terms, however, no one talked about the importance of cultural issues, although such issues continued to exist. Prohibition, the most long-lasting major cultural issue of the previous century, disappeared almost immediately

---

24. See Tip O'Neill, *Man of the House: The Life and Political Memoirs of Speaker Tip O'Neill* (New York: Random House, 1987); Joseph A. Califano, *Governing America: An Insider's Report From the White House and the Cabinet* (New York: Simon and Schuster, 1981); Joseph A. Califano, *Inside: A Public and Private Life* (New York: Public Affairs, 2004).
25. Bob Woodward, *The Agenda: Inside the Clinton White House* (New York: Simon & Schuster, 1994), p. 165. See John F. Harris, *The Survivor: Bill Clinton in the White House* (New York: Random House, 2005), pp. 78-79 and 451.
26. Morris P. Fiorina, *Culture War? The Myth of a Polarized America* (New York: Pearson Longman, 2005).

from the political scene when Roosevelt became President. This created the impression that economic issues clearly were at the forefront, and cultural issues were secondary and were used primarily to hold the members of the "base" on the farther ends of the spectrum in place. Why did this change occur?

This book will argue that, in fact, the major reason that cultural issues are so important today is the lack of choice on economic issues. It will argue that much of middle-income and lower-income emotional resentment at the cultural values of the upper class with family income over $75,000 a year really reflects resentment at the economic policy of the government responsive to this class.

UNDERSTANDING AMERICAN POLITICAL DEVELOPMENT REALISTICALLY

The major purpose of this book is to address the questions raised in the last two paragraphs. It will attempt to illuminate and explain the evolution of the United States from the strange political world of the 1930s to the strange political world of the early 21st century. The book will give the most attention to the long process of realignment that stretched from the early 1950s through the early 1990s and to the demographic and institutional factors that shaped its outcome. However, Chapters 2 and 3 will examine the historical development of the Democratic and Republican coalitions that existed before and during the New Deal and created the starting point for change. It does not have space for a comprehensive exploration of the data on individual attitudes and voting, but, instead, focuses on the institutional questions of party coalitions and the strategies of presidential candidates. The sub-headings of sections in Chapters 2, 3, 6, 7, and 8 will include names such as Woodrow Wilson, Franklin Roosevelt, Harry Truman, Adlai Stevenson, John Kennedy, Jimmy Carter, Ronald Reagan, Bill Clinton, and George W. Bush.

The book will, first of all, focus on the conflict between North and South that was the key question of the Constitutional Convention. It also will emphasize the religious and ethnic conflict among European-Americans that permeated American society. These two conflicts shaped American political culture and party politics for nearly 200 years.

The basic disappearance of both the North-South conflict and the great antagonisms among the European-American religious and "racial" groups from the 1950s through the 1970s obviously had a most profound impact upon the party system. The impact is all the more profound because the transformation was largely unrecognized and because the implications for centuries-old political assumptions have not been rethought. We need to clarify our thinking as we move into a new century in which different conflicts and different problems will be coming to the fore. This book is intended to contribute to that process.

In broader perspective, the old party coalitions dissolved because the South inevitably became politically competitive as it, under pressure, changed its centuries-old treatment of blacks. Yet paths of historical evolution are not inevitable, and this seems particularly true of the coalitions that developed in the late 1990s. If the alternative paths are not properly appreciated, we are unlikely to see the alternatives that are open today and in the future.

Understanding the politics of the past is, unfortunately, not a simple task. Politicians always engage in spin, but opposing politicians and skeptical journalists usually try to inform the attentive public about the real motivations behind the real policies. With the passage of time, however, memories fade, and we are left with the words of politicians and come to take them seriously. James Madison was the great party organizer and strategist of his time — the Karl Rove of his day as he created the Jeffersonian Republican Party. Unfortunately, his spin has now become political philosophy — or, really Political Philosophy. His "Republicanism" has become "republicanism." This is a general problem, but it is especially great if some aspect of politics is so sensitive that it was not discussed at the time or was discussed in code words.

The political discourse of the 20th century featured two great taboos. One was the nature of the Constitutional Convention and the Constitution it produced. Scholars could only hint that the convention was a velvet military coup d'état against the Articles of Confederation, a coup led by the man who controlled the army. This meant that scholars could not discuss George Washington's motivations — his absolute obsession with national security, coupled with his strong desire for a federal government (really a confederate government in domestic affairs) that could not threaten slavery in the South, including at Mount Vernon. Scholars, let along those writing for a general audience, had to treat Alexander Hamilton and James Madison as independent giants, not the persons they really were: the chief political aides of Washington for the North and South respectively, the former 28 years old in 1785 and the latter 34.

Since the Progressive historians of the first four decades of the 20th century wanted to increase the economic power of the federal government, they naturally claimed that the Founders were driven by economic considerations and intended to establish a strong central government. In fact, the Convention deliberately created the government that Washington wanted — one that had already been proposed by Thomas Jefferson in a letter to his fellow Virginian slaveholder, James Madison, in December 1786. The goal of the Philadelphia meeting, Jefferson wrote, should be "to make us one nation as to foreign concerns & keep us distinct in Domestic ones."[27]

The institutional checks and balances of the Constitution were not the expression of an abstract philosophy about how best to organize government, but were designed to give each section of the country a veto on domestic policy.[28] The great unspoken decision at the Convention was to maintain an equal number of slave and non-slave states. The granting of two Senators to each state thus gave each section the same number of Senators. The power to confirm appointees and treaties

---

27. "From Jefferson," December 16, 1786, in Robert A. Rutland, ed., *The Papers of James Madison* (Chicago: University of Chicago Press, 1975), vol. 9, p. 211.
28. The decision to break the unspoken rule on the equal number of states with the admission of California in 1850 helped lead to the Civil War. See Barry R. Weingast, "Political Stability and Civil War: Institutions, Commitments, and American Democracy," in Robert H. Bates, ed., *Analytic Narratives* (Princeton: Princeton University Press, 1998), pp. 150-153 and 157-158.

in the Senate gave each section a veto. The strange runoff in the presidential election in the House of Representatives gave each state a single vote and, therefore, each section the same number of votes and a veto in an Electoral College election that was not expected to produce a majority. The Vice President was given a tie-breaking vote in the Senate, therefore creating two vetoes, one for each section, if the President and Vice President were always from a different section.

As a result, each section was given the autonomy in domestic concerns that Jefferson proposed and institutional guarantees to try to protect this autonomy. Even after the Civil War, the North soon gave the South autonomy to treat the former slaves as if it had won the Civil War. This autonomy lasted for an improbable three-quarters of a century. The latter point was especially difficult to acknowledge directly and was hidden in code words such as "federalism," "states' rights," and "minority rights," and in an unwarranted glorification of "Madisonian democracy." In the past, the reason for the code words was understood, but over time younger generations were less likely to appreciate the true meaning of a number of them.

The second great taboo of the 20th century was the disastrous impact of World War I and World War II on relations among European-Americans and the ability of the United States to have a reasoned foreign policy.[29] Woodrow Wilson's entry into World War I, his anti-German and anti-Irish propaganda, and then his policies during the Versailles Conference and the Red Scare in 1919 produced a rejection of the League of Nations by the representatives of the offended groups. It led to an isolationist stance in European affairs in the 1930s that made the United States ineffective in international relations during the interwar period. Then during and after World War II, Roosevelt and Truman faced almost insuperable problems in introducing a policy — any policy — on the postwar settlement in Germany. For geographic reasons, the lack of a policy toward Germany made the conduct of policy toward the Soviet Union almost impossible and led to the terrible McCarthyism of the decade from 1946 to 1955, also a phenomenon based on ethnic antagonisms.

One of the driving motivations of politicians from the 1920s onward was a desire to bring the European-Americans together. Those "present at the creation" (the title of Secretary of State Dean Acheson's autobiography) believed that conflicts in Europe had to be ended if the conflict among European-Americans was to be solved. They knew they had to change the diverse "racial" identities among the European-Americans and create a common identity.

Those striving to end the divisions between the Southern Protestants and the Northern Protestants and among the various "races" in the North and create a common white identity decided in the postwar world that it would be advantageous to make the discussion of the divisions a taboo subject or, at least, one conducted in code words. This may well have been a successful strategy but once the whites were united and had to face new problems, they had little of the social and political under-

---

29. The person who came the closest to expressing this in public was George F. Kennan, but even he could not write about his childhood in German-American Milwaukee during World War I or about ethnic politics being the reason for his great suspicion of democracy in foreign policy. George F. Kennan, *Memoirs* (Boston: Little, Brown, 1967).

standing necessary to do so in a sophisticated manner. The creation of the whites was such a key and unappreciated element in party alignment that it is given two entire chapters at a transitional point in this book.

Many of an older generation will feel very uneasy about such a frank discussion of matters that were so taboo during much of their lifetime. However, the North-South conflict has been so completely ended and the "racial" identities of European-Americans so completely erased that the old taboos are no longer needed. The consequences of maintaining the taboos have become so negative that it is vital to lift them.

UNDERSTANDING THE RELATIONSHIP OF CULTURAL VALUES AND ECONOMIC INTERESTS IN POLITICS

This book is not written by an historian, but by a political scientist. Moreover it is written by a political scientist who primarily is a comparative theorist of the older generation. As a consequence, the perspective of its author is far removed from that found in much of the scholarly literature or the media on the driving forces of contemporary American politics. This is particularly so on the relationship of cultural values and economic interests in politics.

The belief that moral values were all important in the 2004 election came from the nature of the campaign and then from the way the exit polls were interpreted. Two articles in *The New York Times* based on the exit polls were especially influential.[30] But the press coverage of the 2004 election only reflected a growing emphasis by scholars and other observers on the rise in the importance of cultural values and a decline in that of economic factors in voters' decisions in American politics. In 1992, a Clinton adviser, James Carville, had a famous sign in his office: "It's the economy, stupid." Instead the statistical data suggested, in the title of a famous article, "It's Abortion, Stupid." Now, scholars are moving to the position, "It's Religion, Stupid."[31]

---

30. Todd S. Purdum, "An Electoral Affirmation of Shared Values," and Katharine Q. Seelye, "More Values Cited as a Defining Issue of the Election, *The New York Times*, November 4, 2004, pp. 1 and 4.
31. Alan I. Abramowitz, "It's Abortion, Stupid: Policy Voting in the 1992 Presidential Election," *The Journal of Politics*, vol. 57, no. 1 (February 1995), pp. 176–186. For an early argument that values were already crucial in the 1970s, see Everett Carll Ladd, with Charles D. Hadley, *Transformations of the American Party System: Political Coalitions from the New Deal to the 1970s*, 2nd ed. (New York: W. W. Norton & Co., 1978). The argument became very widespread in the 1990s both in the scholarly and non-scholarly literature. See, for example, Ben J. Wattenberg, *Values Matter Most: How Democrats or Republicans or a Third Party Can Win and Renew the American Way of Life* (New York: Free Press, 1995). The argument on religion can be found in James L. Guth, Lyman A. Kellstedt, Corwin E. Smith, and John C. Green, "Religious Mobilization in the 2004 Election," paper presented to the American Political Science Convention, September 1-4, 2005, Washington, DC.

These assumptions about the overwhelming priority of cultural values must, however, be treated with the greatest of caution. Political analysts from the time of the Greeks have understood that cultural issues and economic interests are not independent. It is necessary to return to their insights. Economic interests, let alone status interests, are not part of the state of nature but are shaped and even defined by world-views imbedded in particular cultures. But, by the same token, economic and status differences have a major impact on cultural identifications and the acceptance of cultural values.

The differences in average income and cultural values of adherents of the different Protestant religions in America have already been mentioned. But, of course, cultural identities, values, and beliefs may also be associated with psychological tensions that derive from difficult economic and social conditions. Politicians often try to mobilize voters by deflecting these tensions onto other groups or issues. "Scapegoat" is a word with origins in biblical times. Psychological tensions or status concerns are a standard part of the interpretation of the popularity of Hitler in Germany in the 1920s and the 1930s, the appeal of the Know-Nothing Party in the United States in the 1850s, the long-term success of Prohibition as an issue in the United States, and the extreme racism of low-income Southern whites.[32]

This book is not the place for a sophisticated analysis of the relationship among cultural issues, economic interests, and psychological tensions. Nevertheless, several simple and basically uncontroversial points are crucial to keep in mind when we think about contemporary politics.

First, cultural differences do not lead automatically to conflict. The Caribbean island of Trinidad has a large population of Muslims and Hindus from the Indian subcontinent, but they peacefully live together intermixed in the same neighborhoods. They still observe their traditional religious practices. The Hindu funeral pyres stand by the sea, quite visible to everyone. Even more visible are the differing Muslim and Hindu symbols in the yards of adjoining houses on the same block in the neighborhood. The Muslims and Hindus of Trinidad also support the same political party.

The level of conflict associated with cultural differences can also vary from time to time in the same place. The differences between Catholics and Protestants were long associated with violent wars in Europe and with major political conflict in the United States. Now they are seldom explosive. The striking thing about places such as Serbia and Rwanda is that people of different religions and ethnic groups lived peacefully together in the same villages for decades.[33] Human-interest stories from

---

32. For the classic works on this subject, see (for Hitler) Erich Fromm, *Escape From Freedom* (New York: Farrar & Rinehart, 1941); for the Know-Nothings, David Brion Davis, *The Slave Power and the Paranoid Style* (Baton Rouge: Louisiana State University Press, 1969); for prohibition, Joseph R. Gusfield, *Symbolic Crusade: Status Politics and the American Temperance Movement* (Urbana: University of Illinois Press, 1963); for lower-class racism in the South, Dollard, Miller, Doob, Mowrer, and Sears, *Frustrations and Aggression*. The classic, if extreme, argument for the general importance of underlying psychological tensions from childhood is Harold Lasswell, *Psychopathology and Politics* (Chicago: University of Chicago Press, 1930).

Iraq today often feature Sunni and Shiite neighbors who now are highly antagonistic to each other, but once were quite friendly.[34] The same phenomenon is found throughout American history.

Consequently there must be a reason extraneous to cultural identities and values that sometimes makes them the center of major conflict — sometimes violent in the streets, sometimes merely emotional at the ballot box. The Catholic-Protestant conflict in Northern Ireland has been much slower to lose its intensity than in the rest of Europe, and this cannot reflect simply the nature of the Catholic and Protestant religions. An association of Catholicism with Irish nationalism is one factor, but the combination of Scottish nationalism and Presbyterianism is not the explosive combination today that it was during the British civil wars.

A large number of political scientists are now exploring why cultural and religious differences that for a long time did not lead to dangerous conflict suddenly do. One factor clearly is the way that values and interests are distributed in a community. Imagine a community with 100,000 people that has 50,000 Protestants and 50,000 Catholics (or 50,000 blacks and 50,000 whites or 50,000 English speakers and 50,000 French speakers). Imagine that the community has 50,000 affluent people and 50,000 who are poor. If the Protestants and Catholics each include a similar mixture of affluent and poor, the situation is likely to be peaceful, especially if social mobility is possible. If all the Protestants are affluent and all the Catholics are poor (or the reverse), the conflict has the potential of being very violent, especially when the lower income group becomes educated enough to feel that it deserves upward social mobility — and is denied it.

This is not a hypothetical argument. A key factor in the unrest of the Catholics in Northern Ireland was their justified belief that religious discrimination helped to contribute to their poverty. Educated blacks in the American South in the 1950s had a similar conviction. The difference between the better-off Sunnis (and affluent Christians) and the poorer Shiites was a key factor in the Lebanese civil war, as it is around Baghdad in Iraq today. The upwardly mobile French Canadians who wanted to move to Montreal in the mid-20th century found that those with a native knowledge of English had a major advantage, and the Pashtun speakers of Afghanistan faced the same problem with the Farsi-speaking elite in Kabul.

The overlapping of differences in values, identities, and interests has also sometimes been important in the United States in realms other than black–white relations. Frederick Jackson Turner, the historian who emphasized the role of the frontier in American history prior to the 20th century, was surely right when he insisted that there was "such a connection of the [ethnic] stock, the geographic conditions, the economic interests, and the conceptions of right and wrong, that all have played upon each other to the same end."[35]

---

33. For a particularly poignant scholarly study of such a village in Bosnia, see Tone Bringa, *Being Muslim the Bosnian Way: Identity and Community in a Central Bosnian Village* (Princeton, NJ: Princeton University Press, 1995), pp. xix-xx and 4-6.
34. See, for example, Sabrina Tavernise, "Sectarian Hatred Pulls Apart Iraq's Mixed Towns," *The New York Times*, November 20, 2005, p. 1.

Resentments in which cultural identities and values overlap with economic interests are especially likely to be expressed in political conflict. When such overlapping occurs, politicians often have been able to link ethnicity and/or conceptions of right and wrong to economic grievances in a way that generates votes for themselves. As shall be seen, for example, Thomas Jefferson and James Madison chose foreign policy toward England as their cultural issue when they created the first American political party. The issue was politically effective because they could accuse the ethnic English economic elite of favoring a pro-England policy and betraying American national interest and republicanism because of their economic interests and preference for English institutions. The issue touched both ethnic and economic resentments among the non-English who lived away from the coast.

Since the cultural values are likely to be more emotional than economic interests in conflicts in which the two overlap, the political conflict is likely to be expressed in those terms: Protestants vs. Catholics, Sunni vs. Shiite, French vs. English in Quebec, non-Chinese vs. Chinese in Southeast Asia, policy toward France and England in early America. One should never assume, however, that a major conflict that seems to be overtly about religion, ethnicity, and/or language does not also involve non-cultural issues.

This fact always must be kept in mind in analyzing the increase in the importance in cultural issues in the United States at the present. The United States is a relatively well-integrated society, and it has been extremely open to upward mobility for members of the repeated waves of immigrants who arrive to take the lowest-paying jobs in the economy. Only when the number of educated blacks with blocked upward social mobility reached a critical mass in the mid 20th century was there widespread violence.

The question is whether the current prominence of cultural issues arises from the inherent importance of cultural issues today or whether they are important because the two parties provide no economic choice and both are responsive to the wealthiest quarter of the population, those with household incomes over $75,000 a year. In fact, the further question is whether economic grievances are being displaced on cultural issues.

Kenneth Wald raises the key question about the red state–blue state conflict in a matter-of-fact manner when he writes about the difference between the United States and Europe in a book on religion and politics in the United States:[36]

> In most other advanced industrial societies, political conflict commonly centers on questions about the distribution of economic resources and burdens. Such issues are not unknown in American political life, but they must share the national agenda with controversies that touch more directly on moral values and religious doctrine. The passion that suffuses such issues as abortion rights, school prayer, equal rights, pornography, and other moral concerns seems notably lacking when Americans confront questions such as tax rates, national health insurance, labor union rights,

---

35. Frederick Jackson Turner, *The Significance of Sections in American History* (New York: Henry Holt and Company, 1932), pp. 48–49.
36. Kenneth D. Wald, *Religion and Politics in the United States*, 4th ed. (Lanham, Mary: Rowman and Littlefield Publishers, 2003), p. 27.

or tariff protection. Moreover, at a time when the politics of religious concern seems to be weakening in other advanced societies, it has gained a renewed foothold in American politics.

This statement is purely descriptive, and it could, of course, have been expressed in the opposite manner. In the United States, intense and often emotional political struggle centered on economic issues during most of the New Deal period. In recent decades the conflict over economic issues has become less intense. The key question is that of cause and effect. Are religious issues more important in the United States because American culture is different, or are religious issues more important because conflict over economic issues is suppressed?

As late as 1978, Everett Ladd, a scholar who correctly saw that the party system was changing, had no sense the Republican Party was to become the home of the Evangelical Protestants. "At the activist level," he said, "the Republicans remain remarkably the party of upper-middle class white Protestants."[37] Two years later one of America's most distinguished journalists, David Broder, wrote a book on generational change in which the chapter on the new right dealt only with the new economic conservatives and did not mention the Evangelicals.[38] I will suggest that Ladd and Broder were closer to the truth about the major Republican activists than is suspected today. These activists entered politics in the 1960s with Barry Goldwater, who was economic conservative but a libertarian on cultural values. Unlike their mentor, however, the Goldwater Republicans of the future were willing to sacrifice his cultural libertarian position to win support for his economic program.

The results of the 2000 election certainly give reason for pause. The national popular vote was so close that one can look at areas won by each candidate without elaborate statistical adjustment. Data are available on the Congressional districts and they show, of course, that the Democrats won the poor black and Hispanic districts. However, Bush won 45 of the 50 white Congressional districts with the lowest household income and 92 of the 125 next lowest, a total of 137 of 175 of the poorest white districts. While Bush did well in wealthy Southern districts, Gore won 71 of the 100 Congressional districts outside the South with the highest household income and 29 of the next 50 wealthiest. As will be discussed in chapter 9, Bush scored a major victory over Kerry in 2004 among middle-income whites. Perhaps the income differences are an accidental reflection of cultural difference, but there are real reasons to wonder, all the more so since Bush passed a prescription drug program and the Democrats pushed for fiscal responsibility. As the conservative columnist George Will reported in November 2005, federal spending grew twice fast under President Bush as under President Clinton, 65% of it not associated with national security.[39]

The relation between economics and culture is always complex, but the question must be addressed, not simply dismissed with the assumption that

---

37. Ladd, *Transformations of the American Party System*, p. 259.
38. David S. Broder, *Changing of the Guard: Power and Leadership in America* (New York and Schuster, 1980), pp. 160-188.
39. George Will, "Grand Old Spenders," *The Washington Post*, November 17, 2005.

"values matter most." If an economic crisis develops, it will occur in very difficult political conditions. The population now is highly alienated by the choices it faces. The quadrennial National Election Study, the central survey of political science for half a century, has asked many of the same questions about alienation for many decades, and the standard political science study of the 2000 election by Paul Abramson, John Aldrich, and David Rohde reports the changing level of political effectiveness over a long period of time. Table 2 shows the result of a scale that combines the reaction to two statements. "Public officials don't care much what people like me think," and "People like me don't have any say about the government does." In 1956 and 1960, the population generally saw government as responsive, but this had changed by 1980 and has not changed back since.

Table 2: Sense of Political Effectiveness, United States, 1956–2000

Level of Effectiveness	1956	1960	1980	1984	1988	1992	1996	2000
High	64%	64%	39%	52%	38%	40%	28%	35%
Low	15%	15%	30%	23%	32%	34%	47%	40%

Source: Paul R. Abramson, John H. Aldrich, and David W. Rohde, Change and Continuity in the 2000 Election (Washington: CQ Press, 2001), pp. 87–88.

In 1980, the population had every reason to feel dissatisfied with government. The economy and stock market had performed poorly for over five years, the US could not free its hostages in Iran, memories of Vietnam and Watergate remained strong, and the population was highly disappointed with Jimmy Carter as President. It is therefore remarkable that the figures for 2000 figures were even worse than 1980 ·spite eight straight years of strong economic growth.

The National Election Study data from the 2004 election are not available at the this book goes to print, but all the public opinion polls published in the spring 'mmer of 2005 show growing public disenchantment not only with the Con- 'd the President, but also with the priority that politicians give to values ᶠ concrete economic problem. The public opinion surveys after the death of ·ive Terri Schiavo in March 2005 showed real public exasperation with 'ho intervened in this case rather than focus on economic problems.

OPTIONS FOR THE FUTURE

comparative government who long participated intimately in the
nerican relations not only has unusual perspectives, but also
the future. The first involve US foreign policy. After World
ericans and British-Americans of the North came to be dis-
ated in the Republican Party. The German-Americans
ationship between East Germany and West Germany, as
. The British-Americans, while suspicious of Germany,
v in the party and the country as a whole. The Demo-
much more unsympathetic to the reunification of
coincidence that all five Republican Presidents of

the postwar period had a pro-détente policy and that all but Reagan in his first term reduced military spending. All four Democratic Presidents prior to Bill Clinton raised military spending, each quite substantially, and all had serious confrontations with the Soviet Union.

The Republican Party found it politically useful to balance its pro-détente policy with hard-line rhetoric toward the Soviet Union and defense, while the Democratic rhetoric emphasized arms control and global cooperation. The difference between rhetoric and real policy in both parties was a stabilizing factor in foreign policy, but the reunification of Germany left both parties with rhetoric alone. The role of the ideological activists of both parties on foreign policy was greatly strengthened — and at a time when the nominating process gave special power to these activists in determining the nominee of each respective party. It is quite possible that this is the root cause of the Iraq War.

A second important question for a person interested in US foreign policy and/or comparative political theory is the disaster that has marked American nation-building in places such as Vietnam, Latin America, Africa, Russia, and Iraq. Anyone who reads serious books about Iraq is horrified at the inexperienced staff of the Coalition Provisional Authority. The only difference in the disaster that produced perhaps ten million deaths in the former Soviet Union — a number that continues to rise because of the abnormally high mortality rates among adults — was that the "nation-builders" included a large number of ideological neo-classical economists who had no knowledge whatsoever about building a market, let alone a state.[40]

Yet, if those involved in such nation-building exercises were modest enough to acknowledge their ignorance, they could justly reproach the intellectual community. Where is the sophisticated literature that they should be reading? There are many reasons for the lack of attention given to the theory of the development of states and the relationship of the state development to markets and democracy. One reason, however, is that those examining the political development of the United States usually are not interested in broader development questions and that those interested in broader development issues do not examine the lessons of American political development. As a result, we do not apply the real lessons of the experience of the country that we should know the best when we think of nation-building.

Those who do examine the American experience for these purposes do so from a highly idealized Progressive point of view. The major catch phrase of nation-building is "civil society," a phrase defined as would a modern Progressive. Yet the great success of the United States in the decades after the Civil War must have rested to some extent — I would say, to a very great extent — on the Robber Barons, the urban political machines, the corruption, the de-democratization, the tariffs, and the "mediocre" Presidents of the time. Yet anyone reading the scholarly literature and particularly the literature for the general reader will conclude that American developments after the Civil War were so seriously counterproductive that they must have prevented the United States from having a major role in the 20th century. The

---

40. For an insider's view marred only by excessive tact, see Joseph E. Stiglitz, *Globalization and Its Discontents* (New York: W. W. Norton, 2002). The current life expectancy is 59 years for men and 66 for women.

time has come to abandon the Progressive mythology and look seriously at the American historical development, including those aspects of it that would not be discussed favorably in a high school ethics class.

This book has that purpose. It will argue that even in the United States the formation of national identity has been a long, long process. Indeed, the effort failed in 1861 and American national identity was preserved (or perhaps restored) in the South only at the cost of a terrible war that cost over 600,000 lives. The book will treat the democratization from the 1820s to the 1860s as a major mistake that predictably destabilized the country. It almost produced a successful fascist-like Know Nothing Party, but it surely contributed to the onset of the Civil War as the elite strove to bring the explosive popular forces under control. The reduction of democracy after the Civil War, often by those who claimed they were democratizing, was stabilizing. That it took over 175 years to end the autonomy of the South in repressing its blacks should be a lesson to those who think that autonomy in Iraq will end quickly and will not be associated with some extremely unhappy consequences for many living in the various autonomous regions.

Most of the readers of this book will be concerned with American political developments in the early 21st century. The present dichotomy between red states and blue states is politically unhealthy, all the more so because it rests largely on a politics that overtly centers only on differences in cultural values. The great advantage of political conflict based on disagreement over economic questions is that compromises of various types are possible. So long as the economic conflicts center on fairly marginal questions (and they should, as both parties move toward the center), the political sphere should not be marked by intense and lasting emotion. By contrast, although some compromises can be made on an issue such as abortion, there cannot be a compromise on the fundamental question.

Fortunately, the present party coalitions and strategies do not seem permanent. If value issues are, in fact, crucial, both parties have major internal conflicts on value questions. The economic conflicts within the two parties are, if anything, more severe. By the actions of the two parties, if not always their rhetoric and ideology, the Democrats may well have returned to the economic position marginally to the right of the Republicans (or at least of George Bush) that they held before 1933.

But, of course, Bush has not made difficult choices in moving to the left. Rather, he has tried to finance both the old Republican tax programs and his new expenditure programs through a deficit. If the deficit is brought under control by economic growth, then the President's policy will seem a brilliant Keynesian policy. If an economic crisis occurs, then the Republican or Democratic parties will face extremely difficult problems unless one or both of them substantially changes its posture.

After two straight losses in presidential elections and six straight losses in Congressional ones, the Democratic Party has begun to debate party positioning in future elections. Yet the debate centers solely on cultural issues. The middle class to which the party must be responsive continues to be defined as those in the professional and managerial stratum. In fact, those in the professional and managerial jobs are generally in the upper strata of the population if "upper strata" are defined reasonably — say, the top quarter of the population by income. Those with a family income of over $100,000 a year in 2000 were in the top 11 percent of the population, while those with a family income over $75,000 were in the top quarter.[41] The median income was $45,000. Those who had been in these income brackets received a monthly Social Security check of over $1600, while the average Social Security payment was $922 in 2003.[42] Approximately half of Social Security recipients received less. Although the descendants of many old Democrats have moved into the top one-quarter of the population in household income, someone else must by definition be clustered around the median. Large numbers of these people live in the red states or red areas. If the Democratic Party does not find a way to represent them and receive more of their votes, its claim to being a middle class party will only intensify resentment and alienation.

Let us hope that one or both parties find a way to represent the economic interests of the middle income in a sustainable way. Let us hope that a major third party is not necessary. Alienation can be dangerous. In the 1840s and 1850s, when the Democrats and Whigs did not respond to the strong anti-Catholic feelings of their supporters, really to their anxieties and insecurities during the first stages of industrialization, large numbers of the electorate voted for the Know-Nothing Party and this produced a dynamics that made civil war very difficult to avoid.

The first stages of globalization of the economy may produce similar insecurities, especially when a revered chairman of the Federal Reserve Board acknowledges he has no real idea about the nature of derivatives in hedge funds, why long-term interest rates are so low, or why market forces have not led to a reduction in the size of the American trade balance rather than permitting its continual rise.[43] In 1992, George H.W. Bush and Bill Clinton were quite respectable candidates, but 23% of white males cast a ballot for the highly implausible H. Ross Perot — and in an election with an unusually high turnout.

The support for Perot in 1992 will be discussed at length later in this book, but it clearly reflected major long-time discontent derived from economic grievances and the apparent effect of immigration and outsourcing on wage levels that focused for the moment on the bipartisan endorsement of NAFTA. If economic conditions take a real downturn in the current decade, especially in conjunction with a defeat in Iraq or the Middle East in general, the political consequences of the underlying alienation could be much stronger than in 1992.

But, of course, before we engage in serious thinking about the future, we must understand how we reached the strange and unnatural party alignment that most now take for granted. The basic American political culture and system of party alignments rested on assumptions that persisted for over 200 years or were suppressed. The formation of the "whites" — the movement to a sense of community between the

---

41. *Statistical Abstract of the United States, 2004–2005* (Washington, DC: US Government Printing Office, 2004), p. 443. For an expression of utter contempt at Clinton's leading pollster who was describing such people as middle class and emphasizing the need to direct policy at "the suburban swing" and "the suburban married couples," see Robert B. Reich, *Locked in the Cabinet* (New York: Alfred A. Knopf, 1997), pp. 320 and 330.
42. *Statistical Abstract of the United States, 2004-2005*, p. 349.
43. For a frightening analysis of the trade deficit by Alan Greenspan, see Greg Ip, "Greenspan Sees No Policy Edge to Fix Trade Gap," *The Wall Street Journal*, November 15, 2005, p. A2.

North and the South and among the European-American ethnic and religious groups required a fundamental party realignment, but the destruction of the underlying rules of the game that made the realignment inevitable also made the reestablishment of optimal new rules extraordinarily difficult. The mistakes that have been made may have high costs in any crisis. The first purpose of the book is to contribute to a greater understanding of the old assumptions and the changes that undermined them.

CHAPTER 2. THE "IRRATIONAL" NORTH–SOUTH COALITION AFTER THE CIVIL WAR

We still see the decades after the Civil War through the eyes of the Progressives of the early 20th century. In this view, a series of incompetent Presidents, perhaps with the exception of Grover Cleveland, presided over an era of corruption, abandonment of blacks, rule in the Northern cities by undemocratic political machines, and domination of Congress and state government by the new corporations. Fortunately, in this image of American history, the democratic Progressives led by Theodore Roosevelt and Woodrow Wilson cleaned up government, at least temporarily, and set the United States on the correct path.

In fact, the Progressive version of history was part of the political struggle of the time, and it is remarkably misleading. The Progressives were members of the urban "middle class," really people in the top 10 to 15 percent of the white population in income and status. Most were towards the top of that stratum. They were fighting against the industrial elite to create a more pluralistic elite in which they would have an important role. This was a highly desirable development in American history, but it was a stage, a stage that actually came at the "right" time. The base of American 20th century greatness was built by the "corrupt" Presidents after the Civil War.

Political scientists now see democracy not so much as the result of mass pressure as of a "pact among elites" — a phrase that comes from the negotiated "reforma pactada" in Spain after Franco's death between democratic forces and elite elements tied with Franco. Giuseppe Di Palma writes that the best example of a transition to democracy propelled by popular forces or civil society is Costa Rica in 1949 and that it is the only example. In this view, the different warring elements of the rural, urban, regional, military, and political elite come to fear each other more than the population, they are overcome with "weariness," and they see democracy — or a form of democracy — as a way to prevent any one group in the elite from having too much power. The crucial element, Di Palma insists, is that the more radical forces agree to negotiate with and provide guarantees to the conservative forces behind the old regime.[1]

This analysis, however, has crucial implications that almost always are forgotten. First, political philosophers have always understood that there is a reason that the Greek word for "the people" (*demos*) is at the root both of "democracy" and "demagogue."[2] Until a broad educated and propertied popular base can be created, a populist demagogue may be able to use the democratic mechanism to mobilize popular resentments and establish a dictatorship. When World War I destroyed the developing elites of Europe, the result was not a world safe for democracy but one unsafe for democracy throughout Europe from Russia to Spain. The American Civil War, as will be discussed, can also be attributed to premature democratization.

A second prerequisite for a pact among elites is the existence of strong elites who can make a pact. Such elites take a long time to form. The US always had strong political elites in the states, but it did not have a national political stratum to control democratic forces in the middle of the 19th century. The end of the century seemed even more dangerous. The Ellis Island immigration coincided with the evolution of a new industrial elite, the destruction of military force at the state level in the Civil War, the sharp reduction of popular power at the ballot box, and the Republican tendency to nominate and elect military figures as presidential candidates. The Progressives continued to restrict popular democracy, but tried to ensure controlled competition among the elites with democracy limited to those with a significant amount of property.

Nevertheless, both those interested in nation-building and in the party realignment in the 1970s and 1980s have another set of questions. How did the Progressives and their predecessors achieve the controlled democracy that accomplished their purposes? The reduction of the suffrage clearly was important, but so were the strange party alignments that emerged. Both the Republican and the Democratic parties seemed as unstable as the Whigs before them, but both were to survive at least a century and a half.

The Republicans were especially vulnerable. A Radical Republican leader, Thaddeus Stevens, pointed to the basic problem in 1867:[3]

> If impartial suffrage is excluded in the rebel States, then every one of them is sure to send solid rebel representative delegations to Congress and cast a solid rebel electoral vote. They, with their kindred copperheads of the North, would always elect the president and control Congress.

---

1. Giuseppe Di Palma, *To Craft Democracies: An Essay on Democratic Transitions* (Berkeley: University of California Press, 1990), pp. 8 and 166. For civil society, pp. 37 and 38. His discussion of the necessary members of a pact comes in pp. 86-108. For his warning that foreign efforts to prevent such an alliance with the conservatives may retard democratization, see p. 191. The book was published in 1990, but perfectly describes the American role in Russia in the early 1990s and in Iraq after 2003.
2. J.S. McClelland, *The Crowd and the Mob: From Plato to Canetti* (London: Unwin Hyman, 1989), pp. 1–3.
3. Quoted in Paul Kleppner, *The Third Electoral System, 1853–1892: Parties, Voters, and Political Cultures* (Chapel Hill: University of North Carolina Press, 1979), p. 84.

In modern language, Stevens was predicting that the Democrats would follow a modern red-state strategy to unite the South and Midwest, the home of the Copperheads.

The blacks in the South were, in fact, disenfranchised, and the South continued to have as many Electoral College votes as before. In the 1880s the former slave states had 76% of the Electoral College votes necessary for victory. Yet, despite this Democratic advantage, the Republicans won 10 of the 14 Presidential elections from 1876 through 1928, and they might have done even better. They lost the 1912 election when Theodore Roosevelt broke away from his party and formed a third party. They would have won in 1884 if 600 voters in New York had shifted from Grover Cleveland to James G. Blaine. Charles Evans Hughes would have defeated Wilson in 1916 if 2,000 voters in California switched to him.

The major reason Thaddeus Stevens was wrong was that the South did not form an alliance with the "Copperheads" and the rural-oriented populists of the Midwest. Instead, the Southern Democrats allied with the three industrializing states of New York, Connecticut and New Jersey. Coalitions are based on policy choices, and *The Wizard of Oz* presented the choices well. To have an alliance with New York (Emerald City), the Democrats needed to follow the yellow brick road — that is, support the gold standard (adopt a tight money policy). To ally with the West (Kansas), the Democrats had to click their silver shoes, the color of Dorothy's shoes in the book before they became a photogenic ruby in the movie. They needed an inflationary pro-silver policy.

The Democrats, like the Republicans, followed the gold standard instead of the looser money policy that most Midwestern and Southern voters wanted. The Democrats clicked their silver shoes by nominating the bizarre William Jennings Bryan only when they had no chance to win and when they wanted to prevent their Midwestern Congressional delegation from being decimated.

The Southern Democrats' failure to ally with the Midwestern Copperheads creates several mysteries. First, why did the Democrats choose a losing coalitional strategy when the Republicans seemed in a hopeless political position? Second, since the Republicans also adopted the gold standard, why did a powerful third party not arise in the South and Midwest to challenge the two major parties? Why was American political development so different from Argentina, a commodity-exporting country with an economic and social profile similar to that of the United States?

Most important from the perspective of this book, what residues of a strange Southern–New York party alignment that persisted through the New Deal period still exist today? Now the moderate Progressives of the Northern suburbs are in the Democratic Party and support a modern version of the gold standard. The Republicans have put together the alliance of the South and the populist William Jennings Bryan, and they support a modern version of his pro-silver policy. Yet, their respective rhetoric does not reflect the reality, and many questions are raised. The past is the place to start.

THE DEMOCRATS' CHOICES AFTER THE CIVIL WAR

Prior to the Civil War, the Federalists, the Jeffersonian Republicans, the Whigs, the Democrats, and even the Know Nothings were all bisectional parties. This was a significant factor in holding the country together. When the Whig Party collapsed because of the inability of its leaders to handle nativist emotions and when an all-Northern Republican Party replaced it, the Civil War ensued.[4]

If anything, Thaddeus Stevens underestimated the Republicans' political problem after the war. Lincoln won only 40% of the national vote in 1860 and only 54% of that in the non-slave states. In 1860 he barely won California, Illinois, Indiana, and Oregon, and without them the election would have been thrown into a House runoff where either a compromise candidate or a compromise policy almost surely would have prevented the Civil War. In 1864, Lincoln did better in the Midwest, but he lost New Jersey and won New York by 7,000 votes, Pennsylvania by 20,000, and Connecticut by 2,500. The Republicans won in 1860 because of the Panic of 1857, and they seemed certain to lose in the next economic downturn if the Southern states were back in the Union and were all voting Democratic.

If the whites succeeded in disenfranchising the former slaves, however, the Electoral College and its winner-take-all policy ensured that the South would not lose any power in presidential selection. In the typical year of 1904, the former slave states cast only 22% of the national popular vote, but received 36% of the votes in the Electoral College. The Confederate states alone cast 10% of the vote for President and received 25% of the Electoral College vote.

On the surface, Republicans did not have a hopeless position in the South. According to the 1870 census, blacks constituted 42% of the population of the former states of the Confederacy and 43% in 1880. The blacks would vote Republican if allowed to cast a free vote. This is why Radicals such as Stevens were so eager to use military force to guarantee blacks the suffrage granted them by the 15th Amendment.

Unfortunately, the winner-take-all distribution of Electoral College votes within each state meant that black suffrage had to be fully guaranteed if the Republicans were to benefit. It did not matter whether the Republicans received 40% of the vote in a Southern state or 20%. In either case they would receive no Electoral College votes. If they could not obtain enough black votes to obtain a plurality in some states, partial success would not help. This was a major reason the Republicans gave up the effort and sought to negotiate compensation from the Democrats. This is why E. E. Schattschneider called the Electoral College "the bulwark" of the solid

---

4. Many believe that that the Whigs collapsed because of the slavery issue, but the Democrats were just as divided on this issue. More recent scholars have emphasized that the Whig Party was actually destroyed by the Know Nothing Party because it ignored anti-Catholic nativism. See William E. Gienapp, *The Origins of the Republican Party, 1852–1856* (New York: Oxford University Press, 1987), and Michael F. Holt, *The Rise and Fall of the Whig Party: Jacksonian Politics and the Onset of the Civil War* (New York: Oxford University Press, 1999).

Democratic South.[5] He knowingly was using shorthand. He really meant the Electoral College with the winner-take-all distribution of votes.

Once it became clear that the Democrats would receive all the Electoral College votes of the South, the Democrats faced a basic decision on electoral strategy. In 1876, 185 Electoral College votes were needed for victory, and the slave states had 138. Hence the Democrats had to obtain 47 votes in the non-slave states. New York, Connecticut, and New Jersey had 50, while the eight trans-Mississippi states had 39. However, the Democrats often won Indiana with its 15 votes and surely would do so with a rural-oriented strategy. After the 1880 reapportionment, 201 Electoral College votes were required for victory in 1884, and the former slave states had 153. The Democrats only needed an additional 48 votes, and the Connecticut–New Jersey–New York bloc and the eight trans-Mississippi states, even without Indiana, each had 51.

The Southern Democrats had the crucial decision. If they were united, they could ally either with the Midwestern or the Eastern wing of the party.[6] C. Vann Woodward discussed the choice of the South in the language of the time: "It was plain that the reunion was a forked road, that the right fork led to the East and the left fork to the West. Between the right-forkers and the left-forkers the debate raged for months."[7] The right-fork strategy was to follow the yellow-brick road, while the left was to click the silver slippers.

Political economy theory strongly suggests that the Democrats should have chosen the left-fork Midwest strategy after the Civil War. Many scholars think the crucial long-term difference between the Democratic and Republican parties was their respective position on the tariff. From the first days when the Democratic Party was formed in the 1830s, it favored a low tariff and the Whig Party wanted a higher one.[8] The Republicans, as the representative of the industrializing North, followed the same pro-tariff policy as the Whigs.

If the South wanted a partner for a low-tariff coalition, the commodity-exporting West was the obvious choice. In 1870, the Confederate states were 9% urban and the Border states 22%. The West and Midwest other than California, Illinois, Michigan, and Ohio were 15% urban, and even these four states were only 25% urban. By contrast, the three core states of the right-fork strategy — Connecticut, New Jersey, and New York — were 47% urban in 1870.

As Table 1 shows, both the industrial states of the East and the North Central States continued to urbanize rapidly. The South still remained overwhelmingly rural,

---

5. E. E. Schattschneider, *Party Government* (New York: Farrar & Rinehart, 1942), pp. 221–223.

6. Another potential problem existed: the Democratic presidential candidate had to receive the vote of two-thirds of the convention delegates, and the large states of the Old Midwest might join the East to veto a nominee with less than a majority. However, the two-thirds rule could always be replaced by a simple majority in the Convention. The Southern Democrats could achieve their goal by threatening to form a new party with the Populists of the Midwest.

7. C. Vann Woodward, *Origins of the New South, 1877–1913* (Baton Rouge: Louisiana State University Press, 1951), pp. 48–50.

8. Thomas B. Alexander, *Sectional Stress and Party Strength: A Study of Roll-Call Voting Patterns in the United States House of Representatives, 1836–1860* (Nashville: Vanderbilt University Press, 1967).

and the Prairie and Mountain were little more urban. Since the price both of cotton and grain dropped sharply in the decades after the Civil War, the Southern and Midwestern voters shared a common interest in a low tariff policy, an inflationary policy to make debts easier to pay, and regulation of railroad prices. They had the same perceived grievances against the railroads, the banks, and the East. Populist campaign rhetoric should have been highly attractive to the voters of both regions.

Table 1: Rural–Urban Breakdown on Population, Selected Regions, 1880 and 1900

Region	Percentage Urban, 1880	Percentage Urban, 1900
South	11%	15%
North Central	27%	45%
Prairie & Mountain	16%	27%
CT, NJ, NY	55%	71%
Total US	28%	40%

Note: *South: The 11 Confederate states, but three most southern border states (Kentucky, Missouri, and West Virginia: North Central: Illinois, Indiana, Michigan, Ohio, and Wisconsin; Prairie and Mountain: Colorado, Idaho, Iowa, Kansas, Minnesota, Montana, Nebraska, Nevada, North Dakota, South Dakota, Utah and Wyoming.*
Source: *Historical Statistics of the United States Colonial Times to 1970 (Washington: US Government Printing Office, 1975), part 1, pp. 24-37.*

The Midwestern strategy also seemed to promise the Democrats a safer margin of victory in the Electoral College, for it probably would garner at least some of the Electoral College votes of the other Midwestern states. These included the 22 of Illinois, the 15 of Indiana, the 13 of Michigan, the 23 of Ohio, and the 11 of Wisconsin. A rural Populist might even win a few Electoral College votes in the rural states in northern New England. If the Democrats nominated a strong candidate from Illinois, Michigan, or Ohio, the party might have done quite well in the popular vote.

By contrast, the New York strategy led to precarious Democratic victories at best. The Democrats won a total of 24.7 million votes and the Republicans 24.0 million in the presidential elections from 1876 through 1892. Yet, the Democrats had Electoral College victories in only two of the five elections. When the Democrats won in 1884 with Governor Grover Cleveland of New York, their right-fork strategy produced victory in only four non-slave states: New York, Connecticut, New Jersey, and Indiana. The three Eastern states cast a total of 1,565,000 votes, and Grover Cleveland took all three with a *combined* margin of 6,650 votes. In 1888, Cleveland was defeated because he lost his home state of New York by 14,500 votes out of 1,320,000 cast.

THE DEMOCRATS CHOOSE THE YELLOW BRICK ROAD

The Democrats nominated a conservative former governor of New York for President in 1868 and a conservative New York publisher in 1872. Indeed, their 1864 candidate, General George McClellan, was born and raised in Pennsylvania. All three men lost, but the Democrats can hardly be criticized for adopting this or any other strategy. Lincoln was winning the war in 1864, and the South could not vote. Immediately after the war, the Democratic Party had the stigma of lukewarm support for the Civil War. So long as US troops were guaranteeing that Southern blacks could vote, no strategy had a real chance of success.

The 1876 election was quite different. Commodity prices had collapsed in the Panic of 1873, and the resulting economic depression seriously weakened the Republicans. The Republican 108-seat House margin in 1872 was transformed into a Democratic 84-seat margin in the 1874 off-year election. Republicans had held the Presidency for 16 years, and the Democrats had every reason to expect victory in 1876.

Instead, the Democrats nominated a conservative New York governor, Samuel Tilden, and he lost the 1876 election by one Electoral College vote, 185 to 184. In immediate terms Tilden lost because 20 disputed Electoral College votes were awarded to his opponent, Rutherford Hayes, but Tilden should not have needed these votes. The Midwest suffered heavily from the Panic of 1873, but Tilden received only 15 of the 118 Electoral College votes of the non-slave states that stretched from Ohio to the Pacific Ocean. Only one of those 118 votes was disputed. Hayes was no radical, but he came from a small town in Ohio and was less conservative. The Midwest had no reason to support Tilden.

Despite the disaster in the 1876 election, the South continued its right-fork strategy. In the 15 presidential elections from 1876 to 1932, the Democrats nominated the New York governor six times, the New Jersey governor twice, and another New Yorker or Pennsylvanian three times. These Democrats were consistently more conservative than their Republican counterparts, even Franklin Roosevelt judging by the Democratic Party platform in 1932. Indeed, since the Democrats had nominated a Pennsylvania general and two prominent New Yorkers in 1864, 1868, and 1872, this meant that Eastern conservatives were nominated in 14 of 18 elections.

The Democratic nomination of Eastern conservatives who had little appeal in the Midwest and West essentially meant that these areas were being conceded to the Republicans. In essence, the Democrats were offering the Republicans a basically solid bloc of Electoral College votes in the Midwest and West in exchange for a solid bloc of Electoral College votes in the South.

Only after the Panic of 1893 did the Democrats choose the left-fork strategy with William Jennings Bryan of Nebraska in the elections of 1896, 1900, and 1908. However, Bryan was not a serious candidate. He was 36 years old in 1896 and had served only four years in Congress before he ran for the Senate in 1894 and lost. He always held to the anti-modern cultural values he was to show in the 1920s when he was a lawyer on the anti-evolution side in the Scopes Monkey Trial. Bryan's famous last sentence in his speech to the 1896 convention, "You should not press down upon the brow of labor this crown of thorns, you should not crucify mankind upon a cross of gold," typified a campaign that was like "a religious revival."[9] Bryan was a fundamentalist religious candidate.

---

9. Richard J. Jensen, *The Winning of the Midwest: Social and Political Conflict, 1888–1896* (Chicago: University of Chicago Press, 1971), pp. 275–277.

In addition, this short citation from Bryan's statement about a cross of gold obscures a crucial fact: the "you" referred to England. "Instead of having a gold standard because England has it, we will restore bimetallism, and then let England have bimetallism because the United States has it ... We will answer their demand for a gold standard by saying to them, 'You shall not press down ... etc."[10] Bryan was suspicious of England in his foreign policy and was to resign as Wilson's Secretary of State as the latter tilted toward England in World War I. Bryan was also a typical populist in being anti-immigrant, although he muted the theme. He was entirely lacking in credibility as a presidential candidate and was certain to do badly in the East.

Indeed, Bryan even lost four of the five former slave states that stayed with the Union — the first time any of these Border States ever voted Republican. It seems highly probable that Bryan was nominated only to destroy the Populist challenge in the Midwest and to win back some of the Congressional seats in the area that the Democrats lost in 1894. The Democrats succeeded in achieving these limited goals, but when they had a chance to win in 1912, they nominated the conservative governor of New Jersey, Woodrow Wilson.

The Southern conservatives explained frankly one reason they preferred the right-fork strategy. A left-fork alliance would have had to be based on populist themes. If the Democrats in the South supported a populist national presidential strategy, this would promote and legitimate such views in the South. Voters' turnout would be stimulated among the poorer farmers, and such farmers would also vote for state and local candidates as well. The South tolerated Bryan only because he pre-empted the Populists in the short run and because they had already learned how to suppress low-income turnout by institutional means.

The *Charleston News and Courier* clearly expressed the attitude of the Southern conservatives in December 1878 when it discussed the position that the South should take on the 1880 Democratic platform:[11]

> We see no hope that a platform will be framed that is acceptable to both East and West ... With one section or the other the South must go, and our fixed opinion is that *the permanent interests of the South lie with the East rather than with the West*. The aim of the South being to ... avoid whatever is revolutionary in politics, sociology, or finance, the South must go with the East, despite its aggregating self-assertion, rather than join hands with the West, which is learning the A.B.C. of statesmanship.

The South had another compelling reason to support conservative Democratic presidential nominees. The President had few powers in the domestic sphere other than appointing Supreme Court Justices. A conservative Democratic President, like a Republican President, would appoint conservative Supreme Court Justices. Hence whichever party was elected, the Supreme Court appointees would interpret the

---

10. William Jennings Bryan speech of July 8, 1896, in Arthur Schlesinger, Jr., ed. *History of American Presidential Elections, 1789–1968* (New York: Chelsea House Publishers, 1971), vol. II, pp. 1845–1850. The statement is on p. 1850.
11. Quoted in Woodward, *Origins of the New South*, pp. 49–50.

Constitution in a way that prevented federal protection of the former slaves in the South. The same interpretation would also prevent federal social welfare measures, and this would make conservative Republicans and conservative Northern Democrats happy to cooperate with the South. The bipartisan cooperation on the Court was embodied in an unwritten rule that the Senate would not confirm a nominee for the Supreme Court if it gave either party more than six of the nine members.[12]

But even though the Republican Party was basically conservative, the populist Midwestern and Western wings of the party pushed it leftward on the political spectrum. To be sure, the Republican Party was not very far left, but it was to the left of the Democrats. The Republicans normally nominated a Midwesterner for President and a Northeasterner for Vice President. The Midwesterner was never a radical, but Benjamin Harrison from Indiana was typical in being to the left of the Democratic Grover Cleveland of New York with whom he competed in 1888 and 1892. Theodore Roosevelt was to the left of Woodrow Wilson in 1912. The Republicans also enacted some legislation that the Midwest wanted. Not coincidentally, the Sherman of the Sherman Anti-Trust Act was a Republican Senator from Ohio.

THE ABANDONMENT OF THE INDUSTRIAL WORKER

Since the Republicans conceded the South to the Democrats and the Democrats usually conceded most of the Midwest and the West to the Republicans, the competition for the presidency normally centered on a few states that were much more urbanized and industrialized than either the South or the Midwest. The Ellis Island immigrants poured into the three right-fork states of Connecticut, New Jersey, and New York, and this accelerated their urbanization and industrialization.

But if party competition in the North was concentrated in a few industrial states, what were to be the issues on which this competition would be centered? In fact, as shall be discussed in the next chapter, the party coalitions in the North were primarily based on ethnicity and religion. The Republican Party was essentially the party of the Northern Protestants, especially those who had not come from the South. The Northern Democrats were the party of the non-Protestant immigrants and the Southern migrants.

The non-Protestant immigrants and their children became the core of the construction force that created America's major cities. They then became the major part of the labor force within the factories of these new cities. As early as 1860, 50% of the people in Chicago were foreign-born. The same was true of 47% of the residents in Detroit, 51% in Milwaukee, 48% in New York City, 50% in San Francisco, and 60% in St. Louis. This figure ranged from 35% to 45% in Boston, Buffalo, Cleveland, New Orleans, Newark, Pittsburgh, and Rochester.[13] In addition, a large portion of the "native-born" population in these cities was composed of children of immigrants.

---

12. Letter of Jerry A. Mathews to Claude G. Bowers, October 31, 1932, Bowers mss. II, Indiana University. Mathews had been correspondent of the *New York Sun* in Washington and was told this by Senator Bailey of Texas.

Table 2: Size of White Population, 1890 and 1910, By Origin and Region

Region	Origins	1890	1910
North	Native Stock	8,891,000	11,076,000
	Foreign-Born or Foreign-Stock	8,231,000	14,284,000
North–Central	Native Stock	12,252,000	16,276,000
	Foreign-Born or Foreign-Stock	9,661,000	13,003,000
West	Native Stock	1,490,000	3,575,000
	Foreign-Born or Foreign-Stock	1,383,000	2,968,000
South	Native Stock	11,483,000	18,561,000
	Foreign-Born or Foreign-Stock	1,351,000	1,986,000
Total	Native Stock	34,116,000	49,488,000
	Foreign-Born or Foreign-Stock	20,626,000	32,241,000

Source: *Historical Statistics of the United States, part 2, p. 23.*

Table 3: Percentage In Cities with over 100,000 People Born Abroad or with One or Two Parents Born Abroad, 1910, By Region, in Percentages

Region	Cities with Population of 500,000+			Cities with Population of 100,000–500,000		
	Foreign Born	Parent(s) Born Abroad	Total	Foreign Born	Parent(s) Born Abroad	Total
New England	35.9%	38.3%	74.2%	35.5%	38.2%	73.7%
Mid-Atlantic	35.8%	36.6%	72.4%	28.3%	39.9%	68.2%
East North Central	35.6%	41.4%	77.0%	21.6%	35.1%	56.7%
West North Central	18.3%	35.6%	53.9%	21.9%	33.2%	55.1%
South Atlantic	13.8%	24.1%	37.9%	5.4%	9.6%	15.0%
East South Central	—	—	—	5.5%	13.4%	18.9%
West South	—	—	—	8.2%	21.9%	30.1%
Mountain	—	—	—	18.2%	28.7%	46.9%
Pacific	—	—	—	24.7%	29.1%	53.8%

Source: *Thirteenth Census of the United States Taken in the Year 1910: Abstract of the Census (Washington: US Government Printing Office, 1913), p. 92.*

The combined number of foreign-born and foreign-stock continued to rise after the Ellis Island immigration began in the 1890s. (See Table 2.) In 1890, 20.6 million of the 54.7 million white persons in the United States were either immigrants or their children. This figure increased to 32.2 million of the 81.7 million white persons in the United States in 1910.[14] Immigrants and their children constituted a particularly high percentage of the population in New England, the North Atlantic states, and the Old Midwest, and especially in their large cities. (See Table 3.)

---

13. *Population in the United States in 1860: Compiled from the Original Returns of the Eighth Census* (Washington: Government Printing Office, 1864), pp. xxxi–xxxii.
14. *Historical Statistics of the United States: Colonial Times to 1970* (Washington: US Government Printing Office, 1975), part 1, pp. 116–117.

In essence, therefore, the right-fork strategy of the Democrats meant an alliance of the South with the political machines built on the non-Protestant immigrants in key Northeastern states. Since the South was the poorest rural region in the country and the immigrants were the poorest urban workers, the natural right-fork strategy seemed to be the left-wing economic policy advanced by Franklin Roosevelt in 1933. But, of course, the South elite chose a right-fork strategy precisely because it did not want a left-wing economic policy. In particular, it did not want a definition of the powers of the federal government that permitted such an economic policy.

As a result, the Cleveland and Wilson Democrats favored drastic economy in government spending, a balanced budget, a sound currency, and a laissez-faire economic system. "[Their] intention," Walter Lippmann wrote in 1932, "is to repeal government favors rather than to increase positive government action."[15] Lippmann distinguished between "Cleveland and Wilson Democracy," "Bryanism," and the "kind of collectivism which progressives like Senator La Follette believe in." "Cleveland and Wilson democracy" meant the eastern wing of the Democratic Party. The Bryan Democrats favored what is now called "deficit spending" and "loose money," while La Follette, although not a socialist, believed in the welfare state.

There were several reasons that the Northern Democratic political machines accepted the Cleveland policy. First, of course, the party alignments and the nature of the American political system gave the urban Democratic machines relatively little choice unless they could transform the party system. The Supreme Court was using the provision in the 14th amendment outlawing the seizure of property without "due process of the law" (that is, without a trial) to declare social welfare measures unconstitutional. This interpretation had to be transformed if such measures were to be enacted, and it was the essential provision of the right-fork alliance.

Second, the institutional interests of the political machines pushed them, and also the officials of the trade unions, in a conservative direction. In Europe the close relationship of the unions with a social-democratic party gave lower union and political officials an excellent opportunity to move upward in the political hierarchy. Nothing similar existed in the United States. The trade unions had to rely on the dues of their members, while the political machines received kickbacks from the developers and those to whom they gave patronage jobs.

For this reason, the political machines had a very symbiotic relationship with the urban developers and industrialists. As a number of scholars have argued, the urban machines were very useful in providing the immigrants with what later were called constituent services.[16] Few have asked where the money came from to finance these services, but the political machines' main source of funds were the developers. The machines provided the developers with a stable political order that included a more or less disciplined work force, and the developers paid for these services with

---

15. Column of July 1, 1932, in Walter Lippmann, *Interpretations, 1931–1932* (New York: Macmillan Co., 1932), pp. 308–310.
16. Robert F. Merton, *Social Theory and Social Structure: Toward the Codification of Theory and Research* (Glencoe, IL: Free Press, 1949), pp. 71–81. For the debate on the issue, see Bruce M. Stave and Sondra Astor Stave, ed., *Urban Bosses, Machines, and Progressive Reformers* (Lexington, MA: Heath, 1971).

what critics termed "corruption," but what really was informal "taxation." Radical candidates might disturb the labor discipline being offered by the machines.

The relationship between machines and developers was also useful for immigrants. The precinct captains and ward bosses served as intermediaries between the new immigrants and the government, but they could help the immigrants to obtain jobs not only in the machine and the government, but also in the private sector. The machines created many opportunities for upwardly-mobile immigrants, but they did not fight effectively, if at all, for government social welfare measures. Indeed, if the federal government provided services as an entitlement, then the workers would not need those provided by the party machines and trade unions.

If the state and national Democratic candidates could trust the machines to deliver the immigrant urban vote without making policy commitments, then the swing voters in the North were largely found in the Protestant middle class. Since the Democrats generally were more conservative than the Republicans, they had a natural attraction to middle class voters, but only if they disassociated themselves from the non-respectable political machines and immigrant voters. As David Mayhew emphasized, the Democratic presidential candidates did so by taking an anti-machine position.[17]

In fact, the conservative Democratic Party cooperated with Northern Republicans in destroying the power of the political machines. Grover Cleveland was a leader in civil service reform. Woodrow Wilson became a Progressive when he was elected New Jersey governor, but this merely meant that he had betrayed his promises to the Newark party boss who had been the major factor in his nomination. Indeed, Wilson also attacked the base of the Democratic Party in his writings. In 1902, he published a five-volume scholarly history of the American people, his position as President of Princeton University printed under his name on the title page. Describing the mid 1880s, he wrote,

> The cities were filling up with foreigners of the sort the Know Nothings had feared, men who had left their homeland dissatisfied not merely with the governments they had lived under, but with society itself, and who had come to America to speak treasons elsewhere forbidden.

Wilson denounced the "anarchistic" strikes of the period and expressed total approval of Cleveland's decision to suppress the Pullman Strike by sending troops the governor of Illinois did not think necessary.[18]

Wilson was scathing in his description of the new immigrants who began arriving in great numbers during the 1890s:[19]

> Throughout the century men of the sturdy stocks of the north of Europe had made up the main strain of foreign blood which was every year added to the vital

---

17. David R. Mayhew, *Placing Parties in American Politics: Organization, Electoral Settings, and Government Activity in the Twentieth Century* (Princeton: Princeton University Press, 1986), pp. 318–320.
18. Woodrow Wilson, *A History of the American People* (New York: Harper & Brothers, 1902), vol. 5, pp. 186 and 239–240.
19. Wilson, *A History of the American People*, vol. 5, pp. 212.

working force of the country, or else men of the Latin–Gallic stocks of France and northern Italy; but now there came multiples of men of the lowest class from the south of Italy and men of the meaner sort out of Hungary and Poland, men out of the ranks where there was neither skill nor energy nor any initiative of quick intelligence; and they came in numbers which increased from year to year, as if the countries of the south of Europe were disburdening themselves of the more sordid and hapless elements of their population.

These writings of Wilson circulated in his presidential campaign of 1912, including to his main rival for the Democratic nomination, Champ Clark.[20] His opponents did not use the book against Wilson, and they must have thought it would win him more votes than it would lose.

When Wilson ran for President, he had to move to the left on economic policy to position himself between Theodore Roosevelt and William Howard Taft — or at least Taft as Roosevelt and Wilson were inaccurately describing him. Wilson claimed he was to the left of Taft, but he reassured conservatives that he was not as far left as Roosevelt.

The difference between Wilson and Theodore Roosevelt was striking. As a Southerner by birth and heritage, Wilson introduced systematic segregation, including separate toilets, in government buildings south of the Mason-Dixon line, including in Washington, DC.[21] The Republicans were the party of the blacks, and neither Roosevelt nor Taft had done this. Unlike the Republicans, Wilson also was very reluctant to accept women's suffrage.[22] In 1912 Roosevelt campaigned for social welfare measures — child labor protection, workers' compensation, an increased health program, a minimum wage for women, and so forth. The former President argued, "We are face to face with new conceptions of the relations of property to human welfare.... Property [is] subject to the general right of the community to regulate its use to whatever degree the public welfare may require it."

Wilson denounced Theodore Roosevelt's program as paternalistic and an enslavement of the workers. Wilson's own campaign was, he proclaimed, "a second struggle for emancipation.... If America is not to have free enterprise, then she can have no freedom of any sort whatever."[23] The "new freedom" that he advocated featured an attack on governmental and private restrictions on the market. The gov-

---

20. For example, Senator Pettigrew of South Dakota forwarded a letter to Clark that pointed to the reactionary passages in the book, and it remains among the few letters that survived in Clark's papers, together with a letter of outrage from the Polish community. George Williams to H. P. Pettigrew, December 14, 1911, and Cornelius H. Fauntleroy to Champ Clark, March 16, 1912, Champ Clark Papers, Folders 18 and 30, Western Historical Manuscript Collection.
21. See the discussion in Joel Williamson, *The Crucible of Race: Black/White Relations in the American South Since Emancipation* (New York: Oxford University Press, 1984), pp. 364–398.
22. A member of Wilson's Administration and head of the Wilson organization in Missouri wrote in his diary with relief that they had managed to stave off pressure at the 1916 Democratic platform for a plank in favor of women's suffrage. Breckinridge Long 1916 diary, Breckinridge Long papers, Library of Congress.
23. Arthur S. Link, *Woodrow Wilson and the Progressive Era 1910–1917* (New York: Harper, 1954), pp. 19–22.

ernment intervention that Wilson wanted to limit included the tariff, which Roosevelt defended as necessary to protect worker wages.

In retrospect, the 1912 election seemed to offer an exciting choice between Roosevelt, Wilson, and Taft, but the voters did not see it that way at the time. Whatever Roosevelt's words, he had been President for seven years, and people knew his record in office. Turnout in the non-Southern states was rather low in 1912 (68% compared with 76% in 1908 and 69% in 1916).[24] Moreover, six percent of the voters found the three candidates so conservative that they voted for the Socialist candidate, Eugene Debs. If voters had thought Debs had a chance to win Electoral College votes, he surely would have received a higher percent of the popular vote, perhaps a much higher percent. Despite the increase in population, the total number of votes for the three main candidates in 1912 (13.9 million) was actually lower than that cast for the two main candidates in 1908 (14.1 million) and much lower than the 17.7 million of 1916.

THE ESTABLISHMENT OF RESTRICTIONS ON DEMOCRACY

The greatest apparent mystery of the party alignments after the Civil War is how the politicians succeeded in maintaining them. In W. W. Rostow's phrase, the American economy entered the takeoff phase in 1843 and, despite periodic downturns in the business cycle, it had very rapid, sustained growth until the Great Depression. In the majority of populous countries, this period is marked by major political instability. Extreme populist movements arise that are variously labeled "fascist," "Communist," or "fundamentalist." They normally establish dictatorships unless they are suppressed by the military who themselves establish dictatorial regimes.

The decades prior to the American Civil War correspond to this general pattern of political disorder. The US introduced full democracy for white males in the two decades before the economic takeoff. The old political elite did not know how to contain the emotions of the period, and new politicians emerged to exploit them. This was the meaning of David Donald's assertion that the Civil War was, in substantial part, produced by "excess democracy."[25]

24. Walter Dean Burnham, "The Turnout Problem," in A. James Reichley, ed., *Elections American Style* (Washington: Brookings Institution, 1987), p. 113.
25. David Herbert Donald, *An Excess of Democracy: The American Civil War and the Social Process* (Oxford: Clarendon, 1960), esp. pp. 17 and 22. Reprinted in David Herbert Donald, *Lincoln Reconsidered: Essays on the Civil War Era*, 3rd. ed (New York: Vintage, 2001), pp. 44–62. In a letter to me on August 15, 1997, Professor Donald asserted he was "delighted to learn" the essay was remembered and that "I still think that (with some modifications perhaps) it has validity." He reaffirmed the point in an e-mail of November 12, 2005. Others agreed. The top historian of the Antebellum Democratic Party, Roy Nichols, wrote that politics were in such a "disorganized state ... [that] a maximum number of politicos were disturbed and disoriented." Roy F. Nichols, "The Kansas–Nebraska Act: A Century of Historiography," in Joel H. Silbey, ed., *National Development and Sectional Crisis, 1815–1860* (New York: Random House, 1970), pp. 204–205.

In broad historical perspective the decades after the Civil War should have been as turbulent. The bitter anger from the Civil War remained strong. The new party coalitions provided no protection to the most dissatisfied elements of the population, the poor and middle-income farmers and the new urban workers. The Ellis Island immigration was larger than that of the 1840s and 1850s, even in percentage terms, and it was almost exclusively non-Protestant. Yet, there was no Know-Nothing Party, no significant fascist or socialist party, and no military coup.

Of course, everyone knows about one measure taken by the South to stabilize the situation: it deprived blacks of almost all influence at the ballot box. Federal troops tried to ensure that former slaves could vote during Reconstruction, but by the mid-1870s, the North had essentially given up these efforts. Southerners first used large-scale violence to accomplish their goal — and continued to use violence when "necessary."[26]

Nevertheless, violence offended the sensibilities of the North and even of the Southern middle class, and it could not be used against poor Southern whites. The right-fork strategy did lead to poor white dissatisfaction, and it *did* lead to the rise of a number of populist parties or movements. Turnout remained so high in the 1880s that fusion or independent candidates for governor and Congress had a real chance for victory.[27]

If the conservative political status quo were to be maintained, voter turnout needed to be lowered further. The solution was to change voting rules in a way that could be defended as universal. The 15th Amendment only outlawed discrimination directed specifically against blacks, and the Supreme Court declared that measures affecting low-income whites and blacks alike were constitutional. The requirements of a new constitution in Mississippi in 1890 provided the model: two years residence in the state, self-registration four months before the election, a poll tax in which any unpaid past taxes had to be paid before voting was permitted, a written Australian ballot that constituted a literacy test, and an additional formal test of literacy and "understanding" the constitution that could be applied in an arbitrary manner against blacks.[28]

The most effective laws used to reduce turnout in the South are seldom recognized today because they are still in place and are universally accepted. The first was the establishment of an official state ballot that lists all the candidates — the so-called Australian ballot. In the past, the United States had an ideal system for the literate or semi-literate voter: a voter brought his own ballot to the polling box or urn, one usually provided by a party organizer, and it only contained the name of the candidate or candidates for whom he was voting. When the United States introduced a

---

26. For example, the great white "riot" in 1898 in Wilmington, North Carolina, ended substantial black voting in the largest city of the state at that time. David S. Cecelski and Timothy B. Tyron, *Democracy Betrayed: The Wilmington Race Riot of 1898 and Its Legacy* (Chapel Hill: University of North Carolina Press, 1998).

27. J. Morgan Kousser, *The Shaping of Southern Politics: Suffrage Restriction and the Establishment of the One-Party South, 1880–1910* (New Haven: Yale University Press, 1974), pp. 26–27.

28. V. O. Key, Jr., *Southern Politics in State and Nation* (New York: A. A. Knopf, 1949), pp. 537–538. Kousser, *The Shaping of Southern Politics*, pp. 139–145.

government ballot that listed all the candidates, it could have followed the practice of Latin America and Asia and placed non-verbal symbols, colors, and/or photographs to help the semi-literate, but this was seldom done.

The second measure that limited turnout was the requirement that voters be registered, but voluntarily and not by the government. Such registration meant that prospective voters not only had to have a fairly high degree of literacy, but also the self-confidence to deal with government bureaucrats. In most developed countries the local government has the responsibility of identifying voters and registering them before the election.[29] Instead, the new registration procedures in the United States were deliberately made more complicated to discourage the less educated.

Since the Mississippi requirements applied to everyone, the US Supreme Court asserted in *Williams v. Mississippi* in 1898 that they were not covered by the 15th Amendment. This decision effectively ended legal challenges to voting restrictions, and other Southern states followed the Mississippi example either in whole or in part. Southern turnout began to fall rapidly. In 1876, 75% of eligible voters in the South cast their ballots in the presidential election, but only 65% in 1880, 58% in 1896, 44% in 1900, and 29% in 1904. It remained in the 20% to 30% range through 1948 — indeed, in the 24.5% to 26.5% range from 1932 to 1948.[30]

Other measures not directly related to suffrage were also used to reduce the power of the blacks. In particular, Southern politicians called the Democratic Party a private group and introduced primary elections in which only its members could vote. The party often chose not to admit blacks.[31] Hence, the Democratic primary became the only meaningful election, and even blacks who succeeded in registering — for example, in the larger cities — could only vote in general elections that had no impact on the outcome.[32]

The restriction of democracy in the South led to another mystery: why did the North, and especially the Republicans, tolerate it?[33] The basic answer is that the

---

29. This can have a major impact on turnout. When Canada shifted from enumeration immediately before the election to an earlier compilation of the list, turnout dropped, especially among younger voters. Louis Massicotte, Andrei Blais, and Antoine Yoshinaka, *Establishing the Rules of the Game: Election Laws in Democracies* (Toronto: University of Toronto Press, 2004), pp. 66–82, especially 78–79. I owe the information about the effect of the change to a private communication from Professor Blais.

30. Walter Dean Burnham, "The Turnout Problem," pp. 113–114.

31. Michael Perman, *Struggle for Mastery: Disenfranchisement in the South, 1888–1908* (Chapel Hill: University of North Carolina, 2001), pp. 299–320.

32. Darlene Clark, *Black Victory: The Rise and Fall of the White Primary in Texas*, new ed. (Columbia Mour: University of Missouri Press, 2003); Steven F. Lawson, *Black Ballots: Voting Rights in the South, 1944–1969* (New York: Columbia University Press, 1976), pp. 23–54.

33. A large literature explores the abandonment of the Southern blacks by the Republicans. Stanley P. Hirshson, *Farewell to the Bloody Shirt: Northern Republicans and the Southern Negro, 1873–1893* (Bloomington, Ind.: Indiana University Press, 1962); Vincent P. De Santis, *Republicans Face the Southern Question — The New Departure Years, 1877–1897* (Baltimore: Johns Hopkins University Press, 1959); Xi Wang, *The Trial of Democracy: Black Suffrage and Northern Republicans, 1860–1910* (Athens: University of Georgia Press, 1997), pp. 196–197.

Democratic right-fork strategy protected the basic interests of the Northern Republicans.

First, the Southern alliance with the East in presidential politics meant that the Democrats could not compete effectively with the Republicans in the Midwest and West. Hence the Republicans could offset their losses in the South with a powerful position in the Midwest. Their campaign contributors among the Northern economic elite also were more than contented with an arrangement that prevented strong government regulation of the economy or social welfare.

Second, the inability of a populist party to win Electoral College votes in the South meant that populist parties could not compete effectively in the Midwest. There were not enough Midwestern Electoral College votes for them to win a majority in the Electoral College. Without Electoral College votes in the South, the Populists could, at best, force a runoff in the House of Representatives. In a runoff, the Democratic-Republican alliance would have been decisive.

The third reason the Northern Republicans tolerated Southern restrictions on turnout is that they wanted to use the same techniques to reduce turnout in the North, especially among immigrants. Indeed, Progressive Republican intellectuals were deeply worried by universal male suffrage well before the new wave of Ellis Island immigration. Charles Francis Adams, Jr., a grandson of John Quincy Adams and a son of the vice presidential candidate of the Free Soil Party in 1848, was blunt in 1869 about his fears of universal suffrage: "Universal suffrage can only mean in plain English the government of ignorance and vice — it means a European, and especially Celtic, proletariat on the Atlantic coast; an African proletariat on the shores of the Gulf, and a Chinese proletariat on the Pacific." In 1878, the famous historian Francis Parkman wrote an article entitled "The Failure of Universal Suffrage." The next year a liberal reformer reported that "expressions of doubt and distrust in regard to universal suffrage are heard constantly in conversation, and in all parts of the country."[34]

A number of steps were taken to reduce the turnout of the poor voters in the North, especially the immigrants. The right to grant citizenship was taken from the states and given to the federal government. It became more difficult.[35] Civil service reform had a similar consequence, for a reduction in the patronage jobs controlled by the machines reduced the amount of labor at their disposal for poll work. A decline in machine income lessened their ability to create the carnival-like atmosphere that had drawn men into the city and to the polls.[36]

In addition, the Northern states adopted virtually all the measures to restrict suffrage that were used in the South, although not usually as a complete package.[37] Some even employed poll taxes, and many had a literacy test. All introduced the Australian ballot and self-registration. Supposedly these steps were taken to stop fraud by the political machines, but the lack of non-verbal symbols on the ballots bespoke

---

34. The various statements are quoted in Michael E. McGerr, *The Decline of Popular Politics: The American North, 1865–1928* (New York: Oxford University Press, 1986), pp. 45–47.
35. Daniel J. Tichenor, *Dividing Lines: The Politics of Immigration Control in America* (Princeton: Princeton University Press, 2002).
36. McGerr, *The Decline of Popular Politics*, pp. 76–90.

of other motivations. Indeed, the Progressives even pushed for the initiative and referendum that required still higher levels of literacy.

The residency and registration requirements in the North could be fully as complicated as in the South. In 1961 John Bailey, the chairman of the Democratic National Committee and a party leader in Connecticut, testified about registration rules introduced at the turn of the century in his state and still in effect in the 1960s:[38]

> In my own State of Connecticut, it is very difficult for a person to become a voter. We have constitutional requirements, first that they have to read part of the Constitution in the English language; secondly, that they have to be brought to the townhall because voters can only be made by a majority of the members of the board of selectmen in the town.... You can't delegate the authority.... There are three selectmen. Two of them have got to be present at one place, and the people have to present themselves [to read part of the Constitution even in] the city of Hartford where are some 85,000 or 90,000 voters.... If you are made a voter in Hartford and then you move to West Hartford, you then have to go through the whole procedure again.

The sub-committee chairman, Senator Estes Kefauver from the former Confederate state of Tennessee, was incredulous.

Table 4: The Democratic and Republican Presidential Vote, 1908–1940,
Total Number and Percentage

Year	Turnout	Northern Turnout	Democrat Total Vote	Democrat Percent	Republican Total Vote	Republican Percent
1908	65.7%	76.1%	6,406,874	43.3%	7,676,598	51.6%
1912	59.0%	67.7%	6,294,326	41.8%	3,486,343	23.2%
1916	61.6%	69.1%	9,126,000	49.2%	8,547,000	46.1%
1920	49.2%	57.3%	9,134,000	34.1%	16,152,000	60.3%
1924	48.9%	57.5%	8,387,000	25.8%	15,724,000	54.0%
1928	56.9%	66.7%	15,004,000	40.8%	21,433,000	58.2%
1932	56.9%	66.2%	22,878,000	57.4%	15,760,000	39.6%
1936	61.0%	71.4%	27,751,000	60.8%	16,679,000	36.5%
1940	62.5%	72.9%	27,343,000	54.7%	22,334,000	44.8%

Source: Walter Dean Burnham, "The Turnout Problem," in A. James Reichley, ed., *Elections American Style* (Washington: Brookings Institution, 1987), pp. 113–114.

Voter turnout in the North did not fall as rapidly or as far as the South, but it declined very precipitously. From 1876 through 1896, approximately 85% of eligible

---

37. See the discussion in Frances Fox Piven and Richard A. Cloward, *Why Americans Still Don't Vote and Why Politicians Want it That Way* (Boston: Beacon, 2000), pp. 45–93. For an incredibly detailed description of the voting rules in each state over time, see Jerrold C. Rusk, *A Statistical History of the American Electorate* (Washington: CQ Press, 2001), pp. 13–36.

38. "Nomination and Election of President and Vice President and Qualifications of Voting," Hearing before the Subcommittee on Constitutional Amendments of the Committee of the Judiciary, United States Senate, 87th Congress, July 13, 1961, pp. 538–539. This hearing was chaired by Senator Estes Kefauver of Tennessee, and this document and many documents and other materials on such subjects and Electoral College reform are found in his papers in the University of Tennessee.

Northern voters voted in the presidential elections. This figure fell to 82.6% in 1900, 76.1% in 1908, 67.7% in 1912, and 57.3% in 1920.[39]

One factor in the 1920 decline was the introduction of women's suffrage. Many women did not take advantage of their new right, particularly immigrant women. One reason that Republicans so strongly supported the 19th Amendment and that Democrats like Wilson resisted was that both knew it would double the votes of old-line Republican Protestants, but would not have the same impact on the votes of Democratic immigrants. Indeed, as Table 4 indicates, the total Republican vote rose 90% between 1916 and 1920, while the total Democratic vote did not increase at all, despite women's suffrage.

THE DEMOCRATS SHIFT TO THE LEFT SIDE OF THE POLITICAL SPECTRUM

The Democrats had as little chance for victory after the Panic of 1893 as the Republicans after the Crash of 1929. When foreign policy and nativist issues — and then the split in the Republican Party — gave them a good chance in 1912, they abandoned William Jennings Bryan. As will be discussed in the next chapter, they also refused to nominate Speaker of the House Champ Clark of Missouri, as they returned to the right-fork strategy with Woodrow Wilson of New Jersey. Economic issues were not decisive in the 1912 and 1916 elections, and they were no more important in 1920.

Table 5: Democratic Victories in House Elections, 1916–1928, By Region

Type of State	1916	1918	1920	1922	1924	1926	1928
Confederacy	100 (N=104)	101 (N=104)	97 (N=104)	97 (N=104)	101 (N=104)	101 (N=104)	98 (N=104)
Border	36 (N=48)	30 (N=48)	15 (N=48)	34 (N=48)	28 (N=48)	33 (N=48)	18 (N=48)
Non-Slave	80 (N=283)	58 (N=283)	19 (N=283)	72 (N=283)	55 (N=283)	59 (N=283)	49 (N=283)
Mid-West	34 (N=127)	17 (N=127)	3 (N=127)	23 (N=127)	19 (N=127)	21 (N=127)	15 (N=127)
Northeast	33 (N=123)	31 (N=123)	12 (N=123)	41 (N=123)	28 (N=123)	32 (N=123)	29 (N=123)
Pacific–Mtn	13 (N=33)	10 (N=33)	4 (N=33)	8 (N=33)	8 (N=33)	6 (N=33)	5 (N=33)
Total	216 (N=435)	189 (N=435)	131 (N=435)	203 (N=435)	184 (N=435)	193 (N=435)	165 (N=435)

Notes: *Confederate: Alabama, Arkansas, Florida, Georgia, Louisiana, Mississippi, North Carolina, South Carolina, Tennessee, Texas, Virginia; Border: Delaware, Kentucky, Maryland, Missouri, Oklahoma, West Virginia; Middle West: Illinois, Indiana, Iowa, Kansas, Michigan, Minnesota, Nebraska, North Dakota, Ohio, South Dakota, Wisconsin; Northeast: Connecticut, Maine, Massachusetts, New Hampshire, New Jersey, New York, Pennsylvania, Rhode Island, Vermont; Pacific–Mountain: Arizona, California, Colorado, Idaho, Montana, Nebraska, North Dakota, Oregon, Utah, Washington, Wyoming.*

Source: *Calculated from Congressional Quarterly's Guide to US Elections, 4th ed. (Washington: CQ Press, 2001), vol. 2, pp. 1012-1046.*

In 1916, Wilson adopted the slogan "He kept us out of war." As his chief political aide noted in his memoirs, Wilson did not promise that he would continue to keep the country out of war, but many voters understandably drew that conclusion.[40] When Wilson entered World War I in 1917, a month after his second term began, and harshly criticized German-Americans and Irish-Americans, this produced heavy Democratic losses in the 1918 Congressional election. He then launched the Red

---

39. Burnham, "The Turnout Problem," pp. 113–114.
40. Indeed, Wilson told Tumulty in April 1917 that he always expected war, but wanted to wait until the public was ready for it. Joseph Tumulty, *Woodrow Wilson: As I Know Him* (Garden City, NY: Doubleday, Page, & Co., 1921), pp. 250–259.

Scare against the German-Americans in 1919 and agreed to a peace treaty at Versailles that many ethnic groups damned. The Democratic losses continued throughout the decade, as Tables 4 and 5 document.

The stagnation in the total number of Democratic votes in the presidential elections of 1920 and 1924 was particularly alarming. As the Republican totals remind us, the number of votes for each party should have risen sharply in 1920 because of the ratification of the 19th Amendment, even for the party that received a lower percentage of the vote. As Table 6 shows, the Democrats did especially poorly in states with the largest number of German-Americans and Irish-Americans.

Table 6: Percentage of Democratic Presidential Votes in States with the Most German-Americans and Irish Americans, 1908–1932

States	1908	1912	1916	1920	1924	1928	1932
Total Democrat	43.1%	41.8%	49.2%	34.2%	28.8%	40.8%	57.4%
Irish States							
Massachusetts	34.0%	35.5%	46.6%	27.8%	24.9%	50.2%	50.6%
Connecticut	35.9%	39.2%	46.7%	33.3%	27.5%	45.6%	47.4%
Rhode Island	34.2%	39.0%	46.0%	32.8%	36.5%	50.2%	55.1%
New York	40.7%	41.3%	44.5%	27.0%	29.1%	47.4%	54.1%
New Hampshire	37.6%	39.5%	49.1%	39.4%	34.7%	41.0%	49.0%
New Jersey	39.1%	41.2%	42.7%	28.4%	27.4%	39.8%	49.5%
Delaware	45.9%	46.5%	47.8%	42.1%	36.8%	33.8%	35.3%
Pennsylvania	35.4%	32.5%	40.2%	27.2%	19.1%	33.9%	45.3%
Nevada	45.7%	39.7%	53.4%	36.2%	22.0%	36.2%	69.4%
California	33.3%	41.8%	46.6%	24.3%	8.2%	34.2%	58.4%
German States*							
Wisconsin	36.7%	41.1%	42.8%	16.2%	8.1%	44.3%	63.5%
Minnesota	33.1%	31.8%	46.3%	19.4%	6.8%	40.8%	59.9%
Nebraska	49.1%	43.7%	55.3%	31.3%	29.6%	36.2%	63.0%
Illinois	39.0%	35.3%	43.3%	25.5%	23.4%	42.3%	55.2%
Iowa	40.6%	37.6%	42.9%	25.5%	16.4%	37.6%	57.7%
South Dakota	35.1%	42.1%	45.9%	19.8%	13.4%	39.2%	63.6%
Michigan	32.5%	27.4%	43.9%	22.3%	13.1%	28.9%	52.4%
Ohio	44.8%	41.0%	51.9%	38.6%	23.7%	34.5%	49.9%
North Dakota	34.8%	34.3%	47.8%	18.3%	7.0%	44.5%	69.6%
Colorado	48.0%	42.8%	60.8%	35.9%	22.0%	33.9%	54.8%

*Note: New York and New Jersey ranked 7th and 8th on the list of states with the most people either born in Germany or with a parent born there. Many of these were Jewish rather than ethnic Germans and in any case these states were distinguished by their high numbers of Catholic immigrants. They have been replaced by two states — North Dakota and Colorado — that ranked somewhat lower in percentage from Germany, but they both had very large numbers of people from the Volga region of Russia who actually were ethnic Germans.

Source: For ethnic distribution of states in 1910, Thirteenth Census of the United States Taken in the Year 1910: Abstract of the Census (Washington: US Government Printing Office, 1913), pp. 166-169, 893-895, and 803. For presidential votes, see CQ's Guide to US Elections, vol. 1, pp. 665-673.

In 1924, domestic economic issues again came to the fore as a new collapse in commodity prices created great suffering in the rural areas. Neither the Democrats nor the Republicans responded, and Robert La Follette of Wisconsin was able to achieve real success with a new Progressive Party. He won a total of 16.6% in the country as a whole and 33% in Wisconsin and the non-slave states beyond the Mississippi River. He also did quite well in the ten largest cities in 1924, winning 23.6% of their vote.[41]

The Democrats nominated an Irish Catholic, Al Smith, in 1928 in an effort to restore their ethnic coalition destroyed by Woodrow Wilson during the war, by their 1920 campaign, and then by the challenge of the Catholic La Follette. Nevertheless, Smith's economic policy was quite conservative, and this alone made him unattractive to the La Follette supporters of 1924. This conservatism may have cost him as much among rural Progressive voters as his Catholicism and position on Prohibition.

Smith made his own economic views absolutely clear when Roosevelt moved to the left in economic policy after his inauguration in 1933. Smith damned him for accepting the radical Midwestern ideas on currency, and he helped to found a conservative, anti-New Deal organization called the American Liberty League. In 1936, he denounced Roosevelt's "betrayal" of the Democratic Party.[42]

No doubt, the attitude of those such as Smith was the major reason that Roosevelt had taken an ambiguous position on economic policy during the 1932 campaign. He vaguely suggested that the government should be more vigorous in combating the Depression, but his concrete policy promises were quite conservative. Mitchell Palmer, Woodrow Wilson's Attorney General who used troops against trade unions, was given the responsibility of drafting the Democratic platform. It was thoroughly orthodox.

Since the big city bosses generally favored the renomination of the Catholic Al Smith, Roosevelt had to seek delegates for the 1932 convention elsewhere. He decided to put together a coalition of the South and the West, hoping to win at the convention with Bryan's left-fork strategy. Roosevelt ultimately obtained the nomination by giving the vice presidency to John Garner, the candidate of Texas and California, a symbol of the coalition between South and West, although a conservative one.[43] As Walter Lippmann wrote in January, Roosevelt had mastered "the art of carrying water on both shoulders." Lippmann warned that "it is not easy to say with certainty whether his left-wing or his right-wing supporters are the more deceived." [44]

Roosevelt defeated Hoover 57.4% to 39.6% in 1932, but he did not arouse great enthusiasm. The voter turnout in the North actually fell to 66.2% from 66.7% in the 1928 election. The rural La Follette voters of 1924 did, however, sense that Roosevelt was in the Bryan tradition. Roosevelt won 59.4% of the vote in the Prairie states and 58.3% in the Mountain and Western states. Yet, although he was the governor of New York, Roosevelt only won the industrial states from Massachusetts through

---

41. David Burner, "Election of 1924," in Schlesinger, *History of American Presidential Elections,* vol. 3, p. 2487. Oklahoma was populated almost wholly by Southerners and is counted as a border state. La Follette received only 14 percent of the vote in the other four old Midwestern states — Illinois, Indiana, Michigan, and Ohio. The state in this group with the largest Progressive vote was Ohio, the most German-American of the four states.
42. Christopher M. Finan, *Alfred E. Smith: The Happy Warrior* (New York: Hill & Wang, 2002), pp. 305–317.
43. Columns of June 26, 1932, and July 4, 1932, in Lippmann, *Interpretations, 1931–1932,* pp. 298–301 and 312–314.
44. Column of January 8, 1932, in Lippmann, *Interpretations, 1931–1932,* pp. 260–262.

Ohio by a 50.4% to 45.8% vote. He lost two — Connecticut and Pennsylvania — to a candidate from Iowa who was presiding over the Great Depression. The urban immigrants were resentful that Roosevelt had replaced Smith, and they were not convinced he would change policy.

An indirect indication of the nature of the 1932 election in the populous Eastern and Midwestern states was provided by a public opinion poll conducted by a major magazine, *Literary Digest*. In 1936 the journal was to predict the victory of the Republican Alf Landon, and this fiasco led to its demise. The magazine conducted the poll by telephone, and the sample was badly biased because many poor voters no longer had a telephone. Yet, *Literary Digest* had used the same technique in the past and had an excellent record of predicting presidential elections. The reason, as Everett Ladd points out, is that Northern Democratic and Republican voters were not that differentiated in their incomes prior to 1936, and hence in their telephone ownership.[45] This was even true in 1932. Neither the rich nor the poor expected the aristocratic Roosevelt to lead economic warfare against his "own class."

When Roosevelt was inaugurated, however, he introduced a highly experimental and dramatic economic policy that made the phrase "the first 100 days" a cliché in American politics. Roosevelt sharply increased government controls of production with the NRA (National Recovery Act) and established a jobs policy as a form of relief. He began running large deficits as John Maynard Keynes was advocating. By any normal criteria, Roosevelt had moved the Democratic Party far to the left. Instead of being to the right of the Republicans on the economic spectrum, the Democrats were now on the left side.

Several factors were important in Roosevelt's decision. One was almost surely personal. Franklin Roosevelt always acted as if he were competing with Theodore Roosevelt for a better historical legacy. It was a difficult task, for Theodore's face was on Mount Rushmore. In domestic policy, Theodore was on the left wing of the more left-wing party, and Franklin would not find it easy to achieve a more impressive domestic record than his cousin with a traditional Democratic program.

A second reason was Roosevelt's fear of being outflanked on the left, as occurred with the Liberal Party in Great Britain. The Socialist Party of Eugene Debs had won from 3% to 6% of the vote in every election from 1904 to 1920. In 1924, Robert La Follette of Wisconsin was spectacularly successful with his Progressive Party. If Roosevelt remained to the right of the Republican Party and did not end the Depression quickly, a new more left-wing Progressive Party or Labor Party might well seriously challenge him in 1936. Huey Long of Louisiana was of special concern, for he could challenge the Democrats in the North as well as the South.[46]

Roosevelt's shift to the left clearly was popular with a large segment of the population. Turnout in the North had been 66.2% in 1932, but it rose to 71.4% in 1936. His percentage of the popular vote in the non-slave states rose from 53.9% to 58.5%

---

45. Everett Carl Ladd with Charles D. Hadley, *Transformations of the American Party System: Political Coalitions from the New Deal to the 1970s* (New York: W. W. Norton & Company, Inc., 1975).

46. T. Harry Williams, *Huey Long* (New York: Knopf, 1969). He was assassinated in 1935.

and from 50.4% to 57.3% in the industrial states from Massachusetts to Ohio. In all, 16.9 million people in the North voted for Roosevelt in 1932 and 21.3 million in 1936. In short, only when Roosevelt introduced his radical measures during his first term was he able to mobilize real popular enthusiasm. His move to the left after coming to office also created for the first time a strong economic differentiation between Democratic and Republican voters. This is why the telephone public opinion poll of the *Literary Digest* that was so successful in 1932 was a complete failure in 1936.

THE CHANGE IN THE SUPREME COURT AND THE CONFIRMATION OF THE NEW PARTY COALITIONS

Whatever Roosevelt's calculations in 1932 and 1933, one fact was certain. Most of the regulatory and social welfare measures he wanted to introduce were not constitutional by the precedents the Supreme Court had established during the previous half century. Roosevelt could never institutionalize the New Deal unless he could induce or force the Supreme Court to change its interpretation of the Constitution.

The old Court interpretation actually corresponded fairly closely to the intentions of the Founding Fathers, but the thoughtful defenders of the old Court interpretations did not simply focus on the original intent of the Founders.[47] Many, such as Robert A. Taft, the son of President William Howard Taft, thought a major expansion of the role of the federal government in the economic realm was incompatible with political freedom.[48] Roosevelt made the opposite case: a government that could not respond to the desires of the majority on matters such as social welfare was undemocratic.

In his relatively short State of the Nation speech on January 6, 1937, Roosevelt used the word "democracy" or "democratic" 22 times. He argued that "democratic forms" would be overthrown if they were not effective, but that such democratic forms could be as effective as (even "superior" to) "more extreme forms of government ... without the spiritual sacrifices which those other forms of government exact."[49] In his Second Inaugural Address, delivered two weeks later, Roosevelt emphasized "the power to govern." He returned to the theme of democracy: "The essential democracy of our nation and the safety of our people depend not upon the absence of power but upon lodging it with those whom the people can change or continue at stated intervals through an honest and free system of elections."[50]

---

47. Nothing is as strange as the notion in the United States that modern Americans must be bound by decisions made by semi-democrats who were absorbed 220 years ago with writing a minimalist document that would allow each region, especially the slaveholding South, to accept a common constitution. The American system of gradual constitutional change by Court change is actually an excellent method of preserving restraints but permitting change.
48. A very clear expression of his view was presented in a speech at Ardmore, PA, October 21, 1936. Robert A. Taft Papers, Box 1291, Library of Congress.
49. *The New York Times*, January 7, 1937, p. 2.
50. *The New York Times*, January 21, 1937, p. 1.

A great myth has been created that the Supreme Court has enormous power in guaranteeing constitutional restraints on the President and Congress. Yet, as the man who soon was to become chairman of the Republican National Committee noted in 1934, "the Supreme Court ... is the weakest of the three coordinate branches of government."[51] The reason is that the Constitution does not specify the number of Supreme Court Justices, and a President with a majority in both Houses can change that number, even from 9 Justices to 19 by a regular law with a bare majority. If someone attempts to filibuster the change, a simple majority can abolish the filibuster. The President can then appoint 10 new Justices with any view of the Constitution so long as the Senate will confirm them.

On February 5, 1937, Roosevelt did, in fact, propose that the President be allowed to appoint an additional Supreme Court Justice for each sitting Justice over the age of 70, a total of six at that time. It was clear that those appointed would declare that the government regulation and social welfare measures of the New Deal were constitutional. Everyone assumed that Roosevelt with his huge new majority could easily enact a compromise measure that expanded the Court by two members.

In actuality, one conservative Justice changed his position on April 12, 1937, when the Wagner Act on trade unions unexpectedly was declared constitutional. This change in position created a 5 to 4 majority in favor of the New Deal measures. The majority was strengthened when another conservative Justice resigned on May 18, the day that the Senate Judiciary Committee was voting on the bill to expand the Court. The Committee voted against the bill, and capital wags quickly declared that "a switch in time saves nine."[52]

The standard history of the 1937 "court packing," written shortly after the event, treats the failure of Roosevelt's proposed law as a great defeat for the President. In fact, Roosevelt surely achieved exactly what he wanted. He often talked about the Liberal government of Herbert Asquith in England and its sharp reduction of the power of the House of Lords in 1911. The House of Lords had been resisting a pension law, and Asquith had called and won a special election in January 1910 on the issue of the power of the House of Lords.[53] The Prime Minister threatened to expand the size of the House of Lords if it would not agree to a reduction of its power to block legislation. After the election, it agreed to do so.

---

51. Henry Fletcher, quoted in William E. Leuchtenburg, *The Supreme Court Reborn: The Constitutional Revolution in the Age of Roosevelt* (New York: Oxford University Press, 1995), p. 85. Leuchtenburg's reexamination of this battle is far superior to the earlier, long-standard work on the subject done at the time. Joseph Alsop and Turner Catledge, *The 168 Days* (Garden City, NY: Doubleday, Doran, 1938).
52. The remark was spreading rapidly through Washington society in the week of June 9, 1937. See "Supreme Court Crack," in Raymond Clapper Papers, Box 8, Library of Congress. The witticism became a section heading in Alsop and Catledge, *The 168 Days*, p 135.
53. For a contemporary description of the battle, see A. Lawrence Lowell, *The Government of England*, new ed. (New York: Macmillan, 1912), vol. 1, pp. 423–436. For evidence about Roosevelt's earlier interest in the Asquith experience, see Leuchtenburg, *The Supreme Court Reborn*, p. 95.

Roosevelt followed precisely Asquith's path in the mid-1930s, even using a pension law, his Social Security law, for the crucial test. His closest political adviser, James Farley, wrote in his diary that Roosevelt was "very happy" about the change in the interpretation of the Wagner Act and looked like "the Cheshire Cat had swallowed the canary." Then when the other conservative Justice resigned, the President was in "very good humor and not at all disturbed by all the agitation precipitated by the Supreme Court controversy."[54] Roosevelt's top speechwriter, one of his closest aides, notes that "of all the ways open to him, Franklin does seem to have chosen the one most upsetting to judicial dignity."[55]

Instead of being a defeat, Roosevelt's transformation of the Supreme Court was his greatest domestic victory and his greatest domestic achievement. Roosevelt had succeeded in democratizing the party system by shifting one of the parties to the left (to be sure, the rather moderate left by European standards) and by enacting social welfare for the population. He then changed the Constitution to legitimate for the first time the right of the federal government to respond to the majority on such questions.

The result was not, of course, what Robert Taft feared. He himself was elected Senator from Ohio in 1938, and after several months in Washington, he declared that his fears had been excessive.[56]

> I spoke and talked against planned economy and government regulation, and expected to find the government here operating in accordance with the theory of a planned and regulated economy so beautifully outlined by New Deal writers. But, as a matter of fact ...machinery is whirring in every direction, but without any balance-wheel.

Two months later Taft spoke more colorfully at the Gridiron Club: "I came down to Washington prepared to meet a raging New Deal lion, and instead I find a rather sleepy and confused lion enjoying an over-dose of social, and political, security."[57]

The Republicans themselves moved to the left after the 1936 election and accepted the general principles of the New Deal. Indeed, in 1937 the conservative Vice President, John Garner, told Roosevelt's first Director of the Budget, also a conservative, that there was no hope of a reversal:[58]

> It seems to me that we are going to get in a position where it will be impossible for *any President* to get from Congress sufficient legislation to materially reduce the

---

54. James Farley diary, April 12, 1937, and May 18, 1937, James A. Farley Papers, Roll 3, Library of Congress.
55. Rexford G. Tugwell, *The Democratic Roosevelt: A Biography of Franklin D. Roosevelt* (Garden City, NY: Doubleday, 1957), p. 392.
56. Robert A. Taft guest column in *The Washington Post*, February 1939. Attached to letter of Harlan Miller to Robert Taft, February 1, 1939, Robert A. Taft papers, "Remarks – 1939" Folder, Box 1293, Library of Congress.
57. Robert A. Taft speech to the Gridiron dinner, April 15, 1939, in Robert A. Taft papers, Box 1292, Library of Congress.
58. John Garner letter to Lewis Douglas, September 9, 1937, Lewis W. Douglas papers, Box 252, Folder 13, University of Arizona. The italics are Garner's.

activities that are and will have been built up. It is nearly impossible now to get Congress to reduce expenditures and more unnecessary bills, prompted by considerations of personal interest and carrying drafts on the Treasury, have been passed in the last two years than in any other two year period in the history of the Congress: showing you the trend of the Congressional mind is to give little thought to dollars and cents in the matter of public policy.

THE CONSEQUENCES FOR THE OLD DEMOCRATIC COALITION

The shifting of the national Democratic Party to the left side of the spectrum was quite popular among the broad population of the South. Indeed, because the South was the poorest region in the country, it benefited disproportionately from many New Deal policies — e.g., rural electrification and the Tennessee Valley Authority. Nevertheless, the change in the Supreme Court interpretation of the powers of the federal government annulled the central provision in the North–South "pact" of the 1870s and 1880s. When the Southern elite wanted a weak federal government that could not impose its will on the states, it had logically allied with the Democratic Party, the more right-wing of the two parties. But now, of course, the Republicans occupied that position on the spectrum.

From a strictly logical point of view, the change in the position of the Supreme Court need not have benefited blacks. The new interpretation proclaimed that the due process clause of the 14th Amendment did not prevent the majority in Congress from enacting legislation that legalized trade unions or taxed people to fund pensions. If so, why should the Court prevent the majority in the states from enacting laws to regulate the economy by requiring segregated facilities? One Roosevelt appointee to the Court, Felix Frankfurter, took precisely this position, even on political questions.

Of course, the Court's failure to apply the 15th Amendment on black voting rights to obvious cases of discrimination against black voters had been hard to defend on any intellectual grounds. These decisions were almost certain to be overturned. But, in addition, Southern politicians understood full well that, logical or not, liberal Justices who reflected Northern Democratic values were likely to interpret the 14th Amendment so as to protect blacks on issues such as the "separate but equal" doctrine and segregation. On this case, the new interpretation actually followed the "original intention" of those who drafted the 14th Amendment during Reconstruction.

The change in the position of the Northern Democratic Party and of the Supreme Court was accelerated by political and demographic changes taking place within the black population of America. Historically the blacks had voted overwhelmingly for the Republican Party. They were not only grateful for emancipation, but were making a rational political calculation. The Democratic Party was the party of the South and the party positioned on the conservative side of the political spectrum. The Republican Party, even after Reconstruction, was marginally more sympathetic.

Franklin Roosevelt never showed any major interest in blacks when he was governor of New York.[59] He had been a member of the Wilson Administration and had been the official responsible for introducing segregation into the building of the War Department and State Department. After suffering polio in 1921, Roosevelt began going to Warm Springs, Georgia, to rebuild the strength of his legs. He bought land in the area, typically only some 80 miles from the plantation near Roswell, Georgia, where Theodore's mother had been raised. He treated Georgia as his adopted home, developed a real feel for the white political culture, and followed local mores in dealing with blacks.[60]

Despite the Depression and Hoover's neglect of the blacks during his Administration, Roosevelt still lost black precincts in Chicago to Hoover 75% to 21% in 1932, in Cincinnati 71% to 29%, Cleveland 82% to 17%, Knoxville 70% to 30%, and Philadelphia 71% to 27%. Despite the Depression, Roosevelt did worse than Smith in black precincts in Chicago, Cleveland, and Knoxville.[61] Only in New York City did Roosevelt actually win in black areas in 1932, and then by a narrow 51% to 46% margin. Even in the Roosevelt landslide of 1936, the Republicans still received strong black support. (See Table 7.)

The black response to Roosevelt's movement of the Democratic Party to the left actually took some time, partly because most of Roosevelt's changes were cautious and subtle. He often simply acted, Southerners complained, as if blacks were "as good as anyone else." Without prior announcement, more blacks were seen marching in the inaugural parade. They were regularly invited to White House meetings and receptions. Woodrow Wilson's portrait was not hung at the 1936 convention. This was primarily a gesture to German-Americans, but knowledgeable blacks also appreciated it. Then Roosevelt created a major controversy by insisting that a black minister open one of the sessions of the 1936 Democratic Convention.[62]

Table 7: Percentage of Blacks Who Voted Republican in 1932 and 1936 Presidential Elections, Five Northern Cities

City	1932	1936
Chicago	77%	51%
Cleveland	76%	38%
Philadelphia	73%	34%
Pittsburgh	48%	17%
Detroit	50%	25%

Source: Samuel Lubell, *The Future of American Politics*, 2nd ed. (Doubleday: Garden City, 1956), p. 53.

---

59. Nancy J. Weiss, *Farewell to the Party of Lincoln: Black Politics in the Age of FDR* (Princeton: Princeton University Press, 1983), pp. 17–22.
60. See the discussion in Frank Freidel, *F. D. R. and the South* (Baton Rouge: Louisiana State University Press, 1965), pp. 1–33. For example, the black servants had an adjoining house with facilities, and hence they did not have to use the bathrooms in the main house.
61. Weiss, *Farewell to the Party of Lincoln*, pp. 10 and 30–31.
62. Weiss, *Farewell to the Party of Lincoln*, pp. 40–45 and 185–186.

Roosevelt took very few concrete actions to help blacks directly until the eve of World War II. He did insist in the 1930s that race not be a factor in the distribution of relief jobs and aid and, despite the poor enforcement of this pledge, a substantial number of blacks did make it to the rolls of the Works Progress Administration (WPA) and the CCC (Civilian Conservation Corps). A scattering of low-level black advisers and officials were appointed in the various government departments.

Nevertheless, the President was frank in telling black leaders that Southerners controlled Congress and that he had to appease them.[63] All of his social welfare measures were locally administered, and this inevitably had an impact. They also had provisions, usually demanded by Congress, that excluded most blacks or reduced their benefits. Even the Social Security Act did not cover occupations such as farm labor and domestic help, where most blacks were employed. Pensions were based not on need or on the principle of equal treatment, but on contributions that reflected wage level. Federal pensions thus were much higher for the well-to-do than the poor, and black wages were lowest of all.[64]

Roosevelt moved more rapidly during the war. In 1944, the Supreme Court reversed an earlier unanimous decision and in *Allwright v. Smith* decreed that a primary is an integral part of the election process and that blacks could not be excluded from it. The administration also pushed for the integration of the military outside of the South during the war, and it created some symbolic units that featured highly trained blacks — for example, the Tuskegee air unit of black pilots. One can choose to emphasize the great inequality and discrimination that continued to exist or the progress that was achieved, but progress was, in fact, achieved.[65]

The South did feel reassured when Roosevelt replaced the left-wing Henry Wallace as Vice President by the moderate Harry Truman in 1944. Everyone knew that the Vice President almost surely would become President in the relatively near future.[66] Truman came from the former slave state of Missouri and from a pro-Confederate family. All politicians knew that he enjoyed telling off-color jokes about blacks.[67]

Sophisticated Southerners understood, however, that the question was not whether change would occur, but how fast. Indeed, even before the attack on the Court in 1937, Roosevelt had had the 1936 Democratic Convention repeal the requirement that the Democratic nominee must receive the vote of two-thirds of the delegates. Instead, only a simple majority was needed. Roosevelt surely was looking

---

63. For the testimony of the head of the NAACP, see William F. White, *A Man Called White: The Autobiography of William White* (New York: Viking Press, 1948), pp. 169–170.
64. Robert Lieberman, *Shifting the Color Line: Race and the American Welfare State* (Cambridge: Harvard University Press, 1998), pp. 67-117. Ira Katznelson, *When Affirmative Action was White: An Untold History of Racial Inequality in Twentieth-Century America* (New York: W. W. Norton, 2005), pp. 25-52.
65. For a good discussion of the combination of pluses and minuses, see Katznelson, *When Affirmative Action Was White*, pp. 80-112. See also Sherie Mershon and Steven Schlossman, *Foxholes & Color Line: Desegregating the U.S. Armed Forces* (Baltimore: Johns Hopkins University Press, 1998).
66. Walter Lippmann, "Today and Tomorrow: President Truman," *The New York Herald Tribune*, April 17, 1945, p. 25.
67. For examples and a discussion of his racist prejudices, see Richard L. Miller, *Truman: The Rise to Power* (New York: McGraw Hill, 1986), pp. 325-330.

forward to what might be a difficult re-nomination of himself for a third term in 1940, but the South knew that the change would reduce its ability to block a liberal candidate in the future.

Moreover, the migration of blacks out of the rural South was accelerating and was certain to have political consequences. As Table 8 shows, this migration had begun during World War I and had continued in the 1920s. Most of the migrants went to Southern cities, but many moved to the North, especially to the "Middle States" of New York, New Jersey, and Pennsylvania and to Illinois, Michigan, and Ohio of the old "Northwest." Blacks had constituted only 2.5% of the population in twelve large Northern cities in 1910, but this figure rose to 7.4% in 1930 and 8.2% in 1940.[68] In the Confederate states, one-third of blacks lived in urban areas in 1940. The process of black migration accelerated during the 1940s because of the war and then the postwar mechanization of cotton harvesting. By 1950, 45% of blacks in Confederate states lived in urban areas, and 12% of the people in the twelve large Northern cities were blacks.

Table 8: Percentage of Blacks in the States and Large Cities of the East and Midwest, 1900 to 2000

Year	Former States of the Confederacy	Former States of the Confederacy Who Live in Urban Areas	Seven Large Eastern and Midwestern States	Twelve Large Cities of Seven Large States
1900	38.1%	14.6%	2.0%	2.4%
1910	35.3%	18.3%	2.0%	2.5%
1920	32.5%	22.7%	2.7%	4.3%
1930	25.8%	29.1%	4.1%	7.4%
1940	28.0%	33.7%	4.6%	8.2%
1950	24.8%	45.2%	6.4%	12.0%
1960	22.7%	55.4%	8.5%	19.8%
1970	20.3%	64.1%	10.5%	27.4%
1980	19.6%	71.7%	11.9%	32.2%
1990	19.5%	75.8%	12.8%	35.5%
1999	20.0%	—	13.8%	—
2000*	19.5%	—	13.2%	34.4%

Note: The seven large states are Illinois, Indiana, Michigan, New Jersey, New York, Ohio, and Pennsylvania. The large cities are those with at least 250,000 population in 2000: Buffalo, NY; Chicago, IL; Cincinnati, Ohio; Cleveland, Ohio; Columbus, Ohio; Detroit, MI.; Indianapolis, Ind.; Newark, NJ; New York City, NY; Philadelphia, Pa.; Pittsburgh, Pa.; and Toledo, Ohio.
Source: A variety of census volumes, 1910-2000.
* The introduction of a "2-race" category reduced the number of blacks.

As blacks moved from the rural South into Northern and even Southern cities, the quality of their education gradually improved. The cruder means of preventing black turnout could not be used in the larger Southern cities, and the blacks became politically more active. In the North, Democratic politicians could no longer avoid responding to the new black members of their local coalition.

---

68. The large cities are those with at least 250,000 population in 2000 in Illinois, Indiana, Michigan, New Jersey, New York, Ohio, and Pennsylvania: Buffalo, NY; Chicago, IL; Cincinnati, OH; Cleveland, OH; Columbus, OH; Detroit, MI; Indianapolis, IN; Newark, NJ; New York City, NY; Philadelphia, PA; Pittsburgh, PA; and Toledo, OH.

Ironically, it was to be Harry Truman who showed Southerners that they were justified in their fears. Truman had been a steadfast supporter of the New Deal in the Senate in the 1930s, and he focused almost exclusively on this point in his 1940 re-election campaign.[69] Truman was, however, a member of "the Club" in the Senate, and Democratic insiders understood that he was not a radical.

Truman's top political adviser, Clark Clifford, caught the essence of Truman's policy in an August 1948 memorandum: The President, he said, should be presented "as a crusader rallying the people to *save* the tremendous social gains made under the New Deal and *carried forward* by his administration."[70] (The emphases are mine.) Truman's major contribution in social policy was to introduce administrative order into the disorganized Roosevelt programs and expand the coverage of programs such as Social Security.

Truman's reputation as a strong New Deal President was based primarily on his opposition to conservative Republican rhetoric and his 1948 campaign against the "Do-Nothing 80th Congress." The aspect of that campaign of greatest political importance, however, involved civil rights. As a President from a slaveholding state, Truman felt that he had a special need to reassure Northern voters that he was committed to civil rights. The left-wing Henry Wallace had decided to run for President as a third party candidate in 1948 and would win a significant number of votes in the large urban centers. Truman wanted a large black turnout to offset these losses.

Indeed, Truman's advisers feared that blacks might vote for Wallace or even return to their earlier Republican identification. Governor Thomas Dewey had promoted anti-discrimination laws in New York that applied to blacks as well as Ellis Island immigrants, and he was likely to be the Republican candidate for President in 1948. Truman's adviser, Clark Clifford, sent the President a memorandum insisting that he must take preventive action by proposing a federal fair employment law and a federal commission to oversee it:[71]

> It is inconceivable that any policies initiated by the Truman Administration no matter how "liberal" could so alienate the South in the next year that it would revolt. As always, the South can be considered safely Democratic. And in formulating national policy, it can be safely ignored. The only pragmatic reason for conciliating the South in normal times is because of its tremendous strength in Congress [but] since the Congress is Republican ... and the Democratic President has, there-

---

69. This statement is based on an examination of his surviving speeches from the campaign and from copies of newspaper articles about the campaign, both found in Truman's Senatorial papers at the Harry S. Truman Presidential Library.

70. Clark Clifford, "Memorandum for the President: The 1948 Campaign," August 17, 1948, p. 32; Clifford Political File, Box 22, Harry S. Truman Presidential Library. Republished in Dennis Merrill, *Documentary History of the Truman Presidency* (University Publications of America, 1996), vol. 14, "Running From Behind: Truman's Strategy for the 1948 Presidential Campaign," pp. 332-339.

71. Clark Clifford, "Memorandum for the President," November 19, 1947, Clark Clifford papers, Political File, pp. 3 and 12. Harry S. Truman Presidential Library. These words, like nearly all the memorandum, came verbatim from a memorandum of September 18, 1947, sent him by James H. Rowe, a liberal Roosevelt adviser. These two memoranda both are in Merrill, *Documentary History of the Truman Presidency*, vol. 14, pp. 29-104.

fore no real chance to get his own program approved by it ... he has no real necessity for "getting along" with the Southern conservatives.

Truman did issue an executive order that officially ended discrimination and segregation in the military. He did present a civil rights bill to Congress in the early months of his second term, but everyone understood that a Southern filibuster could and would prevent the enactment of any major civil rights legislation. Nevertheless, many Southerners understood that Truman's behavior showed that any President, Democratic or Republican, actually felt he could safely ignore the South. Strom Thurmond, a South Carolina governor who had been generally progressive and had even proposed the abolition of the state's poll tax, decided that it would profitable to run for President on a third party ticket.[72]

Truman did try to heal the wounds within the Democratic Party by sponsoring a successor in 1952, Adlai Stevenson, who was moderate if not conservative with respect both to civil rights and New Deal legislation. This did not, however, prevent the Republican candidate, Dwight Eisenhower, from winning four Confederate states in 1952 and five in 1956. Then when a Southern President, Lyndon Johnson, introduced the Great Society and conducted a foreign policy that provoked a radicalization of elite youth, a fundamental party alignment began in earnest. This will be discussed in Chapters 7 and 8.

---

72. Jack Bass and Marilyn W. Thompson, *Strom: The Complicated Personal and Political Life of Strom Thurmond* (New York: Public Affairs, 2005).

Chapter 3. The Ethnic and Religious Character of Parties in the North

The logic of the old North–South party coalitions was stark: if the former Confederate states were to be solidly Democratic, then the outcome of the election would be decided in the non-Confederate states. If electoral competition in the North did not focus on economic issues, it had to center on other factors. In particular, the absence of economic competition inevitably made cultural questions especially important.

In essence, the two major political parties in the North were coalitions of different religious groups, and church officials served as part of the political organization of "their" party. The Democrats in the North essentially were the party of Protestant migrants from the South and non-Protestant immigrants. The Republicans were the party of the Protestants who did not come from the South. Since ethnicity usually was closely associated with religion, the parties also were coalitions of ethnic groups. But when ethnic groups were divided between Protestants and Catholics, as were the Germans, the people voted on a religious basis.

Ethnic and especially religious differences among Protestants generated great emotion throughout the 17th and 18th century, but the old antagonists joined together in the mid-19th century to direct their hostility toward the new Irish and German Catholic immigrants. The word "race" was applied to the peoples from the different countries of Europe, and it implied the same racist prejudices and emotions that it did in the mid-20th century.

Then just as Northern Protestants were becoming more accustomed to the Catholic Irish and Germans, a new wave of German Catholics fled Otto Bismarck's anti-Catholic *kulturkampf* and came to the United States. An even larger group of non-Protestants began arriving from southern and eastern Europe – the so-called Ellis Island immigrants, notably Italians, Poles, and Jews from the Russian Empire. They were considered even worse than the earlier Catholics.

On balance, the new non-Protestant immigration actually should been beneficial for American social peace. The Civil War, whatever its short-run and long-
range causes, was a terrible conflict among the country's Protestants. It cost over
600,000 deaths in a country of 31 million people, 15 million of them adults. It left
intense bitterness. If huge non-Protestant immigration created pressures for the
Protestants to come together, that was a healthy development. It surely was no
accident that the three Presidents from 1901 to 1921 — Theodore Roosevelt, William
Howard Taft, and Woodrow Wilson — all had personal backgrounds that symbolized the reconciliation of the Protestants of the North and the South.

The great tragedy for the European-Americans after the Civil War was the
change that occurred in European international relations at the end of the century.
Europe had largely been at peace for nearly a century after the Napoleonic wars.
Britain and Germany were allies throughout the century, and the British-Americans
and German-Americans could unite behind the foreign policy followed by Britain
and Germany. The two countries were involved only in short wars with countries
such as Russia and France that had few immigrants in the United States. The only
conflict in Europe that really mattered in American politics was the demand for independence in Ireland.

In the 1890s, however, the relationship between Germany and Britain became
increasingly hostile and a great war broke out between the two in 1914. This was a
disaster for American domestic ethnic peace. Judging by the immigration quotas
based on the 1920 census, British-Americans and German-Americans together constituted over 55% of the white population in 1920, nearly 65% if those from eastern
and southern Europe are excluded. The British-Americans and German-Americans
reacted to American policy toward their homelands with the same emotion that
Cuban-Americans display toward US policy toward Cuba today.

The Republican Party coalition was based primarily upon the British-American
and German-American Protestants, and the growing conflict between Britain and
Germany put particular strain upon that coalition. In 1912, the Democrats seemed
likely to win large numbers of Republicans from one wing of the party or the other,
depending on the nominees of the two parties. When Theodore Roosevelt split from
the Republicans and ran as the candidate of its English wing in a new Progressive
Party, the Republicans were threatened with extinction. Roosevelt was so serious
that his party ran candidates in almost all Congressional districts in 1912. If he won,
he wanted a fundamental realignment in which his new party would become permanent and would win an increasing number of Southern as well as Northern votes.
Since his mother was born in the South and his father in New York, he seemed well
positioned to achieve this goal.

In response, the Democrats nominated a fervent Anglophile and critic of the
Ellis Island immigrants, Woodrow Wilson. Wilson undercut Roosevelt's support
among the British-Americans and achieved victory himself in 1912. Once in power, he
strongly tilted toward Britain in World War I during his first term and then entered
the war at the beginning of his second term. Even before American entry into the
war, Wilson damned critics of his policy, a large number of them Germans and Irish,

as disloyal and even traitorous. He continued to do this in the postwar Red Scare of 1919. The Democratic candidate in 1920, James Cox, followed a similar path.

Wilson's policy put enormous strains on the Democratic coalition, and the Democrats suffered crushing defeats in 1920 and 1924. In 1924, the success of a new Progressive Party headed by a Catholic isolationist, Robert La Follette, raised the possibility that the Democrats would be the party to disappear. The Democrats first moved to prevent this by nominating an Irish Catholic, Al Smith, in 1928. Then Franklin Roosevelt coopted the Progressive economic program and reassured the German-Americans with his isolationist policy toward Hitler.

Wilson's intensification of ethnic conflict among the European-Americans also did great harm to American foreign policy and domestic peace. This was the key factor in the defeat of the League of Nations in 1919, the isolationism of the 1930s, and then the McCarthyism of the late 1940s and early 1950s. After World War II, the entire political stratum felt a great need to end these conflicts. As will be discussed in the next two chapters, they used both foreign and domestic policy to create a new European-American community.

CREATING "NATIONAL" AND "ETHNIC" IDENTITIES

The nature of identity in the past is extraordinarily difficult to discuss because of the lack of sound evidence. We can see how earlier writers identified themselves or wrote about the subject, but we can seldom be certain how widely or deeply these identities were shared by those who didn't write. Indeed, the writings of political intellectuals often do not reflect existing identities, but are attempts to create new ones — or at least to change the relative importance of existing identities. Everyone has multiple identities — "group memberships," to use the language of an earlier generation[1] — but the strength of these identities varies from person to person and from time to time. Gender is the most obvious example of a timeless identity whose political salience has changed greatly over time. National or ethnic identities are no different, except that they are far more transient in nature.

The "national" identities that result from state boundaries are especially problematical, for boundaries have been very unstable over the long centuries of industrialization. In the late Middle Ages, Europe had "500 more or less independent political units" and probably just as many identities, at least among the elite.[2] European borders and identities changed constantly during the next 450 years because of small or large-scale wars. "Regional" identities often were stronger than "national" ones, and for a long time after the Reformation, religious identities were almost surely more important than national ones.

---

1. David B. Truman, *The Governmental Process: Political Interests and Public Opinion* (New York: Knopf, 1951).
2. Charles Tilly, "Reflections on the History of European State Making," in Charles Tilly, ed., *The Formation of Nation States in Western Europe* (Princeton, NJ: Princeton University Press, 1975), p. 15.

National identity is still evolving in Europe. The early 21st century is likely to witness a slow and prolonged growth in the strength of the "European" identity and a decline in identification with "regional" units such as Germany or Italy. Indeed, if the present nation-states gradually lose power to Brussels, people increasingly may come to identify with older "nations": Scotland, Catalonia, Bavaria, Tuscany, Brittany, and so forth.[3] Unless the effort to create a European identity fails, the process will be very uneven from group to group, and generational differences will be enormous. The creation of national identities in the past in Europe went through a process of analogous length and uncertainty.

Long-term identity in the Third World remains even more uncertain. "Countries" such as Sudan and Congo have essentially been non-existent. Many "Sudanese" still consider themselves Arabs or Muslims on the one hand or Blacks or Christians on the other. Even in Nigeria, the most developed country in Africa, the self-identification of "Ibo" and "Yoruba" is often more meaningful than "Nigerian." Borders in Africa have been stable for fifty years, but if the centuries-long experience of Europe is any guide, a half century of stable borders guarantees nothing about the long-term outcome.

The way in which specific identities survive and become consolidated can be quite arbitrary. Ernest Gellner argues that "it is not the aspiration of nations which create nationalism; it is nationalism which creates nations." At another point he makes the same point in slightly different language: "nationalism is not the awakening of nations to self-consciousness: it invents nations where they do not exist."[4] This view was not original with Gellner, but was implied in an old witticism: the difference between a language and dialect is that a language is the dialect with the largest army behind it. Gellner may exaggerate, but even a partial critic, Benedict Anderson, insists national communities are "imagined" in the sense of being created.[5]

Ideology and myth about American exceptionalism to the contrary, nation-building in the United States and the formation of American national identity has had much in common with the experience of Europe and the Third World. Gellner's view that nationalism "invents nations where they do not exist" seems almost to have been written with the United State specifically in mind.

Richard Merritt discovered in a careful content analysis that articles in the colonial press only used collective designations such as "the colonies" in the first part of the 18th century. "America" was first used in the British press (the English had to distinguish among their growing number of colonies), but those articles written in the colonies began to refer more often to "America" only in 1763. The word "Amer-

---

3. For a doctoral dissertation that explores this, see Seth Jolly, "A Europe of Regions? Regional Integration, Sub-National Mobilizations, and the Optimal Size of Nations (PhD dissertation, Duke University, 2006).
4. Ernest Gellner, *Thought and Change* (Chicago: University of Chicago Press, 1964), p. 174. In a book published after his death in 1995, Gellner summarized the debate on nationalism and placed himself "firmly" on the side of those who "believe in the Creation of Nations." Ernest Gellner, *Nationalism* (New York: New York University Press, 1997), pp. 92 and viii.
5. Benedict Anderson, *Imagined Communities: Reflections on the Origin and Spread of Nationalism*, revised edition (London: Verso, 1991).

icans" came to predominate only in 1773.[6] It may well be that the identity of "American" was no more universal in 1773 than "Nigerian" or "Yugoslavian" were in 1973. Thomas Jefferson always said he thought of himself as a Virginian, not an American. The Civil War that occurred 85 years after the revolution was, first of all, a rejection of American identity.

"Tribal" or "ethnic" identities are created as much as "national" ones, and this too happened in America. "German-American" was typical. Until the 1870s, no Germany existed, only many different states (e.g., Prussia) with their own identities. The Catholic German states often were at war with the Protestant ones, and the Germanic peoples from the Northwest could hardly understand the language of those from the Southeast. But in America they were all Germans.

Actually the Germans in America were colloquially called the Dutch. This not only was a corruption of "Deutsch," but also recognized that the early "Dutch" and the early northwestern "Germans" were similar. Theodore Roosevelt liked to use colloquial language and referred to Irish as "micks," Italians as "dagos," and Chinese as "Chinks." Even at the end of the 19th century Germans were still "Dutchmen" for him.[7] Ronald Reagan was nicknamed "Dutch," and it may not be a coincidence that he was particularly concerned about the Berlin Wall and went to the Bitburg cemetery despite protests that some SS troops are buried there. He devoted nine pages in his autobiography to the latter visit, most from his diary. The words "abortion," "life," "pro-life," or *Roe v. Wade* are not in the index because these subjects are not even mentioned in the 726-page book.[8]

Similarly, Polish-speaking peasant immigrants had lived in three different countries — Russia, Germany, and Austro-Hungary. No sense of Polish nationalism existed in the countryside where they lived, and they became Poles only in the United States.[9] The mass of "Italian-Americans" came from Sicily or elsewhere in southern Italy where people did not understand "textbook" Italian, the language spoken in Fiorello LaGuardia's home city of Milan in northern Italy.[10]

The process of creating new identities continues today. "Hispanics," "Asian-Americans," and even "blacks" are almost totally artificial concepts. Created in the name of cultural pluralism, multiculturalism, and diversity, they actually are melting

6. Richard L. Merritt, *Symbols of American Community, 1735–1775* (New Haven, Conn: Yale University Press, 1966), pp. 140 and 54–59.
7. Christian Gellinek, *Those Damn "Dutch": The Beginning of German Immigration in North America During the Thirty Years War* (Frankfurt: Campus Verlag, 1996), and A. G. Roeber, "'The Origin of Whatever is Not English Among Us': The Dutch-Speaking and the German-Speaking People of Colonial British America," in Bernard Bailyn and Philip D. Morgan, eds., *Strangers within the Realm: Cultural Margins of the First British Empire* (Chapel Hill: University of North Carolina Press, 1991), pp. 237 and 222. Thomas G. Dyer, *Theodore Roosevelt and the Idea of Race* (Baton Rouge: Louisiana University Press, 1980), p. 30.
8. Ronald Reagan, *An American Life* (New York: Simon and Schuster, 1990), pp. 376–384.
9. Robert E. Park and Herbert A. Miller, *Old World Traits Transplanted* (New York: Harper and Brothers, 1921), p. 135.
10. The classic statement of the paradoxes of this phenomenon is found in a famous autobiography. Jerre Mangione, *Mount Allegro: A Memoir of Italian American Life* (Boston: Houghton Mifflin, 1943), pp. 50–53.

pot terms intended to end the great cultural diversity of the immigrants coming from Asia, Latin America, the Caribbean and, increasingly, Africa. Not incidentally, these new identities also had the great advantage of fusing European-Americans into another artificial group, the "whites."

But efforts to create new identities also can fail. As the Protestant Irish intermarried with the English, many intellectuals tried to invent new terms that would combine them and the English-Americans into a single "ethnic group." The new identity was variously called Anglo-Saxon, British-American, and Anglo-American, but no label was accepted even as a common identity was being formed.

The Germanic background of simple English words became the base for another movement to create a "Teutonic" identity that included both British-Americans and German-Americans. It might well have succeeded if Britain and Germany had continued to be allies in international affairs, but it collapsed as the relations between the two countries deteriorated at the end of the 19th century.

The effort to give the English, non-English British, and Germans a common identity only succeeded after World War II when they all became "whites." Indeed, the white identity even "melted" them together with the people from eastern and southern Europe whom they had treated with such contempt in the Immigration Law of 1924. Anyone looking at real skin colors will understand that the white identity, like the black, is as artificial as Asian-American.

THE FORMATION OF AMERICAN IDENTITY AND THE AMERICAN REVOLUTION

So far as can be judged, the early American colonists identified themselves primarily not with England, but with their respective religions. The different colonies had been settled in the mid-17th century by people from the different warring sides of the English civil war, and each side had its own religion. The pro-Royalists who settled the South were Anglican, while the anti-Royal forces of New England were Puritans. The neutrals who came to Pennsylvania had adopted the pacifist Quaker religion.[11]

These intense hostilities from the civil war had faded somewhat by the time of the American Revolution, but they were still strong and emerged in a variety of settings. Thus, in the late 1760s and early 1770s before the revolution, the Anglican Church wanted to appoint a bishop in the New World, but this produced enormous anxiety in New England. In the words of the historian Carl Bridenbaugh:[12]

> That a sinister Episcopalian influence was felt throughout the land, the Dissenters sincerely believed. They detected it in the rush of Anglican placemen to America and the news that the Church of England needed outlets for a surplus of

---

11. For an excellent discussion of the different regions from which the English had come and the impact on the areas in the colonies they settled, see David Hackett Fischer, *Albion's Seed: Four British Folkways in America* (New York: Oxford University Press, 1989).
12. Carl Bridenbaugh, *Mitre and Sceptre: Transatlantic Faiths, Ideas, Personalities, and Politics, 1689–1775* (New York: Oxford University Press, 1962), p. 258.

young curates; they detected it in lay and clerical intrigues against the charter governments of New England; they detected it in the prelatical opposition to dissenting efforts to Christianize and educate the Indians; they detected it in the encouragement of Roman Catholicism in Canada; they detected it in the renewal of the old game of proselyting; they detected it in the curt denial of the legitimate requests of the New York Lutherans and Presbyterians for incorporation. In the London and American press they found confirmations, often lurid, always interesting, of their worst fears.

According to John Adams, "the apprehension of Episcopacy contributed ... as much as any other cause, to arouse the attention not only of the inquiring mind, but of the common people, and urge them to close thinking on the constitutional authority of parliament over the colonies." In Adams' words, this was "a fact as certain as any in the history of North America."[13]

The Congregational ministers of New England were a powerful force in the small towns and villages, and they naturally were highly agitated about the change in the religious and intellectual climate in the larger coastal cities. As Alice Baldwin correctly emphasized, they were key political organizers in the countryside — the mullahs of the American Revolution, so to speak. Since suffrage was given to the propertied, farmers elected most of the New England legislators and were the real base of the revolution in the region.[14]

Other groups in turn were just as suspicious of the New England Puritans. When Adams himself passed through New York on his way to the First Continental Congress in Philadelphia in August 1774, the powerful Philip Livingston, a brother-in-law of John Jay, was not even polite enough to hide his own suspicions:[15]

> [Livingston] says if England should turn us adrift we should instantly go to civil Wars among ourselves to determine which Colony should govern all the rest. Seems to dread New England.... Hints were thrown out ... of the Goths and Vandalls.

According to the highly sympathetic editor of George Washington's papers, the first President, an Anglican vestryman, seemed to retain "perhaps subconsciously, the old Cavalier-Roundhead prejudice."[16]

With the end of the British civil war, excess rural population in England moved to a burgeoning London. As a result, the great majority of immigrants to the New World in the 18th century were not Englishmen, but Irish, Scots, and Germans. By one reasonable estimate, some 300,000 whites immigrated to the colonies from 1700 to 1775, a disproportionate number in the 25 years before the revolution, especially in the 10 years after 1765. Only 44,000 of the 300,000 were estimated to be English, and a high percentage of them were "transported" (exiled) convicts.[17]

---

13. Bridenbaugh, *Mitre and Sceptre*, p. 233. Bridenbaugh agrees with Adams.
14. Alice M. Baldwin, *The New England Clergy and the American Revolution* (Durham, N. C.: Duke University Press, 1928).
15. Diary entry of August 22, 1774, in L. N. Butterfield, ed., *Diary and Autobiography of John Adams* (Cambridge: Harvard University Press, 1962), vol. 2, p. 107.
16. John C. Fitzpatrick, *George Washington Himself: A Common Sense Biography* (Indianapolis: Bobbs Merrill Company, 1933), p. 335. See p. 337 for Edward Rutledge's letter to John Jay of June 29, 1776, about New England demagoguery.

Each non-English group also had its own religion or religions. The Germans were Lutherans or Mennonites. The Scots and Protestant Irish were officially Presbyterian, the national church of Scotland, but there were too few Presbyterian ministers to serve the interior. As a result, many Irish and Scots in the interior switched to religions that relied on lay preachers, notably the Baptists. The Germans were not involved in ancient conflicts with the English, but this was not true of the non-English in Great Britain:[18]

> [They] had brought with them to the New World ancient ethnic identities that were almost tribal in nature. Each of the colonies' separate peoples had a firm conviction, rooted in bloody ancestral memories, that certain other peoples were their folk enemies to be battled at every opportunity.
>
> Within the British Isles, the English, Scots, Irish, and Welsh had been at each other's throats, literally and figuratively.... The English millions regarded [the] much less numerous ethnic outgroups in Scotland, Wales, and Ireland as crude, hill country tribes — in one sense comic, in another contemptible. In their turn, the Scots, Welsh, and Irish thought the wealthy and self-important English arrogant and domineering.

Carl Becker, one of the foremost historians of the early 20th century, reports that the non-English British immigrants still thought that way about the English elite who dominated New England and the coastal areas of other colonies:[19]

> The Scotch-Irish or German dweller saw himself as a Westerner.... The Western imagination had conjured up the specter of a corrupt and effete "East": land of money-changers and self-styled aristocrats and a pliant clergy, the haunt of lawyers and hanger-ons, proper dwelling place of [indentured] "servants" and the beaten slave, a land of cities, scorning the provincial West and bent on exploiting its laborious and upright people. And who could doubt that men who bought their clothes in London would readily crook the knee to kings?

The English elite also retained their attitudes toward the non-English from their homeland. George Washington began his career as a teenage surveyor in the West serving the new immigrants. He described them as "a parcel of barbarian's and an uncouth set of people."[20] Washington became one of the members of the English elite most knowledgeable about the West, and over 30 years later his attitudes were the same. Those in the Virginian interior, he wrote in 1784, were "foreign emigrants,

---

17. Aaron S. Fogleman, "Immigration, German Immigration, and 18th-Century America," in Eberhard Reichmann, LaVern J. Rippley, and Jorg Nagler, eds., *Emigration and Settlement Patterns of German Communities in North America* (Indianapolis; Max Kade German-American Center, 1995), p. 5. Bernard Bailyn, *Voyagers to the West: A Passage in the Peopling of America on the Eve of the Revolution* (New York: Knopf, 1986).
18. Robert L. Kelley, *The Cultural Pattern in American Politics: The First Century* (New York: Alfred A. Knopf, 1979), pp. 34–35.
19. Carl Lotus Becker, *Beginnings of the American People* (Boston: Houghton Mifflin Co., 1915), p. 175. For a longer discussion of the culture of those in the Borderlands in Britain and then in the American colonies, see Fischer, *Albion's Seed*, pp. 605–782.
20. Warren R. Hofstra, "'A Parcel of Barbarian's and an Uncooth Set of People:' Settlers and Settlements of the Shenandoah Valley," in Warren R. Hofstra, ed., *George Washington and the Virginia Backcountry* (Madison, Wisc.: Madison House, 1998), pp. 87–114.

who can have no particular predilection for us" and who might become "as uncon-nected with us, indeed more so, than we are with South America."[21] The Constitu-tional Convention was but two-and-a-half years in the future.

John Adams was little different. New England had few non-English, and it had little contact with other colonies before the revolution. Old prejudices remained. On the eve of Adams' trip to Philadelphia for the opening of the First Continental Con-gress, a friend felt it necessary to warn him ("just a hint") to be polite to those of "Dutch or Scottish or Irish Extraction" whom he would meet, many of whom were "worthy and learned men."[22] As always, "Dutch" included "Germans." The friend surely had reason to think that the warning was needed, and, of course, prejudices among the non-educated were greater.

As the number of immigrants became much larger, they and their children had to move into the interior to find affordable land. The further they moved into the interior, the more the leaders in the colonial capitals near the coast feared losing control of them. This was a fear that lay behind the desire to have a common "American" identity.

In broader perspective, the "American" Revolution was not the result of some deep American yearning for independence. Rather, it was an effort to create and instill a new common American identity among those with relatively little in common. If Britain had offered home rule in 1775 and the resulting formalization of American identity, it would have been accepted, but the offer several years later came after the new elite had taken the houses and land of fleeing or "cleansed" Tories. Home rule at that stage would have required the restoration of the property rights of the latter.

The concern about the interior and about the relations of the immigrants and Indians with England and Spain was also a crucial factor in Washington's intense desire in the 1780s for a strong central government in the foreign and security realm. When James Madison (aged 36) and Alexander Hamilton (aged 30) invited the col-onies to send delegates to Philadelphia in May 1787, everyone knew two facts. First, Washington's national organization of former army officers was holding its con-vention in Philadelphia at precisely the same time, and many of them were calling for Washington to conduct a coup. Second, Madison and Hamilton were Washington's two chief political aides, Madison for the South and Hamilton for the North. It was an invitation not to be refused.

---

21. Letter to Jacob Reed, November 3, 1784, in W. W. Abbot and Dorothy Twohig, eds., *The Papers of George Washington, The Confederation Period* (Charlottesville: University Press of Virginia, 1992), vol. 2, p. 121.
22. "From William Hawley," July 25, 1774, in Robert J. Taylor, ed., *Papers of John Adams* (Cambridge: Harvard University Press, 1977), vol. 2, p. 120.

RELIGIOUS AND RACIAL CLEAVAGES AND THE CULTURAL ISSUES OF THE
FOUNDING FATHERS' PARTIES

Obviously, no one would underestimate the significance of cultural issues in the
party politics of the last decade. Yet, many attribute this fact to the growth in the
importance of "post-materialist" values in post-industrial society. Without question,
societal evolution does brings new interests and values to the forefront, but it is a
major mistake to think that cultural issues are new. They often were even more emotional in elections prior to the 1990s, including those involving the Founding Fathers.
Sainted figures such as Jefferson and Adams essentially called each other traitors.

Jefferson and Madison deliberately created an opposition party in the early
1790s to run in the first competitive presidential election, first expected in 1792 and
then in 1796. They knew that otherwise Alexander Hamilton, with the support of
Washington, would select a ticket that did not include them. In 1796, the slave states
had only 65 Electoral College votes, and Jefferson was to lose 12 of them both in 1796
and 1800. Adams would almost surely win the 39 votes of New England. Jefferson
and Madison, his chief political organizer, had to win at least half the 34 electors of
the non-slave states of the Mid-Atlantic region ("the middle states"). The big prizes
were New York with 12 electors and Pennsylvania with 15.

Unfortunately for Jefferson and Madison, an alliance of slaveholders of the
undemocratic South with the small farmers of democratic Pennsylvania and New
York was economically and politically unnatural. Jefferson and Madison were
required to overcome the economic differences with a cultural issue.

New York and Pennsylvania were the states with the largest number of Americans who were not of English origin, and the inland South had much the same ethnic
mix as Pennsylvania. The Dutch had originally settled in New York (New
Amsterdam), and the wave of 18th century immigrants had generally arrived in Philadelphia and moved westward to mid-Pennsylvania before turning in a southwesterly
direction. The estimates for the number of non-English in New York in 1790 range
from 42% to 54%, and those for Pennsylvania from 65% to 80%. The figures for the
South vary by state, but are in the 30%–40% or 50%–65% ranges.

The lower figures for the non-English in 1790 were those of an American Historical Association study that was part of the effort to establish the national origin
quotas in the late 1920s. The higher ones were more recent calculations by two
scholars, Forrest McDonald and Ellen Shapiro McDonald.[23] Given its purpose, the
American Historical Association study was not likely to underestimate the number
of English, but neither estimate is really "accurate." People were too mixed both in

---

23. Forrest McDonald and Ellen Shapiro McDonald, "The Ethnic Origins of the American
People, 1980," *William and Mary Quarterly*, vol. XXXVII, no. 2 (April 1980), pp. 180 and
198. This source also describes the 1931 study well and indicates the reasons for the
different estimates. For the calculation of the national origins quotas, see Margo J.
Anderson, *The American Census: A Social History* (New Haven: Yale University Press,
1988), pp. 144–149.

Britain and in the colonies. The higher McDonald numbers surely, however, are politically more relevant from our point of view.

Nearly all the significant cities at the time of the revolution were on the coast, and all were engaged in international trade. All the Borderland peoples, including those with more English ancestors than non-English, shared a deep suspicion of these cities and the men who dominated them. Jefferson and Madison used this suspicion as the base for their cultural issue in forming their new party. England and France were at war for much of the 18th century, and French support had been crucial in the American Revolution. War erupted again between the two in 1793 after the French king was beheaded, this time with Spain allying itself with Britain. George Washington negotiated the Jay Treaty with Britain in 1794 and then the Pinckney Treaty with Britain's ally, Spain, in 1795. The treaties normalized trade relations and essentially supported Britain and Spain in their war with France. In exchange, Britain abandoned ten illegal forts it maintained on American soil in the North, and Spain allowed American shipping to pass down the Mississippi River to the Gulf of Mexico. Both abandoned covert aid to the Indians in the American West.

The ethnic English coastal elite both in the North and the South approved the development of commercial relations, and the treaties also were highly favorable to the South and West both because of the end of foreign support for the Indians and the opening of rivers to the Gulf of Mexico. In the battle to create their new Republican Party, however, Jefferson and Madison "forgot" the advantages of the treaties to their supporters. Instead, they damned Washington's and the Federalists' foreign policy as an illegal and dangerous betrayal of France.[24]

Since the federal government had few powers in the domestic sphere, foreign policy was an appropriate focus for the 1796 election. Jefferson did not, however, engage in an abstract geostrategic debate about American policy toward Britain and France. Rather, he used the war as a cultural issue to appeal to the ethnic and religious prejudices of the non-English in Pennsylvania, New York, and the West against the ethnic English elite. He hoped to stir emotions sufficiently to give local politicians a reason to join his new Republican Party and to help win their states' Electoral College votes for him.

The Republicans charged that the ethnic English elite in the large coastal cities supported England because of their selfish desire for trade with England and because of their traitorous love of England and its political institutions. They claimed that England had "bought and corrupted the government" and that the Federalists were willing accomplices. They called the Federalists "the Anglo-Monarchical Tory

---

24. The issue went back to the first days of the First Congress. The first bill introduced was a tariff to finance the federal government, and the main issue was not its general level, but the grant of most-favored-nation status to Britain (that is, the same level of tariffs as to other countries). Those such as Madison thought the Britain should pay higher tariffs until it addressed American grievances about observance of the peace treaty. For an early discussion of this thesis, see Joseph Charles, *The Origins of the American Party System: Three Essays* (Williamsburg, Va.: Institute of Early American History and Culture, 1956). One of the essays, originally published in *William and Mary Quarterly*, XII, 1955, pp. 581-630, was "The Jay Treaty: The Origins of the American Party System."

Party," which consisted of "the admirers of British tyranny." Vice President Adams from democratic Massachusetts was said to want "an aristocratical form of government." [25] Nothing was said about the truly aristocratic government in the South that Jefferson and Madison never tried to change.

Jefferson went further in a letter to a foreigner in 1796. The letter was leaked to the press, although apparently not by Jefferson.[26]

> Our politics has wonderfully changed since you left us. In place of that noble love of liberty and republican government which carried us triumphantly thro' the war, an Anglican, monarchical and aristocratical party has sprung up, whose avowed object is to draw over us the substance as they have already done the forms of the British government ... Men who were Samsons in the field & Solomons in the council ... have had their heads shorn by the harlot England.

The Samson and Solomon whose head Jefferson thought shorn by the harlot England was George Washington himself.

The Federalists responded by saying that Jefferson favored France because he was an extreme democrat and because he was an atheist who liked the French revolutionaries' attack on religion. Federalists habitually used terms such as "Jacobins," "the French faction," "the anti-American gallic faction," the "associates of these French incendiaries," "traitors who have sold their country and are ready to deliver it to the French."[27] Jefferson's policy, they said, would lead to the guillotine of the French Revolution. The Founding Fathers were calling each other traitors and doing so in terms even more emotional and extreme than the accusations made by both parties in the 2004 election. Adams pushed through the Alien and Sedition Acts to try to curtail Republican dissent.[28]

The emotions became so strong that George Washington feared for the political stability of the country. In a letter written a month before his death in December 1799, he told the Secretary of War of his fears about the immediate future: "I have for sometime past, viewed the political concerns of the United States with an anxious and painful eye. They appear to me, to be moving by hasty strides to some awful crisis."[29] He seemed to have reason for concern.

---

25. Richard N. Rosenfeld, *American Aurora* (New York: St. Martin's Press, 1997), pp. 70, 91, and 94. This is a lively account of the contents not only of the republican newspaper, the *Aurora*, but also the opposition press.

26. Thomas Jefferson to Philip Mazzei, April 24, 1796, in Barbara B. Oberg, ed., *The Papers of Thomas Jefferson* (Princeton: Princeton University Press, 2002), vol. 29, p. 82. Before sending the letter Jefferson had crossed out another phrase, "lions in the fields and councils," which he apparently had replaced by that about Samson and Solomon. See p. 83, n8 of this volume. For the history of the controversy about the leaking of the letter, see pp. 73–81.

27. Rosenfeld, *American Aurora*, pp. 70, 72, 75, 80, and 94.

28. Alexander DeConde, *The Quasi-War: The Politics and Diplomacy of the Undeclared War with France, 1797–1801* (New York: Charles Scribner's Sons, 1966); James M. Smith, *Freedom's Fetters: The Alien and Sedition Laws and American Civil Liberties* (Ithaca, NY: Cornell University, 1956); John C. Miller, *Crisis in Freedom: The Alien and Sedition Acts* (Boston: Little, Brown, 1951).

In fact, America avoided the extreme political instability of most post-colonial regimes in the 20th century, but its politics over the next fifteen years were very tense. Adams tilted to England in his "phony war" with France, while Jefferson and Madison were to tilt to France. The latter two tried to change British behavior with different types of economic boycott, but succeeded only in harming the American economy more than the British. Madison, whose re-nomination and reelection in 1812 were in danger because of the costs of his economic boycott at home, seems deliberately to have provoked the War of 1812 for electoral purposes.[30] If this was his goal, he was successful. In fact, the Federalists carried their opposition to the war to a point where they lost their viability as a national political party.

Only scholars working on American history of that period remember the Jefferson–Adams conflict on policy toward England and France and the cultural issue built upon it, but the issue still echoed in the 20th century. Two Anglophiles who wanted to support Great Britain in World War I, Theodore Roosevelt and Woodrow Wilson, long detested Jefferson. Even today a President with little apparent interest in history but with roots in Connecticut is allied with England in a war in Iraq in which he and his supporters direct their fire at France rather than other strong opponents of the war such as China, Germany, and Russia.

Surprisingly, the intense emotions associated with the War of 1812 and the disappearance of the Federalists did not result in instability in the relations between New England and the South. On the contrary, "a Era of Good Feeling" ensued in which there was no party competition. The Virginian James Monroe selected the top leaders of all regions for his cabinet, including the son of John Adams, John Quincy Adams, as Secretary of State and heir apparent. Even though Monroe's presidency was to feature the crisis over the admission of Missouri to the Union and the Panic of 1819 with its many bank failures, no one challenged Monroe in the 1820 election or tried to introduce party competition.

ANDREW JACKSON, THE ETHNIC BASE OF THE DEMOCRATS AND WHIGS, AND THE CATHOLIC IMMIGRATION

The British defeat of Napoleon in 1815 meant that policy toward Britain and France was no longer a relevant issue for the United States. That policy could no longer, therefore, be an important cultural issue in American politics. Many American political scientists have argued that competing parties were required by the logic of the American political system, either because of the Electoral College or the problems of organizing Congress or both, but no party arose to replace the Federalists for 20 years. The US really became a no-party state. The disappearance of the

---

29. "To James McHenry," November 17, 1799, in Dorothy Twohig, ed., *The Papers of George Washington, Retirement Series* (Charlottesville: University Press of Virginia, 1999), vol. 4, p. 410.
30. J. C. A. Stagg, *Mr. Madison's War of 1812: Politics, Diplomacy, and Warfare in the Early American Republic, 1783–1830* (Princeton: Princeton University Press, 1983).

major cultural issue of the first party system and the simultaneous disappearance of its two parties do not seem a coincidence.

When political parties were formed again in the early 1830s, Andrew Jackson and his political organizer, Martin Van Buren, chose to re-create Jefferson's and Madison's coalition for their new Democratic Party. Martin Van Buren was the leading politician from New York and Jackson was a slaveholder from Tennessee; hence they personally represented the states of the South and the most populous of the Middle States. In addition, however, they also deliberately appealed to the same non-English peoples as Jefferson and Madison, again using a cultural issue. Indeed, the South had become much more democratic by this time, and the Democrats needed the ethnic cultural issue for the Southern non-English voters in the interior as well as for voters in the North.

The Democratic Party had long held an annual Jefferson–Jackson dinner to honor its founders and quietly to acknowledge that it remained a Southern party at its base. When Franklin Roosevelt repositioned the party to the left in 1933, his partisans were eager to recast Jefferson into a representative of the economic interests of the small farmer and Jackson into a representative of the working man.[31] Jefferson, however, represented the small farmer only to the extent that he promoted the expansion of the West into which they could migrate. In fact, Jackson was quite conservative in his economic policy, much more so than the Whigs, and he did poorly among ethnic English subsistence farmers and workers in New England and upper New York in 1828.

Jackson's first biographer, a man who actually lived in Jackson's time, insisted that "[no] man will ever be able to comprehend Andrew Jackson who has not personally known a Scotch Irishman. More than anything else he was a North-of-Irelander." In the words of this biographer, "[Jackson] was of Black Protestant Ulster stock, at a time when the Presbyterian poor of Ulster hated British rule almost as much as did the Catholic Irish."[32]

Jackson and Van Buren used their own personal background as a cultural issue by which to appeal to the non-English. The first six Presidents, who occupied the White House for 40 years, were all ethnic English. By the 1830s, the descendants of the first Scotch, Protestant Irish, and German immigrants had roots in America for over a century. They were upwardly mobile and were intermarrying with the English. They wanted to be accepted by the ethnic English, not to condemn them. In this respect, their position was like that of the Irish Catholics in the mid 20th century.

It was these desires that Jackson represented. He had married a well-to-do English woman, and he had been the great general who defeated the English in the War of 1812. He was a powerful symbol of the success of the Scotch-Irish, and his election as President would be the culminating symbol of their respectability. Jackson occupied the same role for the Protestant Irish that John Kennedy was to

---

31. The classic such book is Arthur Schlesinger, Jr., *The Age of Jackson* (Boston: Little, Brown, 1945). For a recent book with this thesis, see Sean Wilentz, *The Rise of American Democracy: Jefferson to Lincoln* (New York: Norton, 2005).
32. James Parton, *Life of Andrew Jackson* (New York: Mason Brothers, 1860), vol. III, p. 685, and vol. I, p. 33. Quoted in Kelley, *The Cultural Pattern in American Politics*, pp. 146–147.

occupy for the Catholic Irish in 1960. Van Buren was a member of the other great non-English immigrant group — officially Dutch, but really northwestern Germanic (Deutsch). Jackson named him secretary of state and heir-apparent and supported another Scotch-Irishman (John Calhoun) for Vice President.

The Whig Party was created at the same time as the main opponent of Jackson and the Democratic Party. The party had a politically intelligent economic policy. Industrialization had begun immediately after the end of the War of 1812, and thus the tariff for the first time became more than a revenue measure and acquired policy significance. The new industrialists wanted a tariff for protectionist reasons, while consumers and farmers had an interest in low tariffs. The Whigs advocated a reasonably high tariff to promote industrial growth, but offered the resulting revenue to Western agricultural interests as "internal improvements."

The economic issue was not, however, strong enough to ensure a Whig victory. The Whigs, almost by default, were the party of the ethnic English, and their leaders emphasized the point in choosing an English name for it. Nevertheless, the ethnic English were in the minority in the country. The Whigs needed to adopt a cultural issue that reached out to other groups, but its leaders never succeeded in doing that. Their original foolish choice of the name of an English party was symbolic of a problem they never were to overcome. In a statement of the time that historians still often cite, "the Whigs died of respectability."

After World War II, scholars were absorbed with the great problem of ending the consequences of the Civil War for blacks, and, consequently, they emphasized slavery as the issue that tore the Whig Party apart. The problem with this interpretation is two-fold. First, the Democrats had cleavages on the issue that seemed even greater than the Whigs in the 1850s, and they did not split. Second, the New England Republicans, the Conscience Whigs foremost among them, accommodated themselves with extreme ease to the subjection of the blacks after the Civil War. This subjection lasted virtually unchallenged for over three-quarters of a century.

We need to re-examine the politics of the 1840s and 1850s in a serious manner. The leading scholars of the 1930s for the first time moved beyond the differing moral explanations of the war previously advanced by Northern and Southern historians. The scholars of the 1930s did not see the Civil War as inevitable, but the result of a political process gone wrong. Their precise analysis of the "blundering generation" of the 1850s may be flawed. I would point to the aging generation of Henry Clay, Martin Van Buren, and Daniel Webster as the one that made the most important blunders. Nevertheless, an exclusive or even primary emphasis on the moral outrage of the Northern Whigs is not really tenable.

As William Gienapp strongly emphasized, the Republicans did not destroy and replace the Whigs. The Know Nothing Party played this role.[33] The Know Nothings had not been an anti-slavery party — they actually were to be the second party in the South in 1856 — but an anti-Catholic one. The problem that first tore the two-party

---

33. William E. Gienapp, *The Origins of the Republican Party, 1852–1856* (New York: Oxford University Press, 1987).

system apart was the wave of Catholic immigration into the Northern cities and the immediate entry of the Catholics into the Democratic Party.

In Ireland and Germany, the Catholics had been bitter enemies of the Protestant Irish and Germans who had formed the base of the Democratic Party. Now the Protestants' own party, the party of Andrew Jackson, was actively recruiting and mobilizing their ancient Catholic enemies. The Irish Catholics themselves were in charge of the Democratic political machines of Northern cities, and these machines seemed to represent all the evils that rural people associated with cities since at least the time of Sodom and Gomorrah.

From a modern perspective, the entry of Catholics into the Democratic Party should not have caused an insuperable problem for the United States. Historically antagonisms among different ethnic groups have gradually faded in the United States as members of a new group become better educated and begin to intermarry with other groups. In the 18th century, the Northern Protestant Scots and Irish were considered thoroughly disreputable by the English, but a century later they were becoming a respectable part of the Republican coalition. This, of course, was to take place with the Ellis Island immigrants as well. Today they are simply white, together with the Protestants.

As the children and grandchildren of immigrants become upwardly mobile, many of them naturally transfer their allegiance to the old English party, perhaps in connection with intermarriage. As the Catholic Irish and Germans became Democrats, the children of the Protestant Irish (Scotch-Irish) and Germans should have increasingly become Whigs. The great political disasters of the mid 19th century in America began not with an intensification of feelings about slavery but with the failure of the Whig leaders to understand the need to attract the Protestant supporters of the Democrats. Henry Clay's great defect as a political leader had always been his failure to understand the need for cultural and symbolic issues in politics. Now at the end of his life, Clay did not realize that he could unite the Protestants both of the North and the South by taking a moderately anti-Catholic position.

The collapse of the second party system of the Democrats and Whigs began with the Mexican War of 1845. The invention of the telegraph and the approach of the railroad to the Mississippi River made it inevitable that the United States would acquire the three great Pacific ports of Puget Sound, San Diego, and San Francisco, as well as the land needed to build railroads to them. The Mexican government could barely control the area around Mexico City, and there were virtually no Spanish speakers in Texas or the other parts of the Mexican Southwest. If the United States did not take the ports, Britain or France might even do so.[34]

Nevertheless, the Mexican population totaled some 7 to 8 million people, while the United States had 23 million whites. The Mexicans were at least nominally Catholic, and none spoke English. A large proportion were native-Americans. The

---

34. For a book emphasizing the importance of the ports, see Norman A. Graebner, *Empire on the Pacific: A Study in American Continental Expansion* (New York: Ronald Press Co., 1955), pp. 3–5. In 1838, French seized control of Vera Cruz on the Gulf of Mexico south of Texas to force the Mexican government to take a desired action.

acquisition of Mexico would transform the religious, ethnic, and linguistic balance in the United States. The Democratic President, James Polk, skillfully avoided this problem. American troops occupied Mexico City, and the United States could have acquired all of Mexico, either as a territory or a colony. Polk, however, drew the border only 25 miles south of San Diego and then extended it eastward to acquire the minimum amount of land (and Mexicans) necessary for the construction of a railroad line from New Orleans to San Diego.[35]

Unfortunately, however, some Southern politicians talked about the need to expand the slave territory if slavery were to be preserved, and Northern Democratic leaders gave them some meaningless verbal support for coalitional reasons. This opened the party to the charge that the Democrats were trying to acquire Catholics because they would vote Democratic. In the emotional language of time, the Democrats were charged with serving the interests of the "Papal Power." The aging Democratic leaders were no more sensitive to the political problems of immigration and the political tensions of industrialization than the aging Whig leaders.

At the elite level, the Whigs were the party of the railroad magnates, the Southern plantation owners, and the New England cotton manufacturers. All had reason to favor the annexation of Texas and the land from Texas to the Pacific. At the mass level, the Whigs could have embraced expansion westward from Texas as Manifest Destiny, but opposed expansion southward from Texas on religious and ethnic grounds. They could have explicitly used foreign policy to denounce the Democrats as "the Papal party."

With such a strategy, the Whigs could have used the appeals of national unity and religion to draw together the Northern and Southern Protestants and become the dominant American party for the rest of the century. Instead the Whigs thought they must attract the new Catholics in order to avoid becoming even more of a minority party than they already were. In New York, they even supported state aid to Catholic parochial schools.

The Whigs failed in their goal of attracting Catholic voters, but succeeded only in angering their own English base by their efforts. The battle between the English King and the Catholic Church had been a key element in the English civil war, and Catholics still could not vote in England in the early 19th century. Many English-Americans remained highly anti-Catholic, and in the 1850s they began voting for an openly anti-Catholic party, the American or Know-Nothing Party. In the mid-1850s the Know-Nothings even swept English Massachusetts. Large numbers of the Scotch-Irish and German Protestants also supported the Know-Nothings.

The new Republican Party rose as an all-Northern party that combined the economic positions of the Whigs and, in a polite manner, the anti-Catholic themes of the Know-Nothings. It deliberately courted the Protestant Irish and Germans of the North by adopting the name of their old Jeffersonian Party, and to a substantial degree

---

35. The American ambassador to England spoke of the "outlandish population" of Mexico, and the public wanted little to do with them. Frederick Merk, *Manifest Destiny and Mission in American History: A Reinterpretation* (New York: Alfred A. Knopf, 1963), pp. 135, 183, and 185.

it succeeded. But the new Republicans also tried to deflect the tensions of early indus-trialization in the North from the Catholics onto a mythical "Slave Power." This was a brilliant electoral strategy, but not one that promoted national unity.

THE BRITISH-GERMAN CONFLICT AND THE STRAIN ON THE REPUBLICAN COALITION

The great ethnic (or "racial") problem for American party coalitions in the early 20th century would have been totally unexpected a few decades earlier — a conflict between the British-Americans and the German-Americans. The Protestant German-Americans had been part of the Democratic coalition under Jackson and Van Buren, but they had moved to the Republican Party in the North as the rapidly-rising number of German Catholics became Democrats. However, since Protestant and Catholic German-Americans were reasonably equal in number by the end of the 19th century, both parties had a strong incentive to treat them with care.

In the 1870s the relationship between the German-Americans and the British-Americans seemed likely to become even closer. Germany and Britain had tradi-tionally been allies against France, and the two countries had excellent relations under Wilhelm I, who ruled from 1858 to 1888. Britain supported Germany in its war with France in 1870, and the United States adopted the same position. Wilhelm's son and heir apparent, Frederick, was the son-in-law of Victoria and even more pro-English than his father. He even seemed to favor movement toward constitutional monarchy.

The friendly relations of England and Germany were not based on geostrategic calculation alone. After the end of the English civil war, the English had invited a man from the German principality of Hanover to be its king — the future George I. The civil wars had ended in a decisive rejection of the Pope and Roman Catholicism, and the English choice of a German king symbolized a simultaneous rejection of 300 years of French rule and its cultural impact on England and its culture. The Hanover dynasty, renamed Windsor during World War I for political reasons, still remains in place.

The Germanic origins of older English words showed that the Germans and English had common roots in the past, and the Hanover dynasty naturally wanted attention drawn to this fact. It had the strongest interest in emphasizing the affinity of the Germans and the English. The result was a well-developed theory that did focus on the "Anglo-Saxon" or "Teutonic" ancestors of the modern English. English democracy and civilization, it was argued, did not come from Rome through the three-century French domination of England after 1066, but from its Anglo-Saxon heritage. The democracy and economic vigor of German medieval towns were seen as typical of this Teutonic civilization.[36] Queen Victoria strongly supported this theory after her marriage to Albert of Saxe-Coburg.

Of course, if the British and the Germans descended from the same people, so did British-Americans and German-Americans. Since these two groups each consti-tuted approximately one-quarter of the European population in the United States, it would be highly stabilizing if they saw themselves as part of the same family. Not surprisingly, "by the 1890s the Teutonic origin doctrine was the dominant historical viewpoint in Great Britain and the United States." A formal movement even arose in the United States to create a "Teutonic" identity that embraced both groups, and Theodore Roosevelt was one of its warm supporters.[37]

The Teutonic movement probably would have succeeded if German and English relations had continued to be warm. However, when Wilhelm I died in March 1888, Frederick was suffering from cancer and ruled for only three months. His son, Wilhelm II, was Victoria's grandson, but was nationalistic and much less well inclined toward Britain. Relations between Britain and Germany gradually deteriorated, and England gradually formed a collective security arrangement with its traditional enemies, France and Russia. The alliance was directed against Germany and Austro-Hungary.[38]

Conflict between Germany and Britain, let alone war between the two countries, was disastrous for American politics. In the 1890s, those of Germanic origin constituted by far the largest number of recent immigrants in America, particularly since those from Switzerland and Austria were normally ethnic Germans. (See Table 1.) Indeed, most Danes, Norwegians, and Swedes were Lutherans, and the Scandinavians tended to ally with the German Lutherans in American politics and voted Republican.[39]

Table 1: Country of Origin of the Foreign White Stock, 1900

Country	Total Stock	Foreign Born	Foreign Parent
England & Wales	2,628,948	933,390	1,695,558
Scotland	680,997	233,473	447,524
Ireland	4,990,778	1,615,232	3,375,546
Canada	2,562,330	1,172,860	1,389,470
Germany	8,003,351	2,663,204	5,340,147
Austria	824,400	432,764	391,636
Switzerland	294,272	115,581	178,681
Norway	814,910	336,379	478,531
Sweden	1,124,018	581,986	542,032
Denmark	341,488	153,644	187,844
Poland	710,156	383,392	326,764
Russia	774,444	486,346	288,098
Italy	738,513	483,963	254,550

Source: Twelfth Census of the United States Taken in the Year 1900. Population, Part 1 (Washington: Census Office, 1901), pp. cxciv–cxcvii.

36. For good surveys of early English writing on the German-English link, see Reginald Horsman, *Race and Manifest Destiny: The Origins of American Racial Anglo-Saxonism* (Cambridge, MA: Harvard University Press, 1981), pp. 9–24, and Stuart Anderson, *Race and Rapprochement: Anglo-Saxonism and Anglo-American Relations, 1895-1904* (Rutherford, NJ: Fairleigh Dickinson University, 1961), pp. 37–45. Also see Hugh A. MacDougall, *Racial Myth in English History: Trojans, Teutons, and Anglo-Saxons* (Hanover, N.H.: University Press of New England, 1982).

37. For the movement, see Edward N. Saveth, *American Historians and European Immigrants, 1875-1925* (New York: Columbia University, 1948), pp. 13–31. The quotation is from Anderson, *Race and Rapprochement*, p. 45.

38. See, for example, Paul M. Kennedy, *The Rise of the Anglo-German Antagonism, 1860–1914* (London: Allen & Unwin, 1980).

The Protestants from Great Britain were becoming increasingly integrated with each passing generation, and Woodrow Wilson was not politically inaccurate when he spoke in the early 20th century of "the Anglo-American race."[40] Yet, the British-Americans felt very insecure at this time and saw their cultural and political hegemony under severe threat. The Irish Catholics were becoming the dominant political force in Eastern cities, and the relatively recent Germans immigrants often retained the use of the German language. Finally, the Ellis Island immigration from eastern and southern Europe began to grow in the 1890s.

The wave of immigration from southern and eastern Europe that began in the late 1880s was larger both in absolute and percentage terms than that in the 1830s and the 1840s. The average number of immigrants was 496,000 a year from 1889 to 1893, but then fell to 269,000 a year because of the economic depression. The number rose to 551,000 a year from 1899 to 1903, 960,000 a year from 1904 to 1909, and 1,035,000 a year from 1910 to 1914.[41] Those from eastern and southern Europe alone totaled 160,000 a year from 1889 to 1893, 395,000 from 1899 to 1903, 810,000 from 1904 to 1909, and 720,000 from 1910 to 1914. The great majority of these immigrants were either Catholics or Jews.

Such an influx of new immigrants, especially at a time of growing tension in Europe, put enormous strain on the American political structure. Since the Republican Party was based largely on the Protestant Germans and British-Americans, any conflict between Britain and Germany was especially dangerous to it. The German-Americans dominated the Republican Party in the Midwest and much of the West, while the British-Americans constituted the core of the party in the East. The Republicans usually had tried to balance their presidential ticket with a candidate from each of the regions, and the alliance between Anglophile Theodore Roosevelt of New York and William Howard Taft of Ohio was only the most recent example of this policy.

Roosevelt abandoned any thought of the Teuton movement as England and Germany became antagonists, and he became increasingly jingoistic in support of England. Roosevelt shared Wilson's attitudes about "hyphenates," (e.g., those like the "Irish-Americans" with a hyphen between their two identities), and his favored ethnic group in American society, the "English-speaking race," was very close to Wilson's "Anglo-American race." Roosevelt had a long historical memory. A half century later, his daughter recalled that she still could hear her father and his close friend, Senator Henry Cabot Lodge, "speaking of Jefferson as if he were an extremely obnoxious man who behaved in the most deplorable manner." She reported "they felt quite passionately against Jefferson."[42]

---

39. Paul Kleppner, *The Third Electoral System, 1853–1892* (Chapel Hill: University of North Carolina Press, 1979), pp. 153–155 and 158–165.
40. Although Wilson was the first major politician to embrace the phrase, he did not invent it. For a reference to its use in 1839, see Anderson, *Race and Rapprochement*, p. 26.
41. *Historical Statistics of the United States, Colonial Times to 1970* (Washington: US Government Printing Office, 1975), vol. 1, pp. 105–106.
42. Henry Brandon Interview with Alice Roosevelt Longworth, July 1967, Henry Brandon Papers, Box 18, Folder 1, Library of Congress.

When Roosevelt decided to run again for President in 1912, first for the Republican nomination and then as a third party Progressive candidate, he believed that he could mobilize the British-Americans against William Howard Taft, who was from the party's German-American wing in the Midwest. Taft won the key test vote at the convention by a 567 to 507 margin, but the Republican organizations in the Confederate states attracted only those interested in patronage and more corrupt rewards. Taft won them 197 to 52 on the key test vote, and Roosevelt took the delegates outside the Confederacy by a 455 to 370 margin. This was a fact he emphasized when he ran as a third party candidate.

The enormous ethnic tensions within the Republican Party would give the Democrats a real opportunity if they developed the right strategy. Although the conflict between British-Americans and German-Americans was far too sensitive to mention publicly, the Democrats knew that they must try to attract either the Protestant German-Americans or British-Americans from the Republicans in the 1912 election. The traditional right-fork strategy meant, in effect, an alliance with the more English-American states, while the Bryan left-fork strategy meant an alliance with the more German-American states.

THE DEMOCRATS' CHOICE BETWEEN AN ANGLOPHILE AND NEUTRALIST POSTURE

The conflict between Britain and Germany caused no internal coalitional problem for the Democrats so long as they adopted a neutralist position. The South always supported any presidential foreign policy in exchange for its autonomy in domestic affairs, and the two large immigrant voting-groups of the Democrats, the Irish Catholics and German Catholics, both wanted a neutralist foreign policy.

One candidate for the 1912 nomination was Champ Clark of Missouri, Speaker of the US House of Representatives. Besides his enormous political experience and skills, Clark had two great personal strengths as he sought Protestant support in a presidential race. First, he had been born in Kentucky and had lived in and represented Missouri. Both were classic Border states, and Northern Protestants wanted to reconcile with Southern Protestants.

Second, Clark came from a German-American section of Missouri near St. Louis, and he had the expected dedication to neutrality in the conflict between Britain and Germany. He had been an anti-imperialist with respect to the acquisition of Hawaii and the Philippines in the 1890s. After World War I broke out in 1914, he was a leading opponent of American involvement, although a relatively quiet one because he was a Democratic Speaker of the House and the President was also a Democrat.

Clark's leading opponent at the Democratic Convention was Woodrow Wilson. Wilson was an even more powerful symbol of unity between the North and South. He had been born and raised in a Confederate state, and he had received his PhD at the University of Virginia. Yet, he had received his undergraduate education at Princeton, and he returned to the North to work, ultimately as president of Princeton and governor of New Jersey.

Unlike Clark, Wilson had always been a pronounced Anglophile. Wilson's father was a well-known Scotch-Irish Presbyterian minister, and his mother was born in Carlisle, England, although of Scottish origins. Woodrow completely identified with the unification of English and non-English British-Americans into what he called "the Anglo-American race." His view of Jefferson was identical to Roosevelt's. Even when a student at the University of Virginia, Wilson refused to visit Jefferson's nearby home at Monticello on principle because of Jefferson's pro-French leanings. As a college professor he described Jefferson as "not a thorough American because of the strain of French philosophy that ... weakened all his thought."[43]

Wilson as a nominee would be a typical right-fork governor (although one with only two years of political experience before becoming President). He moved to the left to position himself between Theodore Roosevelt and William Howard Taft, a position already occupied by Champ Clark as a Midwesterner. Wilson's supporters also argued that it was important for national unity to elect the first President born in the South since 1848. They could also quietly point to the advantages of a strong Anglophile who had damned the Ellis Island immigrants in undercutting the appeal of Theodore Roosevelt.

At the 1912 convention, Clark gained a majority of votes on early ballots, but a two-thirds majority was required. At his high point on the 10th ballot, Clark led Wilson by 556 votes to 350, a majority of the 1094 delegates. He had 506 of the 804 delegates (63%) from the regions of the country in which competitive elections were held, the non-slave states and the Border States.[44] In the past, a candidate with a majority normally received the extra needed votes, for a majority always could abolish the two-thirds rule in mid-convention as William Jennings Bryan had threatened to do in 1896.

This time Wilson and Clark had similar domestic views, and one would have thought the anti-England Bryan of Nebraska would have supported the candidate from neighboring Missouri who shared his foreign policy views. If so, Clark surely would have been nominated. Instead, Bryan supported Wilson. An understanding had probably been reached that Bryan would be named Secretary of State so that Wilson could go into any European crisis with a neutral posture. Wilson finally won on the 46th ballot.

Wilson's victory in 1912 is taken for granted as the inevitable result of the split in the Republican Party. This is a mistake, for voters usually make a strategic decision in three-way races. That is, the Republicans normally would have eventually chosen between Taft and Roosevelt to prevent a Democratic victory. In 1912, Wilson's pronounced Anglophile position and the importance of ethnicity in that year's election made it easy for English and Scotch-Irish Republican voters to cast

---

43. Harley Notter, *The Origins of the Foreign Policy of Woodrow Wilson* (Baltimore: Johns Hopkins University Press, 1937), pp. 27 and 158.
44. *Congressional Quarterly's Guide to U.S. Elections*, 4th ed. (Washington: CQ Press, 2001), vol. 1, p. 601.

their ballot for their favorite Republican in full awareness this would help elect Wilson.

It is fascinating to speculate on the consequences of a Clark nomination, for American and perhaps world history might have been very different. He surely would have won the 167 Electoral College votes of the Confederate states and the border states of Kentucky, Missouri, and Oklahoma. He needed another 99 Electoral College votes; the 10 most German-American states had 130 votes and the other non-Border states beyond the Mississippi River had 49. Clark likely would have lost some of the urban Midwestern states, but he should have had an easy Electoral College victory in a two-candidate race, if not necessarily a popular majority.

In a three-way race with Clark, Roosevelt likely would have run an intensely anti-hyphenate race, and conservative Republicans would have had a choice between helping to elect the moderate "hyphenate" Democratic candidate or preventing their party from being replaced by a more radical Progressive one. Clark probably would have won, but then would have faced a very uncertain Republican response in 1916. Of course, the European powers would have had to react to a US President with a very different foreign policy than the strong pro-English position Wilson was to adopt in his first term. Their reaction is unpredictable. But since the prolongation of the war resulted in the breakup of the Austro-Hungarian Empire, the Communist victory in Russia, and the instability in Germany that led to Hitler, the consequences of the various choices could have been monumental.

THE DISASTROUS IMPACT OF WILSON'S POLICY ON THE DEMOCRATIC COALITION

When Woodrow Wilson was elected President, few expected a major, long-term war in Europe. If a war did occur, everyone assumed the United States would not become involved. As the historian Ernest May wrote, "owing to the large English and German elements in the population, government leaders assumed that the nation could never take part on either side without bringing on a civil war at home." In the first months of the war, President Wilson himself told the German ambassador, "We must be absolutely neutral, because otherwise our mixed population would fall into another war."[45]

Such American neutrality would have been easy if the war were a short one, but the United States had fundamental decisions to make when the war lasted for years. The rights of neutrals to trade with belligerents during war had been a central foreign policy concern for the United States from the beginning of its history. In 1800, the country did not have the power to enforce its neutral rights, but this was not true in 1914. The United States was perfectly placed to compel each side to accept free American trade with the other. Or if it chose, the United States could

---

45. Ernest R. May, *The World War and American Isolation, 1914-1917* (Cambridge, MA: Harvard University Press, 1959), pp. 34 and 118.

force both sides to accept a cease-fire, either through economic pressure or a threat to intervene on the other side.

In actuality, Wilson tilted entirely to the British side. He made the right of Americans to travel on British ships, eventually even armed merchant marine ships, a cause of war. Yet, he allowed munitions sales to Britain and gradually moved toward government loans to pay for them, the latter really not permitted by international law. He accepted the British boycott of food and raw materials sent to Germany, both dubious acts in international law. When Britain lay mines far from German ports and stopped American ships on the high seas, the United States tolerated the actions even though they were highly illegal by international law and a gross interference with neutrals' rights.[46]

The most dangerous aspect of Wilson's policy was his insistence on protecting the right of Americans to sail on combatant ships. Even a pro-Wilson scholar described the policy in the following terms: [47]

> Wilson decided to take a stand against the submarine when he could conceivably have accepted the German decree as he had earlier the British mine-laying proclamation. He then elected to separate his demands upon Germany from any made upon Britain, insisting that the Germans obey international law regardless of what their enemies did. And he chose to threaten war if Germany failed to comply. In each case he had at least one alternative, usually one recommended to him by Bryan as more apt to preserve the peace. He rejected these options.

Wilson's reaction when a British passenger ship, the *Lusitania*, was sunk in May 1915 so alarmed Bryan that he "resigned because Wilson had chosen to close the avenues of retreat, to threaten war, and to stake America's prestige on the success of his diplomacy."[48] The Germans promised not to attack passenger ships. The real political explosion occurred in February and March 1916 when the Administration extended its guarantees of the right of safe American travel to include armed merchant ships. Champ Clark told a press conference that Congress by a two or three to one margin wanted to warn Americans not to take merchant ships and that it did not want the government to protect them. Wilson vehemently insisted, and Congress retreated.[49]

---

46. See John Milton Cooper, Jr.'s two surveys of the literature, "World War in American Historical Writing," in John Milton Cooper, Jr., ed., *Causes and Consequences of World War I* (New York: Quadrangle Books, 1972), pp. 3–44, and "World War I: European Origins and American Intervention," *The Virginia Quarterly Review*, vol. 56, no. 1 (Winter 1980), p. 9. Marion C. Siney, *The Allied Blockade of Germany, 1914–1916* (Ann Arbor, Mich.: University of Michigan Press, 1957).

47. May, *The World War and American Isolation*, p. 137.

48. May, *The World War and American Isolation*, p. 156. May is cited almost exclusively in this chapter because he has a quite balanced position. It is easy to find authors who treat Wilson as flawless, as well as those who consider him a total cynic eager to find any excuse to go to war in his second term. After World War II, the effort to bring German-Americans and British-Americans together led to an unspoken compromise: Wilson's policy in World War I should not be criticized, but the rejection of the League of Nations should be blamed on his inflexibility, not the German-Americans. This was politically adroit, but the reverse criticisms were more accurate.

One reason why Congress was uneasy about challenging Wilson was that he had intensified his attacks on hyphenates at home. He first concentrated on alien groups, but included naturalized Americans among them and ultimately anyone who challenged the foreign policy of the government. In November 1915, the President expressed "grave concern" about "men who loved other countries better than they loved America ... and had forgotten that their chief and only allegiance was to the great government under which they live." "It is high time that the nation should call to a reckoning" these people "who speak alien sympathies." [50]

In his State of Union speech on December 7, 1915, President Wilson went further:[51]

> The gravest threats against our national peace and safety have been uttered within our own borders. There are citizens of the United States ... born under other flags but welcomed under our generous naturalization laws to the full freedom and opportunity of America, who have poured the poison of disloyalty into the very arteries of our national life; who have sought to bring the authority and good name of our Government into contempt, to destroy our industries wherever they thought it effective for their vindictive purposes to strike at them, and to debase our politics to the uses of foreign intrigue...

> [They] have brought deep disgrace upon us and have made it necessary that we should promptly make use of processes of law by which we may be purged of their corrupt distempers...I urge you to enact such laws at the earlier possible moment....

> I am urging you to do nothing less than save the honor and self-respect of the nation. Such creatures of passion, disloyalty, and anarchy must be crushed out. They are not many, but they are infinitely malignant, and the hand of our power should close over them at once....

> There are some men among us ... who, though born and bred in the United States and calling themselves Americans, have so forgotten themselves and their honor as citizens as to put their passionate sympathy with one or the other side in the great European conflict above their regard for the peace and dignity of the United States.... No laws, I suppose, can reach corruptions of the mind and heart; but I [must express] the even deeper humiliation and scorn which a self-possessed and thoughtfully patriotic American mind must feel when he thinks of them and of the discredit they are daily bringing upon us.

It required at least five minutes to read the whole section of the speech aloud.

These were remarkable words. America was not to be at war for 16 months, and Wilson emphasized the point in his State of the Union speech, "We have stood apart, studiously neutral." That is all that those with "alien sympathies" were proposing. They were saying Wilson had not been neutral enough, although some, like Eugene

---

49. Arthur S. Link, *Wilson: Confusions and Crises, 1915–1916* (Princeton: Princeton University Press, 1954), pp. 142–174.
50. Woodrow Wilson, "An Address on Preparedness to the Manhattan Club," November 4, 1915, in Arthur S. Link, ed., *The Papers of Woodrow Wilson* (Princeton: Princeton University Press, 1980), vol. 35, p. 172.
51. Woodrow Wilson, "Annual Message to Congress," December 7, 1915, in Link, *The Papers of Woodrow Wilson*, vol. 35, pp. 306–307.

Debs, who was supported by six percent of the voters in 1912, were socialists who called for strikes to get better wages for workers. Those who supported Great Britain were never accused of "alien sympathies," only those who supported Germany or the Irish rebels.

If Wilson had simply tilted toward Britain but acted in a way to keep the United States out of war, he would have found a politically adroit way of balancing the conflicting pressures under which he operated. Wilson was publicly more moderate on the war than the Republicans. Theodore Roosevelt denounced Wilson for cowardice and weakness for not supporting Great Britain more strongly. The Republican nominee, Charles Evans Hughes, was somewhat more moderate than Roosevelt, but essentially followed his line.

Those like Roosevelt and Hughes were responding to many voters, especially among the British-Americans, who felt intensely on the subject. Nearly 20 years later, the editor of the *Boston Herald* recalled "the anti-Teutonic fury that swept the English-Americans in Boston."[52] Wilson's supporters used the slogan, "He kept us out of war," and this convinced many "hyphenates" that he was the lesser evil and that his attacks on them and his tilt to Britain were politically necessary.

The states that Hughes carried in 1916 were 63% urban, while the states that Wilson won were 45% urban. Wilson lost the Eastern states north of Maryland, including his own New Jersey, by a 140 to 4 Electoral College margin. These were the states that were the most strongly English-American. Wilson in turn did very well in the states west of the Mississippi, many of them with a large German-American population, but he lost the more urban states of the Old Northwest except for Ohio, a state with large numbers both of German-Americans and Southern migrants. The West Coast had long been highly anti-Chinese and anti-Japanese, and Wilson had encouraged California to exclude Japanese from owning land, even though this was a violation of the Japanese-American Treaty.[53] Wilson won the election only because he carried California by 3,500 votes.

Even before Wilson's inauguration, Germany declared unlimited submarine war within a restricted area. When four American ships in that zone were sunk, Wilson called for Congress to declare war. It responded positively. The Administration quickly moved to build support for the war and suppress criticism of it. It convinced the Congress to pass a series of laws — the Alien Act, the Alien Enemies Act, the Espionage Act, the Sedition Act, the Selective Service Act, and the Trade with the Enemy Act — that achieved this end.[54]

---

52. Letter of Frank W. Buxton to William Dodd, July 6, 1933, William Dodd Papers, Box 40, 1933 Correspondence — B, Library of Congress.
53. Arthur S Link, *Woodrow Wilson and the Progressive Era 1910–1917* (New York: Harper, 1954), pp. 84–85.
54. Harry N. Scheiber, *The Wilson Administration and Civil Liberties, 1917–1921* (Ithaca, NY: Cornell University Press, 1960). H. C. Peterson and Gilbert C. Fite, *Opponents of War, 1917–1918* (Madison: University of Wisconsin Press, 1957). See Michael E. McGerr, *A Fierce Discontent: The Rise and Fall of the Progressive Movement in America, 1870-1920* (New York: Free Press, 2003), pp. 279–283. John Higham, *Strangers in the Land: Patterns of American Nativism, 1860-1925* (New Brunswick, NJ: Rutgers University Press, 1955), pp. 196–250.

George Creel, the head of the Committee on Public Information, wrote in his memoirs, *How We Advertised America*, that the Administration did not introduce legal censorship because it believed that the "desired result could be obtained without paying that price that a formal law would have demanded." Creel declared that it is "better far to have the desired compulsions proceed from within than apply them from without."[55]

The Administration did not use moral suasion alone to achieve self-censorship. When many super-patriotic, anti-German groups arose, the government did not discourage them.[56] Instead the Committee on Public Information had a speakers' corps and produced a series of films that were even more strident than Wilson's words. The Administration paid for ads calling upon citizens to report to the Justice Department, "the man who spreads pessimistic stories ... cries for peace, or belittles our efforts to win the war."[57]

Whatever one thinks substantively about Wilson's policies during and then after the war, they were disastrous for future ethnic peace and especially the Democratic coalition. His entry into war so soon after the election led many German-Americans and Irish-Americans to doubt Wilson's honesty, and it created enormous bitterness among them. Then German leaders were not permitted to play any role at the Versailles Peace Conference, and Germany was effectively disarmed and forced to pay high reparations. During the war the President enunciated the principle of national self-determination, but neither the German-speaking Austrians nor the large number of such Germans on the borders of the new Slavic east European countries were given the right to decide whether they would prefer to join Germany. Naturally, Britain would not agree to Ireland having the right of self-determination.

Wilson had based his wartime policy on neutrals' rights, even the right of Americans to sail on armed ships of belligerents. Yet, at the Versailles Conference, he sponsored a new League of Nations that assumed the concept of neutrality was outmoded. All members were obligated to unite against the aggressor in collective security. In short, they were obligated not to be neutral. German-Americans naturally thought the League was meant to legitimate Wilson's World War I policies — indeed, that his support of the League of Nations indicated he never believed his words about neutralism and neutrals' rights during his first term. They assumed that the same American political forces that defined the aggressor during the war would prevail in any future conflicts.

Then Wilson Administration further angered German-Americans by launching the Red Scare against them in 1919 and 1920. The Germans seldom expressed open

---

55. George Creel, *How We Advertised America* (New York: Harper and Brothers, 1920), pp. 5, 16–17, and 24.
56. For a vivid description of these activities, see Frederick C. Luebke, *Bonds of Loyalty: German-Americans and World War I* (DeKalb, IL: Northern Illinois Press, 1974), pp. 225–265. This is a remarkably good book, especially in the many political cartoons that it reprints and that give a sense of the times that a modern reader really cannot believe without such visual evidence.
57. Quoted in David M. Kennedy, *Over Here: The First World War and American Society* (New York: Oxford University Press, 1980), p. 62. A long chapter (pp. 45–92) of this book analyses the various steps taken to suppress dissent.

opposition to the treaty, but their silence reflected their fear, not their indifference.[58] The Irish-Americans had no such inhibitions, and they even persuaded the House of Representatives to pass a resolution that rather mildly supported the Irish-American position on Irish independence.[59]

Ratification of the treaty required the votes of two-thirds of the Senate — 64 Senators. Only 39 approved without reservations, and 12 with relatively minor changes. The treaty received unqualified support from 34 of 51 Senators in the South and West, but from only 5 of 44 Senators in the Northeast and Midwest.[60] The Senators with large numbers of German-American or Irish-American voters usually were either direct opponents or strong reservationists who likely would always try to avoid a choice. The leader of the reservationists, Henry Cabot Lodge, was typical. His state of Massachusetts contained so many English-Americans and Irish-Americans that any definitive choice would have deeply offended great numbers of his voters.

Not surprisingly, the Democrats paid a high political cost for Wilson's policy. The 1918 Congressional election was scheduled for November 5, even before the war was to end on November 11. Wilson, despite the advice of his top political adviser, decided to make support for the Democrats in the Congress a vote of confidence on his conduct of the war. A top Wilsonian Progressive and a future American ambassador to Germany later described the results:[61]

> The people of the United States were compelled under their constitution to hold an election in November, 1918, at a moment when war heats disqualified great race blocs from intelligent voting. It was natural that the German-Americans should have voted against the then president of the United States ... It was equally natural that the Irish should vote against the president because, somehow, he had not been able to defeat England at the same time Germany was defeated.

The Democrats won 80 seats in the non-slave states in 1916, but only 58 in 1918 and 19 in 1920. The Midwest had 127 seats, and the Democratic total fell from 34 to 17 to 3 in these years.[62]

The Democrats provided a final insult to the German-Americans in the 1920 presidential election. The Democratic candidate, Governor James Cox, came from Ohio, a state with many German-Americans. Like Senator Warren Harding, also from Ohio, Cox naturally had supported neutrality prior to American entry into war; but then during the Red Scare of 1919, he decided he needed to compensate to be a

---

58. Austin J. App, "The Germans," in Joseph P. O'Grady, ed., *The Immigrants' Influence on Wilson's Peace Policies* (Lexington: University of Kentucky Press, 1967).
59. Joseph P. O'Grady, "The Irish," in O'Grady, *The Immigrants' Influences on Wilson's Peace Policies*, pp. 56–84. For the House resolution, see pp. 67–71.
60. Thomas N. Guinsburg, *The Pursuit of Isolationism in the United States Senate from Versailles to Pearl Harbor* (New York: Garland Publisher, 1982), p. 34.
61. "Quoted in "Modern History's Greatest Blunder," *Chicago Daily News*, February 10, 1933, in Dodd Papers, Box 40, 1933 Correspondence — D, Library of Congress.
62. The Midwest is defined here as the Old Midwest (Illinois, Indiana, Michigan, Ohio, and Wisconsin) and the trans-Mississippi agricultural states (Iowa, Kansas, Minnesota, Nebraska, North Dakota, and South Dakota). The three Democratic Congressmen in the Midwest were from three urban districts in Chicago.

viable contender for the Democratic presidential nomination in 1920.[63] As Ohio governor, Cox sponsored a state law to ban instruction of German language in school — after the war was already over, but during the Red Scare. This was necessary, he said, because "every germ of Prussian poison must be squeezed out of the organic law of Ohio."

Cox even refused a compromise to permit instruction in German in private and parochial schools. The exclusion of private schools from the prohibition was "artful, insidious and apparently deliberate in its attempt to deceive the people of the state." Since "the teaching of German to young people was a menace to the ideals of the republic," its retention in private schools "would leave places of refuge for breeding treason." The Catholic Church in Ohio strongly wanted the right to teach German in parochial schools. Thus, in taking his position, Cox was directly challenging the German-American Catholics who were a key element of the Democratic base in the Midwest.[64]

Then in 1920 Cox chose Franklin Roosevelt as the Vice Presidential nominee. Roosevelt was a 38-year-old Anglophile who had been Assistant Secretary of the Navy in the Wilson Administration and ardently supported America entry into the League of Nations. Rightly or not, people assumed that his policy was not far from Theodore's.

During the campaign, Harding ran on the slogan "Return to Normalcy," which implied ethnic peace, but Cox deliberately copied Wilson's tactic of associating the German-Americans with treason. The "largest single group" of opponents of the League of Nations, he said, were "the frankly disloyal": "those who were pro-German before the war, pro-German when the actions of the Kaiser made it impossible that we remain neutral, and pro-German during the war." The other three types of opponents were the "munitions makers," the "radical Socialistic and Communist forces," and those who do not believe "various racial entities have not attained the ideal under the Treaty." The example he cited of the latter was Ireland.[65] In closing his campaign, Cox said, "Every traitor in America will vote tomorrow for Warren G. Harding."

Harding won 65% of the vote in the North in 1920 to Cox's 29%. The 1924 election was even worse. Harding died in office and his Vice President, Calvin Coolidge of Vermont and Massachusetts, succeeded him. The Republicans naturally nominated Coolidge in 1924, and the Democrats nominated a candidate as offensive to its base as Cox. John W. Davis had been Solicitor General from 1913 to 1918 and, as such, was deeply involved in the legal measures against dissent. He then was named ambassador to Great Britain from 1918 to 1921, the period of the Versailles Treaty.

The third party candidate, Robert La Follette of German-American Wisconsin, had been an isolationist during the war and in 1924 adopted a highly liberal domestic

---

63. For the position of Cox and Harding prior to April 1917, see Roger Babson, *Cox: The Man* (New York: Brentano's, 1920), pp. 54–56.
64. James E. Cebula, *James M. Cox: Journalist and Politician* (New York: Garland Publishing, 1985), pp. 90–91.
65. Donald R. McCoy, "Election of 1920," in Arthur M. Schlesinger, Jr., ed., *History of American Presidential Elections* (New York: Chelsea House, 1971), vol. 3, p. 2429.

policy at a time of economic depression in the farm belt. The Democrats received only 28.8% of the national popular vote and only 20.3% from Pennsylvania to the Pacific. If Illinois, Indiana, and Ohio — the three states with a very large number of migrants from the South — are excluded, the Democrats had only 15.7% of the vote. Clearly they had lost the German Catholics and large number of Irish-Americans as well as the traditional Republican Protestants.

THE REBUILDING OF THE DEMOCRATIC ETHNIC COALITION

Robert La Follette's vote in 1924 was drawn from both parties, but Coolidge's vote for President was only 4% lower than the Republican percentage in Congressional races, while Davis' vote was 13 percent lower.[66] Since La Follette was a French Catholic who had done well in the largest cities as well as the rural areas, the Democrats were threatened with the loss of their entire Catholic Northern base. Like the Republicans a dozen years earlier, and like the Whigs, they were in danger of disappearing.

In 1928 the Democrats decided that their first priority was to bring the Catholics back to the party. They nominated an Irish Catholic, Al Smith, who had risen in Tammany Hall politics to become governor of New York. Smith was a strong advocate of the repeal of Prohibition, a position that was simultaneously a political gesture to the German-Americans — who understood that the 18th Amendment had been passed as an anti-German measure.

Smith was a failure by traditional standards. He lost the election by a 58% to 40% margin and won only 97 Electoral College votes. He even lost four Confederate states (Florida, North Carolina, Tennessee, and Virginia), all the Border States, and his own state of New York. Nevertheless, Smith was successful in re-energizing the electorate. Turnout rose in the North from 57.6% to 66.7%. Many came to the polls to vote against him, but the total Democrat vote rose from 8.4 million in 1924 to 15.0 million in 1928. Smith was also successful in bringing the Catholics back to the party. Indeed, he stimulated many women Catholics to vote for the first time.

Franklin Roosevelt had succeeded Smith as governor of New York in 1928, winning the state by 25,000 votes as Smith lost it by 103,000 votes. When Roosevelt was re-elected by 725,000 votes in 1930, he became a favorite for the 1932 Democratic nomination. He needed, however, to end the link in the minds of German-Americans and Irish-Americans between himself and Wilson's foreign policy. He was chosen to write the "Democratic" article on foreign policy in the July 1928 issue of the influential magazine, *Foreign Affairs*, and declared that "it is beside the point at this time to agitate the question of our membership in the League ... A majority of American voters has been opposed." In 1932 he completely repudiated the League and also

---

66. David Burner, "Election of 1924," in Schlesinger, Jr., ed., *History of American Presidential Elections*, vol. 3, p. 2488.

implicitly American involvement in "strictly European political national difficulties."[67]

Herbert Hoover had condemned Japan when it conquered Manchuria in 1931, but he did not intervene. Roosevelt did not even criticize Japan, and he secured the nomination at the convention by making an agreement with the isolationist William Randolph Hearst on selecting John Garner as his Vice President. Texas was the most German-American Southern state, and Garner's district included a substantial number of them.

Roosevelt, as discussed in the previous chapter, actually did better in the German-American states than the large Eastern ones. In large part, the Midwest must have felt that its Eastern coalition partners had abandoned them in foreign policy during the war and in domestic policy in the 1920s. They were, therefore, perhaps more willing to believe Roosevelt's Bryan-like strategy in his struggle for the nomination. Perhaps the Catholics in the Eastern states were disillusioned that Smith was not re-nominated.

When Roosevelt was elected in November 1932, Germany was a peaceful, if unstable, democracy. Roosevelt identified fully with the Navy, and the Navy thought that an eventual war with Japan was inevitable. There are a number of signs that Roosevelt was thinking about eventual action against Japanese expansion that might make the US dominant in the Pacific and help unite the European-Americans in a war against them.

Unfortunately, by the time Roosevelt was inaugurated in March 1933, Hitler had come to power. Nothing could have been worse from the perspective of American ethnic politics and of Roosevelt's hopes for a landslide win that would give him a mandate in 1936. The President followed a policy of reassuring the German-Americans and Irish-Americans with a thoroughly isolationist policy prior to the fall of France in June 1940. Even then, he lost 8 Midwestern states in 1940 and 10 in 1944. These included 6 of the 10 most German-American states in 1940 and 7 in 1944. American support for the war, especially for the demand of unconditional surrender, was far weaker than described in the mythology about the unity of the "greatest generation."[68]

The ethnic conflicts that had plagued the United States and its foreign policies continued after the onset of the war. The differences over the treatment of Germany led Roosevelt to avoid any decisions on the postwar settlement during the war and then led Truman to the same policy during the first two years of his Administration. Nevertheless, the conflicts erupted again in the McCarthyism that continued into the early 1950s.

The Democrats were to suffer another great loss during the war and especially in 1946 in the strip of states from Pennsylvania to California. These states had 201 seats

---

67. For 1928, see Franklin D. Roosevelt, "Our Foreign Policy," *Foreign Affairs*, vol. 6, no. 4 (July 1928), p. 580. For an excellent and detailed discussion of his 1932 speech, see Charles A. Beard, *American Foreign Policy in the Making, 1932–1940: A Study in Responsibilities* (New Haven: Yale University Press, 1946), chapter 5 and especially pp. 75–76 and 84.
68. Steven Casey, *Cautious Crusade: Franklin D. Roosevelt, American Public Opinion, and the War Against Nazi Germany* (New York: Oxford University Press, 2001).

in the 1930s and 200 in the 1940s, and the number won by the Democrats declined from an abnormal 165 in 1936 to 90 both in 1938 and 1940, and to 62 in 1942. The Democratic seats rose to 75 in 1944 and fell to 38 in 1946. Even their victories usually came in large cities with relatively low numbers of German-Americans. In 1948, two new parties—Henry Wallace's left-wing Progressive Party and Strom Thurmond's segregationist States' Rights Party—were to break away from the Democrats and run as independent candidates in the 1948 election.

Truman's ability to win attract voters from Pennsylvania to California in the 1948 election and to increase the number of Democrats' seats from 38 to 83 likely stemmed in large part from his decision to rebuild Germany in the Marshall Plan and to defend Berlin against the 1948 Soviet blockade. But whatever the cause of the 1948 results, the Democratic Party clearly was not in danger of collapse, as it had been in 1924. In fact, some state elections — notably Adlai Stevenson's upset election as governor of Illinois in 1948, and by a huge landslide — indicated that the party had other strategies it could follow to preserve itself.

Nevertheless, the political elites of both parties had already decided that the costs of the racial conflicts among the European-Americans were far too high for a country that wanted to be a super-power in Europe. They had decided, although without articulating the point in public, that it was crucial to end these conflicts. The key action was to abolish the whole concept of different European-American races and to change the warring Europeans into a single, common race, the whites. The complex way in which this was done, including with foreign policy actions, will be the subject of the next two chapters. But, of course, if the two parties had basically been coalitions of people of different European races and religions, a transformation in the centrality of these identities was certain to create major problems for the coalitions that had gone back for over a century and a half.

CHAPTER 4. THE MAKING OF "THE WHITES" AND PARTY CHANGE: CHANGING IDEAS OF RACE

Once Franklin Roosevelt repudiated the post Civil War agreements with the South, new party alignments were inevitable. Yet, even then, the pace of realignment was extremely slow. Fifteen years passed between Roosevelt's victory over the Supreme Court and Eisenhower's victory in four Confederate states in 1952. Only in 1980, 43 years after 1937, did Reagan's election signify that the South had become predominantly Republican and then only at the presidential level.

There were many reasons for the length of the process. Of course, nearly two hundred years of history were being reversed, and old attachments and habits of thought died slowly. Politicians had to grope for new solutions, but they could not test new presidential election strategies except once every four years. There were only nine presidential elections between Roosevelt's death and Reagan's victory, and most took place under such different conditions that political strategists found it difficult to draw broad lessons from them.

In addition, the parties had been ethnic and religious coalitions of European-Americans before the Civil War and remained so in the North after that war. The deep divisions among European-Americans significantly complicated the transition to a new realignment. The Republicans, first and foremost, were the party of the Northern Protestants, but the Protestants of the North and the South had been deeply divided since the Civil War period — and even since the British civil wars. If the Republicans — the party of Lincoln — were to win in the South, then this lingering bitterness would have to be overcome.

If the Republicans won Southern states, however, the Democrats in turn had to win compensatory victories in the North if they were to remain competitive. This meant the Democrats would need to win more Northern Protestant votes. Yet the strong prejudices and hostility of the Protestant European-Americans to non-Protestant European-Americans made such a task very difficult. The refusal of Congress to change the 1924 immigration quotas for southern and eastern Europe until 1965 showed that the old suspicions were dying slowly.

Memories of the New England Protestant hostility toward the Irish Catholics and of discrimination against the Ellis Island immigrants, especially the Jews and Italians, still survive among a significant number of people. Memories of the intense antagonisms among the Protestant European-Americans have, however, virtually disappeared among the American population as a whole and even to a large extent within the scholarly community. People show real surprise when they are told that descendants of British-Americans and German-Americans constituted some 50 percent of the white population prior to World War II, that the German-Americans were nearly as numerous as the British-Americans, and that they had a highly antagonistic political relationships from 1910 to 1955, including that expressed in McCarthyism.

The key reason that the earlier conflicts among European-Americans are forgotten is that one technique to end them was to make their discussion almost completely taboo, even for scholars. One might talk about the parochial interests and influence of the Polish-Americans, a group that actually had almost no influence on foreign policy in the 1930s and 1940s, but not that of German-Americans, let alone British-Americans. Criticism of Wilson's entry into World War II, questions about Roosevelt's personal commitment to collective security before 1940, and postwar party divisions on the reunification of Germany were sensitive in the extreme.

The taboos also applied to a discussion of earlier periods. The strength of the religious divisions among English-American colonists in the 17th century and their relationship to the English civil wars got little attention in the specialized histories of the colonial period and none in broader discourse among the educated. George Washington's comment about the "foreign emigrants" in the Shenandoah Valley "who can have no particular predilection for us" was never cited, and the American Revolution was never treated as a war to establish a new national identity that would embrace them."[1]

Least of all do members of younger and middle age generations other than a few scholars understand that European-American groups thought of each other as "races." As has been discussed, the phrase "race, creed, or color" accurately reflected a sharp distinction between "race" and "color." Northerners always had racist attitudes towards blacks, but they also had "racist" attitudes toward other European-American groups that were associated with the same emotions and prejudices as "racism" towards "people of color" with which we are familiar today.

Matthew Jacobson correctly writes about "the fabrication of race" and the "invented category" of race. "Race," he says, "resides not in nature but in politics and culture." This is as true of the "white race" as of others. Jacobson is right to insist that "a significant strand of twentieth century American political life ... is the story of how

---

1. "To Jacob Reed," November 3, 1784, in W.W. Abbot and Dorothy Twohig, eds., *The Papers of George Washington, The Confederation Period* (Charlottesville: University Press of Virginia, 1992), vol. 2, p. 121.

'racial politics' ceased to concern the white races of Europe and came to refer exclusively to black–white relations and the struggle over Negro civil rights."[2]

The fundamental party realignment of the mid-twentieth century was to depend on the end of "racial politics" that concerned "the white races of Europe." In practice, the North accepted the South's definition of race based on color of skin precisely at the time that it began to emphasize the evils of racism. Indeed, instead of including gradations such as "mulatto" that are widely used in Latin America, the North adopted the definition of "black" and "white" that was introduced to define the subjects of the segregationist Jim Crow laws at the turn of the century. This meant that very light-skinned "tans" became "black" and that swarthy colors became "white." But this process, which will be discussed in the next chapter, cannot be properly understood unless we first understand the way that our grandparents and great-grandparents thought of "races" and "whites." This is also necessary, in my opinion, if we really want to destroy "racism" today.

THE EARLY SOUTHERN CREATION OF "WHITES"[3]

The concept of "white" first arose in America in connection with the introduction of slavery.[4] Yet it had little reality so far as "white" adult males were concerned. "White" was hardly the word to describe the color of the skin of a man who had worked in the fields for years in the sun. "Leathery brown" was more accurate, even more in the South than in the North. Gary Taylor points out that European art from the days of the cave dwellers gave "whites" a reddish brown skin, an appropriate color for those who worked outdoors.[5] This may have been one reason that "white" was not as central an identity as is now assumed.[6] Another factor was that the only "real" whites were women who did not work outdoors, and men did not want to give them the highest status.

Even the distinction between African slave and white non-slave was not clear-cut, especially in the South. Many, if not most, European immigrants came to the colonies as indentured servants or as exiled convicts. The Europeans working in the tobacco fields often did not live in much better conditions than black slaves except that their bondage was limited to a set number of years. Indeed, black slaves, "servants," and convicts might work in the fields together. The mortality rate was so high

---

2. Matthew F. Jacobson, *Whiteness of a Different Color: European Immigrants and the Alchemy of Race* (Cambridge, MA: Harvard University Press, 1998), pp. 247, 1, 4 and 9.
3. Donald Fred Tingley, "The Rise of Racialistic Thinking in the United States in the Nineteenth Century" (Ph.D. diss, University of Illinois, 1952).
4. For the debates on the subject, see Theodore W. Allen, *The Invention of the White Race* (London: Verso, 1994), pp. 1–24. A book that explores in detail the way that the issue emerged in England in the decades before the arrival of the first colonists is Gary Taylor, *Buying Whiteness: Race, Culture, and Identity from Columbus to Hip-Hop* (New York: Palgrave Macmillan, 2005).
5. Taylor, *Buying Whiteness: Race, Culture, and Identity From Columbus to Hip-Hop*, pp. 29–35.
6. See Richard Dyer, *White* (London: Routledge, 1997), p. 57.

that the length of servitude for the Europeans was often just an academic concept, until enough black labor was available for the servants to be sent to Western lands.

The coastal English continued to see those in the interior as foreigners after the revolution, and they made little distinction between the non-English immigrants and the Borderland English. Indeed, the prejudices survived into the 21st century in stereotypes about hillbillies, rednecks, crackers, and white trash.

Nevertheless, the South received relatively few immigrants after the 1830s other than in a few ports such as New Orleans, Louisville, and especially St. Louis. The descendants of the older European immigrants increasingly intermarried, and the 1830s Romantic conception of separate races built on language and cultural differences, let alone the later concept of race based on "blood," had little relationship to the reality of the European-Americans of the South. People who originally descended from different ethnic origins began to see themselves as having a common identity, "white."[7]

The sense of a common identity was further strengthened by the belated introduction of universal white male suffrage in the South and a reduction in the gerrymandering that was aimed at reducing the influence of the interior. The property requirement for suffrage had not been motivated simply by fear of the poor. The poor were disproportionately the "foreigners" who lived in the interior, and that was an important consideration. The granting of the vote to these foreigners was a powerful symbol that they were no longer foreign, but equal members of the community. Officially, they were superior to the free blacks, who still couldn't vote. This was done quite consciously and was defended as a necessary step if the non-English Europeans were to be used in the militia to control black rebellions.[8]

The real issue regarding color in the South centered on the persons who were partly European and partly African in origin. "Mulatto" (or, colloquially, "yellow") was widely employed in Latin America for those of mixed origin, and it was used in the United States as well.[9] Indeed, it was an official racial category in the 1850 and 1860 census. In 1860, 86.7% of Negroes were identified as "black" and 13.3% as "mulatto," percentages that were 69% and 31% respectively in the North.[10]

---

7. George M. Fredrickson, *White Supremacy: A Comparative Study in American and South African History* (New York: Oxford University Press, 1981).
8. For the democratization of the South, see, for example, Chilton Williamson, *American Suffrage: From Property to Democracy, 1760–1860* (Princeton: Princeton University Press, 1960). Fletcher M. Green, *Constitutional Developments in the South Atlantic States, 1776–1880* (New York: W.W. Norton, 1966). Fletcher M. Green, *Democracy in the Old South, and Other Essays* (Nashville: Vanderbilt University, 1969). For the tie between slavery and suffrage, see Williamson, *American Suffrage*, p. 232, and Alexander Keyssar, *The Right to Vote: The Contested History of Democracy in the United States* (New York: Basic Books, 2000), pp. 38 and 46.
9. See, for example, Anthony W. Marx, *Making Race and Nation: A Comparison of South Africa, the United States, and Brazil* (Cambridge: Cambridge University Press, 1998), pp. 65–76. Carl N. Degler, *Neither Black Nor White: Slavery and Race Relations in Brazil and the United States* (New York: Macmillan, 1971). Joel Williamson, *New People: Miscegenation and Mulattoes in the United States* (New York: Free Press, 1980). Virginia R. Dominguez, *White by Definition: Social Classification in Creole Louisiana* (New Brunswick, NJ: Rutgers University Press, 1986).

After the Civil War, the South could have evolved even further in the Latin American direction. "Mulatto" was retained in all the US censuses from 1870 through 1930, except for 1900, and the census of 1890 used "Quadroon" and "Octoroon" at the direction of Congress.[11] "Negroes" of mixed background could feel very torn about their identity.[12] Homer Plessy of the famous 1896 *Plessy v. Ferguson* Supreme Court case that endorsed the "separate but equal" concept was very light-skinned — an "octoroon" in the language of the Louisiana law.[13] He argued that the state did not have the power to define race. The Court could have agreed, but did not.

The approval of legal segregation by the Supreme Court in *Plessy v. Ferguson* was a key event in the formation of a white identity. A considerable amount of de facto segregation was inevitable in the South after the Civil War because the slaves had been denied education and hence had a low economic and cultural level. Yet the rules of segregation usually were customary rather than legal. Behavior toward blacks varied with circumstances, and many of the Southern elite were willing to continue that practice. A Charleston newspaper in 1897 called for "first-class cars for first-class passengers, white and colored" and added, "To speak plainly, we need, as everybody knows, separate cars or apartments for rowdy or drunken white passengers far more than Jim Crow cars for colored passengers."[14]

The great political problem in the South was that the lower income whites had lost a great deal in the years after the Civil War. The upwardly mobile, who had managed to buy a slave or two, lost most of their wealth. They then suffered greatly from the long decline in commodity prices that began in 1873. Psychologically, emancipation of the slaves and then the guarantee of black suffrage in the 15th Amendment ended the legal status of poor whites as superior to blacks in this respect. The poor whites responded to their worsening psychological and economic situation by supporting radical populist parties and engaging in radical actions against former slaves.[15]

The 1880s and 1890s were the period in which new voting rules were introduced to restrict voter turnout of poor whites and blacks and destroy the populist parties.

---

10. Kenneth Prewitt, "The Census Counts, the Census Classifies," in Nancy Foner and George M. Fredrickson, eds., *Not Just Black and White: Historical and Contemporary Perspectives on Immigration, Race, and Ethnicity in the United States* (New York: Russell Sage Foundation, 2004), p. 150. For the 1860 figures, see *Population of the United States in 1860 Compiled from the Original Returns of the Eighth Census* (Washington, D.C.: Government Printing Office, 1864), p. x. In 1850, the percentage of mulattos was 11.1% nation-wide and 29.0% in the North.
11. For a list of all the "racial" census categories from 1830 to 1930, including the Asian ones, see Melissa Nobles, *Shades of Citizenship: Race and the Census in Modern Politics* (Stanford: Stanford University Press, 2000), pp. 44 and 187–188. For Congress and quadroons and octoroons, pp. 56–57.
12. For an extended discussion of one such "black" writer, Jean Toome, see Matthew P. Guterl, *The Color of Race in America, 1900–1940* (Cambridge, MA: Harvard University Press, 2001), pp. 154–183.
13. Nobles, *Shades of Citizenship*, pp. 56–57.
14. Quoted in C. Vann Woodward, *The Strange Career of Jim Crow*, 3rd rev. ed. (New York: Oxford University Press, 1974), pp. 49–50. The first edition of Woodward's famous book was published in 1955, but the most developed and refined version of the thesis is found in the third revised edition.

These also were the years in which those who wanted a strict legal system of segregation emerged victorious. The cause-and-effect relationship between these two developments is unclear, but the two must have been linked in an evolution that stretched over a quarter of a century. The new voting rules implied an equality between blacks and poor whites, and one that reduced turnout of both, but legal segregation again put poor and middle-income whites in the same social category as the well-to-do whites and reassured them. In the words of Vann Woodward, "the Negro was now pressed into service as a sectional scapegoat in the reconciliation of estranged white classes and the reunion of the Solid South." The Negro became an "approved object of aggression."[16]

Woodward's classic book is controversial, especially for points not covered in this chapter, but no one would dispute his central point. Segregation became far more formalized and comprehensive in the legal system at the turn of the century.[17] The corollary is so taken for granted that almost no one mentions it: instituting a system of legal segregation depended on a legal definition of "white" and "Negro." The definitions of Negro varied somewhat from state to state, especially at first, and so did the behavior that was required to be segregated. Nevertheless, in each locale, it had to be legally clear who could and could not sit at the front of the bus and who was excluded from specific institutions.

Other problems of definition remained. The Alabama Supreme Court decided (wrongly, in the opinion of the US Supreme Court) that an Armenian was not white. In another case the Alabama Court showed confusion about whether a Sicilian (Italian) was white.[18] Yet eventually a reified dichotomy between whites and Negroes in the South was developed. It had broader implications, if for no other reason than that the US Census Bureau had to satisfy politicians of both regions. In 1930, the Bureau finally accepted the "one-drop" rule in its purest form. "A person of mixed white and Negro blood should be returned as a Negro," enumerators were instructed, "no matter now small the percentage of Negro blood."[19] The census takers had to use this definition in the North as well as the South.

Of course, gradations among whites persisted even in the South. The South, other than Louisiana, had few Catholics, and many Southerners continued to be highly anti-Catholic and anti-Semitic. This meant that through most of the 20th century they did not really think of themselves as being part of the same white com-

---

15. For a comprehensive discussion of the radicalism in politics and in behavior, see Joel Williamson, *The Crucible of Race: Black/White Relations in the American South Since Emancipation* (New York: Oxford University Press, 1984), pp. 189–195 and 224–258. For a survey of the waves of segregation, see 253–256.
16. Woodward, *The Strange Career of Jim Crow*, 3rd revised edition, pp. 82 and 81.
17. For a discussion of the controversy, see John W. Cell, *The Highest Stage of White Supremacy: The Origins of Segregation in South Africa and the American South* (Cambridge: Cambridge University Press, 1982), and Howard N. Rabinowitz, "More than the Woodward Thesis: Assessing *The Strange Career of Jim Crow*," in Howard N. Rabinowitz, ed., *Race, Ethnicity, and Urbanization: Selected Essays* (Columbia: University of Missouri Press, 1994), pp. 23–41.
18. Jacobson, *Whiteness of a Different Color*, p. 4.
19. Nobles, *Shades of Citizenship*, p. 118.

munity as Catholics. One has the impression that Jimmy Carter, at great political cost to himself, never fully felt comfortable with the Irish-American Tip O'Neill or the Italian-American Joseph Califano (or the Jewish-American Michael Blumenthal).[20] But over time the "white" identity continued to become stronger. In 2004, North Carolina re-elected a Catholic Democratic governor by a wide majority in a state that voted solidly for Bush for President and for the Republican Senate candidate. No one noticed that he was Catholic. The issue was explicitly raised in the 2005 gubernatorial race in Virginia because the Catholic Democratic candidate personally opposed the death penalty for moral reasons. He still was elected.

THE DEVELOPMENT OF EUROPEAN-AMERICAN "RACES"

Northerners, like Southerners, always thought of themselves as white, but in one key respect their experience was very different. The number of immigrants who entered the South in the 19th century was relatively small, and the immigrants of the 18th century gradually melded together. The North, by contrast, received a large number of Irish and German Catholics in the 19th century, together with Protestant immigrants from the Scandinavian countries. This gave Northerners a heightened sense of ethnic diversity.

The new Catholic immigration into the North began at the same time as the Romantic Movement in Europe and the creation of the first emotional nationalism on the continent. The Romantic Movement emphasized the unique nature of peoples, their *Volkgeist* or folk-spirit, but this spirit was based on culture, religion, national character, and language, not genetic ties.[21] In the United States this general set of attitudes was expressed in the use of the word "race" for the different European peoples coming into the country.

Because of the cultural — usually linguistic — basis of "race," the number of races in the United States could be quite large. A middle-level American official wrote during World War I that the war presented "a wonderful chance in this country to weld the twenty-five or thirty races which compose our people into a strong, virile and intelligent people.... [A] splendid race of new Americans." One of the foremost scholars on the subject looked at American attitudes towards 40 races.[22]

Many of the 25 to 40 "races" could be relatively small, but many of them simultaneously also were considered part of broader races. The larger races included "English," "Saxon" or "Anglo-Saxon" (Protestant British), "Teuton" (German),

---

20. See the discussion in Chapter 8, pp. 205-206.
21. Hans G. Schenk, *The Mind of the European Romantics: An Essay in Cultural History* (London: Constable, 1966). The subtitle of the work defines the nature of the phenomenon, and Schenck focuses entirely on the Romantic concept of peoples as cultural entities.
22. Emory S. Bogardus, *Immigration and Race Attitudes* (Boston: D.C. Heath, 1928), p. 25. Quoted in Michael McGerr, *A Fierce Discontent: The Rise and Fall of the Progressive Movement in America, 1870–1920* (New York: Free Press, 2003), p. 291.

"Celtic"(Irish Catholic), "Romance" or "Latin" (French, Italian, and Spanish), "Slavic" (east European), and "Semitic" (Jew).[23] Some of these labels aggregated smaller races, and any people we might now call an "ethnic group" was called a race. Finally, all of these smaller and aggregated races of European-Americans were considered part of an overarching group, the "whites."

Peoples from outside Europe were, of course, also called races, but lack of familiarity resulted in awareness only of aggregated races whose definition was not fixed. "Turko-Mohammedan," "Asian," or "South American" were sometimes used. However, a more sophisticated person such as Eleanor Roosevelt understood that these groups needed to be subdivided. In 1933, she wrote about the war between the Japanese and Chinese in 1933 as one involving "the yellow races," but "races" was plural.[24]

Although a number of books deal with the development of the concept of race in the United States, the subject remains very murky. The old intellectual debates about "race" can be studied, but it is very hard to know how people actually thought about themselves and others. In particular, the relative importance of the different level of races in their minds is especially obscure. After all, people think of themselves as blue-eyed, brown-eyed, or some variant, but that difference has never been politically relevant. For us, the real question is the political salience of the white identity.

At a minimum, it is clear Northerners did not see a simple dichotomy between "whites" and "Negroes." Instead, they ranked the "races" in a hierarchical manner. Woodrow Wilson's "sturdy stocks of the north of Europe" were at the top, sometimes termed the "Nordic" races. Within northern Europe, the Teutons and Anglo-Saxons originally were at the very top, but as British-German relations deteriorated, only the Anglo-Saxons remained at the pinnacle. In Anglo imagination, the Teutons became a domineering race, not as high in status as they themselves believed.

The French of the Romance or Latin race were a step lower, and many thought the Latin element that three centuries of French rule had introduced into English culture had polluted the superior Teutonic culture of the original inhabitants. Much lower on the scale were the Catholic Irish, "the white niggers," as they were sometimes called. Yet even the Irish had been uplifted a bit by centuries of English rule. The "races" of eastern and Southern Europe were certainly below them, and then came the American Indians. The African races and most of the Asian ones were at the lowest level, although Theodore Roosevelt was one who greatly admired the Japanese. But since races were ultimately defined by culture, they could rise over time as their cultural level rose. This included blacks.

This definition of "race" to include European-American "ethnic groups" survived for a surprisingly long time, especially in the North. The phrase "race, creed, or color," was often used, and the words "race" and "color" were not redundant. As has been

23. Edward N. Saveth, *American Historians and European Immigrants, 1875–1925* (New York: Columbia University Press, 1948). Also see Stuart Anderson, *Race and Rapprochement: Anglo-Saxonism and Anglo-American Relations, 1895–1904* (Rutherford, NJ: Fairleigh Dickinson University, 1981), pp. 63 and 91.
24. Mrs. Franklin Roosevelt, *It's Up to the Women* (New York: Frederick A. Stokes, 1933), p. 239.

seen, a Kansas City firm answering a survey in the 1930s could describe its employment practices as "no colored hired in office [and] no discrimination as of race."[25]

As late as World War II, Americans spoke of European races without self-consciousness. In 1933, Franklin Roosevelt referred openly to Felix Frankfurter's Jewish "race" to his face, and Frankfurter did not seem offended.[26] General Dwight Eisenhower in 1942 mentioned "the English race" in a memorandum, while the American Ambassador to Germany in 1938, Hugh Wilson, referred to "the portions of the German race outside of and adjoining the boundaries of Germany."[27] The head of the US Military Mission in Moscow in World War II, General John R. Deane, wrote to General George Marshall in 1944, "The individual Russian is a likable person. Their racial characteristics are similar to our own."[28]

As was obvious in Deane's comment about Russians and in Theodore Roosevelt's use of "English-speaking race" to refer to Americans, the concept of race in the first half of the 20th century still often was as cultural in character as it had been a century earlier. The concept had, however, become hopelessly confused because of Charles Darwin's theory of evolution and the survival of the fittest. Race could also be a biological term, and many people began, allegorically or not, to use words like "flesh," "stock," and "blood."

Nevertheless, language and religion also remained an important element of "race," and even a scholar who tended to emphasize the physical component in the definition of race still acknowledged that scholars used "race" and "nationality" interchangeably.[29] The result, in the words of Reginald Horsman was "to jumble race, nation, and language into a hodgepodge [often] of rampant radical nationalism."[30] Language and religion usually were usually most important.

---

25. Claudia D. Goldin, *Understanding the Gender Gap: An Economic History of American Women* (New York: Oxford University Press, 1990), pp. 147 and 249, n14.
26. Frankfurter memorandum of conversation with Franklin Roosevelt, March 8, 1933, Frankfurter papers, Reel 60, Library of Congress.
27. Eisenhower memorandum of November 8, 1942, in Harry C. Butcher, *My Three Years with Eisenhower: The Personal Diary of Captain Harry C. Butcher* (New York: Simon and Schuster, 1946), p. 178b. Hugh Wilson to Cordell Hull, October 11, 1938, in Hugh R. Wilson, Jr., *A Career Diplomat, The Third Chapter: The Third Reich* (New York: Vantage Press, 1961), p. 56.
28. John R. Deane to George C. Marshall, December 2, 1944, George C. Marshall papers, Box 63, Folder 31, George C. Marshall Research Library, Lexington, Virginia. Those who were anti-Russian spoke of Russians as "Orientals," obviously again not a definition based on skin color. For discussion of such images of the "Asiatic" Russians at the turn of the century, see Anderson, *Race and Rapprochement*, p. 69.
29. Anderson, *Race and Rapprochement*, p. 19.
30. Reginald Horsman, *Race and Manifest Destiny: The Origins of American Racial Anglo-Saxonism* (Cambridge, Mass: Harvard University Press, 1981), p. 26.

THE CHANGING CONCEPT OF WHITES IN THE NORTH

It is extremely difficult to understand the process by which European-Americans in the North came to develop a purely "white" racial consciousness. The redefinition of race in the United States was so sensitive that even specialists could not publicly discuss it while it was under way. Only after a white identity was universally internalized among European-Americans — too internalized, many scholars are beginning to recognize — was it possible to write books about the creation of the white race. It is not an accident that all the books cited in this book on this subject were published in the last dozen years: *The Invention of the White Race* (1994), *Towards the Abolition of Whiteness* (1994), *How the Irish Became White* (1995), *White* (1997), *Whiteness of a Different Color* (1998), *Making Whiteness* (1998), *The Color of Race in America, 1900–1940* (2001), *Not Just Black and White* (2004), *Buying Whiteness* (2004).

Of course, identity never is precise in nature. The author of a book entitled *How the Irish Became White* reported that his own maternal grandfather, born in 1896, "was either 'Austrian,' 'Polish,' or 'Jewish,' depending on the context."[31] All European-Americans were always "white," but that was only one of their racial identities. They were members not only of some 40 races, but also of intermediate groupings that later were called "panethnic identities"[32] — for example, "Slavic" or "Romance."

Even then the word "white" could be somewhat fuzzy in general usage. In 1862, an educated English-American, who surely would have called the Irish white, if pressed, casually distinguished in his diary between the Irish and "the laboring class of whites."[33] In the 1920s, a careful student of language, H. L. Mencken, wrote in a matter-of-fact manner of "black and other non-Nordic writers."[34] That grouping actually expressed the logic of the 1924 Immigration Act. A new phrase, "the Caucasian race," was invented to classify people, in Matthew Guterl's phrase, who were "absolutely white." Only in the late 1930s, he reports, were Jews and Italians given that status.[35]

Language also was fluid. Noel Ignatiev's book is entitled *How the Irish Became White*, but its thesis suggests a different title, *How the Irish Changed Themselves Into Whites*. Precisely because their original status in America reflected their negative image, they strove to see themselves as whites and to have others see them as "white." Modern scholars tend to emphasize that the Irish were psychologically driven to feel

---

31. Noel Ignatiev, *How the Irish Became White* (New York: Routledge, 1995), p. 196, fn 16.
32. See, for example, John Itzigson, "The Formation of Latino and Latina Panethnic Identity," and Yen Le Espiritu, "Asian-American Panethnicity: Contemporary National and Transnational Possibilities," in Foner and Fredrickson, *Not Just Black and White*, pp. 197–216 and 217–234.
33. Ignatiev, *How the Irish Became White*, pp. 35 and 166. The diary is Nicholas B. Wainwright, ed.., Sidney G. Fisher, *A Philadelphia Perspective: The Diary of Sidney G. Fischer Covering the Years 1834–1871* (Philadelphia: Historical Society of Pennsylvania, 1967), p. 439.
34. Quoted in Jacobson, *Whiteness of a Different Color*, p. 5.
35. Guterl, *The Color of Race in America, 1900–1940*, p. 188.

superior to the blacks, but surely it was more important to them at the time to be considered more equal by the older immigrant groups.

Sometimes the Irish were successful. In some contexts they even were seen as Anglo-Saxons — for example, in California when the issue was the relationship of European-Americans with Asians and Asia. Matthew Jacobson reports the cynical but undoubtedly accurate comment of an Irish activist, "The moment a Teuton or Celtic achieves fame ... he is hailed as a new product of 'Anglo-Saxon' civilization.... But if he winds up in the police court, he is regarded simply as a drunken German or Irishman."[36]

Indeed, general images evolved over time. Mark Twain, writing in anti-Irish Hartford, Connecticut, in 1875, treated Huck Finn more positively than he did Huck's drunken father. Huck even had a close Anglo-Saxon friend, Tom Sawyer. Nevertheless, Huck was also on friendly terms with a black, and he headed off for the territory at the end of the book because he feared Aunt Emily would "civilise" him. Twain, no doubt, thought of the New England Irish as being similarly disinclined to be civilized.

Alas, Huckleberry Finn probably succumbed to "civilisation" after all. Despite Twain's fears, Huck was so likeable that some "lace Irish" woman almost certainly managed to entice him into marriage. Even if his wife was not fully respectable, they surely had "lace Irish" children. By the late 1930s, one of the most popular books and movies in American history, *Gone with the Wind*, even had an Irish O'Hara owning a Southern plantation in Finn's time.[37]

The process of full assimilation was never rapid. Speaker of the House Tip O'Neill, who was born in 1912 in the Boston area, reports in his autobiography that "I knew I was Irish even before I knew I was American." O'Neill had a tremendous drive to see that "his people" were accepted by the people he saw and detested at Harvard, but it is hard to believe that he ever had much of a reason to think of himself as "white" as a young person.[38] The non-Irish in turn almost always thought of Tip as a "mick" rather than as a white.

Scholars have begun to explore when the variety of multiple European-American races in the North disappeared and a single "white race" with a number of "ethnic groups" was formed. They have not reached a consensus. Most date the first major scholarly use of "ethnicity" in the American context to 1941, and the changes in the 1940 census headings point in that direction. One scholar reports, however, that some Jewish-American intellectuals first used the word "ethnic" at the time of World War I.[39]

---

36. See Matthew F. Jacobson, *Special Sorrows: The Diasporic Imagination of Irish, Polish, and Jewish Immigrants in the United States* (Cambridge, MA: Harvard University Press, 1995), p. 190.
37. Guterl, *The Color of Race in America*, pp. 185–188.
38. Tip O'Neill, *Man of the House: The Life and Political Memoirs of Speaker Tip O'Neill* (New York: Random House, 1987), pp. 6–7 and 378.
39. Victoria Hattan, "Ethnicity: An American Genealogy," in Foner and Frederickson, *Not Just Black and White*, p.42.

The Jewish-Americans, however, had a special problem because their "race" was usually defined in religious terms, but they had come to America from a variety of countries and spoke a variety of languages. Thus, some concept such as "ethnic group" made special sense for Jewish-Americans, but it is likely that the Gentile emphasis on a Jewish race wiped out any sense on their part of the diverse origins of Jewish immigrants in Europe.

Without any question, a key event in the development of a single white race was Hitler's tortured concept of a pure "Aryan race" and then the implications he drew for the "Jewish race." Developments in Germany led many Western scholars to demonstrate that "races" in Europe actually had hopelessly intermixed genetic origins and cultural heritages.[40] Intermarriage in the United States made the idea of pure races even more impossible in the New World.

Educated Americans who became young adults in the 1930s may already have learned that Hitler's use of "race" for Europeans had made it too explosive to apply to European-Americans in public. Nevertheless, the statements cited above show that officials born in the late 19th century retained their old definition of "race" and used it regularly in talking with others. The casual statement by the Kansas firm in the 1930s that it did not hire colored or discriminate on the basis of race shows the usage certainly was not limited to older members of the elite. It was to be the 1940s before the old phrase "race, creed, or color" was definitively replaced by the more ambiguous "race, creed, color, or nationality (and/or national origins)."

The replacement of the emotional word "race" by the less emotional "ethnic group" in describing European-Americans was a highly desirable step forward. The new emphasis on white identity was another matter, for the Southern definition of race was as absurd as Hitler's. A former dictator of Haiti allegedly once said that Haiti was 90 percent white in its population. When challenged on such a ridiculous statement, he answered simply that Americans called a person of mixed European and African background "black" and that he called them "white."

It would have been natural to denounce segregation in the South on the same grounds used against Hitler's "Aryan race." "Blacks" were too mixed in their genetic, let alone cultural, heritage for the Southern legal definition to make any sense at all. Indeed, those who dealt with the sale of slaves could readily identify them by their tribal and language origin in Africa. Their diversity of language was considered a factor that reduced the danger of a slave revolt. Different accents continued into the 20th century.

If *Plessy v. Ferguson* were to be explicitly overturned as occurred in *Brown v. Board of Education* in 1954, the Court could easily have referred to the literature on the confused concept of race and said that Plessy was right after all in his argument that government should not be defining "race." Indeed, some of the new literature on "whiteness" is beginning to call for the outright abolition of the concept of race based

40. Among those who wrote for a mass audience and received widespread attention were Jacques Barzun, *Race: A Study in Modern Superstition* (New York: Harcourt, Brace, and Co., 1937); Ruth Benedict, *Race, Science, and Politics* (New York: Modern Age Books, 1940); and Ashley Montagu, *Man's Most Dangerous Myth: The Fallacy of Race* (New York: Columbia University, 1942).

on color. Vron Ware and Les Back, for example, write of "the fervor with which we proclaim our commitment to abolishing whiteness."[41] Their argument is quite convincing for the concept of "blacks" as well.

If the term "race" were to be retained in the 1940s and 1950s, then a return to the cultural definition of the past would have seemed preferable. Theodore Roosevelt's "English-speaking race" or perhaps "American race" made the most sense. As shall be seen, no one had yet advocated affirmative action, and the American Civil Liberties Union was demanding that any reference to race be removed from application forms or even from the census. It was several decades before anyone expected large numbers of Asian immigrants.

Nevertheless, the use of "white" had many tactical advantages. First, it had taken nearly a century to consolidate the new common identity of American, and the attempts to create Anglo-Saxon and Teutonic identities had failed. Those in the 1950s who had been told for 40 years that they were "Yugoslavians" still thought of themselves as Serbs, Croatians, and so forth. "White race," by contrast, was a census category that Northerners already embraced as a secondary identity and that those in the South accepted as their primary identity.

Second, Southerners might feel more comfortable about Northerners and more willing to see them as part of the same "white" community if that was a commonly accepted identity. Northern acknowledgement of persistent "white racism" in the North as well as the South would make it easier for the South to accept change in its treatment of blacks.

Third, and perhaps most important of all, acceptance of the Southern definition of "white" and then the reformers' emphasis upon "white" racism were important steps in erasing European-American racial identities. The new "whites" included not only Woodrow Wilson's "men of the sturdy stocks of the north," but also the "men of the lowest class from the south of Italy and men of the meaner sort out of Hungary and Poland." It was utterly unjust to blame the Ellis Island immigrants for slavery, but they received compensation: they now were considered equal members of the "white" (or "white male") ruling class along with the Boston Brahmins and the Southern plantation owners.

---

41. Vron Ware and Les Back, *Out of Whiteness: Color, Politics, and Culture* (Chicago: University of Chicago Press, 2002), p. 12.

CHAPTER 5. THE MAKING OF "THE WHITES" AND PARTY CHANGE: THE TRANSFORMATION OF RACE

So many people had an interest in moving away from the old concept of European-American races that the process of creating "whites" was partly spontaneous. Sometimes, however, people acted more deliberately, either directly or by indirection. "Multiculturalism" supposedly was developed to emphasize diversity, but its obvious effect was to destroy diversity among immigrants such as "Asian-Americans" and to imply a single European culture and history. The emphasis on "white" racism implied that all European-Americans were alike and were "whites." The records and written forms needed to achieve affirmative action had a "white" category that all the non-favored European-American groups such as Italians and Poles were forced to mark.

These are the sort of actions that Matthew Jacobson had in mind when he wrote about "the fabrication of race" and the neglected "strand of twentieth century American political life" of how "'racial politics' ceased to concern the white races of Europe and came to refer exclusively to black–white relations."[1]

It is not clear how many of those who developed these various concepts and requirements were conscious that they were ending conflicts among European-Americans — indeed, had this as one of their conscious motives — but the changes could and would have been reversed if their melting pot consequences had not been wanted.

The government itself was an active participant in the process of creating "whites." The first definitive change in the meaning of "race" came in the official labels of the 1930 and 1940 census. In 1910, statistics on Negroes and whites were placed under the heading "color," and Negroes were officially divided between "black" and "mulatto." In 1920 and 1930 the heading was "color" or "race," but statistics on "mulatto" were only collected in 1920, not in 1930. In 1930, the Census

---

1. Matthew F. Jacobson, *Whiteness of a Different Color: European Immigrants and the Alchemy of Race* (Cambridge, MA: Harvard University Press, 1998), pp. 247, 1, 4 and 9.

Bureau accepted the most extreme Southern definition of "black": the so-called "one-drop rule." In 1940, "race" became the only heading in the published returns. Negroes were called "colored" in the 1940 census, to emphasize the point.

Then in the 1960s it was the government that insisted Europeans list themselves as "white" on a great variety of official documents whose purpose was to provide assistance to those in other categories. Indeed, when the government began to expand the attack on discrimination against blacks, the NAACP strongly opposed the inclusion of race on application and reporting forms. Many from the Ellis Island immigrant groups reminded policy-makers of the long history of discrimination against them. The inclusion of "race" in early state non-discrimination laws on "race, creed, and color" had explicitly been intended to protect Ellis Island immigrants, and they were nervous about being included in the "white" group that now was being defined as the discriminators. Government officials certainly became aware of the complaints, if they had not thought through the implications beforehand. Changes that created whites were never reversed, but only strengthened. [2]

Similarly while the repeal of the national origin quotas in 1965 eventually opened up massive immigration from Asia, it was presented almost entirely as a measure to treat all European-Americans — all whites — as alike. President Truman could not have been more explicit about the national origins quotas when he vetoed the McCarran-Walter Immigration Act of 1952. He flatly declared that any idea that "Americans with English or Irish names were better people and better citizens than Americans with Italian or Greek or Polish names ... is utterly unworthy." Senator John Kennedy cited these words of Truman directly in promoting his immigration bill in 1957, and they had special meaning coming from a man with an Irish name who was running for President. Lyndon Johnson repeated them again when opening his drive to enact the Immigration Law of 1965.

The Immigration Law of 1965, the Voting Rights Act of 1965, and the movement toward affirmative action in 1966 occurred in an extremely short time. The black revolution had begun seriously in the spring and summer of 1963 and clearly was a catalyst. All the responses dealing with the revolution had the effect of lessening the traditional political conflict among European-Americans and of defining ethnic politics as "Black–White" in nature. It is not a coincidence that the period from 1968 to 1980 was precisely the period of striking party realignment.

FOREIGN POLICY AND THE INTEGRATION OF EUROPEAN-AMERICANS

Sometimes government officials and activists were quite aware of what they were doing. Without doubt, the key figures in the foreign policy establishment were consciously determined to end the "civil war" in Europe and also the tensions among

---

2. See Hugh Davis Graham, *Collision Course: The Strange Convergence of Affirmative Action and Immigration Policy in America* (New York: Oxford University Press, 2002), and John David Skrentny, *The Ironies of Affirmative Action: Politics, Culture, and Justice in America* (Chicago: University of Chicago Press, 1996).

European-Americans that continued even after World War II. They could not discuss their policy publicly, but Dean Acheson could have called his autobiography "Stopping Soviet Aggression" instead of "Present at the Creation."[3] There was a reason for his choice.

Indeed, since divisions among the European-Americans had such an adverse impact on foreign policy from the 1910s through the 1940s, those in the foreign policy establishment were the first to try to end the conflicts in Europe and among European-Americans. This effort actually began in the 1920s and 1930s. State Department personnel were almost all British-Americans, and during World War I the Department openly discriminated against German-Americans, anyone with German names, and anyone suspected of anti-British feelings.[4] After the United States refused to join the League of Nations, British-Americans generally were opposed to American involvement in collective security actions in the 1920s and 1930s.

In part, of course, the American political and foreign policy establishment was simply following the British policy line at the time, but, more fundamentally, it had expected World War I "to weld the twenty-five or thirty races [into a] splendid race of new Americans." Instead the war severely divided them, and the establishment wanted to heal these wounds. They favored active participation in international relations, but not measures that would cause ethnic conflict in America.[5]

Franklin Roosevelt, as Wilson's assistant secretary of navy for eight years, shared this concern. Roosevelt was an Anglophile, but it is not clear whether he shared the British government's assumptions about appeasement in the mid 1930s or was closer to the views of Winston Churchill and Anthony Eden. Yet, so long as Britain and France were not ready to engage in serious collective action against Germany, Roosevelt's best foreign policy strategy under the assumptions either of the British government or Churchill was to try to reassure the German-Americans and to let them convince themselves that Hitler was different from the Kaiser.

Whatever Roosevelt's secret predictions of the future, all his actions indicate that he adopted a strategy Wilson ascribed to himself in 1917. When Wilson called for a declaration of war in April 1917, he told his chief political adviser, Joseph Tumulty, that "from the very beginning I saw the end of this horrible thing, but I could not move faster than the great mass of our people would permit." He had, he said, worked "to make every part of America and the varied elements of our population understand that we were willing to go to any length rather than resort to

---

3. Dean Acheson, *Present at the Creation: My Years in the State Department* (New York: Norton, 1969).
4. The assistant secretary of state for personnel was Breckinridge Long, a man renowned for his anti-Semitic and anti-Slavic views whom Roosevelt had placed in charge of refugee policy in 1939. When appointed assistant secretary of state for personnel (and Asia and Russia) in January 1917, one of his first actions was to conduct a purge of those thought to be pro-German. See 1917 diary, Breckenridge Long Papers, Box 1, Entries of March 1, 1917, March 3, 1917, and March 16, 1917. Library of Congress.
5. See, for example, Melvyn P. Leffler, *The Elusive Quest: America's Pursuit of European Stability and French Security, 1919-1933* (Chapel Hill: University of North Carolina Press, 1979).

war.... Now we are certain that there will be no regrets or looking back on the part of our people."[6]

Unfortunately, Wilson seriously underestimated the amount of antagonism to his foreign policy, and hence he concluded that any opposition must have sinister roots. Roosevelt's behavior made it clear that he was intent on showing that he did not think any opponents were disloyal. Roosevelt also realized that this was a wise electoral policy for himself, especially since he was so closely associated with Wilson.

Roosevelt's attempts to reassure the German-Americans and Italian-Americans took many forms. The President was almost compulsive in his efforts in the 1930s to demonstrate that he was committed to non-intervention. He extended his earlier policy of not criticizing the Japanese to Hitler and Mussolini. Until November 1938, he would not even permit his wife to criticize Hitler's treatment of Jews.[7] Lest he be seen as praising the Axis by omission, Roosevelt also did not criticize other dictators such as Stalin. When he began criticizing the Axis in the late 1930s, he did so with the vague term "the dictators" that applied to Hitler's potential targets in the East as well as to Hitler himself.

Roosevelt's diplomatic moves in Europe also were remarkable for the extent of their isolationism. Six months before the invasion of Austria in March 1938, Roosevelt withdrew the American ambassador who favored collective security and left the post open. In 1938 and 1939, he also had no ambassador in the Soviet Union as it pushed for collective security. His ambassadors in Britain, France, Germany, and Italy all favored appeasement, and the first three (and perhaps the fourth) almost surely wanted to encourage Germany to move eastward and conquer the Soviet Union. Then, after the invasion of Poland, Roosevelt convinced many in the British Foreign Office that he wanted Britain to accommodate itself to Hitler.[8]

When Hitler conquered the Low Countries and France in June and July 1940, Roosevelt did switch to what is correctly called an "undeclared war" against Germany.[9] Nevertheless, he still continued to try to reassure the German-Americans, both directly and indirectly. The German-Americans feared a return to the persecution and even prosecution of World War I, but the President never used Wilson-like words even to suggest that non-citizen Europeans were a potential threat. He never hinted that members of the isolationist America-First movement were at all disloyal.

After Pearl Harbor was attacked, the Administration continually emphasized that the war should always be treated as a war of the whole people — or at least all

6. Joseph P. Tumulty, *Woodrow Wilson as I Know Him* (Garden City, NY: Doubleday, Page, and Co., 1921), p. 257.
7. Blanche Wiesen Cook, *Eleanor Roosevelt* (New York: Viking Press, 1998), vol. 2 (1933–1938), pp. 304–334.
8. These statements about Roosevelt are based on a very great amount of archive research in the papers of the officials and diplomats involved. The amount is only partially suggested by the footnotes of this book. This work will be the basis for a book tentatively entitled *FDR's Policy Toward Europe.*
9. William L. Langer and S. Everett Gleason, *The Undeclared War, 1940–1941* (New York: Harper, 1953).

European-American peoples. Directives to movie studios emphasized this theme, and soldiers with a variety of ethnic names were found in every war movie.

More dramatically, Roosevelt appointed men with pronounced German-American names to top command posts. Dwight Eisenhower was commander in Europe, Chester Nimitz commander of the Pacific Fleet, and Carl Spaatz head of the air force that bombed Europe. Roosevelt never mentioned the ethnic factor, but he certainly was aware of Eisenhower's background. When the German-American George Messersmith, a counselor on postwar foreign policy and an extremely experienced ambassador (the last ambassador to Austria), inquired whether he might be named secretary of the state after the war, Roosevelt replied, "Just think. With Eisenhower and Messersmith, people might ask who won the war."[10]

Even before France had surrendered, the President had signed the Alien Registration Act, more familiarly known as the Smith Act. It required the registration of all non-citizens and authorized arrests for subversion even during peacetime. (Such arrests during war were taken for granted.) In all, approximately 300,000 Germans, 600,000 Italians, and 90,000 Japanese had to register. Still, only 7,164 alien Germans and 3,596 Italians were to be arrested from December 1941 to June 1945, and 1,300 of them were non-resident seamen. Only a tiny percentage of domestic aliens from Europe were interned.[11]

The internment of Japanese-American citizens, the darkest stain on the history of American participation in World War II, had the indirect effect of highlighting the different assumptions about German-American loyalty. The President often is treated as a more passive actor in this decision, but the combination and sequence of events makes it absolutely clear that his role was crucial.

The Japanese-Americans, it seldom is emphasized, were not all treated equally. There were 118,000 Japanese in Hawaii, 20,000 of them non-citizens, and 117,000 in the Pacific states on the Mainland. Hawaii could be attacked again, and sabotage might be costly. Neither of these was true on the Mainland. The local authorities in Hawaii resisted internment, and it never was done. The military also opposed internment on the Mainland, and polls showed little public support except in California. The President never challenged the intensification of the pressure when it easily could have been stopped. It is a reasonable guess that he primarily saw the advantages of a scapegoat to deflect any pressure off German-Americans and Italian-Americans.[12]

---

10. George Messersmith, undated memorandum, Messersmith Papers, number 1888, University of Delaware Library.
11. Roger Daniels, *Guarding the Golden Door: American Immigration Policy and Immigration Since 1882* (New York: Hill and Wang, 2004), pp. 87–88.
12. Francis Biddle, *In Brief Authority* (Garden City, NY: Doubleday and Co. 1962), pp. 212–226. Biddle, who was Attorney General, strongly opposed the internment and provides the numbers and describes the pressures without drawing the logical conclusion of his analysis. For a good short history of the internment of the Japanese on the Coast by one of the leading experts on the subject, see Roger Daniels, *Prisoners Without Trial: Japanese-Americans in World War II*, rev. ed. (New York: Hill & Wang, 2004).

Roosevelt is often accused of refusing to think of the consequences of his wartime actions for postwar Europe, but this is unfair. Messersmith was only one of many with whom he discussed the issue. Roosevelt also is accused of making too many concessions to Stalin, but, except perhaps in the Pacific, this too is unfair. Instead, the President deserves criticism for refusing to try to make concrete agreements with Stalin of any nature. As George Kennan wrote his friend Charles Bohlen in despair in January 1945, "we have consistently refused to make clear what our interests and our wishes were in eastern and central Europe."[13]

The problem was that no intelligent policy could be followed toward the Soviet Union until the United States was willing to make a decision on Germany. Yet everyone understood that any policy toward Germany was certain to produce a political explosion. Over 40% of Germans had voted for Hitler in 1932, and a higher percentage had approved of him in later years. This made it impossible to absolve the German people from responsibility for the regime, but any talk about authoritarian German families, religion, or political culture — and there was a great deal of it during the war — inevitably applied to German-Americans as well.

Moreover, all European-Americans were deeply concerned about the nature of the settlement. The German-Americans and Italian-Americans did not want a draconian peace, let alone the necessary justification for it indicated in the previous paragraph. The Irish-Americans had been allied with the German-Americans during and after World War I and remained highly suspicious of the English. Virtually all other European-Americans came from countries that had suffered grievously from German attacks, and the Jewish-Americans had special reason for suspicion and anger.

Roosevelt's successor, Harry Truman, is praised for his steadfast opposition to the Soviet Union or damned for his provocative policy toward it, but he followed neither policy in his first 20 months in office. Like Roosevelt, Truman was too afraid of the domestic consequences of any policy to do anything. As a former Senator from a state with a mixed British-American and German-American population, Truman had a good sense of the moods of both, and he undoubtedly felt that the passage of time was necessary for emotions to cool and for pressure for action to build.

Unfortunately, a policy of inaction from 1945 to 1947 was a policy, and it meant no reconstruction in Germany and a terrible life for the German people. When Richard Nixon visited Europe in 1947 as a member of the prestigious Herter Commission, he ended his notes on Germany by quoting a private comment made by a fellow member of the Commission, Francis Case of South Dakota, on the trip back to America: "When civilized people capture cannibals, they do not eat them."[14]

By this time, Truman had already changed policy toward Germany with the Marshall Plan. The Herter Commission itself was a result of that policy change. Yet the President was driven to action only when the Republican Party won a smashing

13. Charles E. Bohlen, *Witness to History, 1929–1969* (New York: W. W. Norton, 1973), pp. 175–176. The full exchange of letters is in Kennan's papers at Princeton University and Bohlen's at the Library of Congress.
14. Richard Nixon. Typed Reports of Observations by Country, undated, but fall of 1947. The Herter Committee, Box 1, Folder 17, Nixon Library and Birthplace.

victory in the 1946 Congressional elections. One reason was that many Republicans had begun to use accusations of Communist influence in government as a codeword for an attack on his non-policy on Germany. Not by coincidence, the early "McCarthyism" of 1946 and 1947, in which Joseph McCarthy himself did not participate, was directed primarily at Jewish-Americans who were thought to support the extremely harsh Morgenthau program for Germany. (Morgenthau, Roosevelt's Secretary of the Treasury, was the only Jewish member of the Cabinet.)[15]

Sophisticated postwar politicians understood that the major conflicts in Europe had to end if the conflicts among the European-Americans were to end and American ethnic peace were to be ensured. Non-involvement in Europe had failed, and now the United States intervened vigorously. It was utterly consistent in pushing for a more united Europe: an Iron and Steel Community, united Western zones in Germany, a North Atlantic [Military] Treaty Organization, a European Defense Community, a Common Market, a European Community, and so forth.

The policy began most dramatically with a Marshall Plan whose main unspoken purpose was a change in policy about reconstruction of Germany. All European powers had to participate in drafting the distribution of aid if any of them was to receive funding. Not by the slightest coincidence, no European-American group could complain about the distribution its homeland received since its homeland had agreed to the distribution. Even the East Europeans were invited to participate. The only major group that did not have a homeland in Europe, the Jewish-Americans, was given one in Palestine.

It seemed as if Truman had brilliantly handled the impossible task of reconciling the European-Americans to a stable settlement in Europe. A military alliance in Europe that included Western Germany was another matter. It formalized the division of Europe, and the British Lord Ismay is reported to have said that "the purpose of NATO is to keep Russia out [of Europe], America in, and Germany down."

The German-Americans were as negative about NATO as they were positive about the Marshall Plan. The new Secretary of State, Dean Acheson, who was chosen to preside over the creation of the North Atlantic Treaty Organization, was ostentatious both in his English style of dress and behavior and in his Anglophile policy. Acheson strenuously opposed a unified neutral Germany, and the German-Americans and their representatives believed that he shared Ismay's views.

When the NATO Treaty was presented to the Senate for ratification, nearly 26% of Republican Senators voted against the ratification of NATO in protest, and another 16% joined them in voting for a reservation that would have declared the US had no obligation to give military aid to other NATO members in case of attack. Almost all the Senators from the East and South supported the treaty, as did those in

15. The documentation of this argument will be presented in a book by the author tentatively entitled *The Politics of the Origins of the Cold War*. The first standard treatment of Morgenthau's policy is John Morton Blum, *From the Morgenthau Diaries* (Boston: Houghton-Mifflin, 1967), vol. 3 ("Years of the War, 1941-1945"), pp. 327-420. For a recent study, see John Dietrich, *The Morgenthau Plan: Soviet Influence on American Postwar Policy* (New York: Algora, 2002).

the northern Midwestern states of Michigan, Minnesota, and Wisconsin. (Presumably the support of the large number of the descendants of New Englanders and Scandinavians outweighed the German-Americans.) In the band of 11 states from Pennsylvania to Nevada, however, a full 57% of the Senators, Democratic as well as Republican, voted against the treaty and/or for the reservation.[16] Half the Senators in Idaho, North Dakota, Oregon, South Dakota, and Washington joined the latter group.

Joseph McCarthy was an Irishman who was Senator in the most German-American state and who personally was highly anti-English. He had seldom used the anti-Communist issue from 1946 to the early fall of 1949 when the main target was Jewish-Americans, but tested the theme in local speeches in Wisconsin in the late fall of 1949. He then dramatically raised the charge of Communists in the State Department in February 1950. On January 21, Alger Hiss, a high-ranking member of the English-American establishment, was convicted of perjury in connection with his denial of espionage in the 1930s, and on January 25 Secretary of State Dean Acheson stated publicly that he would not "turn his back on Alger Hiss." British-American diplomats dominated the State Department. McCarthy used Acheson and Hiss as symbols of his attack on the State Department and what he saw as its pro-English bias.

In the long run, NATO was an important step in ending the divisions within Western Europe that had been the real cause of war. Not only were German, English, and Italian troops all placed under an American general, but the countries of Western Europe were said to be a "North Atlantic Community" with the United States. Not even an unreasonable alarmist could think that Britain and Germany would once more go to war. Not by coincidence, this also meant the British-Americans and German-Americans were part of the same community and had no basis for future conflict.

The ethnic base of McCarthyism seemed to suggest that the conflicts from World War I would continue into the indefinite future, but the opposite was the case. The broad educated class became convinced these ethnic conflicts must be ended. Eisenhower's election as President in 1952 was an obvious symbol of reassurance to the German-Americans, but as the leader of forces that had defended England from German attack, he was more than acceptable to the British-Americans. Not surprisingly, each party wanted him as its candidate. John Kennedy explicitly presented himself as an Irish-American Catholic candidate, and his election reassured the Irish. Kennedy's father had been a major isolationist in the 1930s and 1940s, but John, as will be seen, was a fervent interventionist in international relations of the 1950s and 1960s, a major reversal of the traditional Irish-American position.

When Eisenhower won the Republican nomination, he selected a running mate with the middle name of Milhous (the maiden name of Nixon's mother). He then named a Secretary of State, John Foster Dulles, who had headed the major law firm handling trade with Germany in the 1930s; the message to the German-Americans

---

16. The roll calls on the treaty and the reservations are found in *The New York Times*, July 22, 1949, p. 2.

was absolutely clear. Even before the election, observers said Eisenhower would certainly destroy McCarthy and McCarthyism, and so he did.

THE GROWING ACCEPTANCE OF THE ELLIS ISLAND IMMIGRANTS

The efforts in foreign policy circles to end the conflicts among the European-Americans naturally centered on the Western European countries that had been central figures in the international politics of the 1930s and in World War II. The eastern European countries had been treated as pawns in the 1930s, and they were given secondary priority during World War II and the immediate postwar period. By late 1947, there was relatively little that the United States could do to affect their fate until after Stalin's death.

Although the great ethnic conflicts in American political history had always occurred among the European-Americans who were from "the sturdy stock from the north of Europe," the United States also would also have to end discrimination against those from southern and eastern Europe if European-Americans were to become "whites."

The scorn for the Ellis Island immigrants at the turn of the century was not very different from that toward the Protestant Irish (the Scotch-Irish) a century and a half earlier or toward the Irish Catholics from the 1840s onward. For the first time, however, prejudice was combined with legal action. In 1921 and 1924, the Congress almost unanimously sharply limited immigration and created quotas for countries of origin that severely discriminated against the countries of eastern and southern Europe. In the ten years prior to World War, 1,012,000 people a year had immigrated to the United States, including 906,000 a year from Europe as a whole. Of that number, 722,000 came annually from southern and eastern Europe. The 1924 law limited immigration from Europe to 154,000 a year and that from all of southern and eastern Europe to 28,235.[17]

The 20th century discrimination against Catholics and Jews continued well into the postwar period. Even Joseph Kennedy, an extremely wealthy Irish Catholic who had married the daughter of the mayor of Boston, could not overcome the informal barriers that kept the Irish from elite country clubs in the 1930s. He was so angry at such social snubs that he was determined to make one of his sons President — first, his oldest son Joseph and then his second son John, after Joseph was killed in war.

The problem for Ellis Island immigrants was greater because they had arrived more recently. The elite universities established quotas to limit the number of Jewish students. Even officials of the Roosevelt Administration were open in their anti-Semitic remarks. William Bullitt, ambassador to the Soviet Union from 1933 to 1936, was typical. In a letter he knew Roosevelt would see, Bullitt wrote that diplomats in Moscow needed an excellent knowledge of the Russian language to deal with "the

---

17. For a very clear and short description of the decisions and of the quotas in 1921, 1924, and 1939, see William S. Bernard, ed., *American Immigration Policy — A Reappraisal* (New York: Harpers and Brothers, 1950), pp. 22–31.

slippery Jews who dominate [the Foreign Ministry] (now commonly known as the Ghetto)."[18] Bullitt became the President's representative to draft the foreign policy section of the 1936 Democratic platform. He was named Ambassador to France and became Roosevelt's most intimate adviser on Europe for the next five years. When officials in the Administration talked privately or wrote in their own diaries, they could be even less restrained.[19]

The prejudice against the Catholics of the Ellis Island immigration was as great as that against the Jews — or perhaps even greater after Hitler's policy made open anti-Semitism more dangerous in the United States. Polish-Americans, for example, were the butt of the so-called Polish jokes that in every imaginable way suggested their extraordinarily low level of intelligence. There even were new jokes about the Polish Pope who was elected in 1978.

Italian-Americans faced not only the usual prejudices against Catholics but also stereotypes about the Mafia. When Nathan Glazer and Daniel Patrick Moynihan analyzed the reasons that Italian-Americans were not as important in New York City politics in the 1960s as might be expected, they pointed directly to the perceptions of the Mafia, to "the curse of the Mafia."[20] An Italian-American who was upwardly mobile in politics or in business was assumed to have risen on the basis of Mafia connections. In 1950, the future governor of New York, Mario Cuomo, graduated first in his class in City College law school, but not a single Wall Street law firm would give him a job interview.

Of course, rising education levels and upward mobility among members of the new immigrant groups had produced some acceptance by 1950. Developments in the foreign policy also had a positive impact. The World War II propaganda that treated all European-Americans as members of a single community probably was primarily motivated by a desire to reassure the German-Americans. Yet Americans from southern and eastern Europe benefited most in relative status terms when treated like other Europeans.

Then in 1945 the Yalta Declaration, whatever its flaws, declared eastern Europe to be fully ready for democracy. Few in the American educated public would have had such a thought in the 1930s. Those following a policy of appeasement gave no thought to the consequences for the east European peoples, including the Jews. Indeed, many had thought that east Europeans were so backward that German rule would have a civilizing effect. This was no longer possible after the war. The imposition of Communism was treated as the suppression of normal European countries.

---

18. Letter from Bullitt to Judge [Assistant Secretary of State R. Walton] Moore, April 25, 1935. R. Walton Moore Papers, Box 3, Bullitt Folder, FDR Library, Hyde Park, NY. See a similar letter to Moore on June 24, 1934, that is found in the same papers and box.
19. For a famous example involving two high-ranking officials, one of them very close to Roosevelt and the other a most trusted ambassador, see the diary entry of November 28, 1941 in Fred L. Israel, ed., *The War Diary of Breckinridge Long: Selections from the Years, 1939–1944* (Lincoln: University of Nebraska Press, 1966), pp. 225–226.
20. "Introduction to the Second Edition: New York City in 1970," Nathan Glazer and Daniel Patrick Moynihan, *Beyond the Melting Pot: The Negroes, Puerto Ricans, Jews, Italians, and Irish of New York City*, 2nd ed. (Cambridge, MA: MIT Press, 1970), pp. lxvi–lxviii.

The new attitude was expressed in the phrase "Eastern Europe." The atlas might say that Europe ended at the Ural Mountains deep inside Russia, but after the war the boundaries of the East European countries with the Soviet Union became the dividing line between civilized Europe and the semi-barbarian Soviet Union. Already by mid-1945, Averell Harriman, ambassador to the Soviet Union, told Secretary of Navy James Forrestal privately that "the greatest crime of Hitler was that his action had resulted in opening the gates of Eastern Europe to Asia."[21] This also, of course, implied there was little difference between Americans from eastern and western Europe. The focus of the Truman Doctrine in February 1947 on Greece and Turkey led to great emphasis on the Greeks as the founders of Western democracy. The North Atlantic Treaty Organization (NATO) even managed to include Mediterranean Greece and Italy in the "North Atlantic" group of countries — the old Nordic community.

The Greece–Turkey Aid Bill of 1947, the Marshall Plan, and NATO made discrimination against the large southern European groups, Italians and Greeks, highly counterproductive from a foreign policy point of view. Both Greece and Italy had large Communist parties, and it made little sense to spend large amounts of money to defend them from Communism and then offend Italy and Greece by treating their emigrants as being less worthy in comparison with northern Europeans, even Germans with their large quotas.

Truman directly raised the foreign policy issue when he condemned the continuation of the old quotas in the McCarran Act of 1952:[22]

> Today, we are "protecting" ourselves, as we were in 1924, against being flooded by immigrants from Eastern Europe. This is fantastic. The countries of Eastern Europe have fallen under the communist yoke — they are silenced, fenced off by barbed wire and minefields — no one passes their borders but at the risk of his life. We do not need to be protected against immigrants from these countries — on the contrary, we want to stretch out a helping hand, to save those who have managed to flee into Western Europe, to succor those who are brave enough to escape from barbarians, to welcome and restore them against the day when their countries will, as we hope, be free again.

Of course, equal treatment is never simply bestowed as a kindness upon a group subject to discrimination. The group has to become more mobilized and fight for its own rights. This happened after World War II, but the struggle of the eastern and southern Europeans for equal rights is not properly appreciated today. Thus, a 1945 New York law that prohibited discrimination in employment on the basis of "race, creed, color, or nationality" — and other similar legislation that followed — now

---

21. Diary entry of July 29, 1945, Box 2, vol. 2, James Forrestal Papers, Princeton University. An edited form of the Forrestal diary was published in 1951 but it excludes a great amount of sensitive material, including this conversation. Serious scholars cannot rely on these early published sources but need to go to the original material. James Forrestal, *The Forrestal Diaries*, edited by Walter Millis (New York: Viking Press, 1951).
22. *Public Papers of the Presidents of the United States. Harry S. Truman, 1952-1953* (Washington: US Government Printing Office, 1966), p. 443.

tend to be seen only as early steps in the struggle to improve the lot of blacks. In reality, the words "creed" and "nationality" were not simple ornaments but the core of the laws.

One of the most perceptive political observers of the mid-20th century, Samuel Lubell, had a particularly clear understanding in 1952 of the role of the European-Americans in the struggle for civil rights and their self-interest in it:[23]

> Civil rights are popularly thought of as a Negro problem. But what makes the civil rights issue so explosive is not simply that Harlem is on the march. The significant fact is that Harlem's awakening coincides with the "coming of age" of all the other urban underdogs.

Lubell declared that the anti-discrimination laws "are on the statute books because those who suffered discrimination in the past — the children of the 'micks,' 'wops,' 'kikes,' 'niggers,' 'polocks' and other abused groups — are in the mood, and at last have the political strength, to do something about it." The blacks were perhaps the weakest of this group of peoples.

The most outrageous discrimination against the eastern and southern Europeans was the Immigration Law of 1924. As discussed above, 722,000 people a year had come from eastern and southern Europe in the decade before World War I. Table 1 shows the decline to 225,000 a year from 1920 to 1924 and 36,000 a year from 1925 to 1929.

Table 1: Annual Number of Immigrants, 1905–1970

Years	Total Annual Immigration	Immigration from Europe	Immigration from Southern and Eastern Europe
1905–1914	1,012,000	906,000	722,000
1920–1924	555,000	358,000	225,000
1925–1929	307,000	158,000	36,000
1946–1949	154,000	92,000	28,000
1950–1954	220,000	143,000	80,000
1955–1959	280,000	138,000	65,000
1960–1965	286,000	109,000	50,000
1966–1970	374,000	120,000	71,000

Source: *Calculated from Historical Statistics of the United States Colonial Times to 1970 (Washington: US Government Printing Office, 1975), p. 105.*

After Hitler came to power in Germany, immigration did not pose a major problem for those German Jews who could find a sponsor. The number of Jews in Germany was relatively small, and they could enter on the large quota for Germany. When Hitler conquered Austria, Czechoslovakia, and Poland in 1938 and 1939, however, the number of Jews was vastly larger and the quotas were minuscule. Roosevelt and Congress resisted pressure to admit many outside the quotas.

After World War II, a great economic boom occurred in the United States and a huge number of Europeans were displaced from their homes or fled from them.[24]

---

23. Samuel Lubell, *The Future of American Politics* (New York: Harper, 1952), p. 81.

Most of the displaced persons either returned to their homelands or found residence elsewhere in Europe, but approximately one million persons from the Soviet Union and Eastern Europe felt they could not safely return home after the war.[25] All came from countries with low American quotas, and significant numbers remained in refugee camps in Western Europe.

Until 1965, Congress steadfastly refused to change the quota system either by increasing the overall limit, by changing the quotas within Europe, or, the most frequent proposal, by shifting unused quotas (in practice, those of Great Britain and Ireland) to southern and eastern Europe. The basic reason for the reluctance to change the distribution of quotas within Europe was a belief that any change would lead to an increase in total immigration, despite the absolute assurance of advocates of change that this would not occur. The cynicism was certainly justified in 1965.

The major reason for the refusal to increase immigration immediately after the war was that memories of the Depression were fresh and people assumed another would occur after the war. Public opinion polls in 1944 showed that jobs after the war — "JOBS in capital letters," according to a Gallup memorandum — was a bigger concern than winning the war or the nature of the postwar peace. If the war in Europe and the Pacific were continuing, respondents would vote for Roosevelt 51% to 42%; if both wars were over, Dewey would win 50% to 40%; and if only the European war were over, Roosevelt would win 47% to 45%.[26] In May 1945, the Office of War Mobilization and Reconversion estimated that if the Asian War ended within a few months (as it did), the unemployment would reach 10–12 million people, almost as high as during the depression.[27]

The investment community shared this view of the future. The economy and stock earnings boomed after the war. Yet the Dow Jones Industrial average did not respond. It was at 162 on August 8, 1945 (9 points above the year's low) and enjoyed a 32 percent rise to 212.5 in the nine months after the end of the war. Yet it took nearly four years before it broke through to a new high. Instead, in each year from 1946 through 1949, the average returned basically to the 162 level of the end of the war.[28] Only in April 1950 did the average hit a postwar high of 213 and begin its great rise. As Table 1 shows, this fear about the economy kept immigration from Europe in the second half of the 1940s well below the levels even of the late 1920s.

---

24. For a good study that provides not only numbers but also a feel for the situation of the refugees, see Mark Wyman, *DP: Europe's Displaced Persons, 1945–1951* (Philadelphia: Balch Institute Press, 1988). A very thorough year-by-year discussion of Congressional action (and failure to act) over decades is found in Edward P. Hutchinson, *Legislative History of American Immigration Policy, 1798-1965* (Philadelphia: University of Pennsylvania Press, 1981). Pp. 268–366 describes the period after World War II.

25. Robert A. Divine, *American Immigration Policy, 1924–1952* (New Haven: Yale University Press, 1957), p. 111.

26. "66% on Roosevelt," *Time*, vol. XLIV, no. 4 (July 24, 1944), p. 17. The Gallup organization prepared an extremely detailed, 19-page analysis of public opinion and tactics for the Republicans. Opinion Research Corporation, "DEWEY vs. ROOSEVELT: An Analysis of Presidential Election," August 21, 1944. A copy is found in the Everett M. Dirksen Papers, Politics, f. 523, Dirksen Congressional Research Library.

27. "Vinson's Office Hurries to Get Ready for Any Sudden End to Jap War, *The Wall Street Journal*, May 7, 1945, p. 1.

As people became more confident about the postwar economy, some change was permitted in the flows of immigration. Yet a close re-examination of Table 1 shows a number of peculiarities. First, the total number of immigrants remained below the level of the late 1920s, but it rose steadily. Second, the number of immigrants from all of Europe remained below the level of the late 1920s, and soon stagnated. Third, the number of immigrants from eastern and southern Europe rose substantially even though quotas were not changed. They constituted some 50 to 60 percent of the European total.

This surprising combination of facts has several explanations. The increase in total immigration was the result of the lack of limits in the Immigration Law of 1924 on immigration from the Western Hemisphere and the steady increase in that immigration, especially from Mexico. The increase in eastern and southern immigration was the result of a series of ad hoc decisions that did not mention southern and eastern Europe, but that had the effect of benefiting people from that region.

In effect, the American engaged in a quiet policy well expressed in the title of a doctoral dissertation: "The Lingering Death of the National Quota System: Immigration Policy 1952–1965."[29] This policy was enacted in an uncoordinated manner both through executive orders and Congressional action. In 1945, Truman allowed brides and children of servicemen to enter the country outside of the quotas. Many came from Italy and Asia. In 1947, he proposed that 400,000 refugees be admitted to the United States above the quotas over a four-year period.

Although the resulting laws contained micro-compromises to benefit this or that nationality, the final outcome was close to Truman's proposal. A Displaced Persons Law was passed in 1948 to admit 200,000 persons over two years, and another was passed in 1950 to admit another 200,000 persons over the next two years.[30] Congress increasingly passed bills admitting individuals as exceptions, and other *ad hoc* actions were taken — e.g., Eisenhower's "parole" of 31,000 refugees from the 1956 Hungarian Revolt.[31]

In addition, an unknown number of refugees or children of refugees were admitted against the quotas of the countries in which they were residing. The over-subscribing of the German quota in the 1950s did not reflect a sudden desire of Germans to leave what was becoming a very prosperous country. Instead, many of the refugees were concentrated in Germany, and they were having children. The latter were treated, perhaps often and perhaps always, as Germans. The immigration from the United Kingdom declined by half after the 1965 Immigration Act, and it seems likely that the German desire to emigrate was declining as well.

---

28. The Industrial Average was 163 on October 9, 1946, 163 on May 17, 1947, 165 on May 16, 1948, and 162 on June 13, 1949. The figures are found in Phyllis S. Pierce, ed., *The Dow Jones Averages, 1885–1995* (Chicago: Irwin Professional Press, 1996).
29. The dissertation was written by Stephen Thomas Wagner and was accepted by Harvard University in 1986.
30. Hutchinson, *Legislative History of American Immigration Policy*, pp. 273–295.
31. For a listing of the various special acts from 1953 to 1964 and the numbers that resulted (including the 385 admitted outside of quotas on the skilled sheepherders act of 1954), see King, *Making Americans*, p. 232.

Table 2: Size of Annual Quota and Actual Annual Immigration, Selected Countries, 1951–1960

Country	Annual Quota	Annual Immigration	Country	Annual Quota	Annual Immigration
Germany	25,814	34,545	Greece	308	4,844
			Hungary	865	6,455
Ireland	17,756	6,455	Italy	5,666	18,700
			Poland	6,488	12,798
UK	65,361	20,887	Romania	289	1,743
			Spain	250	1,072
			USSR	2,697	4,650

Source: Drawn from Desmond S. King, *Making Americans: Immigration, Race, and the Origins of the Diverse Democracy* (Cambridge: Harvard University Press, 2000), p. 230.

Given postwar conditions, the admission of displaced persons meant the admission of large numbers of immigrants from eastern Europe. As a result, the annual number of immigrants from a series of southern and eastern European countries far exceeded the quotas. (See Table 2.) To maintain the fiction of the quota system, Congress charged the refugees who were admitted above the quotas to the future quotas for the country from which they came and supposedly limited future immigration from it.

Nevertheless, everyone knew that the "mortgages" against future quotas in eastern and southern Europe and the "temporary" stays for those on parole were fictions. The discriminated groups were quietly being treated as equals and the quotas for them were being raised. Nevertheless, there were long waiting lists for Greeks, Italians, and Poles, and there would be major problems if it became easier to emigrate from Communist countries.

THE MOVEMENT TO END THE QUOTA SYSTEM

During the 1950s political pressure began to build for a formal change in the principle of quotas by national origin for European immigration. To be sure, when Congress passed the 1952 McCarran–Walter Act, the first comprehensive immigration law in a quarter of a century, it refused to modify the national quota system. Congress would not even accept the proposal that unused quotas from one country be shifted to another country.[32]

---

32. For a comprehensive survey of evolving arguments made on both sides of the issue over time, see Cheryl Shanks, *Immigration and the Politics of American Sovereignty* (Ann Arbor: University of Michigan Press, 2001).

Truman decided to veto the McCarran–Walter Act. The Act tightened political and security restrictions on applicants, resident aliens, and newly naturalized citizens, and Truman had been engaged in a battle with Congress over loyalty oaths and other internal security questions. This may have been his primary concern with the McCarran–Walter Act, but, as has been seen, he concentrated his fire on the retention of national quotas and the notion that "Americans with English or Irish names were better people and better citizens than Americans with Italian or Greek or Polish names." As John Kennedy began running for President, he directly quoted this statement, and his own Irish name was a special gesture to the non-Irish Catholics he was trying to court. He also spoke frequently to Jewish groups, to draw them in as well.[33]

Kennedy had had a very undistinguished record in Congress, and he decided that he wanted a piece of legislation to take into the 1960 campaign. He chose the immigration issue, no doubt, to consolidate his position in his non-Irish Catholic base. Kennedy always defined politics as the art of the possible, and he was always cautious in defining the possible. In his immigration bill, he tried to achieve little more than the transfer of unused quotes to oversubscribed countries and the abolition of the mortgages of non-quota admissions against future quotas. Yet he absolutely wanted a bill to pass, and he settled for the abolition of mortgages alone, together with a few provisions that aided family reunion.

After this gesture to his supporters, Kennedy hardly mentioned immigration during his campaign. When he became President, he listed a large number of legislative areas that were to be his priorities. They did not include immigration. The list proved to reflect his real priorities, and the interest group leaders who wanted an end to national quotas were increasingly frustrated and disappointed.[34]

Only in the summer of 1963 did Kennedy finally propose legislation that would abolish national quotas, but he was positioning himself for another election. It was unclear whether he was serious in pushing a controversial program that would re-emphasize his Catholicism for Protestants. In 1965, his aide and court historian Arthur Schlesinger, Jr. wrote a history of the Kennedy Administration that was over 1000 pages length but that did not even include the word "immigration" in the index. The index of the most recent major biography of Kennedy lists the word once, but the reference is to immigration in the time of Kennedy's grandfather.[35] In other words, both a biographer who knew Kennedy intimately and another who had gone through all the papers 35 years later found no evidence of real interest in the question.

---

33. For a speech on June 4, 1957, to a Jewish group in which he emphasized the indignities imposed on all the peoples of eastern and southern Europe, see John F. Kennedy, *Let the Lady Hold Up Her Head: Reflections of American Immigration Policy* (Washington: American Jewish Congress, 1957), p. 5.
34. A good sense of their feelings can be gained from Betty K. Koed. "The Politics of Reform: Policymakers and Immigration Act of 1965" (PhD Dissertation, University of California at Santa Barbara, 1999).
35. Arthur Schlesinger, Jr., *A Thousand Days: John F. Kennedy in the White House* (Boston: Houghton Mifflin, 1965). Robert Dallek, *An Unfinished Life: John F. Kennedy, 1917–1963* (New York: Little, Brown, 2003).

Kennedy's political problem was transparent. Catholics and Jews would support him regardless of what he did on immigration. The Country Club Protestants, who favored higher immigration, remained solidly Republican. The Protestants in the red states or in the red areas of blue states had always voted Democratic in the South, and many of them voted for the New Deal in other states. They, however, were the group with the greatest suspicion of Kennedy's Catholicism and his support of civil rights for blacks. Both issues were related to their attitude toward immigration.

Lyndon Johnson had the opposite political problem. The Northern ethnic groups were suspicious of him as a Southerner, and they would see his failure to pass an immigration law as confirmation of their suspicions. Johnson needed to pass legislation that ended the system of low national quotas for southern and eastern Europe. Larry O'Brien, one of Kennedy's key political aides, remained on Johnson's staff, and Johnson had him oversee the bill from the White House. Johnson ensured that Senator Ted Kennedy, a junior member of the Judiciary Committee, be placed in charge of passage of the law in the Senate.[36]

There was another, broader factor involved. The battle of the Ellis Island immigrants and of blacks for civil rights had been linked throughout the postwar period. Now the rising violence of the blacks in 1963 meant that formal segregation and restrictions of black voting rights had to be ended. The federal government seemed certain to pass some legislation in this field. It made little sense, political or otherwise, to move towards equal legal rights for blacks but to retain unequal rights in the immigration law for different groups of whites.

The South that traditionally had been anti-immigrant could not logically resist an insistent Johnson on the end of discrimination against Ellis Island immigrants. After all, the South had long treated all whites as equal under the law. Southern laws on segregation did not require Italians, Jews, or Poles to sit in the middle of the bus. Now the Ellis Island immigrants were the most nervous Northerners about government efforts to end *de facto* discrimination against blacks in the North, and they were potential allies for the South on this issue. The South had every interest to embrace them as fellow whites on an issue that was of great symbolic importance to them, but meaningless to the South. A long-time opponent of immigration, Senator James Eastland of Mississippi, the chairman of the Judiciary Committee, stepped aside for Kennedy.

It surely was not a coincidence that Kennedy introduced a civil rights bill in June 1963 at precisely the same time that he introduced his immigration bill. Many doubted that Kennedy would pass either bill in its original form, but if black action forced the pace of civil rights legislation, then it surely would result in an end of the national origin quotas within Europe. Similarly, the Voting Rights Act of 1965 was signed on August 6 and the Immigration Act of 1965 passed on September 30. The Civil Rights Act of 1964 also went into effect in the summer of 1965. The Immigration Act, in the words of Betty Koed, was "the third leg of that legislative triad."[37]

---

36. Adam Clymer, *Edward M. Kennedy: A Biography* (New York: William Morrow & Co., 1999), pp. 70-71.

In the debates on the Immigration Law of 1965, the end of discriminatory quotas against southern and eastern Europeans did not arouse much controversy. They all had become truly white. The real mystery of the law is that it ended the principle of national origins altogether. As Senator Sam Erwin of North Carolina complained to Ted Kennedy in the Senate hearings, the new bill treated a potential Ethiopian immigrant the same as a potential Irish immigrant. As Erwin discovered, these were politically unwise examples, but they pointed to a real political puzzle. Why did the law treat Europeans, Asians, and Africans all alike?

The answer to this question is that those who feared immigration in the 1960s were really concerned with the immigration from Mexico. Immigration law since 1924 had permitted unlimited immigration from the Western Hemisphere, and hence there were no limits on Mexican immigration. The opponents of large-scale immigration made a limitation on total immigration and Western Hemisphere immigration a condition for passage of the bill. The law established a world-wide limit of 290,000 persons a year, including 120,000 for the Western Hemisphere and a maximum of 20,000 for each country. Having made such a decision, the Congress may have felt that it had to end national quotas altogether to appease people in Latin America.[38] Given the growing problems in Indochina, it was also difficult to discriminate against Asians.

The great problem of the Immigration Law of 1965 — and its great paradox — centered on the preferences given "family unification." Parents, spouses, and children could come in outside the quotas. This was an uncontroversial feature of the bill and had been in the Kennedy bill of 1963 and the Johnson bill of 1965. The non-quota postwar immigrants from eastern and southern Europe had left families behind, and nearly everyone sympathized with them. Moreover, the number of such immigrants would be relatively small, and many quietly thought that their family unification would bring in whites and help maintain the existing ethnic balance when race was defined by color of skin. Since the southern and eastern Europeans had now become whites, it no longer mattered that the new European immigrants would come from outside the Nordic countries.

But people with little knowledge about immigration missed a central point that was not lost on specialists. Older European immigrants would soon exhaust the family members they wanted to bring to the United States. Yet, as soon as new immigrants from Latin America or Asia, the great majority of them young males, became citizens, they would feel a strong desire or obligation to invite their family members

---

37. Koed, "The Politics of Reform: Policymakers and Immigration Act of 1965," p. 148.
38. The clearest and most comprehensive discussion of Johnson's legislative record, including on the immigration bill, is Irving Bernstein, *Guns or Butter? The Presidency of Lyndon Johnson* (New York: Oxford University Press, 1996). It gives an excellent summary of the immigration bill on pp. 252-260. A very full discussion of the politics of the passage of the bill based on comprehensive research in the archives of Lyndon Johnson and other archives is found in Koed, "The Politics of Reform: Policymakers and Immigration Act of 1965," pp. 155-275.

to the United States. Family members, especially spouses, would want to use the opportunity to bring over members of *their* original families.

The process would pyramid — or, to use the customary language, would form a chain reaction. Children of illegal immigrants who were born in the United States were automatically citizens, and they could bring relatives into the country when they became adults.

According to the Immigration Law of 1965, a maximum of 2.9 million persons could be admitted from the world as a whole in a decade, 1.2 million from the Western Hemisphere, and 200,000 from Mexico. Instead, the number of legal immigrants was 4.5 million in the 1970s and the number from the Western Hemisphere was 2.9 million. The number increased rapidly in the 1980s and 1990s. The number of illegal aliens was immense.[39]

Many argue that the major increase in immigrants was an unintended consequence of the law.[40] Surely, however, there were many specialists who knew quite well what would happen and who even favored it. They simply kept quiet to facilitate passage of the law. The need to end the distinctions among the whites was simply too compelling not to do something.

Even if the consequences of the law were unintended, the political elite could have changed the law when the implications of family reunification became clear to everyone. Yet, by this time, it was also clear that the immigration was helping to keep general wage levels stagnant and to further the rapid rise of the stock market from its 1981 lows. Those who did not own stocks and who were being harmed became highly alienated, but they were not politically powerful. This is a question to which we will return in the discussion of Ross Perot in 1992 and then of the problems of the first decade of the 21st century.

AFFIRMATIVE ACTION AND THE REQUIREMENT OF WHITE SELF-IDENTIFICATION

Affirmative action is one of the strangest important actions in the history of American policy-making. As Daniel Bell pointed out in 1973, the "extraordinary [thing] about this change is that, without debate, an entirely new principle of rights has been introduced into the polity."[41] In a very sophisticated analysis of the politics of the introduction of affirmative action, John Skrentny points out that most liberals and civil rights organizations originally opposed affirmative action, while conservatives did not oppose it at the time. In Skrentny's words, affirmative action was "the

---

39. A good short summary is Reed Ueda, *Postwar Immigrant America: A Social History* (Boston: Bedford Books, 1994).
40. For a book that makes this argument in the course of describing what happened from 1965 to 1985, see David M. Reimers, *Still the Open Door: The Third World Comes to America* (New York: Columbia University Press, 1985), pp. 63–100.
41. Daniel Bell, *The Coming of Post-Industrial Society: A Venture in Social Forecasting* (New York: Basic Books, 1973), p. 417. Bell is quoted by John Skrentny, who agrees with him. *The Ironies of Affirmative Action*, pp. 2–6. See Graham, *Collision Course*, pp. 1–12 for a summary of the issue.

construction of white male elites who traditionally had dominated government and business." Another major specialist, Hugh Davis Graham, would emphasize the middle-level officials in the enforcement agencies. He labeled one section of his book "The EEOC [the Equal Employment Opportunity Commission] as a Subversive Bureaucracy."[42]

The fascinating questions about affirmative action involve the transformation of a program with no original thought of racial preference into one based on the concept.[43] Even more surprising was the interaction of the program with the massive increase in Hispanic and Asian immigration and the decision to give new immigrants, even non-citizens, preference in hiring. Nevertheless, these questions are not germane in this book until the later discussion of H. Ross Perot's success in 1992 and its implications.

At this point, only two simple points need to be mentioned. The first is that any enforcement of compliance to anti-discrimination rules, let alone affirmative action in the modern sense, depends on information. Unless the government was simply to react to individual complaints, a procedure that failed in the 1950s and 1960s in the registration of black voters, it was necessary to know the percentage of blacks hired not only by particular government departments, but also by specific government contractors, private firms, and colleges and universities. The only way to collect this information was to have appropriate categories on application and employment forms.

We take for granted that we must indicate our "race" on many forms, but this was deeply controversial in the early and mid 1960s. Civil rights organizations had always opposed the collection of such individual data, and the American Civil Liberties Union had even proposed the elimination of all questions about race from the 1960 census. The Kennedy Administration reaffirmed the policy of not keeping a record of race in federal employment files. When the issue was seriously raised in the mid 1960s, the chief Washington lobbyist of the NAACP, Clarence Mitchell, called the idea "scurrilous." In August 1965 he explained the traditional NAACP position:[44]

> The history of the reason why we do not include this is sadly and surely proven, that the minute you put race on a civil service form, the minute you put a picture on an application form, you have opened the door to discrimination and, if you say that isn't true, I regret to say I feel you haven't been exposed to all of the problems that exist in this country....
>
> It seems to me incredible that the Government of the United States, recognizing that there is a nasty, underhanded little system for keeping track of people through a cute little code system ... would make it easy for discrimination by saying "Oh, no, you don't use obscure little marks. You put a nice big thing which shows this is a Negro so you don't have to put on your glasses to find out".... I am just

---

42. Skrentny, *The Ironies of Affirmative Action*, p. 5, and Hugh Davis Graham, *The Civil Rights Era: Origins and Development of National Policy, 1960–1972* (New York: Oxford University Press, 1990), pp. 190–201 and 239–254.
43. For the way this happened in the Nixon presidency, see Graham, *Collision Course*, pp. 65–88, and Skrentny, *The Ironies of Affirmative Action*, pp. 189–121.
44. Quoted in Graham, *The Civil Rights Era*, pp. 199 and 515, fn 69.

amazed that you people who come from these northern states, where you are exposed to this problem, would fall into the crevasse which has no bottom, of keeping racial statistics.

Yet the collection of information obviously was indispensable for any corrective action against discrimination, and those in the agency created to fight discrimination were the ones to push the introduction of racial identification on forms. The civil rights organizations had no option but to accept the change and hope that it was beneficial rather than the reverse.

This decision inevitably led to another question of critical importance, but that often is unrecognized. Just as the introduction of legal segregation in the South absolutely required a precise definition of who was white and who black, so a question about race on an employment form required categories. If people were going to mark a box on forms, they had to have concrete choices. In practice, the options were chosen almost casually.

The word "black" caused no political problem, all the more so since people could include themselves in the black category as they pleased. The words with monumental consequences for the future were those other than "black" and "white," but they are not germane at this point. It was the word "white" that was itself strange for anyone with any historical perspective. "Affirmative action" first was used in the 1960s in a Kennedy Executive Order that probably was taken largely for symbolic reasons. The phrase was included in one vague reference to government contractors: "The contractor will not discriminate against any employee or applicant for employment because of race, creed, color, or national origin.... The contractor will take affirmative action to ensure that applicants are employed, and that employees are treated during employment, without regard to their race, creed, color, or national origin."[45]

The newly elected Kennedy had not included civil rights among the priority areas he listed for legislative action, and the Executive Order seemed a belated and meaningless measure to suggest action. "Affirmative action" in no way suggested or was meant to suggest that any preference be given to blacks. The phrase "national origin" directly referred to the Ellis Island immigrants, and these largely Catholic groups were Kennedy's primary political base. If anyone was to be given preference, they were the most likely beneficiaries. Johnson used "national origin" in a 1965 Executive Order that vaguely mentioned affirmative action, but it did not imply preference.

Now those of different European national origins were all whites. No information was collected that might suggest that Catholics were underrepresented in a place of employment and perhaps were the subject of discrimination — or Poles or Italians or Jews. Daniel Bell made precisely this point. But why did the representatives of the various white ethnic groups not protest? As Bell pointed out, Jews were small in number and feared that comprehensive quotas would harm them. He did not explore the motives of the various Catholic interest groups, but they exemplified the

---

45. Carl M. Brauer, *John F. Kennedy and the Second Reconstruction* (New York: Columbia University Press, 1977).

normal tendency of such groups to have an upper stratum bias.[46] Those who paid membership dues were so successful that they did not fear discrimination. The more affluent Catholics were far more concerned with being automatically accepted as equal whites.

THE NEW DEFINITION OF RACIAL POLITICS

By the 1950s, the word "race" was used only in its present-day sense, and the only major remaining issue was the definition of the race of the Hispanics. The Spanish had intermarried freely with the Indian population in countries such as Mexico. Mexican immigrants included whites without Indian ancestors, Indians without any Spanish ancestors, and people with the widest variety of mixtures of the two (the mestizos). Other Spanish speakers were descended at least in part from former slaves from Africa — e.g., Puerto Ricans and Dominican Republicans — or from Spaniards living in Europe. Portuguese speakers had to be included because of Brazil. "Hispanic" was more inclusive, and "Latino" included English and French speakers from the Caribbean, Belize, and the Guyanas.

Yet there was a difference between race and racial politics. By the late 1950s, everyone was talking about the racial conflict between Negroes and whites, and the politics associated with black–white relations was becoming increasingly intense. Yet direct political conflict between whites and blacks was relatively unimportant, except in a few locales. Indeed, racial politics was not a major factor even in the South itself for the six decades from 1895 to 1955. "Racial politics" in the South meant the use of the racial card in white politics, or, beginning in 1955, white defiance of the federal government.

The Montgomery bus boycott led by Martin Luther King in late 1955 marked the first really major entry of blacks into Southern politics, and it only slowly was followed by other actions. The sit-in movement began in 1960. Only in the spring of 1963 did King decide to challenge the most reactionary police chiefs in a provocative way in order to provoke violence, receive national television coverage, and force Kennedy to act. In March 1963, he did so in Birmingham with great success, and by the late summer violence was becoming increasingly widespread.

Indeed, in late 1964 and early 1965, King worked directly with President Johnson in planning a march on Selma, Alabama, another city where overreaction was anticipated. Johnson wanted such a dramatic overreaction on the eve of his introduction of a Voting Rights Act.[47] Then, only five days after Johnson signed the Voting Rights Act on August 6, 1965, the first major and spontaneous burning of a

---

46. In E. E. Schattschneider's famous phrase, "The flaw in the pluralist heaven is that the heavenly chorus sings with a strong upper-class accent. Probably about 90 per cent of the people cannot get into the pressure system." E.E. Schattschneider, *The Semisovereign People: A Realist's View of Democracy in America* (New York: Holt, Rinehart, and Winston, 1960), p. 35. See pp. 20-46 for his documentation of this point.

neighborhood occurred. Urban blacks did not want to be forgotten once laws affecting the South were enacted.

When black politicians had become active in politics in the North after World War II, they generally had engaged in the traditional ethnic coalitional politics in which other ethnic groups had long taken part. In 1962 two major scholars, Nathan Glazer and Patrick Daniel Moynihan, wrote a highly detailed and convincing study of New York City politics that was entitled *Beyond the Melting Pot: The Negroes, Puerto Ricans, Jews, Italians, and Irish in New York City Politics.*[48] Published in 1963, it followed the rise and fall of the power of the respective ethnic groups as each increasingly moved to suburbs and was replaced by new groups.

As the sub-title of the book makes clear, the Negroes from the South and the Spanish-speaking Puerto Ricans were separate groups in New York City in 1963, not "blacks." They were simply the two most recent "immigrant" groups to enter into the coalitional politics of the earlier immigrant groups. In the introduction to a second edition, the authors wrote that the 1962 New York campaign for governor in which one of them participated "seemed to be consistent with and to confirm the basic assumptions of the book."[49]

The authors did, however, end the first edition of *Beyond the Melting Pot* with a final paragraph that was vague, but prescient: "Religion and race define the next stage in the evolution of the American peoples. But the American nationality is still forming: its processes are mysterious, and its final form, if there is ever to be a final form, is as yet unknown."[50]

Glazer and Moynihan did not change the text of the first edition when they published a second edition seven years later, but they added a 38-page introduction. They could not hide their shock at the scale of the change that had occurred. The salience of the old conflicts had declined and "race has exploded to swallow up all other distinctions":[51]

> [In 1963] Negroes ... viewed themselves as fighting to improve their position not in an undifferentiated white society, but an ethnically diverse one.... That Negroes were, or were becoming, one group in a society made up of self-conscious groups was the basic assumption of the book.... Where the book failed was in determining what kind of group Negroes would form. As an ethnic group, they would be one of many. As a racial group, as "blacks" as the new nomenclature has it, they would form a unique group in American society.

---

47. David J. Garrow, *Protest at Selma: Martin Luther King, Jr., and the Voting Rights Act of 1965* (New Haven: Yale University Press, 1978), pp. 38–39 and before, and p. 54. See, in general, pp., 31–132. As Garrow writes, the Selma March was a completely "conscious, well-calculated ... effort to evoke public nastiness and physical violence."
48. Nathan Glazer and Daniel Patrick Moynihan, *Beyond the Melting Pot: The Negroes, Puerto Ricans, Jews, Italians, and Irish of New York City* (Cambridge, MA: MIT Press, 1963).
49. "Introduction to the Second Edition: New York City in 1970," Glazer and Moynihan, *Beyond the Melting Pot*, 2nd ed., p. vii.
50. Glazer and Moynihan, *Beyond the Melting Pot*, 1st ed., p. 315.
51. Glazer and Moynihan, *Beyond the Melting Pot*, 2nd ed., pp. viii and xiii. The authors did add some qualifying phrases such as "or it would appear at the moment."

Glazer and Moynihan were, however, still too close to events. In broader perspective, the blacks were not, in fact, simply choosing how to define themselves. The white Establishment was defining them and the political space in which they operated. The Immigration Law of 1965 explicitly said that the difference between Irish, Jews, Italians, Germans, and British did not matter. The anti-discrimination laws did not distinguish between the English-speaking descendants of American slaves, Spanish-speaking Puerto Ricans and, increasingly, new immigrants from Africa. They were all "blacks."

The rules of affirmative action, which by 1970 did include preferential treatment, told all of these European groups that they were whites and that they would be treated alike in employment and college admission — and in such a way that another group (increasingly, other groups) would benefit. The white Establishment was telling blacks, by contrast, that they *were* receiving benefits because they were black, that this was now the most salient ethnic division in politics. The number of people who reported that they had native-American ancestors soared as this became beneficial, and blacks also had a reason to internalize their identity.

None of this is meant to criticize the affirmative action program of the mid-1960s or even Nixon's transformation of "affirmative action" into a program of preferential hiring for blacks. It was a brilliant policy to undercut the driving resentment behind the black revolution, namely that bright and ambitious blacks had been denied the chance to get good jobs. Affirmative action also was a brilliant way to strengthen officially and emotionally the self-concept of "whites." The same was true of concepts such as multiculturalism that merged the diverse European cultures into one. If the effect of strengthening white identity had not been considered desirable, policy would have quickly been modified. It would have been easy to protect Ellis Island and Displaced Person immigrants by basing affirmative action on income or some similar indicator instead of "race" or Hispanic background.

Over time, other issues were to arise that were radically to change the impact of affirmative action and the debate about it. But that is not the subject of this chapter. This is a chapter that does no more than insist that the "white" race and the "white"–"black" dichotomy were deliberately created in the two decades after the end of World War II in order to erase the memory of the cultural differences associated with the old European-American "races." The point that is most important at this juncture in the book is to emphasize that this change undercut the very basis of the old party coalitions.

CHAPTER 6. THE INSTITUTIONAL BASE FOR REALIGNMENT

The demographic changes in the mid 20th century clearly set the stage for a major party realignment. The blacks' accelerating migration from the rural South and their growing voting power had an impact on all political calculations. The increasing upward mobility of Catholics and the transformation of the European-American "races" into whites undercut the ethnic coalitions that extended back to the Civil War period and before.

Nevertheless, changes in social forces do not themselves produce political action. Anyone looking at the balance of political and social forces alone would have predicted a major populist party in the United States in the 1880s and the 1890s and full American neutrality in World War I. As political scientists have strongly emphasized in the last half-century, social forces and group interests are not automatically translated into policy. Indeed, as Mancur Olson insisted, self-interest normally will lead people not to participate in mass action to promote their collective interests.

Collective action to defend democracy is particularly difficult to organize. In a book called *The Logic of Collective Action* but that better should been called *The Logic of Collective Inaction*, Olson emphasized the role of compulsion and side payment in inducing people to participate in collective action. This point is well understood in the literature. It is, however, less emphasized that top government officials and/or military commanders control tax revenues and instruments of repression and hence have an unusual ability to suppress participation that is not in their interest.[1]

A serious political analyst actually finds it easier to explain why there are military coups and controlled elections than why they are so rare in modern industrial societies. In fact, of course, ambitious officials and commanders have overthrown countless democracies. Even when powerful officials do not abolish elections alto-

---

1. Mancur Olson, Jr., *The Logic of Collective Action: Public Goods and the Theory of Groups* (Cambridge, MA: Harvard University Press, 1965). The analysis of the disincentives to resist dictators is in Mancur Olson, "The Logic of Collective Action in Soviet-Type Societies," *Journal of Soviet Nationalities*, vol. 1, no. 2 (1990), pp. 8-33.

gether, they often take actions to distort the ways the rules operate in an effort to give themselves a better chance at victory. After the Civil War, as has been seen, the Democrats and Republicans cooperated to limit the suffrage of blacks and poor whites and to prevent a populist third party from being effective. They ignored the 15th Amendment that "guaranteed" blacks' right to vote. The controls on elections in the Third World often are much tighter.

There even is a major problem in relatively well-functioning democracies not threatened by coups. The theory of democracy assumes that politicians will follow their individual self-interest. Indeed, the very purpose of democratic elections is to give politicians a self-interest in promoting the public welfare. Yet the electoral rules that structure these incentives vary greatly from country to country and from time to time. They are not permanent, and they are not dictated from on high. Instead, politicians have a major role in the process, and they often try to structure rules to benefit themselves.

Outsiders who try to fight politicians on the arcane details of institutional rules face especially great collective action problems precisely because the details are so arcane. Those who transformed the long-time party coalitions in the 1950s and 1960s naturally tried to change the nature of institutions so as to benefit themselves personally. This is one reason the logic of the new rules led directly to those aspects of the new party coalitions most open to criticism. Unless we understand the pressures of the new rules and their consequences, we will not understand why the coalitions took the form they did and what must be done to change the situation.

THE EXPANSION OF VOTING RIGHTS AND THE EFFORTS AT DEMOCRATIZATION

The great domestic achievement of Franklin Roosevelt was to democratize the American political system. He destroyed the Supreme Court's interpretation of the 14th Amendment, an interpretation that denied the majority the right to pass social welfare legislation. He continued the political mobilization of the Ellis Island immigrants that Al Smith had begun in 1928, but, what is most important, he responded to the discontented who had voted for Robert La Follette and his Progressive Party in 1924. In particular, Roosevelt gave the lower and middle income voters a choice on economic policy by shifting the Democratic Party to the left side of the political spectrum.

Yet Roosevelt did very little to change or even challenge the restrictions on voter turnout introduced at the turn of the century. The only significant change was a Supreme Court decision that reversed an earlier Court decision allowing the Democratic Party to exclude blacks from its primary. Roosevelt did have his Justice Department support the change, but even then he characteristically acted by indirection. A white candidate in Louisiana — a future leader, Hale Boggs — had been elected fraudulently in a Democratic primary. The Administration argued that courts could deal with such fraud because a primary, despite past Court rulings, was an integral part of the electoral process. The Court agreed, and in 1944 the precedent that allowed court interference in primaries was used to outlaw the exclusion of blacks from the Democratic primary.

The South itself took the first steps to reduce restrictions on voter turnout — a gradual abolition of the poll tax. The poll tax had been intended to reduce poor white turnout as well as that of blacks, and it had been successful. But since the poor and middle-income whites lived disproportionately in the mountains and the foothills, their lower turnout reduced the power of their regions to influence state-wide elections. Hence, once populism had been destroyed and a Solid Democratic South ensured, the top politicians from the inland areas had a self-interest in abolishing the poll tax. Indeed, Strom Thurmond from upstate South Carolina proposed such a measure as governor, and South Carolina did abolish the poll tax. The number of former Confederate states with a poll tax declined from eleven to five by 1964.

As Table 1 indicates, the percentage of blacks who were registered to vote in the South rose significantly during the 1940s and early 1950s. The declining role of the poll tax probably did help black turnout to some extent, but basic sociological changes were more important. Blacks were increasingly moving to the cities, and their education level was rising. Except in the black belt areas, even the rural whites became less afraid of black voting as the number of blacks in the rural South declined.

During the 1950s the federal government became increasingly involved in the enforcement of the 15th Amendment. The Eisenhower Administration pushed the enactment of the Civil Rights Act of 1957 and then of 1960, both of which focused on voting rights. The 1957 law established the principle that the federal government could and should support court action by blacks to overcome the refusal of communities to register them. The 1960 law increased the power of the federal government in this realm.[2] Eisenhower enforced these laws vigorously, and Kennedy continued the enforcement efforts.

The federal government usually won in court with its challenges to discrimination in voter registration, but recalcitrant local authorities could then simply refuse to register new applicants. The Voting Rights Act of 1965 gave the federal government the right to intervene more broadly. If less than 50% of the persons old enough to vote were registered in a state or county and/or if 20 persons in a county complained to the Justice Department and their complaints were judged to be justified, the law required a series of corrective actions.

States that were subject to the provisions of the Voting Rights Acts were, for example, forbidden to use literacy tests and other subjective means to disqualify voters. They could not introduce any new regulation of any type without federal approval. Moreover, the federal government established examiners in such states, and anyone who had not been registered by local authorities could present himself or herself to an examiner. If that person could persuade the examiner that he or she met

---

2. Richard P. Claude, *The Supreme Court and the Electoral Process* (Baltimore: Johns Hopkins University Press, 1970), pp. 86–107. See the memoirs of the official most deeply involved, Herbert Brownell, *Advising Ike: The Memoirs of Attorney General Herbert Brownell* (Lawrence: University Press of Kansas, 1993).

basic requirements such as age and residency, the examiner would issue a card that those at the polling booth had to accept in lieu of registration. In fact, the examiners normally did not have to act, for the states or counties usually complied with the threat voluntarily.

Table 1: Blacks Registered to Vote, 1940 to 1952

	Percent of Voting-Age Blacks Registered			Estimated Number of Blacks Registered		
	1940	1947	1952	1940	1947	1952
Alabama	.4%	1.2%	5%	2,000	6,000	25,224
Arkansas	1.5%	17.3%	27%	4,000	47,000	61,413
Florida	5.7%	25.4%	33%	18,000	49,000	120,900
Georgia	3.0%	18.8%	23%	20,000	125,000	144,835
Louisiana	.5%	2.6%	25%	2,000	10,000	120,000
Mississippi	.4%	.9%	4%	2,000	5,000	20,000
North Carolina	7.1%	15.2%	18%	35,000	75,000	100,000
South Carolina	.8%	13.0%	20%	3,000	50,000	80,000
Tennessee	6.5%	15.8%	27%	20,000	80,000	85,000
Texas	5.6%	18.5%	31%	30,000	100,000	181,916
Virginia	4.1%	13.2%	16%	15,000	48,000	69,326
Total	3.0%	12.0%	20%	151,000	595,000	1,008,614

Sources: David J. Garrow, *Protest at Selma: Martin Luther King, Jr., and the Voting Rights Act of 1965* (New Haven: Yale University Press, 1978), p. 7. Garrow quotes, among others, V.O. Key, p. 523; Margaret Price, *The Negro Voter in the South*, p. 5 and *The Negro and the Ballot in the South*, p. 8; Donald R. Matthews and James W. Prothro, *Negroes and the New Southern Politics*, p. 148; Richard Claude, *The Supreme Court and the Electoral Process*, p. 107; Luther P. Jackson, "Race and Suffrage in the South since 1940," *New South*, June–July 1948, pp. 1–26.

At the same time, the Supreme Court began to act aggressively to remove other inequities in state electoral laws that reduced turnout or that provided lesser influence to different groups, especially ethnic minorities. In *Baker v. Carr* in 1962, the Court declared that courts could accept cases against unfair apportionment of districts for the election of state legislators. In *Reynolds v. Sims*, it demanded a virtual equality in the number of voters in each district.[3] The Court then decreed that it was unconstitutional to have at-large elections in racially polarized communities that prevented minorities from electing representatives of their own race. That is, in such cases the City Council had to be elected by districts, not at large. The Court then tried to guarantee that Congressional districting would ensure the election of minority representatives to Congress.[4]

Congress and the state legislatures also took a series of actions to extend the franchise and/or to increase popular influence. The Congressional laws of 1957, 1960, and 1965 dealing with black suffrage were only the first effort. In 1971, Congress enacted the first of a number of laws to regulate campaign contributions and expenditures. In 1994, it passed the Motor Vehicle Registration Act that required the states to give those acquiring or renewing driving licenses an easy opportunity to

---

3. Claude, *The Supreme Court and the Electoral Process*, pp. 144–223.
4. A very large literature is devoted to the debate on this subject. A good survey can be found in two books edited by Bernard Grofman: *Political Gerrymandering and the Courts* (New York: Agathon, 1990), and *Race and Redistricting in the 1990s* (New York: Agathon, 1998).

register. Then in 2002 it tried to correct some of the technical problems that had created the Florida vote-counting fiasco.

The political parties also tried to democratize the nominating process, and many of these decisions had to be imbedded in state law. At a minimum, states had to establish the date of a primary, and local authorities had to staff the polling stations. The states or the localities had to design the ballot. It was such local governmental action, paradoxically often by local Democratic authorities, that unintentionally led to major problems in Florida such as the punch card ballots with "hanging chads" or the "butterfly ballot" that so harmed Al Gore.[5]

Virtually all these Congressional and state actions were challenged in the courts, and hence the Supreme Court was required to address a series of questions both of principle and detail. The Court adopted the general rule that federal authorities could regulate state voting laws, but it invalidated certain specific Congressional actions as unconstitutional. (One, for example, was the congressional attempt to regulate so-called "issue ads" during a campaign.) Most questions about the constitutionality or meaning of legislation were quite specific, and the result, as Richard Hasen expressed it, has been a continuing "dialogue between Congress and the Court" as the latter tries to adjust to what the Court considers permissible.[6]

The "dialogue" is certain to continue. The Supreme Court dealt with the 2000 Florida vote issue in *Bush v. Gore*. The majority decided that if the "equal protection" clause of the Constitution dictates equal-sized districts, it also should require equal treatment of voters in the casting and counting of votes. The decision was highly controversial, but liberals generally support its key principle. The Court added, however, that this ruling in the Florida presidential election could not be used as a precedent for later elections. This too was reasonable if it simply acknowledged that the opinions on both sides had been so quickly (and badly) written that their precise wording should not be binding in the future. But the majority decision was most unreasonable if it meant its interpretation of the equal protection clause applied only in this single decision, but to no decisions in the future. Not surprisingly, "myriad cases" that will force the Supreme Court to clarify the matter are making their way through the lower courts.[7]

THE DECLINE IN VOTER TURNOUT AND THE PROBLEM OF ALIENATION

Efforts to democratize the voting process have now been underway for half a century, and they would have been expected to increase voter turnout and influence. This is even more the case since voter turnout in the United States has been strongly correlated with education, and education levels have risen steadily.[8] The average

---

5. For a description of the ballots, see Martin Merzer, *The Miami Herald Report: Democracy Held Hostage* (New York: St. Martin's Press, 2001), pp. 37–43.
6. Richard L. Hasen, *The Supreme Court and Election Law: Judging Equality from Baker v. Carr to Bush v. Gore* (New York: New York University Press, 2003), p. 2.
7. Hasen, *The Supreme Court and Election Law*, p. 66.

voter had approximately 9th grade education in 1950. In 1960, 41.1% of those over 25 years of age had a high school diploma or better and 7.7% a college degree or better. In 2000, 84.1% of the population 25 years and older had a high school diploma, and 25.6% a college degree or better.[9]

The original attacks on the restriction of black voting in the South did, in fact, increase voter turnout, but turnout in the South in presidential elections quickly reached a rather low plateau. In the 1948 election, Southern turnout was 23% of the eligible age group, typical of that in the preceding four decades, but the figure rose to 38% in the 1952 election. Southern turnout remained essentially at that level in the elections of 1956 and 1960, but then increased further to 45% in 1964. Some of the rise in turnout simply resulted from the increased competitiveness of Southern elections, but the Democratic Party in the South also accelerated registration of blacks, confident that they would vote Democratic.

In the North, 64% of voting age Americans went to the polls in 1964, and one would have expected turnout in the South to rise toward this level. Instead, the Voting Rights Act of 1965 only raised Southern turnout to 51% in 1968, and that was the high point for the rest of the century. Southern turnout as a percentage of those old enough to vote remained very stable in the 45%–50% range over the next three decades. (It did increase marginally if the rising number of non-citizens and ineligible felons is taken into account.[10]) Two factors that explain this low turnout are the lower level of education both among blacks and whites in the South and the frequent lack of contested elections in the area. The redistricting that segregated Southern blacks and whites into non-competitive Congressional and state districts may also have played a significant role.

Nevertheless, the most unexpected reasons for continued low turnout in the South surely are the general factors that, whatever their nature, also led to a reduction of Northern turnout. As Table 2 shows, this occurred not only in presidential elections, but in Congressional off-year elections as well. Northern voter turnout in presidential elections fell from the 65% to 70% level from 1936 to 1972 to the 50% to 55% level from 1976 onwards. Turnout in off-year Congressional elections fell from the low fifties in the 1950s and 1960s to the high thirties in the 1980s and 1990s.

Northern voter turnout also either was not affected or was affected negatively by the other reforms that were introduced. At least until 2004, and perhaps not even then, the Motor Vehicle Registration Law did not increase the vote, only the percentage of registered voters who did not vote.[11] Other reforms proved just as unsatis-

---

8. Raymond E. Wolfinger and Steven J. Rosenstone, *Who Votes?* (New Haven: Yale University Press, 1980).
9. *Statistical Abstract of the United States: 2004–2005* (Washington: US Government Printing Office, 2004), p. 141.
10. For the corrections, see Table 3, which is based on Michael P. McDonald and Samuel L. Popkin, "The Myth of the Vanishing Voter," *American Political Science Review*, vol. 95, no. 4 (December 2001), pp. 963–974.
11. For the Census Bureau figures on number of the people who reported being registered and the number of the latter who reported voting, see *Statistical Abstract of the United States*, 2004–2005, p. 256.

factory. Presidential nominations came to be decided in February and March — and then in January 2004 — and, as a consequence, the number of people with a meaningful impact in the primaries was extremely low. The nominating process was less democratic at the end of the 20th century than it was prior to the 1972 reforms. Congressional districts became equal in size, as the Supreme Court dictated, but this seemed only to make them non-competitive in some 90% of the cases.

Table 2: Average Turnout of Voting Age Americans in Presidential and Off-Year Congressional Elections, 1952–2002

	National Turnout		Northern Turnout		Southern Turnout	
Elections	Presidential Years	Congressional Off-Years	Presidential Years	Congressional Off-Years	Presidential Years	Congressional Off-Years
1952–1962	61.2%	43.4%	68.3%	52.4%	38.1%	18.7%
1964–1970	61.4%	44.5%	65.2%	51.4%	47.8%	33.4%
1972–1980	53.8%	35.4%	56.3%	41.4%	45.6%	27.3%
1982–1990	51.8%	34.9%	53.4%	39.4%	46.6%	33.1%
1992–1994	55.1%	36.7%	56.7%	40.3%	50.5%	34.6%
1996–2002	50.1%	32.7%	51.9%	38.0%	46.7%	31.2%

Source: *US Census Bureau data, reported in Statistical Abstract of the United States: 2004–2005 (Washington: US Government Printing Office, 2004), p. 257.*

What explains the decline in turnout seen in Table 2? An intense scholarly debate has centered on this question and even on the extent to which a real decline occurred. As is usual in scholarly debates, it is important to sort out the issues, for some of the debate is artificial.

The first question to be asked is the time period the scholar is discussing. Ruy Teixeira, the author of a 1992 book about "The Disappearing American Voter," begins his analysis with the high turnout of the 1950s and 1960s. He naturally ends with 1988, the most recent election prior to the publication of his book.[12] In fact, 1988 featured the lowest Northern turnout of the 20th century except for the subsequent 1996 election, but Teixeira had no reason to suspect this at the time that he wrote.

By contrast, Teixeira's leading protagonists, Michael McDonald and Samuel Popkin, concede in passing the decline that took place from the 1950s and early 1960s, but emphasize the lack of decline since 1976. (See Table 3.) They point out that the Census Bureau data refers to all residents, including non-citizens and felons who cannot vote. They show that turnout among citizens who are 21 years of age and older and who are not felons has generally not declined. In addition, of course, McDonald's and Popkin's 2001 article naturally includes the high 1992 and moderate 2000 turnouts. Curtis Gans in a still unpublished paper argues that if all the data are examined carefully, McDonald and Popkin exaggerate somewhat in seeing stability in turnout from 1976 to 2000, but they seem right at a minimum that relatively little

---

12. Ruy A. Teixeira, *The Disappearing American Voter* (Washington: The Brookings Institution, 1992).

decline occurred in the presidential elections of these years, let alone 2004, at least if the data are corrected for the factors they discuss.[13]

Table 3: Voter Turnout
Among Those of Voting Age, Those Eligible to Vote, and
Those Eligible to Vote Aged 21 and Over, 1932–2000

	% of Those of Voting Age			% of Those Eligible to Vote			% of Those Over 20 *and* Eligible to Vote		
Year	Total	North	South	Total	North	South	Total	North	South
1932	52.5%			57.0%*	66.2%*	24.5%*			
1936	56.9%			61.0%*	71.4%*	25.0%*			
1940	58.9%			62.5%*	72.9%*	26.5%*			
1944	56.0%			55.9%*	65.1%*	24.5%*			
1948	51.1%	57.9%	23.1%	55.2%	59.1%	23.7%			
1952	61.6%	69.3%	38.3%	62.3%	70.0%	38.9%			
1956	59.3%	66.4%	36.7%	60.2%	67.2%	37.4%			
1960	62.8%	69.1%	39.4%	63.8%	70.1%	40.2%			
1964	61.9%	66.7%	44.9%	62.8%	67.4%	45.6%			
1968	60.9%	63.7%	50.7%	61.5%	64.4%	51.4%			
1972	55.2%	58.5%	44.1%	56.2%	59.6%	44.8%	57.2%	60.8%	46.2%
1976	53.5%	55.9%	46.2%	54.8%	57.1%	47.6%	56.4%	58.9%	49.4%
1980	52.8%	54.6%	46.5%	54.7%	56.6%	48.1%	56.2%	58.7%	49.7%
1984	53.3%	54.9%	48.0%	57.2%	59.2%	51.1%	58.6%	60.7%	52.7%
1988	50.3%	51.9%	45.2%	54.2%	56.0%	48.1%	55.5%	57.5%	49.4%
1992	55.1%	56.7%	50.5%	60.6%	62.9%	54.8%	61.7%	64.0%	56.0%
1996	48.9%	50.3%	45.5%	52.6%	54.0%	48.7%	53.9%	55.3%	49.9%
2000	51.2%	52.5%	47.9%	55.6%	56.9%	52.1%	57.1%	58.5%	53.6%

Sources: Michael P. McDonald and Samuel L. Popkin, "The Myth of the Vanishing Voter," American Political Science Review, vol. 95, no. 4 (December 2001), pp. 963–974. The 1932 to 1944 figures, marked with an asterisk, are from Walter Dean Burnham, "The Turnout Problem," A. James Reichley, ed., Elections American Style (Washington: Brookings Institution, 1987), p. 114.

A second question to be asked about the scholarly debate is the purpose of the emphasis given by specific scholars. McDonald and Popkin perform a very useful service by providing figures from 1948 to 2000 that correct the level of turnout for the number of non-citizens, Americans living abroad, and ineligible felons, as well as the granting of suffrage to 18- to 20-year-olds. (They do, however, create a misleading impression by beginning with 1948, with its abnormally low turnout, rather than with 1936 and 1940.)

If the question is the level of citizen turnout, especially among those 21 years older and above, McDonald and Popkin are quite right to emphasize stability after 1976. But McDonald and Popkin implicitly assume that 1976 is normal and, in addition, that the rise of the number of non-citizens in the United States poses no problems in the evaluation of American democracy. Both of these assumptions are open to real question.

---

13. McDonald and Popkin, "The Myth of the Vanishing Voter," pp. 965–966 and 968. On p. 963, they cite a number of the scholars espousing the opposing interpretation. I am grateful to Curtis Gans for his material.

First, it should not even be assumed that 1960 is the proper standard in comparative perspective. Virtually all advanced industrial nations at the beginning of the 20th century had voter turnout above the 75% level, and so did the United States in the 19th century. European turnout remained at that level, but not the American. The precipitous decline of Southern voter turnout to the 25% level in little more than a decade and the decline of some 15 percentage points in the North to the 65–70% level were, as has been seen, the result of a deliberate and successful effort to reduce turnout among the poor.[14] Turnout in the North temporarily dropped lower in 1920 and 1924 because many women did not take immediate advantage of the suffrage given them by the 19th Amendment, but it returned to the 65% to 70% level in the 1930s.

Second, a high level of alienation in 1976 is quite understandable. The resignation of President Richard Nixon and Vice President Spiro Agnew, the fall of Saigon, the oil crisis, and the resulting economic problems had all occurred within the previous three years. Moreover, the two candidates in 1976, Gerald Ford and Jimmy Carter, were not very exciting, and there were no major substantive issues in that election. But if a high level of alienation explains the decline in turnout from the 1960s to 1976, the failure of turnout to rise above the 1976 level for a quarter of a century logically suggests that the level of alienation remained stable during that period. In fact, as noted in Chapter 1, the standard political science book based on an academic survey that uses the same questions at every election shows basic continuity in the level of public alienation from government from 1980 to 2000. The belief in the responsiveness of government was at an all-time low in 1996, a year in which the economy and stock market were booming and in which, by coincidence or not, turnout was also at an all-time low.[15]

On the surface, the continuation of high levels of alienation in the 1980s and 1990s is very surprising. Ronald Reagan supposedly inspired America, and the economy and especially the stock market grew very rapidly from 1982 to 2000. The United States also had an extraordinarily successful foreign policy during this period. Communist regimes collapsed in Eastern Europe and Afghanistan, and the Soviet Union disintegrated. In short, the United States won the Cold War. In addition, the United States repelled Iraq's invasion of Kuwait and supported the independence of the various peoples of Yugoslavia, all with minimal American casualties.

A whole series of hypotheses could be advanced to explain the continuing alienation through the 1980s and 1990s. These include a stagnation of the average wage, suspicion about outsourcing and free trade, opposition to the rise in immigration, cynicism in the media about politics and politicians and/or a displacement of traditional populist resentment against the economic elite onto politicians. Public

---

14. These are the figures of Walter Dean Burnham in his "The Turnout Problem," in A. James Reichley, ed., *Elections American Style* (Washington: Brookings Institution, 1987), p. 114. Professor Burnham corrected his figures for non-citizens, but did not provide the methodology by which he did this.
15. Paul R. Abramson, John H. Aldrich, and David W. Rohde, *Change and Continuity in the 2000 Election* (Washington: CQ Press, 2001), pp. 87–88.

opinion polls show that the white population has always been opposed to affirmative action for minorities and to immigration policy, while blacks remain convinced that they are still subject to discrimination. Whites strongly favor governmental health care programs that are color-neutral, but are deeply convinced, to a large extent mistakenly, that measures directed against poverty primarily benefit minorities.

Basically, however, the answers to the National Election Study survey should be taken literally. The respondents were asked to respond to two statements: "Public officials don't care much what people like me think" and "People like me don't have any say about what the government does." A very substantial proportion of the population disagreed with these statements in early 1960s, but agreed with them from the 1970s into the 21st century, even in long periods of prosperity. They believed that the two major parties were not offering a meaningful choice on issues that mattered to them.

The third reason not to be complacent about the McDonald and Popkin figures is found in the socioeconomic changes that have occurred among the electorate as voting within the total population has declined. As Table 4 shows, the decline in voter turnout has not occurred evenly over socioeconomic groups. Table 4 focuses on turnout among those with different levels of education, but education is the best surrogate for categories such as income or occupation that are more difficult to measure in a meaningful manner from census data.[16] Table 4 shows that the turnout rate among those with an elementary school education declined 32.2 percentage points from 1964 to 2000, those with a high school diploma 26.7 points, and those with a college degree or better 15.5 points.

Table 4: Voter Turnout in Presidential Elections, By Level of Education, 1964–2000 (in Percentages)

Level of Education	1964	1968	1972	1976	1980	1984	1988	1992	1996	2000
8 Years or Less	59.0	54.5	47.4	44.1	42.6	42.9	36.7	35.1	28.1	26.8
Incomplete High School	65.4	61.3	52.0	47.2	45.6	44.4	41.3	41.2	33.8	33.6
High School Graduate	76.1	72.5	65.4	59.4	58.9	58.7	54.7	57.5	49.1	49.4
Incomplete College	82.1	78.4	74.9	68.1	67.2	67.5	64.5	68.7	60.5	60.3
College Graduate	87.5	84.1	83.6	79.8	79.9	79.1	77.6	81.0	73.0	72.0

Source: 1964–1988: Ruy A. Teixeira, The Disappearing American Voter (Washington: The Brookings Institution, 1992), p. 66. (Calculated from Census Data); 1992–2000: Statistical Abstract of the United States: 2004–2005 (Washington: US Government Printing Office, 2004), p. 256.

The figures of Table 4 must be used with some caution. The reported turnout is somewhat higher than the official data on the number who voted for President. Some people claim that they voted when they actually did not. Nevertheless, others actually went to the poll and are not counted in the total presidential vote. Some left

---

16. The major problem with income figures is that they include some people who are only partly employed (e.g., students, housewives, and retirees), but who may have a much higher socioeconomic standing than their actual income suggests. Occupation figures also mix together people of quite different socioeconomic position.

the presidential line on the ballot blank, while others unknowingly spoiled their ballot in some way — e.g., most famously in 2000 by the failure to punch out the chad completely on a punch card ballot. As a result, the figures of Table 4 should be accurate enough for any practical purposes.

The more basic problem with Table 4 is that which McDonald and Popkin emphasize: the statistics are based on a survey of all residents of the United States, citizens and non-citizens alike. Non-citizens and felons who cannot vote are concentrated disproportionately among those who are less well educated. Nevertheless, we should consider the possibility that the census figures are a more accurate indicator of the health of a democratic political system than the turnout figures for those who are eligible to vote. For example, the incarceration of poor blacks, but not middle class whites, for the use of illegal drugs reduces their political influence. This is often criticized, but never changed.

In addition, if non-voting immigrants and especially illegal immigrants occupy a high proportion of low-level socioeconomic jobs, the interests of the poor, including poor citizens, will not be as fully represented in the political process. For example, prior to the 1970s, the minimum wage generally rose as a percentage of the average manufacturing wage, but in recent decades it has scarcely risen at all. Non-citizens comprise a substantial portion of those who would benefit from a higher minimum wage, and a rapid increase in their number clearly reduces voter support for the minimum wage. Not surprisingly, Congressional and presidential support for the minimum wage has declined, but the tragedy of New Orleans reminds us that not all beneficiaries of that wage are illegal immigrants.

The important question is whether the declining turnout among the lower educated and lower income citizen voters is the result of voter alienation or the cause of it. Almost surely, it is both. Democratic theory certainly suggests that representatives will be guided by the wishes of those who vote, not by the population as a whole. As turnout among the lower socioeconomic groups declines, the political system should be more responsive to those in the higher socioeconomic groups. But as the lower socioeconomic groups become less well represented in the system, their turnout may also decline because of growing alienation. Or, at least, their turnout may decline until their resentment is mobilized by a figure such as Ross Perot and/or a more establishment figure with populist themes.

The Failure of Nomination Reforms

Voters never have a truly free choice in elections except in tiny communities in which everyone knows everyone else, including all prospective candidates. In the United States, voters normally must choose between two presidential candidates even though they may not be enthusiastic about either. As a result, the nature of the choice and the way it is determined are of crucial importance. Indeed, the nomination process not only produces candidates but also forces prospective nominees to choose a program and strategy that will best optimize their chance to be nominated.

Almost all specialists agree with James Ceaser that the nominating system "has generated more dissatisfaction among political analysts than any other American institution."[17] In the past, three or four major candidates normally engaged in a struggle for a party's nomination, and the nomination often was not decided until the eve of the convention or at the convention itself. In the last five elections, by contrast, Michael Dukakis, Bill Clinton, Robert Dole, George W. Bush, Al Gore, and John Kerry were effectively nominated by February or March without facing a single candidate who seemed viable, or even in many cases without facing any serious candidates. Kerry was nominated in January. A very strong case can be made that the current nominating rules have played a major role in reducing the responsiveness of the parties to the voters and producing the polarized politics that everyone deplores.

This is not just the judgment of academics. In 2000, the Brock Commission of the Republican Party, which was composed of the party's highest-level professional politicians, was also highly critical of the Republican (and implicitly the Democratic) nominating procedure. According to the Commission report, "it is clear that the reforms of the 1970s have not, on the whole, worked well." The Commission quoted with approval the following statement by an observer:[18]

> Shamefully for a country whose founders created a governmental system emphasizing the balance of power, coherence, and deliberation, we now have a presidential selection process that is imbalanced, incoherent and lacking civic deliberation. Is it any wonder why well-qualified potential candidates ... avoid entanglement in this haphazard and money-driven frenzy, or why voting in general is on the decline?

The Brock Commission sharply criticized the "front-loading" of primaries and "the need for ever-larger sums of money," precisely the problems that repeated reform efforts had been intended to avoid. Most astonishing of all, this report calling for drastic change was published in May 2000 after the nomination of George W. Bush was guaranteed. The top Republican party professionals obviously were convinced that he would be the third straight Republican who would lose by a substantial margin. They thought it was crucial to transform a nominating process that produced two losing candidates from Texas and one from Kansas, all of them following a red state strategy.

1. The Old Nominating Process and Its Reform

The nominating system that existed from the 1920s to the 1960s was a mixed system that elected some delegates in primaries, but most of them in caucuses. The latter did not have the relatively large public participation that has become normal in

---

17. James W. Ceaser, "Improving the Nominating Process," in Reichley, ed., *Elections American Style*, p. 29.
18. Advisory Commission of the Presidential Nominating Process, *Nominating Future Presidents* (Washington: Republican National Committee, 2000), p. 21.

the Iowa caucuses, but almost always were sparsely attended. The caucuses usually were controlled by professional politicians.[19] The primaries allowed candidates to demonstrate that they had electoral appeal and could organize a campaign — and, hopefully, therefore, a presidency. As a participant in the Hunt Commission of the Democratic Party phrased the point in 1981–1982, "a candidate needs an out of town tryout. He needs a chance to try out his act, to play it, to change it, to hone it, and to fine tune it."[20]

In order to ensure that the primaries could play their role, the parties scheduled them at widely spaced intervals. In 1968 the first primary (New Hampshire) was held on March 12 and the second (Wisconsin) on April 2. Pennsylvania scheduled its primary for April 23 and Massachusetts for April 30. The eleven other primaries were spread out in May and the first third of June with some two primaries occurring every week. The only major defect was the absence of primaries in the South.[21]

In the mixed system, the candidate could choose to run in a relatively small number of primaries in diverse states to demonstrate his appeal. Nevertheless, the professionals made the final decisions. The mayor of Chicago, for example, always had an uncommitted Illinois Democratic delegation under his control, and he did not commit them to John Kennedy in 1960 until the convention. The professionals could overrule the judgment of the primary voters if they judged the winner would not be a good centrist candidate or a good President.

In retrospect, scholars look back at the mixed system of the 1960s with nostalgia. Nevertheless, the system rested on the professionals' control of the caucus, and this control was subject to challenge. The caucuses elected delegates by methods that embodied democratic forms, but usually not the reality of democracy. The caucuses often were scheduled at unannounced and arbitrary times and were held well before the election. Delegates could be required to pay high filing fees.[22] Those caucuses in the South and the Border States, which elected 35% of the delegates to the Democratic Convention in 1948, normally elected no black delegates.

Yet, if activists were truly determined, the low level of attendance at caucuses made it easy for them to gain a majority. Supporters of Dwight Eisenhower in 1952 were the first to use the caucuses effectively against the favorite organization can-

---

19. A good short summary is found in Robert E. DiClerico, "Evolution of the Presidential Nominating Process," in Robert E. DiClerico and James W. Davis, eds., *Choosing Our Choices: Debating the Presidential Nominating Process* (Lanham, Mary.: Rowman and Littlefield, 2000), pp. 3-7.
20. Leslie Israel in Stenographic Report of the Hunt Commission, November 7, 1981, p. 178, Box 1, David Eugene Price Papers, Duke University.
21. The dates and results for all primaries in all states holding primaries from 1912 to 2000 are found in *Congressional Quarterly's Guide to U.S. Elections*, 4th ed. (Washington: Congressional Quarterly, 2001), pp. 320-410. Those in 1968 are found on pp. 351-353. See James W. Davis, "The Case Against the Current Primary Centered System," in DiClerico and Davis, eds., *Choosing Our Choices*, 2000), pp. 37–39.
22. A state-by-state survey of procedures was printed in the report of the Commission on the Democratic Selection of Presidential Nominees that met on the eve of the 1968 decision, *The Democratic Choice*, pp. 73–85. A survey of perceived inequities is found on pp. 19–33. A copy is found in the Eugene McCarthy National File, Box 37, Credential Challenge Committee Folder, Georgetown University.

didate, Robert A. Taft. In 1964, Barry Goldwater was popular among the precinct, county, and district Republican officials who played an important role in delegate election, and his supporters made a quiet but vigorous effort to elect more such officials in 1962 and 1963.[23]

Goldwater and his supporters thought he would be quite popular against John Kennedy in the red states of today. Kennedy was in Dallas in November 1963 in large part because polls indicated he would lose Texas by a large margin, even with Lyndon Johnson on the ticket. Yet, however Goldwater might have fared in November 1964 against an Eastern Catholic, Lyndon Johnson was the first major presidential candidate from a Confederate state since 1850 and as a Texan was attractive to the Southwest as well. Goldwater had no chance against him. Nevertheless, conservative activists continued to win delegates in caucuses even though public opinion polls showed Goldwater would suffer a severe defeat in November.

The major change in the nominating process actually did not emerge from the Republican Party after the 1964 Goldwater debacle, but from the Democratic Party in 1968. The 1960s were a time of political turmoil, and Hubert Humphrey, Lyndon Johnson's Vice President, was nominated in the 1968 Democratic Convention without running in a single primary. Not surprisingly, anti-war radicals attacked the nominating process as undemocratic and demanded change. The Democratic convention in 1968 created a commission to revise the rules by which the candidate would be nominated in 1972.[24]

Austin Ranney, a political scientist who was a member of the McGovern Commission, insisted that no one on the commission wanted additional primaries. This was, he wrote, "about the only matter on which we approached unanimity."[25] In the old system, a limited number of primaries had been a useful and inexpensive adjunct to the caucuses, but primaries were very expensive in an age of television, especially if they became the major instrument for selecting delegates.[26]

The radical activists preferred caucuses for perfectly understandable reasons: they did not have the money needed for a large number of expensive primaries, but they had the time and enthusiasm required for caucuses. They were likely to do better in meetings where a small number of votes would be decisive. The commission tried to institutionalize such a system. The new rules recommended by the com-

---

23. The clearest statement about the delegates and the strategy to win them is found in F. Clifton White, *Suite 3505: The Story of the Draft Goldwater Movement* (New Rochelle, NY: Arlington House, 1967), pp. 48-51 and 97.
24. Although many saw this decision as a meaningless gesture to radicals, Max Frankel correctly reported otherwise in a front-page story in *The New York Times* at the time. The resolution, he wrote, introduced "profound changes on [the party's] future processes" that "will outlive the memory of the bitter confrontations and demonstrations." Max Frankel, "Delegate Fights Transform Party," *The New York Times*, August 28, 1968, p. 1. The quotes are from the continuation of the story on an inner page of the paper.
25. Austin Ranney, "Changing the Rules of the Nominating Game," in James D. Barber, ed., *Choosing the President* (Englewood Cliffs, NJ: Prentice-Hall, 1974), p. 73. The italics are in the original.
26. Anthony Corrado, *Creative Campaigning: PACs and the Presidential Selection Process* (Boulder: Westview Press, 1992), p. 35.

mission required that caucuses be more accessible to rank-and-file citizens. The rules also demanded that delegations contain a large number of blacks and women.

Senator George McGovern of South Dakota chaired the commission that changed the rules, and naturally he understood how activists could use the caucuses to elect delegates who would support him. Experienced politicians discussed the results with wonderment. Caucuses in conservative areas in Georgia were often dominated by black radicals and oddly dressed young whites who defeated delegates pledged to Governor Carter or George Wallace. In Massachusetts, Tip O'Neill had long dominated his Congressional district that included Cambridge, and he was the one major Congressional leader who had taken an anti-war position since 1967. Yet he was not elected as a delegate to the Democratic Convention from his district. He said that the Massachusetts delegation to the Democratic Convention looked like the cast of *Hair*.[27]

The top party leaders analytically agreed with the activists about the caucuses, but obviously drew the opposite conclusion. They believed that primaries were more likely to be won by candidates with name recognition and/or with enough funds for a major television campaign. The professionals thought this was an excellent idea, and they pushed for the introduction of a primary in their own state if it did not already have one. The number of primaries rose sharply and, more importantly, so too did the number of committed delegates elected by them. (See Table 5.) By 1996, 42 states held primaries.[28]

Table 5: Number of Primaries and Percentage of Committed Delegates Elected at Them, 1968–1980

	Democratic Party		Republican Party	
Year	Number of Primaries	Percent of Committed Delegates	Number of Primaries	Percent of Committed Delegates
1968	17	36%	16	36%
1972	23	58%	22	41%
1976	29	66%	28	54%
1980	31	71%	33	69%

Source: Nelson W. Polsby, *Consequences of Party Reform* (Oxford: Oxford University Press, 1983), p. 64.

2. The Paradox of Primary Reform and Campaign Finance Laws

Those who have advocated primaries from the beginning of the 20th century have always, of course, claimed that they were a democratizing measure that let the people choose the candidates. This claim was always challenged, essentially on the ground that the primary voter was not representative of the party members as a whole. Critics argued that the nomination of candidates by professional politicians

---

27. John A. Farrell, *Tip O'Neill and the Democratic Century* (Boston: Little, Brown, 2001), pp. 304–305.
28. Scholars differ in their count of the number of primaries. The usual reason is that territories such as Puerto Rico and the Virgin Islands elect a small number of delegates. Sometimes their primaries are counted, sometimes not.

was actually likely to be more conducive to a democratic outcome. Politicians were, it was said, knowledgeable about public desires and moods and had a strong self-interest in finding the candidates whom voters in November would find most attractive and responsive.

The same type of activists who engineered the reforms in the nominating process also persuaded the Congress to enact limitations on campaign contributions and expenditures. Both because of Supreme Court decisions and loopholes in the laws themselves, the limitations on the expenditures in the November presidential election proved to be largely meaningless. But the unlimited "soft" money that was so important in the November election was far less available in the primaries. The government agreed to match contributions in the primaries if candidates accepted strict limits on their expenditures, and the amount of money available for the campaign was grossly insufficient to finance an ever growing number of primaries in an age of television. Even as candidates beginning with George W. Bush rejected government financing, they found they could not raise enough money independently to solve the problem.

Paradoxically, the combination of campaign finance reform and an expanded number of primaries only served to increase the power of major campaign contributors. In the past, contributors who wanted to support a winner had an interest in waiting until they saw the result of early primaries before they decided whom to support. This meant that during the early primaries, the candidates were auditioning both for the professional politicians and for the contributors. Yet, since contributors were supporting candidates who had shown strength and since the contributors were trying to jump aboard a winning bandwagon, the candidates were not that dependent on contributors.

A national primary financed by the federal government would also give the candidates some independence from financial contributors, but the state-by-state system of primaries established in the 1970s inevitably had a very different impact. The 1980 campaign was the watershed event. As the number of primaries increased, the candidates had insufficient funds to compete vigorously in all primaries. Politicians had to decide whether to conserve money for later primaries or spend to their limits in early primaries in hope of achieving an unstoppable momentum and/or bankrupting their opponents. In 1980, one candidate, George H.W. Bush, budgeted for a long campaign while another, Ronald Reagan, went for a quick victory. When Reagan won, most serious candidates decided that his strategy was the best.

But, of course, if the early primaries were to be decisive, states had no self-interest in scheduling their primaries late in the spring. The states introducing new primaries naturally tended to schedule them relatively early in the primary season, and other states began to move their primaries forward. The timing of primaries in 1972 was very similar to that in 1968, but two states, Florida and Illinois, provided a taste of the future: Florida moved its primary from May 28 to March 14 and Illinois moved its from June 11 to March 21. In 1976, four of 24 states held their primaries before the date of the 1968 New Hampshire primary. New Hampshire, determined to remain the state with the first primary, scheduled its primary on February 24, 17 days before its 1968 primary date of March 12.

In 1980, seven states had primaries before March 12, and 14 primaries were held before April 23, the date of the third primary in 1968. The most important changes occurred in the South, for they reflected a coordinated political strategy. By 1976, Senator Edward Kennedy's supporters had moved the New Hampshire primary forward to February 24 and had scheduled the Massachusetts and Vermont primaries in early March in case he ran for President. The three states had their primaries essentially on the same dates in 1980. President Carter feared that Senator Kennedy would challenge him in the 1980 primaries and that these early New England primaries would give Kennedy the image of an unstoppable front-runner. In order to counteract any such impression, the President persuaded Alabama, Florida, and Georgia to schedule their primaries on March 11, one week after the Vermont and Massachusetts primaries.

After the defeat of Walter Mondale in 1984, the Southern states decided to move almost all their primaries in 1988 to March 8, a date that became known as Super Tuesday. As a result, 19 states with 69% of the delegates needed to win held their Democratic primary by March 8. This pattern was basically repeated in 1992 and then was carried further in the 1990s. In 2000, New Hampshire scheduled its primary for February 11, and the Democratic Party held primaries in 24 states with 2,514 delegates out of the total of 4,339. The Republican Party held primaries in states with 1,320 of 2,006 delegates by this date.[29]

The 1984 Democratic nominating campaign was the last to continue throughout the primary season, and Walter Mondale of Minnesota actually won because he carried nearly all the Southern primaries against his major opponent, Gary Hart. The Southerners were not happy with Mondale, but they were even more disturbed by Hart, who was McGovern's campaign manager in 1972 and who emphasized liberal cultural values. The "Super Tuesday" idea was justified as a way to increase the influence of the South, but its real purpose was to ensure an early nomination and prevent victory by an outsider such as Hart.

The Democratic National Committee scheduled the 2004 New Hampshire primary for a still earlier date, January 27. The Iowa caucus was held on January 19. The Republican primaries and caucuses in the 2004 election were irrelevant because of the certainty of President's Bush renomination, but 14 states held their Democratic primaries and caucuses before the February 11 date of the New Hampshire primary in 2000. A total of 34 states held their Democratic primary or caucus before the March 12 opening date of 1968. A substantial number of states actually chose delegates in caucuses once more, for they increasingly recognized that primaries were expensive to conduct and were a waste of money if all but the first ones were meaningless.[30]

As has been seen, this process of front-loading has been much bemoaned, even by Republican Party professionals, and the criticism is well justified. Probably the most important negative consequence is that the candidates and those who support

29. *CQ's Guide to U.S. Elections*, vol. 1, pp. 641-642 and 404-410.
30. For a list of the dates of primaries and caucuses in 2004 in both parties, Michael L. Goldstein, *Guide to the 2004 Presidential Election* (Washington: CQ Press, 2003), pp. 35–37.

them must make their key decisions well before January of an election year. This has a major impact on the outcome.

An incident in the 2000 Republican campaign was highly revealing: the Bush campaign spent a large amount of money on television ads in the Arizona primary even though Bush's major opponent, John McCain of Arizona, was certain to win his own state. The Bush forces were treated with scorn for wasting money, but this criticism was unjustified. Television time for the Arizona primary and others had to be purchased in the fall of 1999 if the best slots were to be obtained, and McCain was not a candidate at that time. Bush's main opponents were thought to be Steve Forbes and/or Pat Buchanan, and Buchanan had done well in the 1996 Arizona primary against Robert Dole. But, of course, if decisions on the purchase of television time must be made in the fall of the previous year, the money must be raised even earlier, perhaps much earlier.

In the summer of 2005, reporters were beginning to say that Senator Hillary Clinton had already won commitments from the networks of large Eastern financial contributors. As a consequence, it is not clear that Senator Clinton can be effectively challenged for the 2008 nomination by anyone other than a person such as New Jersey Governor Jon Corzine or former Virginia Governor Mark Warner, each of whom is wealthy enough to finance his own campaign.

The process by which the networks of contributors choose their respective candidates has not been well studied, but Robert Rubin of Goldman Sachs headed a Democratic fund-raising group on Wall Street and invited Democratic candidates to meet with his group in 1991. The purpose was to allow the members to assess the acceptability of the candidates. Bill Clinton convinced them that he would follow a conservative fiscal policy as they desired. Since Clinton was by no means a certain winner at this stage, they were not really compelled to court the candidate likely to have the greatest appeal to the electorate. Rather, he was under more pressure to adapt his policy to their wishes. (Clinton's nomination will be discussed in Chapter 8.)

FRONT-LOADING AND THE NATURE OF THE PRIMARY VOTER

The front-loaded system has a series of consequences other than its effect on the timing of campaign contributions. First, candidates are nominated well before the broad population knows much about most of them. Indeed, public opinion polls showed that half the Democrats were still completely unfamiliar with John Kerry in April 2004, three months after he had effectively won. Only two candidates had challenged him, an unknown Vermont governor with no national experience and a one-term North Carolina Senator who was not running for re-election because he would almost surely lose. As a consequence, the competitors are not given a chance to be tested or to improve their technique and appeal. This certainly was the case in 2004 with John Kerry.[31]

In addition, those who participate in the early primaries are not a random sample of the November electorate. The all-primary system was meant to reduce the influence of radical activists, and it did so. Nevertheless, the primary electorate always has been composed disproportionately of activists in a broader sense, and the front-loaded system of primaries increased this tendency. Only those quite interested in politics or activated by a charismatic candidate would pay attention to the campaign in January and February and/or would have any significant knowledge of the candidates' views or personal qualities.

The educated activists in the Democratic Party have largely had the characteristic of the "amateur Democrat" to be discussed in Chapter 8. In the last two decades they have, to a large extent, come from the generation of activists of the 1960 and 1970s, but not the most radical of them. The activists in the Republican Party have been the descendants of the secular Goldwater economic and foreign policy activists of the 1960s, together with the social conservatives with whom they formed an alliance. These tendencies are especially strong in the states in which the early primaries are held.

Both the Democratic and the Republican activists have been vitally interested in cultural issues. But, of course, the activists of the 1960s and 1970s have become the affluent suburbanites of the 1990s and 2000s. The Democratic women are supposedly "soccer moms," but in reality married women are generally as Republican as their husbands. They are soccer moms, too. Although many would not recognize it, especially those who vote for the Democrats, most of the broader activists in both parties are basically economic conservatives. Their main economic interest is to ensure a high level of investment, a high return on capital, and a low interest rate environment that would promote a rising stock market. That inevitably has implications for government policy relevant to labor costs. This focus on the market has made the interests of the activists on broader economic policy very similar to those of the major campaign contributors.

The Republican and Democratic primary voters have tended to differ on the priority that they give to low taxes and a balanced budget, but both want low taxes in comparison with other industrial democracies. They favor de-regulation, relatively free trade, outsourcing, and large-scale immigration, all of which hold down wage levels. They favor a reduction in taxes on capital gains, dividends, and estates, but do not demand a decrease in the regressive nature of Social Security taxes or more equality in the size of the pensions offered.

The radical cultural and conservative economic policy favored both by the Democratic and Republican activists who came to dominate the nominating process of both parties was further strengthened by the choice of the states that were scheduled first in the front-loaded system of primaries. The United States was 79% urban in 2000, and over half the American population lived in 11 states whose urban population averaged 88.7%.[32] Yet the three key early primary contests were Iowa, New Hampshire, and South Carolina — states that were 61.1%, 59.3%, and 60.5% urban respectively. The next important primaries were Michigan, with 74.7% urban population and Virginia with 73.0%. Michigan is considered urban, but its urban

---

31. For a recent study, see William G. Mayer and Andrew E. Busch, *The Front-Loading Problem in Presidential Nominations* (Washington: The Brookings Institution, 2004).

population is actually 4.3 percentage points below the national average. Another early state, Arizona, is 88% urban, but much of its urban population is comprised either of conservative white retirees or of non-citizen, and thus non-voting, Hispanics.

The power of rural states was further strengthened by the failure of the parties to allocate convention delegates to states on the basis of their population. As Table 6 indicates, even the Democratic Party awards fewer delegates to the 8 populous industrial states than their population warrants (the Democrats seem more guided by the number of Electoral College votes), but the situation in the Republican Party is almost literally unbelievable. The Party gives heavy weight to the number of Republican voters in previous elections, and hence the red states have come to have a very heavy preponderance of delegates.

Since George H.W. Bush and Robert Dole did well in the red states in 1992 and 1996, the latter were well represented in the 2000 convention. As Table 6 shows, the Southern, Prairie, and Mountain states had 43.9% of the population in 2000 and 50.4% of the Republican delegates. The eight most populous Northern states had 42.3% of the population and 30.6% of the Republican delegates. Since Clinton had won some of the "red" states in 1996, Bush's sweeping victory in the Southern, Prairie, and Mountain states in 2000 gave the latter still more delegates in 2004. The 8 industrial states now had only 26.7% of the Republican delegates, while the Southern, Prairie, and Mountain states had 53.1%, almost exactly twice as many.[33]

This was the unspoken problem being raised by the Republican Brock Commission in 2000. It endorsed the so-called Delaware plan that required a long primary season and required the thirteen most populous states with 62% of the American population to hold their primaries in June. Obviously this might have little effect if candidates had no funds in June, but presumably the adoption of such a primary schedule would be accompanied by changes in the rules on campaign finance.

Yet, if the delegate structure is not changed, candidates from the large urban states still would have an enormous disadvantage. According to conventional wisdom, pro-choice candidates from the Northeast have no chance in the Republican Party primary because of the power of the religious right. The power of the religious

---

32. These were, together with their percentage of urban population, California (94.4%), New Jersey (94.4%), Massachusetts (91.4%), Florida (89.3%), Illinois (87.8%), Connecticut (87.7%), New York (87.5%), Maryland (86.1%), Washington (82.0%), Texas (82.5%), and Pennsylvania (77.1%). If Pennsylvania were replaced by District of Columbia (100%), Hawaii (91.5%), Nevada (91.5%), Rhode Island (90.9%), Arizona (88.2%), and Delaware (80.1%), the population of these 15 states was almost precisely 50% of the country's population, and 90.4% of their population is urban.
33. The 2000 delegate counts by states are in *CQ Guide to U.S. Elections*, p. 640. The totals of earlier convention years are in the same source. The 2004 totals are in Goldstein, *Guide to the 2004 Presidential Election*, pp. 35-37.

right is probably seriously exaggerated. The distribution of delegates may be more important. This is yet another problem that would be solved by a national primary.

Table 6: Proportion of the Population, Electoral College Votes, Party Members, and Convention Delegates by Party, 1952, 1968, 1988, 2000 and 2004

Type of State	% of the Population		% of Electoral College Votes	% of Democratic Convention Delegates	% of Republican Convention Delegates
	Previous Census	Next Census			
1952					
Southern	31.5%	30.7%	31.5%	32.0%	22.4%
Prairie and Mountain	6.4%	6.7%	9.6%	11.4%	13.6%
8 Large Industrial	45.3%	46.1%	40.0%	36.9%	39.3%
1968					
Southern	30.7%	30.7%	30.5%	27.2%	29.6%
Prairie and Mountain	6.7%	6.7%	10.4%	13.0%	14.1%
8 Large Industrial	46.1%	43.1%	40.0%	38.0%	36.0%
1988					
Southern	30.0%	33.9%	32.0%	30.5%	31.3%
Prairie and Mountain	7.5%	7.9%	11.3%	9.2%	13.7%
8 Large Industrial	43.1%	42.2%	37.9%	39.8%	34.3%
2000					
Southern	33.9%	35.2%	33.3%	28.8%	34.0%
Prairie and Mountain	7.9%	8.7%	11.2%	9.5%	16.4%
8 Large Industrial	42.2%	42.3%	36.8%	38.7%	30.6%
2004					
Southern	35.2%	—	34.2%	31.4%	35.6%
Prairie and Mountain	8.7%	—	11.9%	9.3%	17.5%
8 Large Industrial	42.3%	—	35.7%	38.8%	26.7%

Note: South = Confederacy plus Kentucky, Missouri, Oklahoma, and West Virginia; Prairie and Mountain = Alaska, Arizona, Colorado, Idaho, Kansas, Montana, Nebraska, Nevada, New Mexico, North Dakota, South Dakota, Utah, and Wyoming; 8 Large Industrial = California, Illinois, Massachusetts, Michigan, New Jersey, New York, Ohio, and Pennsylvania.

Sources: Census: Various years of the Statistical Abstract of the United States; Electoral College and Convention Delegates until 2000 are found in CQ Guide to U.S. Elections, vol. 1, pp. 617-641 and 739-771. The 2004 figures are from Michael L. Goldstein, Guide to the 2004 Presidential Election (Washington: CQ Press, 2003), pp. 35-37. The figures don't add to 100% because a small number of delegates are given to the territories.

THE CHANGING IMPACT OF THE SENATORIAL ELECTORS ON THE ELECTORAL COLLEGE

The Electoral College remained unchanged during the second half of the 20th century. Over the years, the major concern about the Electoral College had been that the winner of the national popular vote might not receive the most Electoral College votes. This did occur in the 1888 election, and it almost did so in a number of other elections (e.g., 1948, 1960, 1968, and 1976).[34] Many thought that a repetition of the 1888 election results in the modern world would be a disaster that de-legitimated the new President.

In reality, the most astonishing fact about the 2000 election is that Gore's loss in the Electoral College did not produce any significant discussion of the abolition of the Electoral College. Gore was frequently savaged for losing an election in which he won the most popular votes, and Bush proved able to rule very effectively without a so-called popular mandate. Indeed, Bush was a less effective President in 2005 when he actually did have a "mandate."

If the media had not focused all attention in 2000 on the problems of the vote count in Florida, observers would have given far more attention to a universally known but never-discussed feature of the Electoral College that was crucial in the final outcome. This is the awarding of two electors to each state for its Senators — what we will call the Senatorial electors. This feature of the Electoral College had relatively little impact in the past, but it became crucial when the South became competitive and when the Democrats ceased to compete effectively in the so-called red states.

The problem with the electors awarded for Senators is that the population of the states varies enormously today, but each state receives the same number of Senatorial electors. The number of members of the House of Representatives allocated to the states is more or less proportionate to their relative population, and California with its 33.9 million people in 2000 had 53 members of the House. This was 53 times both the population and the number of House members of North Dakota. Yet, North Dakota's two Senators gave it 3 Electoral College votes, one-eighteenth of California's 55. The 21 least populous states – usually called the small states — had 31.5 million people, 2.3 million fewer than California, but they had 91 Electoral College votes compared with California's 55. The 22 least populous states had 34.9 million people, 1.0 million more than California, and 99 Electoral College votes.

California is, of course, not the only populous state that is adversely affected by the awarding of electors for Senators. A careful reader of Table 6 will have noticed that the 8 industrial states had 42.3% of the population at the time of the 2000 census and received 35.7% of the Electoral College votes after the reapportionment based on that census. In 2000, the 9 most populous states — usually called the large states — had 51.2% of the country's population, and the other 42 (counting the District of Columbia) had 48.8%. The 9 most populous states receive an extra 18 Electoral College votes because they get electors for their two Senators, while the other 42 states were awarded an extra 84 votes for this reason. As a result, the 9 large states had only 241 Electoral College votes, 44.8% of the total in 2000. The other 42

---

34. Actually Kennedy received fewer votes than Nixon in 1960 by the most reasonable way of counting them. According to the accepted figures, Kennedy won the national popular vote by 118,500 votes. However, in Alabama neither Kennedy's nor Nixon's name was on the ballot, only lists of "Democratic" and "Republican" electors. In the Alabama Democratic primary, six of the victorious electors had pledged before the primary not to support the national Democratic candidate. The Democratic electors each won more or less 324,000 votes. If as few as 119,000 of the 324,000 Democratic voters preferred the unpledged electors, and surely the total was larger, then Nixon won the nationwide popular vote. A photo of the ballot can be found in *The Birmingham News*, November 6, 1960, Section B., p. 2. The case is discussed in George C. Edwards, III, *Why the Electoral College is Bad for America* (New Haven: Yale University Press, 2004), pp. 48–51.

had 297 Electoral College votes; that is 55.2% of the total. The 9 most populous states were 89% urban in 2000, while the other 42 states were 69% urban.

George W. Bush with his red state strategy naturally carried a disproportionate number of the rural states, and as a result, he won 30 states to Gore's 21 in 2000. This nine-state margin gave him 18 extra Senatorial electors, far more than his overall margin. If electors had been allocated on the basis of Representatives alone, Gore would have won in the Electoral College by a 225 to 211 vote margin.[35] In 2004, Bush won by 286 to 252 votes in the Electoral College; he carried 31 states and lost 20. Without the 22 extra Senatorial electors, he would have won 224 to 212, a victory that would have been reversed by a shift of 6,000 votes in Iowa, despite his 3-million-vote victory. The Electoral College does, in fact, behave in the most peculiar ways.

There are three reasons that observers have not given attention to the Senatorial electors.[36] One is that these electors originally were not that important. The least populous and most populous states had a similar socioeconomic character in 1787, and each of the least populous ones usually was closely linked economically with a more populous one — e.g., Rhode Island with Massachusetts, Delaware with Pennsylvania, and South Carolina with North Carolina. Historians understood that Senatorial electors were a relatively meaningless gesture to the less populous states, and modern observers have tended to assume this is still the case.

Second, when Karl Mundt and Strom Thurmond of South Carolina were trying to form a red state coalition in the 1950s and 1960s, they wrongly claimed that the winner-take-all rule gives excessive power to the urban minorities of the large Northern states. They proposed a constitutional amendment that would require the distribution of Electoral College votes on a district-by-district basis within the states. Opponents rightly said that the district system would increase the discrimination against the urban areas, but in making the case, they accepted the incorrect claim about the present system.

In addition, John Kennedy was trying to persuade the Democratic Party to nominate him for Vice President in 1956 and for President in 1960, and he was openly pro-

---

35. The impact of the small state bias in the Senate itself is even more dramatic. The 26 least populous states have a majority of Senators, but only 16.5% of the population in the 2000 election. The filibuster rule gives 41 Senators the ability to block Congressional legislation, and they can come from the 21 least populous states with only 11% of the country's population in 2000. Small wonder that Ethanol and other kinds of farm aid have been so popular.

36. Actually, there is a fourth reason. In the 1960s and early 1970s a number of scholars attempted to calculate whether the individual voter in a large or small state had a greater chance to cast the decisive vote in an election. The voter had a greater chance to affect the outcome in a state with low population, but the Electoral College votes affected by a one-vote victory would be less. The scholars concluded, presumably correctly, that the voter in the populous state had a greater chance. The problem, however, is that no voter has any chance to affect the outcome in a state, and the analysis is academic. What is important is whether the social forces in a group of states have more influence. Given the urban nature of the most populous states and the rural and small town nature of most of the least populous states, the important fact is that the rural forces in the least populous states clearly are over-represented because of the Senatorial electors.

claiming the advantage of a Catholic candidate. He had an obvious interest in saying that the large urban states in which Catholics were concentrated were given dispro-portionate power by the Electoral College.[37] Memories of this claim persist among scholars and political observers.

Third, the significance of the small state bias in the Electoral College varies with the distribution of the vote. If there is a landslide, neither party benefits from this or any bias in the Electoral College. Only 5 of the 25 presidential elections in the 20th century were competitive. The bias also does not favor either party if the two split the least populous states. For example, Carter won 99 Electoral College votes in 1976 in states with 10 Electoral College votes or less, while Ford won 106. In essence, Carter swept the "small" states of the South, and Ford won the "small" states in the Prairie and Mountain areas.

As Table 7 indicates, the 1948 and 1960 elections were so close in so many states that the relative impact of the least populous and most populous states paled in com-parison with the basically random outcome in both types of states. Nevertheless, if one party adopts a strategy targeted at the red states and the other has a blue state strategy, and if neither seriously challenges the other in its base, this intensifies the problem of the Senatorial electors.

It should be emphasized that the major negative consequence of the Senatorial electors is not the danger that the candidate with the fewer popular votes in a tightly-divided Electoral College will win because he or she wins the most small states. If that occurs again in the near future, it will be a self-correcting problem. The pressure for a national popular election of the President will become almost irresistible.

The major problem of the Senatorial electors is the persistent effect that the phenomenon has on all elections. Anthony Downs' famous model of party behavior indicates the reasons that parties normally move toward the "center" of the political electorate. Thus, if the Electoral College gives more weight to the more rural and small town voters of the least populous states, this should not give a permanent advantage to the Republicans. Instead, both parties should shift to respond to that weighting. The House of Representatives has a mild rural–small town bias and the Senate has a major one. (The 26 most rural states that elect majority of Senators contain 30.3% of the country's population.) The two parties, but especially the Republicans, give far more delegates to the more rural states. As a consequence, the parties should have no problem in adjusting to the implications of the Senatorial electors in the Electoral College.

---

37. See the 1956 memorandum written by Kennedy aide Ted Sorensen, published in 1960. "The 'Catholic Vote'— A Kennedy Staff Analysis," *U.S. News & World Report*, vol. XLIX, no. 5 (August 1, 1960), pp. 68–72.

Table 7: Percentage Point Differences Between Victor and Vanquished in
Presidential Elections, by Number of States, 1948, 1960, 1976, 2000, and 2004

	1948	1960	1976	2000	2004
	Number of States				
Differences (in Percentage Points)					
10+	16	15	20	29	31
5 to 9.9	7	13	11	9	10
2.5 to 4.9	9	3	6	6	4
Under 2.5	9	16	14	7	6
Distorted Because of Third Parties	7	3	0	0	0
Electoral College Votes at Stake in States with a Margin of < 2.5 Points	176	220	181	69	51

Note: 1968 was another close election, but George Wallace received support in such diverse states, with different consequences
that the margins are not meaningful.
Source: The figures through 2000 are calculated from CQ Guide to U.S. Elections, vol. 1, pp. 675-688. The 2004 figures are
calculated from the Almanac of American Politics, 2006 edition.

But, of course, that is precisely the problem. A political system that is weighted
to favor rural and small town areas both in the legislature and the Presidential
election is not likely to be properly responsive to the values and economic interests
of the metropolitan areas. It is extremely easy to see why the Republican Party (or
the Democratic Party, if it had followed a natural coalitional strategy of combining
the Catholics and Evangelicals in the 1970s) would choose a red state strategy. What
is very difficult to fathom is why the other party would not look for issues that
increase its competitiveness in those overweighted states.

CHAPTER 7. THE ORIGINS OF THE REPUBLICAN RED-STATE STRATEGY

Any concept of "red states" and "blue states" in its modern meaning would have been largely incomprehensible prior to the 1990s. The current Southern red states were, of course, solid Democratic territory until the 1950s. Prior to the New Deal, the Republican coalition combined the red Prairie and Mountain states with the blue states and battleground states of the Old Midwest and the East. The only exceptions were elections in which ethnic or foreign policy issues were decisive.

During the New Deal period, the left-wing Midwestern politicians and activists who had long been in the Republican Party moved to the Democratic Party, and the small farmers who had provided the mass base for the populists gradually disappeared with technological change. As a result, the Midwest came to constitute the conservative wing of the Republican Party, but they were "conservative" in a very different sense than is conveyed by that word today.

Thus, the major Midwestern Republican politicians of the 1940s and 1950s did not come from the Prairie "red states" but from the blue or battleground states of 2004. Three dominant Republican Senators of the 1940s and 1950s were Everett Dirksen of Illinois, Arthur Vandenberg of Michigan, and Robert A. Taft of Ohio. Two others, Senator Joseph McCarthy and Governor Harold Stassen, came from Wisconsin and Minnesota, respectively. Nearly all were more moderate than the conservatives of today. Stassen was more liberal than most, but Taft favored public housing. McCarthy was a Wisconsin moderate who focused on social welfare measures before moving toward his famous anti-Communist position in late 1949. He headed the Wisconsin Stassen organization prior to the 1948 election.[1]

The Republican "Southern strategy" from the 1930s to the mid-1970s was also very different from that of the Republicans in later years. In the 1940s, the Republicans promoted civil rights legislation in Northern states. They were largely trying to court Ellis Island immigrants, but they also saw this as the way to become competitive in the South. In the North the Republicans had been the party of the

"Country Club" Protestants and the "Main Street, Rotary Club, blue-suited" Protestants of smaller towns and cities.[2] They sought the same type of voters in the South, and these were the Southerners who were the most moderate on race relations.

On the surface, the Republican Southern strategy was an intelligent one. The growing number of black votes for the Democrats in the South would inevitably push the more racist white Southerners toward the Republican Party. Just as the Republicans won the nativist vote after 1854 without the crude appeals of the Know Nothing Party, so a modern Republican Party could obtain the racist votes in the South without taking an anti-black position. It simply had to adopt a program on desegregation that was not as extreme as that of black Democratic activists, an easy task.

The first major politician to call for a modern red-state strategy was Senator Karl Mundt of South Dakota. In 1948, Strom Thurmond of South Carolina won 39 Electoral College votes in the South as a third-party candidate, and in the 1950s Mundt traveled several times to South Carolina to appeal for a realignment.[3] More directly, he was asking Strom Thurmond to leave the Democratic Party for the Republican, or, really, was supporting a move that Thurmond had in mind. Mundt argued that "Southern Democrats and rural Republicans in this country have much in common" and "we need to do some political engineering so we can work and vote together."[4]

> We might develop the kind of political realinement [sic] that I was talking about when I spoke to you in Charleston some years ago.... [What is important is] getting the people who think alike in this country and who think conservatively and in terms of a modification and limitation of the powers of the Central Government ... into some kind of political party or political apparatus or political association or political instrumentalities so that they can vote alike for the same candidate on the same ticket regardless of what the party label is or where they live geographically.

---

1. An excellent sense of McCarthy and his evolution can be gained from the scrapbooks of newspaper stories about him in the Joseph McCarthy Papers, Marquette University. He almost never used the anti-Communist issue until he started testing it in local speeches in late 1949 and then on the national level in January 1950, after Dean Acheson asserted he would not turn his back on Alger Hiss. The scrapbooks leave the impression that the Senate Democratic victory in 1948 left McCarthy frustrated and gave him the feeling in 1949 that he needed another issue to be reelected in 1952. From childhood, he had internalized the classic anti-English attitudes of the old Irish, and he genuinely detested Acheson.
2. The latter is a phrase applied to Senator Robert Dole of Kansas. Jake H. Thompson, *Bob Dole: The Republicans' Man for All Seasons*, updated ed. (New York: Donald I. Fine, Inc., 1996), p. 243.
3. Thurmond actually won 38 votes in the four states he carried, but one elector from Tennessee who was pledged to Nixon instead voted for Thurmond.
4. He put his 1956 speech in South Carolina in the *Congressional Record*. Karl E. Mundt, "From South Dakota to South Carolina — An Invitation and a Challenge," *Congressional Record — House*, June 4, 1956, pp. 9442–9448. Mundt's position is discussed in James MacGregor Burns, *The Deadlock of Democracy: Four-Party Politics in America* (Englewood Cliffs, NJ: Prentice Hall, Inc., 1963), pp. 295–300.

Thurmond used this argument as a way to justify leaving a Democratic Party that he said was controlled by Northern minorities. This obviously worked out well for him personally, but when Barry Goldwater followed the Mundt-Thurmond strategy on the national level in 1964, he suffered a crushing defeat. A strategy that might work in the two rural states of South Dakota and South Carolina (they were 59% and 61% rural, respectively, at the time) did not seem viable at the national level for a country that was only 30% rural. Then Nixon continued the traditional Republican Southern strategy and was very negative toward the Evangelical voters. Ronald Reagan was to sweep the blue states as well as the red ones. George H.W. Bush almost duplicated his success in 1988.

In short, a Republican red state alliance based in large part on Evangelicals would have seemed deeply unnatural in 1965 and quite unlikely in 1975. The Republican Party was the Protestant party of the North. But that meant the mainline churches: the Episcopalians, Presbyterians, Lutherans, and Methodists. The members of these churches, especially in the North, were generally far better off than the average Southern Baptist or member of an Evangelical sect. The cultural values of these mainline Northern churches were also liberal. They had opposed slavery and segregation, and they had been the main supporters of women's rights. Both economically and culturally, the Southern Evangelicals seemed to have far more in common with the Northern Catholics than with the mainline Protestants.

Even if the Southern Evangelicals could be attracted to an alliance with the mainline churches, it was very unclear which Republican politicians would seek to form such a coalition. After all, both Reagan and George H. W. Bush won blue states as well as red states. The Republicans inevitably would be forced to make a choice, and they might well decide that there were more Electoral College votes in the blue states. Much, of course, would depend both on the strategy the Democrats chose and on the internal structure of power within the Republican Party.

THE AMBIGUITY OF A SOUTHERN STRATEGY

During the 1950s, everyone understood that legal segregation and the disenfranchisement of the black voter would be coming to an end in the Southern states. Black voter turnout was going to rise rapidly in the area, and blacks in the South were likely to vote as heavily for Democratic candidates as they did in the North. Some whites were certain to shift to the Republican Party simply because they could no longer identify with the party that received 90 percent of the black vote. They would respond as the Northern Scotch-Irish and Protestants had done in the 1840s and 1850s when Catholics began pouring into Andrew Jackson's party. But since the South was rapidly industrializing, the middle classes on whom the Republicans had been relying were also rapidly increasing in size.

In the new circumstances, the Republicans would find it possible to win Electoral College votes in the South. They naturally thought a great deal about how to maximize their votes in the region, as of course, did the Democrats as well. Both parties would have to have some kind of "Southern strategy." The question was — what kind of Southern strategy?

As William Safire discusses in his dictionary on political language, the phrase "Southern strategy" is a simple pejorative "attack phrase attributing racist or at least political motives toward any position taken on desegregation or busing that would be well received by most Southern whites." In Safire's words, "the phrase is firmly fixed in the political lexicon not as a strategy, but as a charge of deviousness and discrimination."[5]

In fact, both the Republicans and Democrats had a variety of different Southern strategies from which to choose. The nomination of a non-partisan figure such as Eisenhower in 1952 was one way for Republicans to make it easy for Southerners to vote for a Republican. Kennedy's selection of Lyndon Johnson of Texas as his running mate in 1960 was a Southern strategy. The same was true of the Democrats' nomination of Jimmy Carter, Bill Clinton, and Al Gore for President and of the Republican choice of the two Bushes from Texas. The South was economically poor and culturally conservative, and the Southern Democrat, Lyndon Johnson, chose to appeal to it on economic grounds and the Southern Democrat, Jimmy Carter, chose to emphasize conservative cultural themes. Both were Southern strategies.

The term "Southern strategy" was first used in a policy sense in the 1950s in connection with Barry Goldwater as he thought of running for President.[6] In the future, conservatives were to depict Goldwater as the precursor of Reagan and George W. Bush, a farsighted visionary who had been unlucky in his opponent and in the circumstances in which he ran. This is misleading. Goldwater did seek an alliance of what would become the red states, but he adopted a very different cultural policy than Reagan's and Bush's.

Goldwater's belief in a weak federal government in the economic realm implied a federal government that would have limited power in attacking segregation in the South. Yet Goldwater was extremely libertarian in his cultural policy. On issues such as equal rights for women and a free choice for women on abortion, Goldwater did not follow most Republican leaders to the right in the 1980s. It is not an aberration that Hillary Clinton began as a supporter of Goldwater in 1964.

Nixon, Reagan, and George W. Bush were each to have different versions of a Southern strategy than Goldwater. Nixon favored the traditional Republican appeal to the Southern middle class and assumed that a denunciation of the Northern cultural radicals on non-racial grounds would win enough extra voters for victory. He distinguished between imposed desegregation and imposed integration, the latter symbolized by school busing. Nixon thought the South would accept the former if the government engaged in respectful negotiation rather than confrontation. Nixon's overall position was suggested by his frequently expressed desire to have the prag

---

5. "Southern Strategy," in William Safire, *Safire's New Political Dictionary: The Definitive Guide to the New Language of Politics* (New York: Random House, 1993), pp. 734–735.
6. This is the testimony of Goldwater himself. See "Southern strategy," in Safire, *Safire's New Political Dictionary*, p. 734.

matic conservative John Connally as his successor. Connally was the former Democratic governor of Texas and an associate of Lyndon Johnson.

In 1969, a political aide in the Nixon Administration, Kevin Phillips, wrote a book entitled *The Emerging Republican Majority*, in which he presented a table about the evolution of voting patterns in Virginia to show that Nixon's Southern strategy was working. (See Table 1.) Since the Southern middle class was growing and was voting Republican, Phillips dismissed the strategy of Goldwater and especially the Goldwater activists with scorn as "'revolutionary' Republicanism." He spoke for Nixon.

Reagan shared Goldwater's absorption with economic and foreign policy questions, and his speeches in the 1970s were devoted almost exclusively to these themes. He never showed any tendency to exploit racial issues, but, unlike Goldwater, Reagan did support a number of the cultural issues of interest to the religious right. In reality, however, Reagan tended either to support rather meaningless symbolic issues such as a constitutional amendment to ban abortion or to emphasize rather ill-defined "traditional values." He had made his reputation as governor by denouncing a rather easy target, the Berkeley radicals of the Vietnam era.

Table 1: Growing Political Power and Changing Party Support, Four Virginia Suburban Counties, 1924–1968

	1924	1936	1948	1960	1968
Total Votes Cast for President	8,000	20,000	39,000	146,000	271,000
Four-County Share of Total Virginia Vote	4%	6%	9%	19%	21%
Democratic Share of the Total Vote for President in Four Counties	70%	68%	43%	44%	31%

Note: The counties are Chesterfield, Henrico, Arlington, and Fairfax.

Source: Kevin Phillips, The Emerging Republican Majority (New Rochelle, NY: Arlington House, 1969), p. 266.

George W. Bush is a President about whom no consensus has formed. But whatever Bush's motives, he has strongly emphasized cultural issues that solidified his support in his Southern political base. But he also has promoted economic programs such as prescription drug coverage and reconstruction of the Gulf Coast that appealed to the economic interests of his Southern base. Two obvious questions arise about the future (other than the impact of the President's Iraq policy, whatever the results of that policy may be). First, what would happen if the Democrats were to return to a Southern strategy that put the poorer Southern whites under cross-pressure by appealing to their economic interests? How would the Republicans respond to that challenge? Second, Bush has had an economic policy that appeals both to the well-to-do and to the poor, but it has not been based on what many consider the necessary hard choices. Is it viable over the long term? The issue of the proper "Southern strategy" is a perpetual one and always depends partly on the actions of the other party.

The Red State Strategy of Barry Goldwater

In one sense, Karl Mundt's 1956 appeal for an alliance between South Carolina and South Dakota was prescient. The two states were to vote together for the Republican candidate in all the presidential elections from 1968 to 2004. Indeed, South Carolina also voted Republican in 1964, but South Dakota voted Democratic that year. Nevertheless, the South Dakota public was always liberal, even populist, on economic issues, and it was to elect 9 Democrats in its 15 Senate elections between 1962 and 2004. George McGovern was its Senator from 1963 to 1981.[7] Mundt actually was seeking new cultural issues to counteract the economic preferences of South Dakotans at a time when the traditional foreign policy appeal that Republicans made to German-Americans was losing its meaning.

In 1964, neither student radicalism nor affirmative action had begun. The major non-economic issue was civil rights, but this was defined as a lack of discrimination (not affirmative action) and the "I have a dream" appeal of Martin Luther King for peaceful integration. Those who wanted to maintain segregation understood the implications of Goldwater's position on economic federalism.

Goldwater believed that the government did not have the power to punish private businesses that discriminated. For this reason he voted against the Civil Rights Act of 1964, but said he would have happily voted for it if it did not contain Titles II and VII that applied to private employers. Goldwater's position on federalism did not, however, reflect a racist set of attitudes. He long had belonged to the NAACP. He was a strong supporter of black rights in principle and voted for the 1957 and 1960 civil rights bills. "I am half-Jewish, and I know something about discrimination," he declared. Goldwater also was deeply committed to a libertarian cultural position on the issues promoted by radicals in the 1960s. In the 1980s he became a very close friend of George McGovern.

In 1964, Goldwater was, of course, not seen as a precursor of anyone, but as a man who himself had a precursor, Senator Robert Taft. The battle between Taft and Eisenhower for the Republican nomination in 1952 had been bitter, and the Midwestern conservatives were angry that they had been defeated at every convention since 1940. Nixon's nomination in 1960 was basically inevitable, but Taft conservatives saw him as far too liberal on economic questions. Goldwater was truly in the Taft tradition in the economic sphere, indeed, the Taft of 1936 who had deeply feared government intervention rather than the more moderate Taft who had become a US Senator in 1938.

Goldwater fundamentally miscalculated attitudes on economic issues both in the South and the North. Some Southern politicians were, of course, quite conservative (Lyndon Johnson privately called them "Confederates"), but poor white Southerners were conservative on cultural issues (especially race) and liberal on eco-

---

7. South Dakota rejected George McGovern as a presidential candidate in 1972 by a 54% to 47% margin, but re-elected him as Senator in 1974 by a 53% to 47% margin. Another Senator, Tom Daschle, was Democratic leader in the Senate from 1987 to 2005.

nomic issues.[8] Many Southern politicians like Johnson either shared this set of ideas or responded to it. The Mountain and Prairie states like South Dakota had given large number of votes to Robert La Follette in 1924 and remained populist on economic questions.

George Reedy, a key political aide to Senator Lyndon Johnson in 1959 and 1960, wrote many memoranda for Johnson that seem intended to give his boss arguments (talking points, in modern jargon) to use to defend his position. Two of these memoranda in early 1960 caught the thinking of many Southern politicians, including Johnson. The Reedy memorandum written in late February 1960 referred to "the unnatural alliance between the Republicans and the Southern Democrats in which the Southern Democrats have to give up their ability to work for a number of things the South needs simply because they have to give up a quid pro quo for Republican help in sabotaging civil rights legislation." Ten days later Reedy wrote a second memorandum that explicitly called for the South to remember its common interests with the West and Midwest and the long-time alliance in Congress that often had been built on those common interests:[9]

> The question which every Southern Democrat should ask himself is NOT whether he is willing to cut his ties to the "civil rights" Democrats, but whether he is willing to cut his ties to the Western and Middlewestern Democrats who have some understanding of his problems and are willing to meet him half way.

In addition to misjudging the economic views of the Southern and trans-Mississippi voters, Goldwater also did not have a foreign policy congenial to the large German-American population in the Midwest to which Taft appealed. Goldwater fervently embraced the cultural issue of anti-Communism, but "anti-Communism" was a word that served a wide variety of purposes. For economic conservatives, it expressed the fear that the New Deal might well lead to full socialism or even Communism. For those interested in foreign policy in the 1930s, "anti-Communism" often implied that Hitler was the lesser evil and suggested the advisability of appeasement. For religious conservatives, Marx's deeply anti-religious attitude, expressed in the charge that religion was the opium of the people, made "Godless Communism" a perfect symbol of everything that was wrong in the modern world. But, in addition, "anti-Communism" in the 1940s often meant that a harsh economic treatment of Germany would lead to Communism in Western Europe and that those who promoted such treatment were serving Communist purposes, perhaps consciously.

Republicans such as Robert Taft, John Foster Dulles, and Richard Nixon always made a strong implicit distinction between anti-Communism and policy toward the

---

8. For the survey data on this in the 1950s and the early 1960s, see Don M. Freeman, "Religion and Southern Politics: A Study of the Political Behavior of Southern White Protestants" (PhD dissertation, University of North Carolina, 1964).

9. Memoranda of George E. Reedy for Lyndon Johnson, February 27, 1960, and March 8, 1960, United States Senate Office Files of George Reedy, Box 430 (1 of 2), Lyndon Baines Johnson Presidential Library. See the discussion of this strategy, above. Carl V. Harris, "Right Fork or Left Fork: The Section–Party Alignment of Southern Democrats in Congress, 1873–1897," *The Journal of Southern History*, vol. XLII, no. 4 (November 1976), pp. 471–508.

Soviet Union. Anti-Communism implied a reconstruction of Germany against a Soviet and Communist threat. Nevertheless, a refusal to negotiate with the Soviet Union meant an acceptance of the division of Europe, especially Germany. Robert Taft thus was consistent in using the anti-Communist theme and in voting against the ratification of NATO that formalized the division of Germany.

Goldwater, by contrast, was deeply suspicious of negotiations and even relations with the Soviet Union. He did not really approve of cultural exchanges with Communist countries and acted as if he would end diplomatic relations with the Soviet Union if that were politically possible. This total rejection of contact with evil was very satisfying to religious fundamentalists, but it was scarcely what the German-Americans of the Midwest region desired. Although seeking to follow Taft, Goldwater was rejecting the Taft foreign policy position that was most appealing to them. Goldwater's policy also frightened suburban Republicans at a time of tension in Berlin and Southeast Asia, and he offended cultural conservatives with his libertarianism. Small wonder he lost in such a landslide.

In the future, Southern conservative activists — really the Goldwater activists and their descendants — offered a new version of what Reedy called "the unnatural alliance." They argued that Great Society measures were primarily designed to help those who wouldn't work (implicitly the blacks) and that these measures would be accompanied by social engineering unwanted in the South. The conservative activists, many of them very secular in their own attitudes, essentially offered to support the religious cultural issues of interest to the poor whites if the latter would forego economic welfare measures of benefit to themselves. The religious televangelists of the 1970s gave way to the secular right-wing radio-evangelists of the 1990s and 2000s, such as Rush Limbaugh, who adopted the conservative cultural position for coalitional reasons. Goldwater never modified his cultural position to achieve his economic goals.

RICHARD NIXON AND THE TRADITIONAL REPUBLICAN SOUTHERN STRATEGY

The politician who was most often accused of a "Southern strategy" with racial overtones was Richard Nixon. In fact, Nixon was the great centrist politician of mid-20th century America, and he was less the sinner than the sinned-against in the political game of distortion and smear. Nixon had enormous personal insecurities (what his closest lieutenants called "his dark side"), and they led him to actions that ultimately destroyed him.[10] Barry Goldwater was to tell the newsman, David Broder, "It was the biggest shock of my life to suddenly realize in a flash, after knowing this guy like a brother, that he was a dishonest man all the way through."[11] Nixon had

---

10. In retrospect, one of the striking features of Nixon's speech accepting his nomination for President in 1960 came at its very beginning: "To stand here before this great convention to hear your expression of affection...is, of course, the greatest moment of my life." Few politicians would have used "affection" in this way on this occasion. Acceptance speech, *The New York Times*, July 29, 1960, p. 9.

absolutely none of Kennedy's sense of humor or irony to lessen his intensity or lighten his appeal.

Yet none of this affected the general policy positions that Nixon took. Politicians do not simply compete for the center. They also strive to "position" their opponents on the extreme end of the spectrum. Jimmy Carter's chief adviser on issues in the 1976 campaign, Stuart Eizenstat, was typical in the language he used in his advice to Carter in early 1976:[12]

> Push [Senator Henry] Jackson to the right as competing with Wallace for the far-right.... Position yourself as the moderate alternative to Jackson-Wallace on one side and Udall on the other. This is easily done by pushing Jackson to the right.

Nixon misrepresented liberals to make them seem further to the left than was accurate, and they in turn placed him too far to the right. So long as the media and many scholars divided the Republicans into two wings — the liberals represented by Nelson Rockefeller and Harvard University's Ripon Society, and the conservatives — then there was no room for moderates. This automatically put Nixon on the right.[13] But James Reichley, an aide in the Nixon and Ford White House and later a scholar at the Brookings Institution, was right that the Republican Party had four different groups: stalwarts (those based on small cities, such as Everett Dirksen), moderates (those such as Thomas Dewey), progressives (those such as Nelson Rockefeller), and fundamentalists (those such as Barry Goldwater, or at least his supporters).[14]

When Nixon first ran for Congress against Jerry Voorhis, he wrote a letter in May 1946 to the liberal Minnesota governor, Harold Stassen, praising "your campaign to liberalize the Republican Party because I feel strongly that the party must adopt a constructive progressive program."[15] In April 1950, as Nixon prepared to run for Senate, the political editor of the Los Angeles Times accurately wrote that he was "liberal, alert, [and] up-and-coming" in his domestic policy position, a politician in the mainstream of the liberal Republican Party of Earl Warren.[16]

11. David S. Broder, *Changing of the Guard: Power and Leadership in America* (New York: Simon and Schuster, 1980), p. 173.
12. Stu Eizenstat to Jimmy Carter, "Florida statement and Positioning Yourself vis-à-vis-Jackson for the long haul," Undated, but clearly written in late Feb. 1976. 1976 Presidential Campaign, Issues Office — Stuart Eizenstat, Box 25, Memos to J.C. Folder," Jimmy Carter Presidential Library.
13. For a book that essentially defines liberal in this way, but that presents a very valuable insight into a group that receives relatively little attention in this book, see Nicol C. Rae, *The Decline and Fall of the Liberal Republicans: From 1952 to the Present* (New York: Oxford University Press, 1989).
14. James Reichley, *Conservatives in an Age of Change: The Nixon and Ford Administrations* (Washington: Brookings Institution, 1981), pp. 22–34.
15. Irwin F. Gellman, *The Contender, Richard Nixon: The Congress Years, 1946–52* (New York: Free Press, 1999), p. 75.
16. Kyle Palmer, "Cutting Teeth is No Fun," *Los Angeles Times*, April 2, 1950, part 2, p. 4. A wide number of observers made the same evaluation a quarter of a century later. For example, Garry Wills wrote in 1969 that Nixon is "more deeply and consistently liberal than Eisenhower.... The authentic voice of the surviving American liberalism." Garry Wills, *Nixon Agonistes: The Crisis of the Self-Made Man* (Boston: Houghton Mifflin, 1969), p. 582.

California voters clearly perceived Nixon this way. He was elected to the House in 1946, defeating a popular incumbent (Jerry Voorhis) by a 56% to 43% margin. In 1948 he won both the Republican and Democratic primaries in his district when he ran for re-election. Then in 1950 Nixon won a 59% to 41% landslide in a statewide Senatorial race against a weak non-incumbent, Helen Gahagan Douglas. Opponents were to describe these early campaigns as McCarthy-like in character, but this is basically incorrect.[17]

In the foreign policy sphere, Nixon's opponents were to depict him as a hard-line cold warrior who cynically took a pro-détente position in 1971 and 1972 for electoral purposes. This was even less accurate. In his first 1946 campaign against Jerry Voorhis, Nixon explicitly supported the "Byrnes–Vandenberg" foreign policy in his campaign advertisements. At this time, both Byrnes and Vandenberg hoped to negotiate a moderate settlement with the Soviet Union on the German question, probably something akin to that adopted with respect to Austria. After the campaign Nixon wrote an answer to a student's letter saying that he and Voorhis had not differed on foreign policy in the campaign.[18]

Nixon's mother was a Quaker named Milhous, a name that indicated she was the product of an earlier intermarriage between a Quaker and a German in Pennsylvania. Nixon always had the foreign policy instincts that would be predicted of a German-American Quaker from the Midwest. Like most major Midwestern politicians, Nixon's use of the anti-Communism issue never had the anti-Soviet foreign policy connotations attributed to it. It was a general cultural issue attractive to conservatives, especially religious conservatives, but its foreign policy content centered on the opposition to American policy in Germany. As has been seen, Nixon privately compared Truman's policy in Germany to cannibalism in late 1947.

It was not simply a desire to balance the ticket on traditional criteria of age and geography that led Eisenhower, the first full German-American President since Martin Van Buren, to select Nixon as his running mate.[19] The two had quite similar views on foreign policy. Eisenhower chose John Foster Dulles as his Secretary of State both because Dulles had ties with Thomas Dewey and because his postwar policy on Germany made him acceptable to the Midwestern wing of the party (and to Eisenhower himself). Dulles had headed the major Wall Street firm that had been heavily involved in business with Germany in the 1930s, and in 1939 he consistently favored American non-involvement in Europe. He was inclined to criticize Britain and France as much as, if not more than, Germany.[20]

---

17. These statements are based on a careful reading of the papers and speeches of these two campaigns in the Richard Nixon Library in Yorba Linda, California. This work supports the similar judgment of the solid book on the early Nixon, Gellman, *The Contender, Richard Nixon.* Gellman's book too is based on these papers and many other sources.
18. The postcard is found in Folder 14 (Pamphlets) and the letter to Nathan Pratt Hause of January 21, 1947 is found in the folder "Letters or Reflections, 1947." Both are in Box 1 of the Nixon 1946 Campaign Collection, Richard Nixon Library and Birthplace.
19. Herbert Hoover was half German and half English Quaker, and he had the expected foreign policy position in the 1930s and 1940s.

In the 1960 election, it was John Kennedy, not Nixon, who talked about the balance of power shifting to the Soviet Union — about a disastrously threatening position in Cuba, a missile gap, and the need for a major increase in military spending.[21] Kennedy named the hawkish Henry Jackson, Senator from Washington, to the post of chairman of the Democratic National Committee.

Nixon, by contrast, insisted in his 1960 acceptance speech at the Republican Convention that "while it is dangerous to see nothing wrong in America, it is just as wrong not to recognize what is right about America.... America is the strongest nation militarily, economically and ideologically."[22] He chose the liberal Henry Cabot Lodge, Jr., of Massachusetts, Ambassador to the United Nations, as his running mate. Lodge, from Kennedy's home state of Massachusetts, was scarcely a wise choice from a geographical point of view, but he was a symbol that Nixon favored the moderate and pro-détente foreign policy of Eisenhower.[23] Nixon also signaled a more moderate course in his acceptance speech at the convention. The *New York Times* gave it the headline, "Nixon Asks that Fight Against Communism Be Waged on Social and Economic Ground."[24]

When Nixon ran for President in 1968, a year of great political disaster for the Democratic Party, he only defeated Hubert Humphrey 43.4% to 42.7%, while George Wallace received 13.5% of the vote. Nixon's percentage of the vote was not that far above Goldwater's 38.5% in 1964. Simple election statistics dictated Nixon's thoughts about the 1972 election and, therefore, his basic strategy in his first term. In particular, he would have to try to win the Wallace vote or, more important, compete simultaneously again with Wallace and with a Democratic liberal. (The assassination attempt on Wallace in May 1972 and his resulting paralysis had a major, but difficult to assess, impact on the election.)

Some Republican theorists wanted to see the Wallace voter as a Democrat in transition to the Republican Party, but Eisenhower had received 57.4% of the vote in 1956 and Nixon himself 49.5% in 1960. The total turnout in 1968 was 4.4 million higher than in 1960, but Nixon received 2.3 million votes fewer than he had in 1960.

---

20. Ronald W. Pruessen, *John Foster Dulles: The Road to Power* (New York: Free Press, 1982), pp. 127–132, 155–161, 168–172 and 178–185, e.g., p. 180.
21. For a collection of his pre-1960 speeches, see John F. Kennedy, *The Strategy of Peace*, edited by Allen Nevins (New York: Harper, 1960), pp. 38–45 (Missile gap) and 99–102 and 183–185 (Conventional weapons).
22. Acceptance speech at the Republican Convention, *The New York Times*, July 29, 1960, p. 9.
23. Lodge was in charge of the campaign to draft Eisenhower and then secure his nomination in 1952, and Eisenhower recommended to Nixon that he choose Lodge. William J. Miller, *Henry Cabot Lodge: A Biography* (New York: James H. Heineman, 1967), pp., 216–252. Given Kennedy's very narrow margin of victory, it is natural to speculate whether another running mate for Nixon — probably Secretary of Labor James P. Mitchell from New Jersey or Representative Gerald Ford of Michigan, both prominently mentioned — would have given Nixon the geographical balance needed for the election. That is quite possible. Austin C. Wehrwein, "Lodge Gets Word He is Nixon Choice for Running Mate, *The New York Times*, July 27, 1960, pp. 1 and 16 (about Ford and the Midwest) and Leo Egan, "Candidate Picks Lodge for Second Place," *The New York Times*, July 28, 1960, pp. 1 and 12 (about Mitchell).
24. *The New York Times*, July 29, 1960, p. 1.

The Wallace voters came from both parties, and it was not certain which way they would move or how much they were supporting Wallace because of racial issues. Wallace was a populist not only on race, but also on economic issues and many other cultural ones. After he repudiated his views on segregation, Wallace was re-elected governor of Alabama with considerable black support.

Those who charged that Nixon had a racist Southern strategy often cited the Kevin Phillips book on "the emerging Republican majority."[25] Phillips ended his book with a map that gave the modern "red states" of the South, Prairies, and Mountain areas to the Republicans — precisely the states on which Goldwater had focused. Critics charged this was proof that Nixon had a Southern strategy that neglected the Northeast and the Midwestern states east of the Mississippi (the Old Northwest). In fact, Phillips was making precisely the opposite case.

As Phillips emphasized, the Confederate, Mountain, and Prairie states had only 189 of the 270 Electoral College votes needed for victory, and he did not try to reach a bare minimum by adding a few kindred states such as Indiana, Kentucky, West Virginia and, perhaps Ohio.[26] Rather he took the red states for granted as the natural Republican base and conceded New York and New England to the Democrats. Yet he then drew the logical conclusion: the states from New Jersey to Iowa, as well as the three states on the Pacific Coast, were the battleground area, especially the suburbia within them. Phillips thought the correct Republican strategy was try to win these battleground areas, and the title of his book showed his confidence that this could be done.

When Phillips condemned "revolutionary Republicanism" — that is, both Goldwater's economic views and the views of the cultural conservatives — he thought that both the Goldwater and the religious right strategy in the South were losing ones.[27] In addition, Nixon seemed genuinely committed to a racially integrated society. When the Congress passed the first Civil Rights Bill in 1957, the Southern leader, Senator Richard Russell of Georgia, pointed specifically to him as one of its strong supporters. The Attorney General, Russell said, "will be constantly pressed by the Vice President of the United States to apply the great powers of the law to the Southern states at such places and in such time and manner as the NAACP, ... of which the Vice President is the most distinguished member, may demand."[28] At the 1960 Convention, Nixon ostentatiously forced the Platform Committee to reverse itself and adopt a more liberal civil rights plank.[29] Nixon told his chief of staff, H. R. Haldeman, that he was particularly liberal on race issues.[30]

---

25. Kevin Phillips, *The Emerging Republican Majority* (New Rochelle, NY: Arlington House, 1969).
26. Phillips, *The Emerging Republican Majority*, pp. 472–473.
27. A conservative political consultant gives an excellent sense of the feelings of conservatives toward Nixon at this time in his book on Reagan's 1976 campaign. Craig Shirley, *Reagan's Revolution: The Untold Story of the Campaign That Started It All* (Nashville: Nelson Current, 2005).
28. Anthony Lewis, "Russell Assails Nixon on Rights," *The New York Times*, August 31, 1957, p. 1.
29. W. H. Lawrence, "Nixon Says Rights Plank Must Be Made Stronger," *The New York Times*, July 26, 1960, p. 1.

Nixon's civil rights record as President was remarkable — really even more liberal than that of Lyndon Johnson. When Nixon came to power, only 6% of black students in the South went to desegregated schools, but this figure had risen into the mid-80s by the time he had left office.[31] Most give the prime credit for the desegregation of the Nixon years to firmer Supreme Court decisions, but the Supreme Court is very sensitive to signals from an Administration when it requires Administration support in implementing its decisions. Nixon and the Southern governors with whom he was negotiating were happy to have firmer Court decisions to strengthen their bargaining position with the Southern voters.

Nixon thought that the South was ready to move towards legal desegregation if an Administration treated the region with respect and as an equal to the North.[32] Those Southerners who did not want to send their children to the local desegregated schools had discovered that the local churches would provide private schools, and hence they were less resistant. In the 1970 elections, the South elected a number of moderate Democratic governors who were willing to cooperate with the Administration on the question. These governors included Jimmy Carter of Georgia.[33]

Nixon's appeals to the Wallace supporters in 1972 contained little of a racist character. His main target was the student activists, both their demonstrations that transcended legal boundaries, and their violation of traditional norms in the sexual realm and the use of drugs. Nixon's own term in this campaign was "the rock throwers and obscenity shouters." Everyone understood that he was talking about the student radicals and protestors who had a permissive life style and were protesting the Vietnam War.

Indeed, Nixon risked offending the Wallace voters in the North by his direct support of integration in the work place. He had publicly opposed bussing since 1964, and he emphasized his opposition again in May 1972. This was an important symbolic issue in itself, but, in addition, it allowed him to emphasize his determination to treat the North and South alike. Liberal white Northerners often called for bussing that they were avoiding themselves by fleeing to the suburbs. By the same token, Nixon was able to persuade the Southerners of his even-handed approach by promoting affirmative action in hiring in Philadelphia.

But whatever the reason, Nixon became the first President to introduce race-conscious affirmative action in hiring, including the establishment of semi-quotas in hiring for firms in Philadelphia with government contracts. Construction workers were a key group supporting Wallace, and Nixon's policy was politically daring. Nixon also moved toward a similar affirmative action policy for universities.

---

30. Quoted in Robert Mason, *Richard Nixon and the Quest for a New Majority* (Chapel Hill: University of North Carolina, 2004), p. 145.
31. Dean J. Kotlowski, *Nixon's Civil Rights: Politics, Principle, and Policy* (Cambridge, MA: Harvard University Press, 2001), pp. 15–37. The figures are p. 37.
32. See the memoir of Nixon's chief political aide for the South, Harry S. Dent, *The Prodigal South Returns to Power* (New York: Wiley, 1978).
33. *Time* had a cover story on the series of governors, but put Carter's picture alone on the cover in response to pressure from Coca Cola. "New Day a'coming in the South," *Time*, May 31, 1971, pp. 14–20.

In other realms, too, Nixon followed a reasonably liberal policy during his Administration. He created the Environmental Protection Agency and endorsed the Equal Rights Amendment for women. He pushed for the enactment of the Occupational Safety and Health Act in December 1970.[34] When New York legalized abortion in July 1970, Nixon did not denounce the action but said it was an issue for the states.[35] He tried to pass a comprehensive family protection program and did index Social Security payments to wages. Even his policy on Native-Americans was liberal.

In short, both in his general strategy and in his Southern strategy, Nixon governed as a moderately liberal eastern Republican. To use language associated with a later President, he tried to reassure "middle Americans" that he felt their pain and anger about the radical student attack on morality, but his basic policy, both domestic and foreign, was designed to appeal to educated suburban voters. In this, he continued to follow the long-term Republican strategy in the South.

THE RISE OF THE RELIGIOUS RIGHT IN PARTY POLITICS

When observers point to the rise of the religious right in the 1970s, they do not mean — or should not mean — that a large-scale religious conversion took place in the United States. Religion has always been important in the United States. Immigrants from myriad countries and cultures had often used their church as their social and cultural base, the place where they could meet people from their homeland and speak their native language. British Americans of the 17th and 18th centuries often brought their fundamentalist Calvinist religion with them to the colonies. This Calvinist religious strain remained strong in the United States because it conveyed a sense of moral superiority to the new non-Protestant immigrants who settled in the city with all its proverbial corruption.

A modern American instinctively thinks of the rise of the religious right as a movement for revolutionary change. In reality, it was a counterrevolution. American society had long featured severe restrictions on cultural and social behavior based on religion. The laws against the consumption of liquor were largely based on the political action of Protestant churches, but most of the other restrictions came from an unspoken and paradoxical alliance between the Catholic Church and the rural and small-town Protestants who deeply feared both the non-Protestant immigrants and the Catholic Church that represented the immigrants. The revolt of the Baby Boomers, first expressed in an attraction to Elvis Presley and rock and roll and then in the sexual revolution, was directed against these religiously based restrictions.

Those under 55 years of age today cannot imagine how culturally conservative the United States was in the 1950s. It was illegal to import, let alone sell, James

---

34. Charles Noble, *Liberalism at Work: The Rise and Fall of OSHA* (Philadelphia: Temple University Press, 1986).
35. William Safire, *Before the Fall: An Inside View of the Pre-Watergate White House* (Garden City, NY: Doubleday, 1975), p. 322.

Joyce's *Ulysses*, D. H. Lawrence's *Lady Chatterly's Lover*, and the relatively mild porno-graphic novels of Henry Miller until 1963. Hugh Hefner was considered a daring innovator when he published *Playboy* in November 1953, but he eliminated all pubic hair from the photographs in the magazine until January 1972.[36] It was illegal to sell contraceptives in Connecticut until 1965. Married people could not be shown in the same bed in movies or television, and the word "pregnancy" could not be used in these media.

A recent book summarizes the conservative character of the first part of the 1960s in a few pages. The Supreme Court outlawed prayer in public schools in 1962 in *Engel v. Vitale* and Bible reading in 1963 in *Schempp v. Murray*. Yet 88 percent of the population held the opposite position in 1965. Only 5 percent of births took place outside of marriage, and single or divorced mothers headed only 10 percent of fam-ilies. "In 1963 a *New York Times* front page headline expressed the mood of time: 'Growth of Homosexuality in City Provokes Wide Concern.'" Boys in school wore short hair, and 80% of the public approved.[37]

Obviously, such books exaggerate "the good old days." The parents of the Baby Boomers had been the teenagers and the young adults of World War II, and millions of men who went to war did not go as virgins. The Kinsey report on sexual behavior focused, after all, on the parents of the Baby Boomers. The grandmothers of the Baby Boomers not only voted for the first time but, far more shockingly, they were in the flapper generation that began using lipstick, which had been associated only with prostitutes. *Their* parents had been the teenagers of the Roaring Nineties. But the restrictions on openly acknowledged behavior could be quite strict, and they inevi-tably had an impact on actual behavior.

The Baby Boom revolt inevitably would have produced a counter-reaction from the forces that had supported the old religiously-based restrictions. The reaction was, however, magnified by political and technological forces extraneous to that rev-olution. Those with secular, urban culture did not simply liberate themselves from religiously-based control. They also, sometimes intentionally but often uninten-tionally, took decisions that impinged on the lives of rural and small town America.

First, of course, the Supreme Court decisions of the 1950s and 1960s directly affected the life of rural and small town America. They imposed change directly, and sometimes perhaps with undue lack of caution and respect in the religious realm. Yet the Court decisions also had an indirect impact. For example, when school desegre-gation began to be seriously enforced in the South in the late 1960s and early 1970s, the more fundamentalist churches often created private schools — "Christian acad-emies" — for parents who wanted to withdraw their children from the public schools. The children received religious instruction, and parents became tied to the churches that were educating their children.[38]

---

36. Russell Miller, *Bunny: The Real Story of Playboy* (New York: Holt, Rinehart, and Winston, 1984), pp. 41 and 183.
37. Steven F. Hayward, *The Age of Reagan: The Fall of the Old Liberal Order, 1964–1980* (Roseville, Calif: Forum, 2001), pp. 6–11.
38. James Davison Hunter, *Evangelicalism: The Coming Generation* (Chicago: University of Chicago Press, 1987).

A second and more important fact was of a technical character — the creation, first, of television and then of the Internet. This gave Court decisions a meaning they would not have had in the past. The youth revolt in life style and the Court decisions on obscenity took place precisely at the time that television was becoming a universal mass media of communication. Before then, unacceptable *avant garde* culture could largely be kept out of the living rooms of conservative Americans. Now television could not fail to report what was occurring, and television programs gradually became more risqué. They could be seen everywhere. The Internet made a broad pornographic culture available (almost inescapable) to children in their homes.

Many scholars explain the religious right by the supposed psychological insecurity and the loss of status of rural and town residents in the face of modernism. As Steve Bruce emphasizes, however, the Evangelicals had genuine grievances against urban liberals. They were defending their culture from real attack. "Family values" had a concrete meaning to them. They rightly thought they were losing control of the transmission of their values to their children.[39]

A third factor that increased the role of the Evangelicals was the introduction of competitive party politics in the South. The Evangelicals constituted some 20% to 25% of the adult population in the United States in 1980, but roughly a quarter of them were black and remained Democratic. Seymour Martin Lipset found that some one-half lived in the South and one-quarter in the Midwest, but many in the Midwest (and in the West) had their roots in the South.[40] The latter included both the recent migrants and the descendants of the "Copperheads" — the Southern majority in the lower Midwest who supported the South during the Civil War. Even today many have enough of a Southern accent to lead people to talk of "the accent line" in the southern Midwest.[41]

In the past the Southern Evangelicals had been a significant political force in local politics — for example, in the enactment of strict "dry" (anti-alcohol) laws. Yet they had no more reason than other elements of the population to vote in the general elections of the Solid Democratic South. Indeed, they had lower education on the average than other white Southerners, and since they were the poor whites at whom the poll tax was directed, they tended to have lower voter turnout than more educated whites.

The growing party competition in the South gave Evangelicals their first opportunity to participate meaningfully in national politics. The question was which party they would vote for. As has been seen, the Southern urban middle class increasingly

---

39. Steve Bruce, *The Rise and Fall of the New Christian Right: Conservative Protestant Politics in America, 1978-1988* (New York: Oxford University Press, 1988), pp. 2–44. The classic statement of the psychological thesis is found in Seymour Martin Lipset, *Politics of Unreason: Right-Wing Extremism in America, 1790-1977*, 2nd ed. (Chicago: University of Chicago Press, 1978), pp. 428–463, and Seymour Martin Lipset and Earl Raab, "The Election and the Evangelicals," *Commentary*, vol. 71, no. 3 (March 1981), pp. 26–28.
40. Lipset and Raab, "The Election and the Evangelicals," p. 25.
41. For a discussion of the "accent line" in Ohio in the 1976 election and Jimmy Carter's success south of it, see Patrick H. Caddell, "Initial Working Paper on Political Strategy," December 10, 1956, Presidential Papers, Staff Offices — Press: Box 4, p. 10, Jimmy Carter Presidential Library.

had been voting Republican, while the rural and small town whites remained the proverbial "yellow dog Democrats" (that is, they would vote even for a yellow dog if it were nominated by the Democratic Party). Almost by definition, most Evangelical Christians fit within this latter category.

Because of their socioeconomic status, Southern Evangelicals on the average were more anti-black and more pro-Deal than the average middle-class Southern voter in the city. As both parties began to court these Evangelicals, would they tend to give greater priority to their economic views (as did black Evangelicals) or to their cultural views? Would they ultimately vote predominantly Republican or predominantly Democratic — or split their vote between the two parties? But both parties had to seek to appeal to them if they wanted a chance to win in the South. The surprising fact is that the national Democrats withdrew completely from the competition.

In practice, the white Southern Evangelical Christians generally retained an allegiance to the Democratic candidates at the state and local levels during a very long period of transition, but were a swing group at the presidential level. The Evangelicals still strongly supported Stevenson over Eisenhower in 1952 and 1956, but many turned against Kennedy in 1960 over his Catholicism. They then returned to the Democratic candidate of 1964, Lyndon Johnson, except in the Black Belt areas of the Deep South. In 1968, they gave many of their votes to the independent candidate, George Wallace, but they rejected George McGovern and his radical cultural supporters in favor of Richard Nixon in 1972. In 1976, a large number were attracted to Jimmy Carter, a born-again Christian, but in 1980 many, although far from all, voted for Ronald Reagan. In 1984, they strongly supported Reagan and in 1988 Bush.

In 1992, a substantial number of Evangelicals supported Bill Clinton from Hope, Arkansas. The 1994 Republican victory in the Congress seemed, however, to reflect an angry sense of betrayal, perhaps over Clinton's emphasis on allowing open gays in the military, perhaps on his retreat from a middle class tax cut and health care reform. Since that time the Evangelicals have been a core voting group for the Republican Party.

In one sense, the white vote in the United States began to normalize in the 1980s and 1990s: the Southern Protestants began voting Republican like the Northern Protestants, and white Evangelicals, too, began to vote for Republicans almost exactly in the same proportions as the white mainline Protestants of the North. Yet "Protestant" includes people with a broad range of values and interests. The mainline Protestant churches did, after all, differ strikingly from the Evangelicals in their theology, cultural values, and average income.[42] The Republican Party was courting the mainstream, middle class Protestants in the South, and this should have made it unattractive to the Evangelicals.

---

42. These differences were to continue. For example, the more fundamentalist churches became very staunch supporters of Israel, while the mainstream churches were moving towards a demand that American companies stop doing business with Israel. For the campaign of mainstream Protestant churches for a divestment of the stocks of such companies, see Julia Duin, "Israel Tries to Stop Pullout of US Funding," *The Washington Times*, September 17, 2005, p. 1.

In addition, the unhappiness of the Evangelicals about the Supreme Court scarcely pushed them in a Republican direction. The Warren of the "Warren Court" was, of course, the Republican Chief Justice appointed by Eisenhower. That was the Court that made decisions on school desegregation, obscenity, and school prayer. Similarly, *Roe v. Wade*, the key decision in 1973 that gave women an unrestricted right to an abortion in the first three months of pregnancy and a virtually unrestricted right in the next three months, was a 7 to 2 decision. The six Republicans on the Court at this time voted affirmatively on the decision by a 5 to 1 margin. When Supreme Court nominee Harriet Miers in 2005 named Chief Justice Warren Burger as her favorite Justice, she caused some consternation among conservatives because he had voted for *Roe v. Wade*. Harry Blackmun, the Justice who wrote the majority decision, was a Nixon appointee, a man whom Nixon claimed was abnormally conservative and supposedly was selected because Nixon wanted to retaliate against Senators who rejected his two Southern nominees, Clement Haynesworth and G. Harold Carswell.

The Evangelical Christians did not, however, simply have a reason to distrust an alliance with the Republicans. They seemed to have a real reason to support the Democrats. To be sure, the Evangelicals had a hearty dislike of the cultural radicals of the Vietnam era who nominated George McGovern, but McGovern's landslide loss in 1972 had seemingly discredited these radicals.

From the perspective of 1973, the Democratic Party seemed likely to return to the alliance that had won it seven of ten elections from 1932 through 1968 and that had almost won it an 8th in the dreadfully difficult election of 1968. The Democrats basically had formed a coalition of the South with Northern Catholics and Jews. The Jews were culturally liberal, but the United States had far more Catholics than Jews. The Catholic Church was leading the battle against abortion in the 1970s, and the born-again Christian Jimmy Carter, nominated by the Democrats in 1976, was more conservative on abortion than Gerald Ford. It was the Democrats' subsequent move to the cultural left and to the economic right in the 1970s and 1980s that pushed the Evangelicals to the Republicans.

In the late 1970s, a number of fundamentalist televangelists became politically active on the Republican side. Jerry Falwell and Pat Robertson and the Moral Majority that they formed symbolized this movement. Many in the media and the scholarly community have explained the rise of the religious right almost exclusively in terms of the organizing role of the new religious right organizations and the ministers of the Evangelical churches. Sometimes religious right voters are depicted almost like sheep who are herded to the polls to vote in the prescribed manner. This is a serious mistake.

Indeed, the literature on the religious right organizations has a strange quality. The organizations and their organizers always seem to be going through cycles of "rise and fall." In the conventional wisdom, a strong showing by a conservative Republican candidate is evidence that the religious organizers were powerful. By contrast, if a conservative Republican candidate does poorly, this shows that the organizers were weakening. Naturally, from this perspective the media generally considered religious organizers very strong in helping to produce the re-election of

George Bush in 2004, but a very knowledgeable observer, Michael Barone, who attributes the rise of turnout in the election largely to organizational factors, says almost nothing about a religious wing in the Republican Party, except in a passing clause.[43]

The problem with the media interpretation of the power of religious organizations is that the very rules of the game of the media inevitably lead to an exaggerated view of the power of interest group leaders — often self-appointed leaders. The media are required to show "balance" on major political and social issues, and the obvious way to "achieve" this is to interview a representative from an organization on each end of the spectrum or one from competing organizations on both sides of an issue.

Thus, on issues such as abortion (or the confirmation of Supreme Court nominees), leaders of several women's organizations are regularly interviewed even though their organizations now seem unimportant. Several recognized "leaders" of the religious right inevitably appear on the other side. A person who frequently appears in such a context comes to be seen as one with a very substantial number of followers who follow his or her lead. The representatives themselves have a strong incentive to claim strong influence and a large following.

All this may have little relationship to reality. When a leading Republican televangelist, Pat Robertson, ran for the Republican nomination in 1988, his activists were quite important in the few remaining states with caucuses. Yet, despite Robertson's very large campaign expenditures, few Evangelical voters supported him in primaries. Similarly, in the summer of 2005, the conservative *Washington Times* reported that the Christian Coalition was moribund, but a Republican consultant cautioned that it never had been as powerful as many in the media thought. "The demise of the Christian Coalition may," he said, "be more about generating fewer press releases now than it did when Ralph [Reed] was there."[44]

Undoubtedly, organization plays a role in turnout, but it seems far wiser to focus on other factors that are related to the grievances of individuals in the religious right, to the strategies of the politicians who seek their vote (or fail to seek it), and to the political arena in which they find themselves. The evidence suggests that religious voters, like others in the modern world, are largely self-motivated in their decision to go to the polls, and they are quite capable of judging national candidates on their own, especially since the cultural issues often are so starkly drawn between the two parties.

Indeed, the power of the religious right as individual voters in the Republican Party may also be seriously exaggerated. The media gave great emphasis to the role of the Moral Majority and the religious right in electing Reagan in 1980, but the hard evidence does not support this claim. In 1982, Paul Abramson, John Aldrich, and David Rohde published the first of a long and distinguished series of books on suc-

---

43. Michael Barone, "Introduction," *The Almanac of American Politics, 2006* (Washington, D.C.: National Journal, 2005), pp. 21–23.

44. Julia Duin, "Christian Coalition Seen as 'Moribund'," *The Washington Times*, October 13, 2005, pp. A1 and A13.

cessive presidential elections based on the University of Michigan's national election surveys. The 1980 survey interviewed over 1500 respondents, and the authors reported that "like [Everett Carll] Ladd and [George] Gallup, we found little evidence that Reagan benefited from the votes of fundamentalists".[45]

> Given the great interest in the role played by fundamentalist Christians in the 1980 election, we explored voting behavior among white Protestants in some detail.... White Southern Baptists, the most fundamentalist of the major Protestant denominations, were more likely to vote for Carter (who was a Southern Baptist) than were members of any other major Protestant denomination. Our analysis of religious views among white Protestants also found little support for the thesis that Reagan benefited from a fundamentalist vote, although Reagan did do especially well among the small number (N=52) who identified with Evangelical groups.

It is fascinating to read the work of top observers such as David Broder, Kevin Phillips, and James Reichley written during or shortly after the 1980 election. As noted in the introduction of this book, Broder's very sophisticated 1980 study of generation change has an entire chapter on "the New Right" that focuses solely on the economic heirs of Goldwater. Reichley's 1981 *Conservatives in an Age of Change* listed "fundamentalists" as one of the four major groups in the Republican Party, but defined it as "a strain relatively new to the Republican Party, nurtured much more than the stalwarts on political and economic theory, and attracting some support from groups like white southerners and Catholics formerly not much drawn to the Republicans."[46] The reference to "political and economic theory" shows Reichley was thinking substantially of Goldwater activists. Phillips in his 1982 *Post-Conservative America* is more inclined to see a social and even religious element in the New Right, but he gives great emphasis to a broad anti-government, free enterprise mood.[47]

The basic problem in interpretation, as Phillips argued, is that liberalism by 1980 "became associated ... more and more with middle class reformism and permissivism" and "most of the *plausible* radical forces in the country were arrayed under the conservative label."[48] (The italics are Phillips'.) Goldwater had refused to compromise his libertarian principles to form a coalition to support his economic views, but a number of persons in the early 1970s — most prominently, William Rusher, publisher of the *National Review* — worked to form an alliance between economic conservatives and social conservatives, perhaps even in a third party.

Some social conservatives were Evangelicals. The end of the poll tax and the mobilizing effects of Jimmy Carter's candidacy had led more of them to register to

---

45. Paul R. Abramson, John H. Aldrich, and David W. Rohde, *Change and Continuity in the 1980 Elections* (Washington: CQ Press, 1982), p. 101. They refer to Everett Carll Ladd, "The Brittle Mandate: Electoral Dealignment and the 1980 Presidential Election," *Political Science Quarterly*, vol. 96 (Spring 1981), pp. 17-18, and George Gallup, Jr., "Divining the Devout: The Polls and Religious Beliefs," *Public Opinion*, vol. 4 (April/May 1981), pp. 20 and 41.
46. Reichley, *Conservatives in an Age of Change*, p. 26.
47. Kevin P. Phillips, *Post-Conservative America: People, Politics, and Ideology in a Time of Crisis* (New York: Random House, 1982), pp. 32 and 47.
48. Phillips, *Post-Conservative America*, p. 31.

vote, and a number of Republican secular fund-raisers had worked to use cultural issues to persuade them to contribute to conservative political bodies and to vote for the Republican Party. These organizers proved to be very skilled and innovative in developing techniques to raise campaign funds by direct mail. In the course of their work they made contact with a number of Evangelical leaders, especially preachers with a substantial television audience, in order to obtain their address lists and develop fund-raising appeals that would be attractive to an Evangelical audience. They were the ones who persuaded two such television Evangelists, Jerry Falwell and Pat Robertson, to form the political religious organization, the Moral Majority.

Nevertheless, the Evangelicals were not the only social conservatives. A number of intellectuals, primarily middle-aged Jewish New Dealers, abandoned the Democratic Party on foreign policy grounds and essentially adopted Goldwater's policy toward the Soviet Union and Communism. George Wallace had not emphasized religious themes, but had directed his fire at the power of the federal government, especially on racial questions, and at the anti-war radicals. His voters were the largest group of "social conservatives" who would have to move quickly to one major party or the other — or to both.

Most important, the alliance prominently included economic conservatives. One right-wing activist told David Broder in the late 1970s, "You know ... for most of the conservatives of my generation, the Goldwater campaign was the thing that got them involved. It did for us what the McCarthy and McGovern campaigns later did for the Democratic Party."[49] As will be discussed in Chapter 9, George W. Bush was known in Texas by his friends as an economic ideologue who had poor relations with the religious right. Karl Rove apparently is a non-believer.

Given Goldwater's libertarian cultural program, his activists almost surely were attracted to his economic and nationalist views. Ronald Reagan had given the most famous speech in the Goldwater campaign, and he continued to make a large number of speeches, especially in the South. Yet he said relatively little about cultural themes, but focused on the desirability of less government spending and regulation and the need for a stronger defense.

The question is whether such a careful, hands-on reporter as David Broder missed the main right-wing political development of his time or whether the type of activists on whom he focused have, in fact, been the most important activists of the Republican Party and continue to be. A study of 6800 major campaign contributors defined as activists found that 59% of the Republicans were mainline Protestants and 11% Evangelicals.[50] The subject requires far more detailed research than it has received, but the latter hypothesis deserves the most serious attention.

Obviously, at a minimum the Goldwater activists were skilled in developing a cultural issue that proved successful in rallying many to their economic banner who would not naturally have been there. If Goldwater was like Henry Clay in being too

---

49. Broder, *The Changing of the Guard*, p. 175.
50. John C. Green, James L. Guth, and Cleveland R. Fraser, "Apostles and Apostates: Religion and Politics Among Party Activists," in James L. Guth and John C. Green, eds., *The Bible and the Ballot Box: Religion and Politics in the 1988 Election* (Boulder, CO: Westview Press, 1991), p. 117.

respectable to adopt an effective cultural policy with which he disagreed, those who came after him were more successful in doing so. We should remember that quite secular radio "evangelists" such as Rush Limbaugh increasingly replaced the religious evangelists in the 1990s.

GERALD FORD AND THE MODERN RED STATE STRATEGY

In retrospect, people date the red state strategy based on the religious right to Ronald Reagan's drive for the Republican nomination during the presidency of Jimmy Carter or, actually, somewhat earlier. Richard Nixon understood that while many Evangelical Christians might vote for him in some contexts — certainly against Kennedy in 1960 and McGovern in 1972 — they did not feel warmly about him. Basically, Nixon was too much a Quaker and an Earl Warren Californian Republican.

The Evangelicals responded to Ronald Reagan, although less for religious reasons than for his personality and general respect for tradition and opposition to the radical students of Berkeley — that is, for the same reasons other voters supported him. Ronald Reagan was, after all, a divorced man from Hollywood who almost never went to church. Some strongly believe that Reagan's television role as a host of the *General Electric Theater* and *Death Valley Days* gave him an association with the Old West and tradition that was of particular importance.[51]

In a more direct sense the first major move of the Republican Party to a modern red state strategy came in 1976 at the end of the presidency of Gerald Ford. Ford himself was a typical moderate conservative Republican, a Congressman from a district in Michigan centered on Grand Rapids. He was more conservative than Nixon, but his election as Republican leader in the House of Representatives testified to his natural instincts as a coalitional politician. Michigan is not a red state, and Ford was the antithesis of the modern ideological Congressman based on the religious right.

Ford became President in 1974 in circumstances he could not have imagined just a few years earlier. The Watergate break-in had occurred in the summer of 1972, but it had had little impact upon the election. By the summer of 1973, however, Judge John Sirica was using the threat of harsh jail sentences to compel lower Nixon staff members to implicate those higher in the Administration. Nixon's top assistants had been forced to resign in 1973, and people began to speculate about the possible impeachment of the President. Then, in August 1973, it was learned that Vice President Spiro Agnew was under investigation. On October 10, he was forced to resign.[52]

The 25th Amendment to the Constitution gave the President the power, contingent on the approval of a majority of both houses, to appoint a new Vice President

---

51. Wayne Greenhaw, *Elephants in the Cornfield: Ronald Reagan and the New Republican South* (New York: Macmillan, 1982), pp. 9–14.
52. Jerry Landauer, "Spiro Agnew Is Target of a Criminal Inquiry: Extortion is Alleged," *The Wall Street Journal*, August 7, 1973, p. 1. The role of the *Washington Post* in Nixon's impeachment is usually exaggerated, while Judge Sirica is given too little credit.

if the office became open. Nixon said that he preferred John Connally, the former Texas Democrat who had become a Republican, but instead he chose the minority leader in the House, Gerald Ford.[53] The reason is not altogether clear, for Ford was a highly credible interim President and his selection reduced any fear that Congress might have had about impeaching Nixon. Apparently, the Congressional Democrats suggested that they were not eager to vote to confirm a renegade from their party. They also likely thought that if Nixon were impeached, Connally would be much more difficult to defeat in 1976 than Ford. When Nixon told Ford of his decision, he warned that he would support Connally for the presidential nomination in 1976. Ford assented.

Nixon was, in fact, to resign 10 months later on August 8, 1974, in the face of imminent impeachment, and Ford became President. This again left the office of Vice President open, and now Ford had the duty to fill it. As a Midwestern moderate conservative who was a typical member of the old Republican Establishment, Ford accurately signaled that he planned to retain the traditional Republican suburban strategy by selecting Nelson Rockefeller, a more liberal New Yorker, to provide a political balance for himself.

The more ideologically conservative forces in the Republican Party — the supporters of Barry Goldwater — organized behind Reagan in the 1976 primaries in an attempt to deny the nomination to Ford. Reagan concluded that the red states, together with his Pacific Coast supporters, could provide the base for a successful effort to win the Republican nomination. In 1976, the Western and Southern states elected 47 percent of the delegates to the Republican convention. In that year, Reagan won 82 percent of the delegates from the West and 73 percent of those from the South. Together with scattered delegates from the Northeast and Midwest, this brought him to within 120 votes of defeating a sitting President in the convention. He had 1,070 delegates and Gerald Ford 1,187.[54]

Reagan's desire to cultivate social conservatives led him to a conservative cultural program, including support for a constitutional amendment against abortion. This amendment was no more than a symbolic gesture, but his delegates were strong enough at the convention to include two sentences in the three-paragraph section on "Women" in the Republican platform. The section began with a reaffirmation of the ratification of the Equal Rights Amendment and treated abortion as a moral and personal issue on which there were many opinions. Nevertheless, the section ended:[55]

> We protest the Supreme Court's intrusion into the family structure through its denial of the parents' obligation and right to guide their minor children. The Republican Party favors a continuance of the public dialogue on abortion and supports the efforts of those who seek enactment of a constitutional amendment to restore protection of the right to life for unborn children.

53. For Connally, see Edward L. and Frederic H. Schapsmeier, *Gerald R. Ford's Date with Destiny: A Political Biography* (New York: Peter Lang, 1989), p. 136.
54. For these figures, see Rae, *The Decline and Fall of the Liberal Republicans*, p. 117. Her "Western" statistics naturally include California, Oregon, and Washington, not just the Red States of our statistics.
55. *The New York Times*, August 16, 1976, p. 17.

The vague first sentence referred to the right of minors to have abortions without parental approval.

In retrospect, the key decisions in 1976 centered on Ford's choice of a Vice Presidential candidate. On October 29, 1975, Ford gave a speech about New York City at the National Press Club which the *New York Post*, with its customary flamboyance, described in a headline, "New York, Drop Dead." The *New York Times*, traditionally more sedate, ran a headline across the whole page proclaiming, "Ford, Castigating City, Asserts He'd Veto Fund Guarantee." The article underneath the headline reported that Ford "spent more than half of his 40-minute address ... castigating the management and tactics of New York City and state officials." Officials told the *New York Times* that Ford's attack on New York City was part of his campaign for 1976, but they did not reveal a key aspect of the story. On the previous day, Ford had met with Rockefeller and indicated (or perhaps asserted) that he wanted a new running mate in 1976. It is hard to believe that Ford did not tell Rockefeller about the speech he planned to make the next day.[56]

Rockefeller's removal from the Vice President slot on the 1976 ticket is fully understandable. Rockefeller had been unnecessarily offensive to Goldwater forces in 1964 and unnecessarily haughty toward President Ford in 1974 and 1975 in suggesting that he should have the key role in developing domestic policy. (The latter behavior, of course, also offended Ford's chief domestic policy advisers.)[57] Yet Ford easily could have chosen another Eastern moderate to maintain the traditional Republican coalition. One obvious choice was one of his Pennsylvania supporters, Senator Richard Schweiker, whom Reagan was to name as his intended choice just prior to the convention.

Ford had another option that would have created a new coalition based on the old one. Former Texas Governor John Connally was an obvious Vice Presidential candidate, and in late July 1976, the *Washington Post* columnist, Marquis Childs, assumed that Ford would choose Connally and that, as a consequence, "a strong ticket will have been forged."[58] Although Connally had been a Democrat, he was a perfect example of the kind of person who was becoming a Republican in the South and whom Nixon and Ford had continued to court.

Ford wrote in his memoirs that Connally had the reputation of being a political operator and that, in any case, he thought he could not challenge Carter in the South. The latter calculation proved to be a mistake. Ford not only won Virginia, but an

---

56. The article on "Ford, Castigating City...," was written by Martin Tolchin, *The New York Times*, October 30. 1975, p. 1. For the political implications, see R. W. Apple, Jr., "City a '76 Issue for Ford; Democrats Doubt Its Value," *The New York Times*, October 31, 1975, p. 1, and James M. Naughton, "President on Coast, Makes New York's Crisis Focus of his Political Campaign; Ford Holds Rockefeller Blameless," *The New York Times*, October 31, 1975, p. A12. For the October 28 meeting, see Robert T. Hartmann, *Palace Politics: An Inside Account of the Ford Years* (New York: McGraw Hill, 1980), pp. 365–372.
57. For a partisan, but highly informative account by a Ford aide connected with Rockefeller, see Hartmann, *Palace Politics*. Hartmann treats Donald Rumsfeld and Dick Cheney as the villains.
58. Marquis Childs, "Can the Democrats Lose in November?" *The Washington Post*, July 27, 1976, p. A15.

additional 3 former states of the Confederacy gave Carter less than 52% of their vote. One of them was Connally's Texas, and another was neighboring Louisiana. If Ford had carried these two states and retained the states he won, he would have captured a majority of the votes in the Electoral College. Reagan was to take all the states of the Confederacy in 1980 except for Carter's own state of Georgia. Another Southerner, Howard Baker of Tennessee, might also have helped Ford in the South, or even in Ohio, where Ford lost by 11,000 votes.

Instead, Ford selected Senator Robert Dole of Kansas as his running mate. By traditional standards, Dole was a most dubious choice. Kansas and three other Prairie states (Nebraska, North Dakota, and South Dakota) had rejected Roosevelt in 1940 and had voted Republican in every presidential election thereafter except the 1964 Lyndon Johnson landslide. Moreover, Dole personally was not an exciting candidate and had only been reelected Senator in 1974 by a 50.9% to 49.1% margin.

The reason that Ford selected Dole is not absolutely clear. Ford himself writes that he was perfectly comfortable with Dole from their work in Congress and that he needed help in the farm states. The first claim surely is right, but the latter argument is unconvincing since Ford himself came from western Michigan. Another factor was probably crucial. Ford notes in passing in his memoirs that he mentioned six potential candidates to Reagan and that the latter had replied that Dole "would be an excellent candidate."[59]

The real story about Reagan's role was more dramatic. On the day Ford was nominated, he told reporters that he would announce his choice the following day and that he would visit Reagan in the latter's hotel, not even at a neutral site. He actually met Reagan at 1:30 A.M., and Reagan's aides told reporters that Reagan had evaluated Dole positively, but had said nothing about the other five options. Hence, Ford had a stark choice either to accept Reagan's advice or ostentatiously reject it — and this in a situation in which Reagan had an interest in Ford losing so that he himself would be a clear choice for the nomination in 1980.[60]

Ford was an instinctive coalitional Congressional leader, and an experienced presidential campaigner surely would have handled Reagan differently. Nevertheless, there was an important nuance in the Dole selection that must have occurred to Ford and his advisors. In his reelection campaign in 1974, Dole had badly trailed his Democratic opponent in the first weeks of September. This opponent was a Congressman who was an obstetrician and, as a doctor, he had carried out a dozen abortions (all for reasons of complications or health, he said). Dole decided to launch a pro-life attack on him. When Dole won narrowly, his victory usually was attributed to this campaign decision. By 1976 he had come to favor a constitutional amendment outlawing abortion.[61]

---

59. Gerald R. Ford, *A Time to Heal: The Autobiography of Gerald R. Ford* (New York: Harper and Row, 1979), pp. 404 and 400.
60. See Charles Mohr, "Dole Choice Conformed to the Wishes of Reagan," and James M. Naughton, "Delegates Voice Doubts on Ford–Dole Prospects," *The New York Times*, August 20, 1976, p. 1.
61. Thompson, *Bob Dole*, pp. 76–88.

The Ford Administration had been paying for abortions for poor women with Medicaid funds, and Carter firmly promised to end this practice if he were elected President. Ford's wife, Betty, was forthright in supporting the Equal Rights Amendment and women's choice on abortion, and Ford himself was ambiguous on the latter issue. Dole had been divorced and had remarried a professional woman, Elizabeth, whose position on women's issues was similar to that of Ford's wife.

Mary King, the person on Jimmy Carter's staff who handled women's issues, wrote an internal memorandum at the time that pointed to the importance of Dole's position on abortion in his Senate re-election race. But she thought that Elizabeth also was an important factor in Ford's decision. In King's view, two wives on the ticket who were "strong assertive women with minds of their own" would "soften the edge of what will likely be a strong anti-abortion position" of the two candidates themselves and the platform.[62] Indeed, in retrospect, Jimmy Carter thought Ford may well have lost the election because he seemed, on balance, more pro-choice than Carter himself.

Whatever the reasons for Dole's selection, and his position on abortion was most probably one of them, there was one aspect of the selection process that at least symbolized the change that was occurring in the Republican Party. Dole came from a Prairie state. One of Rockefeller's strongest opponents on Ford's team was his chief of staff, Dick Cheney, who came from the Mountain state of Wyoming. The red state alliance was to center on Dole's Prairie states, Cheney's Mountain states, and the South. The selection of Dole was a key step on the transition to the red state strategy.

THE PARADOX OF RONALD REAGAN

As early as 1968, the most conservative forces in the Republican Party did not favor Nixon's nomination but wanted Ronald Reagan. Although Reagan was elected governor of California only in 1966, he ran in a number of primaries in 1968, including as a favorite son in Nixon's home state of California.[63] This latter decision alone guaranteed a negative Nixon attitude toward Reagan, and American political history might have evolved very differently if Nixon had not been destroyed by his Watergate decision. A number of times Nixon indicated that he wanted his successor to be John Connally. At a minimum, Nixon certainly would have invested great effort in preventing Reagan from succeeding him.

But, of course, Nixon *was* forced to resign. The new religious right organizations were formed in the years prior to 1980, and they supported Reagan enthusiastically.

---

62. "Memorandum to Hamilton Jordan by Mary King," 1976 Presidential Campaign, Issues Office—Stuart Eizenstat, Box 24. King attached to the memo a piece of research on Dole's Senate campaign. Jimmy Carter Presidential Library.
63. For a record of the primary results in 1968, see *CQ's Guide to US Elections*, pp. 351–353. Since no one seriously challenged Nixon in 1968, the primary totals were generally small, and Reagan's unchallenged victory in California and his relatively small votes gave him marginally more total votes than Nixon.

Many drew a connection between the rise of the religious right and Reagan's election. James Q. Wilson was one of those who insisted that the movement to elect Reagan in 1980 was, indeed, "an authentic social movement." In Wilson's words, "the life and heart of the campaign are not to be found in elite concerns with economic and foreign policy, but in mass concerns with social and moral issues."[64]

Without any doubt, a number of conservative activists saw themselves as part of a social movement to elect Reagan, and liberal activists could best rally their base by agreeing that Reagan was the product of an extremist fundamentalist movement. Reagan's supporters and opponents have also had an incentive to distort him in a similar direction in other respects. Both depict him as a simple man of a few basic principles (ideological precepts, in the eyes of his opponents) who was almost pushed into running for President, either by his growing horror at events (the conservative version) or by the ambition of his wife, Nancy (the liberal version).

In fact, Reagan was a most determined, ambitious man who had expended enormous energy for many years in his drive for the Republican nomination. Having come close to being nominated in 1976 before the Evangelicals were a strong element in the Republican Party, he scarcely needed their support to win the nomination in 1980. He had begun speaking in the small towns of the South from 1965 and 1966 onward, and he did not have a strong challenger in 1980. His nomination was virtually inevitable long before the social movement developed.

Moreover, Reagan's views are easy to misjudge. He first came on the national political scene as a fervent spokesman for Goldwater in the 1964 campaign, and from the beginning he combined many of Goldwater's nationalist and economic themes. These were the major themes in his speeches throughout the 1970s. The leading activists who were supporting him had also entered politics with Goldwater, and Goldwater's cultural policy was libertarian.

Indeed, Reagan himself had warmly supported Franklin Roosevelt and still was endorsing Democrats such as the left-wing Helen Gahagan Douglas in her Senate race against Nixon in 1950. He had been chairman of the trade union of the Hollywood actors and was a divorced governor of California. Only when he became involved in the Democrats for Eisenhower movement in 1952 did he begin his transition to the Republican Party.

As would be expected of a person of his background, Reagan was tolerant on many cultural issues. While governor, he had signed a permissive abortion law, one of the most liberal in existence at the time. He favored the Equal Rights Amendment (ERA) to the Constitution and changed his mind, he claimed, only when his wife Nancy persuaded him to do so as he was running for President in the 1970s.[65] Even then, he was extremely quiet about his change of position, and a leading official of the National Organization of Women who was working on abortion and ERA issues at the time does not even recall Reagan's change 25 years later.

---

64. James Q. Wilson, "Reagan and the Republican Revival," *Commentary*, vol. 70, no. 4 (October 1980), p. 28.
65. Lou Cannon, *Reagan* (New York: Putnam, 1982), pp. 128–133 and 144.

In 1980, American economic conditions and international relations were extremely unsatisfactory, and Carter's approval ratings in 1979 were lower than Truman's in early 1952 and Johnson's in early 1968. From that perspective, almost any credible Republican should have had an easy victory. Reagan actually was seen as risky, and he received only 50.7% of the popular vote.

Since 6.6% of the voters, mainly moderate Republicans, were to vote for a third candidate, John Anderson, Reagan won a 489 to 49 vote landslide in the Electoral College. The Anderson voters knew that they were supporting Reagan rather than Carter in the election, but they wanted to signal their concerns to Reagan. Reagan heard them. He spent much of the campaign seeking to moderate his image, including by a promise to appoint a woman to the Supreme Court.

At the time, many saw Reagan as advancing a relatively extreme policy. The great majority of Reagan's chief lieutenants were, however, either men who had worked well with him in California or persons who had worked in the Ford Administration. Moderates such as Howard Baker and Michael Deaver exercised great power. Almost none of the activists associated directly with Goldwater or the religious right received significant posts.[66] The only person with fairly doctrinaire economic views high in the Administration was David Stockman, Director of the Office of Management and the Budget. Stockman soon left and lamented in his memoirs that Reagan was "a consensus politician, not an ideologue.... He had no business trying to make a revolution because it wasn't in his bones."[67]

In foreign policy, Reagan often used hard-line rhetoric, but his actions were quite moderate. His response to a terrorist attack in Beirut that killed over 200 Marines was to withdraw from Lebanon. He ended his presidency embracing the Soviet leader, Mikhail Gorbachev, in Red Square, and he claimed he always had been determined to negotiate peace. He said privately that a major reason for his military build-up was not to frighten the Soviet Union but to relieve American anxieties about accepting compromise with the Soviet Union.

In the cultural realm, Reagan gave the religious right almost nothing except rhetoric. He continued to favor a constitutional amendment that outlawed abortion, but everyone knew the abortion amendment had no chance of enactment. His first appointment to the Supreme Court was the moderate Sandra Day O'Connor. He eventually would appoint some quite conservative Supreme Court Justices, but in 1996 the executive director of the Christian Coalition, Ralph Reed, spoke both for religious activists and outside observers when he bemoaned, "I can remember having gone through the Ronald Reagan era, when everybody got warm fuzzies in the Roosevelt Room but nobody had any genuine institutional strength or influence."[68]

As has been mentioned, Reagan's wife Nancy declared in 1987 that she "didn't give a damn about the right-to-lifers" and told his chief of staff that the conservative

---

66. For a top Goldwater aide who bemoaned this, see F. Clifton White, *Politics as a Noble Calling: The Memoirs of F. Clifton White* (Ottawa, IL: Jameson Books, 1994), p. 216.
67. David A. Stockman, *The Triumph of Politics: How the Reagan Revolution Failed* (New York: Harper & Row, 1986), p. 9.
68. Sam Howe Verhovek, "Abortion Barely Mentioned, Its Opponents Are Offended," *The New York Times*, August 15, 1996, p. A1.

Pat Buchanan should not be used as a speechwriter: "His ideas are not Ronald Reagan's ideas."[69] Reagan's memoirs implicitly support these words. They concentrate solely on foreign and economic policy and do not mention abortion and the pro-life forces.

Reagan had carried the blue states in 1980 because of Carter's unpopularity, but the 1984 election was a referendum on his own performance. He received 58.8% of the popular vote against a quite reasonable Democratic candidate in Walter Mondale and again swept the major blue states. Clearly the broad population was reassured by his behavior in office and saw his policy as far more nuanced than either his most ardent supporters or bitter opponents claimed.

By the time Reagan left office, the Evangelicals were firmly identified with the Republican Party. Yet it was still difficult to believe that they would define the face of the Republican Party and lead the Republicans to follow a red state strategy. Men and women were for the first time beginning to vote differently, especially those who were not married. The women's movement was skillful in persuading the media to concentrate on the Republican loss of women's votes with its policy, but the Democratic Party was, of course, also losing the votes of men with its policy. Indeed, the statistics on party identification suggested that men were changing their identification rather than women.[70] But however the gender gap was viewed, a party theorist would predict that the Republicans and Democrats would each move toward the center on gender-related questions in an effort to win back their old supporters.

Least of all would one have predicted that the Republicans would follow a policy that largely abandoned the blue states to the Democrats. As Table 2 indicates, Reagan won the former states of the Confederacy and the border states of Kentucky, Missouri, and Oklahoma by a 7.4 million vote margin. He also won a combination of the Pacific Coast states and the Northern states from the Mississippi River through New England — essentially the "blue states" — by a nearly identical 7.5 million votes. Yet the Southern and the three border states had only 161 Electoral College votes in 1988, while the Pacific and Northern states east of the Mississippi had 294.[71] Minnesota and Iowa had a similar profile to the latter group, and they had an additional 18 Electoral College votes.

In short, as the Republicans looked to a future in which they certainly could not continue to sweep the vast majority of all states, they had to understand that a switch of some 4 million voters in the blue states would cost the party almost twice as many Electoral College votes as a similar loss in the South. The logical decision seemed clear enough.

---

69. Donald T. Regan, *For the Record: From Wall Street to Washington* (San Diego: Harcourt, Brace, Jovanovich, 1988), pp. 70 and 77.
70. This was noted at the time in Paul R. Abramson, John H. Aldrich, and David W. Rohde, *Change and Continuity in the 1980 Elections*, rev. ed. (Washington: CQ Press, 1983), p. 290. This source presents an excellent summary and analysis of the various statistics on the subject before and during the election on pp. 289-291.
71. The "Pacific states" in this calculation include California, Hawaii, Nevada, Oregon, and Washington, but not Alaska, which votes as a Mountain state. The three border states of Delaware, Maryland, and West Virginia are included in the "Northern states east of the Mississippi."

The Democrats were, of course, studying the same statistics as the Republicans. Yet, precisely in the mid-1980s a new organization, the Democratic Leadership Council (DLC), was being formed to persuade the Democrats to adopt a Southern strategy. The DLC failed to stop the nomination of Michael Dukakis of Massachusetts in 1988, but its chairman, Bill Clinton of Arkansas, was nominated and elected President in 1992 and a DLC founder, Al Gore of Tennessee, was elected Vice President. In these simple terms, the Southern strategy worked for the Democrats, but the statistics of Table 2 suggest that this is more of a mystery than is usually assumed. The secret to the mystery is that the so-called Southern strategy of the Democrats really was directed at the relatively well-to-do of the large industrial states.

Table 2: The Democratic and Republican Presidential Vote in the Pacific States, the Old Northwest, and the East, 1984 and 1988

	Reagan's Vote in 1984				Bush's Vote in 1988			
	Vote (in Millions)		Percentage		Vote (in Millions)		Percentage	
State	Reagan	Mondale	Reagan	Mondale	Bush	Dukakis	Bush	Dukakis
California	5,467	3,923	57.2%	41.3%	5,055	4,702	51.1%	47.6%
Connecticut	891	570	60.7%	38.8%	750	677	52.0%	46.9%
Delaware	152	102	59.8%	39.9%	140	109	55.9%	43.5%
Illinois	2,707	2,086	56.2%	43.3%	2,311	2,216	50.7%	48.6%
Indiana	1,377	841	61.7%	37.7%	1,298	861	59.8%	39.7%
Maine	337	215	55.3%	43.9%	307	244	55.3%	43.9%
Maryland	880	788	52.5%	47.0%	876	826	51.1%	48.2%
Massachusetts	1,311	1,240	51.2%	48.4%	1,195	1,401	45.4%	53.2%
Michigan	2,252	1,530	59.2%	40.2%	1,965	1,676	53.6%	45.7%
Nevada	189	92	65.8%	32.0%	206	133	58.9%	37.9%
New Hampshire	267	120	68.6%	30.9%	282	164	62.4%	36.3%
New Jersey	1,934	1,261	60.1%	39.2%	1,743	1,320	56.2%	42.6%
New York	3,665	3,120	53.8%	45.8%	3,082	3,348	47.5%	51.6%
Ohio	2,679	1,825	58.9%	40.1%	2,417	1,940	55.0%	44.1%
Oregon	686	536	55.9%	43.7%	560	616	46.6%	51.3%
Pennsylvania	2,584	2,280	53.3%	46.0%	2,300	2,195	50.7%	48.4%
Rhode Island	212	197	51.7%	48.0%	178	225	43.9%	55.6%
Vermont	136	96	57.9%	40.8%	124	116	51.1%	47.6%
Washington	1,052	807	55.8%	42.9%	904	934	48.5%	50.0%
West Virginia	405	328	55.1%	44.6%	310	341	47.5%	52.2%
Wisconsin	1,199	996	54.2%	45.0%	1,047	1,127	47.8%	51.4%
Total	30,362	22,953	56.8%	42.9%	27,050	25,171	51.3%	47.0%

Source: *CQ's Guide to US Elections, vol. 1, pp. 684-685.*

CHAPTER 8. THE ORIGINS OF THE DEMOCRATS' BLUE-STATE STRATEGY

Whatever the problems in understanding the development of the Republican red state strategy, everyone at least recognizes that the Republicans have had a red state strategy. By contrast, neither Democratic nor Republican partisans really want to acknowledge how far the Democrats have moved from the New Deal, let alone how cautious the New Deal was in comparative terms. Democratic partisans want to maintain their New Deal base by proposing expensive programs such as in health care that they do not intend to enact. Republican partisans want to continue to denounce Democratic big spending to overcome the unhappiness of their old Northern base with the new Republican cultural policy.

The evolution in Democratic strategy is particularly difficult to understand because the extraordinary presidency of Lyndon Johnson occurred in the midst of it. Johnson never could have been nominated on his own as a presidential candidate, and his Great Society was the product not only of his own personal New Deal values but also of another accident — a large Congressional majority resulting from Barry Goldwater's nomination and then landslide defeat. Medicare might not even exist today in its comprehensive form without the accidental Johnson presidency. Or it might have been enacted by the Republicans.

If Johnson had not been President, the evolution of the Democratic strategy would look very different. Roosevelt did conduct a revolution that redefined the permissible limits on the power of the central government in the economic sphere, but he utilized those powers in a highly restricted way. In particular, Roosevelt never used his huge majority in Congress from the 1936 election to try to enact further New Deal legislation. Sometimes this is explained by Roosevelt's absorption with foreign policy after 1936, but, in fact, he did little in foreign policy in 1937 and the first half of 1938 when he had his big majority.

Harry Truman never really expanded the New Deal but only consolidated it and expanded the number of people who received benefits such as Social Security. That is, Truman followed much the same policy as would have the Republicans Wendell Willkie and Thomas Dewey. The memory of Harry Truman's domestic record is shaped more by his fervent 1948 campaign against the "Do Nothing" 80th Congress than his actual programs.

Canada often is treated as more conservative than the US because American Tories founded it and because the existence of Quebec requires a weak central government. Yet, even after the US benefited for 20 years from the New Deal and Truman's Fair Deal, Canada had the social welfare program of Great Britain, far more liberal than that of the United States.

Truman's relative conservatism often is attributed to Southern resistance. In fact, Congressmen in the South often reflected the strong populist preferences of the region, and the 1937 change in interpretation of the Constitution meant that Southerners no longer had to worry about preserving the old interpretation. The South did need to cooperate with the Republicans to obtain support for cloture as Truman pushed civil rights legislation in 1949. Yet Truman had taken the initiative in pushing for a bill that could not pass, but that would force the Southern Democrats to form a conservative coalition with the Republicans. An old member of the Senate Club should not have been surprised by this consequence.

There was another, but never-mentioned, factor in the cautious policy that the Democrats followed under Truman and afterwards. During the Wilson Administration, the more conservative Progressives moved from the Republican Party of Theodore Roosevelt to the Democratic Party. During the presidency of Franklin Roosevelt, the Wilson Progressives were joined by those had supported Theodore Roosevelt and Robert La Follette. All these Progressives came from the "upper-middle class," that is, from the top 10 to 15th percentile of the population in education and income. They often were fervent reformers, but their reformist passions seldom focused on income redistribution.

In his history of the Kennedy Administration published less than two years after Kennedy's assassination, Arthur Schlesinger, Jr., described Adlai Stevenson as the person who gave "the tradition of progressive idealism" a "brilliant and exciting expression" in the postwar period. Later he wrote that Stevenson and Kennedy "were in substantial agreement on the great issues of public policy" and that "Kennedy was emerging as the heir and executor of the Stevenson revolution."[1] When Stevenson first was elected Illinois governor in 1948, however, the *New York Times* columnist Arthur Krock wrote that Stevenson was a "new Democrat," a phrase that Krock was using in its modern meaning. Schlesinger did not mention in this book how intensely unhappy he had been with Stevenson's conservatism in 1952.

Schlesinger was using the phrase "progressive idealism" in a very literal sense. His father, Arthur Schlesinger, Sr., had developed a theory of 30-year cycles of reform and conservatism in American history, and in 1939 he had predicted that 1947 would be the most conservative year of the cycle and 1960–1961 would be the beginning of a new period of reform. Arthur, Jr., reported this theory to Kennedy in July 1959, but

---

1. Arthur M. Schlesinger, Jr., *A Thousand Days: John F. Kennedy in the White House* (Boston: Houghton Mifflin, 1965), p. 23.

predicted that "the approaching liberal epoch would resemble the Progressive period of the turn of the century more than it would the New Deal."[2] He told Kennedy that the new Progressive revolt would grow out of "spiritual rather than economic discontent," but he never could have dreamed of the extent to which spiritual and cultural issues would come to dominate politics. The blue-state strategy did not suddenly emerge in the 1990s.

The history of the development of the suburban or the blue-state strategy of the Democratic Party is the history of the gradual increase in the influence of those imbued with the Progressive tradition. The generation of 20- and 30-year-old Progressives who supported Stevenson and Kennedy never enjoyed real success at the presidential level. Kennedy's presidency was too short, and he was followed by a President who was more of a New Dealer than Roosevelt, a candidate in George McGovern who was a La Follette Progressive, and then Jimmy Carter, who had the Progressives' economic views, but not their cultural values.

Stevenson and especially Kennedy had their major impact upon the next generation, those born during or just after World War II. The Democratic Baby Boomers all point to John and Robert Kennedy as their political inspiration and also as their model of what politics should be. Not surprisingly, it was this generation whose presidential candidates and President consolidated the blue state strategy.

THE SOUTH, THE NEW DEAL, AND LYNDON JOHNSON

The Progressive movement of the turn of the century was essentially an urban movement of the Northeast. Woodrow Wilson's adoption of a Progressive position in 1910, although a more conservative one than that of Theodore Roosevelt, had drawn a larger number of Southerners into the movement, but not enough to change its overall character.

The Progressives shared some common enemies with the Midwestern Populists — notably the large corporations and the immigrants — but the Progressives embraced the fiscal conservatism of the gold standard. More important, their distaste for immigrants was part of their general abhorrence of trade unions and the workers who joined them. Their opinion of radical farmers was little higher. The Populists of William Jennings Bryan detested the immorality, secularism, and modern ideas (e.g., Darwin's theory of evolution) of the urban educated class — that is, the social base of the Progressives.

On the surface, Franklin Roosevelt had been a classic Progressive at the beginning of the century, but a more conservative Wilsonian Progressive rather than one associated with Theodore Roosevelt. Yet, as assistant secretary of the Navy, he had not become involved in the domestic policy debates of the Administration, and his views had not become more clearly defined in the debates of the 1920s. According to the conventional scholarly interpretation, Franklin Roosevelt conducted a revo-

---

2. Schlesinger, *A Thousand Days*, p. 18.

lution by putting together an urban Democratic coalition to represent the interests of the urban workers. There clearly is an element of truth in this interpretation, but it is misleading. Insiders in the 1930s, 1940s, and 1950s often talked as if Roosevelt were a La Follette Progressive.

Walter Lippmann, it may be remembered, had remarked on the great ambiguity in the Roosevelt position in 1931 and 1932. Lippmann distinguished between "the Bryan tradition" in the Democratic Party and "Cleveland and Wilson Democracy" — and differentiated both from the "collectivism" of Robert La Follette. James Rowe's memorandum to Truman in 1947 calling for a radical strategy on civil rights casually referred to "the traditional Democratic alliance between the South and the West."[3] As has been seen, Lyndon Johnson's chief political adviser in 1960, George Reedy, emphasized that Southerners in Congress must maintain their alliance with the West. "The question which every Southern Democrat should ask himself is NOT whether he is willing to cut his ties to the 'civil rights' Democrats, but whether he is willing to cut his ties to the Western and Middlewestern Democrats who have some understanding of his problems and are willing to meet him half way."[4]

Lippmann in 1932 pointed to two countervailing indicators of Roosevelt's position. The Cleveland and Wilson tradition was based on the large industrial states of the east, but was very conservative. Roosevelt had been in the Wilson Administration and talked in Wilsonian terms in 1932. The more radical Bryan tradition was based on the populism of the center of the country, and the core of the delegates whom Roosevelt successfully recruited prior to the Democratic convention came from the Midwest, the West, and the South.

From this perspective, Roosevelt actually embraced the Bryan tradition in 1933 — or, more immediately, the La Follette Progressive tradition of 1924. One of the most striking and least-noticed aspects of the 1932 election is how much the voters already seemed to have some sense that this would occur. In 1932 Roosevelt received a landslide 57% of the vote in the West and the Midwest west of Ohio — 59% in the Prairie and Mountains states alone — but only 50.4% of the vote in the large industrial states from Massachusetts through Ohio. He did even better in the Midwest and West in 1936 (60% of the total), but relatively poorly in 1940 and 1944 in the Midwest and Mountain states alone (50% of the total in both years, 49% and 46% respectively in the Prairie and Mountain states alone). Events in Europe were probably the major reason for the decline in Roosevelt's Midwestern vote after 1938, but his conservative domestic policy in 1937 and 1938 may also have been a factor.

If Roosevelt's first term is seen in the perspective of the Bryan and Cleveland–Wilson traditions, it is striking how many of Roosevelt's policies were directed at the rural areas. Anti-Semitic and anti-socialist conservatives pointed to urban Jews such as Felix Frankfurter and Benjamin Cohen as the radical core of the New Deal,

---

3. See pp. 56-57 of Chapter 2.
4. George E. Reedy memorandum of March 8, 1960. US Senate Papers, Staff office Files of George Reedy, Reedy Memos, Box 430 (1 of 2). Lyndon B. Johnson Presidential Library, Austin, Texas.

but, in fact, the high-level radicals in the Administration were Midwestern Progressives — Harry Hopkins, Henry Wallace, and Harold Ickes.

An examination of archives makes it strikingly clear how often Democratic politicians spoke with fervent pride about New Deal policies that were intended to improve the situation in the countryside. Indeed, most of Roosevelt's actual policy achievements had such a component. The New Deal strove to increase farm prices by repressing supply, sometimes by much-decried measures such as the killing of animals but eventually by the establishment of acreage controls tied with parity payments. Almost no farms had electricity in 1930, and the rural electrification program brought electricity to virtually all of them. The Grand Coulee Dam, Tennessee Valley Authority, Boulder Dam, and many lesser projects promoted flood control and/or the storing of water for irrigation. The CCC and other government job programs had a rural element.

By contrast, the trade unions hardly existed as a major political force in the 1930s. The Wagner Act was less a response to a trade union interest group than an effort to create one. Yet trade unions that were strengthened by the Wagner Act were unable to achieve major policy goals either in Roosevelt's second term or the Truman Administration. The most powerful and radical trade unions such as John L. Lewis' Union of Mine Workers had an antagonistic relationship to both administrations. The American Federation of Labor (AFL) was always conservative, and its radical competitor, the Congress of Industrial Organizations (CIO), was mainly known after the war for its purge of pro-Communist elements.

From this perspective, the position of the South in the New Deal has a rather unusual appearance. Southern voting patterns in presidential elections meant little in the period from 1880 until 1950, but Southerners were very important in Congress. It would, however, be wrong to exaggerate their conservatism. They wanted Supreme Court Justices who would support the autonomy of the South in dealing with its blacks. They did not want a major populist party either under the Democratic label or as a challenger to it. But once these interests were served, the South remained the poorest and most rural region in the country, and it benefited from many economic and social programs.

Of course, the Southern Democratic elite was divided, but the economic elite generally was as suspicious of the Eastern economic elite as were the Midwestern farmers. They suffered from the same decline in commodity prices and, except for those who owned banks, they had an interest in inflation. Even those who owned banks had an interest in keeping the poorer whites quiescent. As a result, Southern voting alignments in Congress often were quite different than in the presidential nominating conventions. From the 1880s onward, Southern Congressmen often cooperated with Midwesterners in Congress on economic and social issues that did not have a racial component.

Northern Democrats sometimes explained the failure of Roosevelt to enact New Deal measures in his second term by a change in position among Southern Congressmen. Indeed, Roosevelt encouraged this interpretation by attempting what seemed an extraordinarily quixotic purge of conservative Democrats, especially Southerners, in the 1938 primaries. In fact, Roosevelt was not a quixotic politician, and he must have been making some political calculation in undertaking a hopeless purge in the 1938 primaries. The South had an interest in preventing a populist third party challenge to Roosevelt in the 1936 election, and at a minimum, Roosevelt was signaling it that there were other third party dangers. He implicitly — and in some leaks more explicitly — was telling the South that he would form a third party if it tried to block his nomination for a third term in 1940 as the Southern Republicans had done in the case of Teddy Roosevelt in 1912.

In emphasizing the conservative Southern opposition to his program in his second term, Roosevelt also was presenting a rationale for his own lack of action. Although he still was quite inactive in foreign policy in 1937 and 1938, he was looking forward to 1940. If he wanted a third term, he would have to emphasize foreign policy. Given the international situation, this meant he would have to move to a more anti-Hitler position. He would need to re-emphasize the old alliance of the South and the English-American Northeast instead of an alliance with the La Follette Midwest. This implied a more conservative economic policy.

Without question, Northern commentators in the postwar period adopted the same strategy of blaming conservative presidential action on the South. They treated Adlai Stevenson and John Kennedy as liberals who needed to select conservative Southern running mates to balance the ticket. In fact, archives and the record make clear that Stevenson and Kennedy's two running mates, Senators John Sparkman of Alabama and Lyndon Johnson of Texas, were more liberal on New Deal economic issues than the men at the head of their respective tickets.

After World War II, however, the interests of the South changed as the issue of civil rights became more important and the Northern Democrats could no longer be counted upon to support the Southern filibusters on the subject. As the Midwestern Progressives switched from the Republican Party to the Democratic Party of Franklin Roosevelt and Harry Truman, the remaining Midwestern Republicans became more conservative. They often were willing to work with the Southerners, but in a different policy coalition than before and during the New Deal.

But, of course, to the extent that this was true, the civil rights acts of the 1960s should have changed the overall Southern interests. The federal government removed the restrictions on the ability of blacks and poor whites to vote, and hence the average relative income of the actual Southern voter fell. The rapid postwar industrialization of the South not only increased the size of the Southern middle class that Nixon and earlier Republicans tried to court, but also the number of industrial workers. The South's major argument to Northern and foreign investors was that the South was not unionized and had a low-wage work force. This should have been reflected in their voting behavior. It seemed that Lyndon Johnson, the first President from the Confederacy in 120 years, had found the right Southern strategy for the Democrats.

ADLAI STEVENSON AND THE BEGINNING OF THE SUBURBAN STRATEGY

Few remember unsuccessful presidential candidates fifty years after their defeat. Thomas Dewey and Adlai Stevenson are little more than names for political science majors in college today. Even this book gives almost no attention to the three defeated Republican candidates from 1936 through 1948 — Alf Landon, Wendell Willkie, and Thomas Dewey. Once Eisenhower defeated Robert Taft for the Republican nomination in 1952, a number of factors made him an easy winner over any Democratic candidate in November. Since the Democrats were sure to be defeated, Stevenson receives little attention except as a man who had the misfortune to oppose Eisenhower. His strategy seems of little interest because no strategy could have won.

Nevertheless, Stevenson is worthy of extended attention. It is correct that no Democratic strategy could have won in 1952, but it is wrong to neglect Stevenson's nomination. It seems quite peculiar on the surface. Senator Estes Kefauver of Tennessee actively wanted the nomination and won the primaries in 12 of the 14 states where they were held. He lost only to Hubert Humphrey in his home state of Minnesota and Richard Russell of Georgia in the neighboring state of Florida. Kefauver had become famous in conducting anti-corruption investigations and espoused a liberal New Deal economic position. He did not have a chance against Eisenhower, but he would have excited the party's base.

Stevenson, by contrast, clearly did not want the presidential nomination. He had been elected governor of Illinois in 1948 by 572,000 votes, the largest Democratic margin in Illinois history until that time, while Truman won the state by only 33,600 votes. Truman lost the Chicago suburbs by a vote of 83,900 to 20,969, while Stevenson lost them only by 64,048 to 44,103. Stevenson actually carried downstate Illinois, an unprecedented development in state politics.[5]

Stevenson wanted to run for a second term as governor in 1952. In January, he had even told his good friend George Ball that he thought Eisenhower would "make a pretty good President."[6] Like many others, he believed Eisenhower would be useful in combating McCarthyism and in consolidating Republican support for American involvement in European defense. Stevenson also hoped that he might be in a good position to run for President in 1956, when Eisenhower would be 66 years old.

Why then would the party choose an unwilling sacrificial goat whose nomination might and did cost the party the governorship of Illinois when it had a candidate who was completely willing and whose loss would cost nothing? One reason was that the party establishment had a quite negative opinion about Kefauver. He did not have the appearance of a dignified President (he wore a coonskin hat as part of his campaign), and he was a maverick whose investigations of corruption had annoyed the leaders of some urban political machines.

---

5. John Dreiske, "Illinois Goes to Truman in Demo Shift," *The Chicago Sun-Times,* November 3, 1948, p. 3. The breakdown of votes for governor by city, suburb, and downstate is found on p. 7.
6. George W. Ball, *The Past Has Another Pattern: Memoirs* (New York: W. W. Norton, 1982), p. 115.

But Kefauver's major shortcoming for the party leadership was much more difficult to discuss in public. Senator John Sparkman of Alabama raised it directly only in a personal letter to the head of the Kefauver campaign in Alabama, but even then Sparkman's administrative assistant officially sent the letter so that Sparkman would have deniability if the letter somehow became public:[7]

> I want you to know that we consider you our good friend and always will.... You know and I know that the real fight here on Civil Rights always has been and always will be on the vote to invoke cloture. If ever sufficient votes are obtained to invoke cloture, we will have a FEPC bill passed and any other Civil Rights bill. The Congressional Record will show that on March 11, 1949, Kefauver supported cloture. The vote was 41 to 46 in favor of the Southerners. For your information, Kefauver was the only Southerner in the Senate who voted as he did.

> There has been much pressure on the [Alabama] Senators to use this vote in Senator [Richard] Russell's candidacy. However, both are reluctant to try to bring the Civil Rights question into this fight. However, since this is a matter of record and because of our friendship, I did feel that I should tell you about it.

In short, the Southern Democratic Party, still feeling the effects of Strom Thurmond's defection in 1948 and expecting Eisenhower to be popular in the South, absolutely did not want a Democratic nominee who favored federal civil rights action. That he might be a Senator from a Confederate state only made the prospect worse. By 1952, Truman from Missouri was sympathetic to Southern concerns, and Northern Democrats, who knew it was a losing year, had no reason to resist. The South, after all, had accommodated Northern political needs with Al Smith in the losing year of 1928, and it deserved reciprocity.

To a modern American, the unacceptability of Kefauver to the South and to the party as a whole is perfectly understandable. The Southern acceptance and even desire for Stevenson is, however, a quite major surprise. Stevenson is one of the great icons of Democratic liberals and aroused the excitement of liberal intellectuals even before his nomination.[8] Eleanor Roosevelt was so enthusiastic about him on the eve of the 1960 convention that she asked Kennedy to turn over his delegates, a majority at the convention, to Stevenson and become his Vice Presidential running mate. As governor of Illinois, Stevenson naturally had to support civil rights and propose a state Fair Employment Practices Commission. How then did he satisfy the Deep South as well as the liberal intellectuals?

The basic reason that Stevenson was acceptable to the South is that he actually was quite conservative on questions of civil rights for blacks. Although he had pro-

---

7.   Letter of Edd H. Hyde to Fuller Kimbrell, June 17, 1952, John Sparkman Papers, Box 409, University of Alabama Special Collections, Tuscaloosa, Ala. In his memoirs Kimbrell does not mention this point, but recalls that Sparkman, who was drafting the civil rights plank in the Democratic Platform, already was being "whispered around" as Stevenson's running mate — which he was to become. Fuller Kimbrell, *From the Farm House to the State House: The Life and Times of Fuller Kimbrell* (Tuscaloosa, AL: Word Way Press, 2001), p. 247.
8.   John Bartlow Martin, *It Seems Like Only Yesterday: Memoirs of Writing, Presidential Politics, and the Diplomatic Life* (New York: William Morrow, 1986), p. 143.

posed a state Fair Employment Practice Commission in Illinois, he had not pushed energetically for its passage, and the law had not been enacted. More important for the South, Stevenson did not favor action by the federal government in the civil rights realm. In January 1952, he privately told a top Truman political adviser that, in the words of a close friend who was present, "the states should be responsible for their own civil rights policies and ... the federal government ought not to put the South completely over a barrel."[9]

The contrast between Truman's campaign strategy in 1948 and Stevenson's in 1952 was striking. Truman had deliberately emphasized civil rights, but Stevenson said little about the subject. He talked as if the solution had to be a change in the hearts and minds of people in the North and South. Many of his speechwriters tried to push him to discuss the subject, but he refused. Even in Harlem at the end of the campaign, Stevenson threw away a careful speech that had been prepared for him and instead made relatively brief general remarks at the meeting of blacks. The remarks were notable for saying little about civil rights and for praising his Alabama running mate, John Sparkman.[10] The Democratic majority fell in almost all cities with large numbers of blacks, and the attractiveness of Eisenhower to whites was not the only reason.[11]

Stevenson's admirers argue that he began as a conservative, but moved to the left after the 1952 campaign. A *New York Times* reporter, Anthony Lewis, had a very different view about Stevenson's position on civil rights in 1956 when he was running once more against Eisenhower. Stevenson, Lewis recalled in 1960, was "quite restrained on the civil rights issue" in 1956. He had a key impact on the 1956 platform and, in Lewis' words, the civil rights plank consisted of a "pallid six paragraphs." It included "such gems as the Democratic Party emphatically reaffirms its support of the historic principle that ours is a government of laws and not of men." When a minority sought to include support for the enforcement of *Brown v. Board of Education,* they were heavily defeated.[12]

Stevenson's conservatism was not limited to civil rights. John Bartlow Martin, a Stevenson speechwriter and author of his standard biography, was quite blunt: "Actually [Stevenson] was not so liberal, was a man who favored balanced budgets, feared executive power, looked with favor on business, deplored what he considered labor's excesses."[13] Stevenson' advisers have left an unusually full record of the cam-

9. Ball, *The Past Has Another Pattern,* p. 117. In August 1952, Ball wrote Stevenson a memorandum raising the specter of another Civil War if the North pushed the South too hard on desegregation. The memo likely was meant to provide Stevenson with talking points to support a position he already held. "Ball Memo on Civil Rights," August 15, 1952, George Ball Papers, Box 160, Folder 9, Princeton University.
10. John Bartlow Martin, *Adlai Stevenson of Illinois: The Life of Adlai E. Stevenson* (Garden City, NY: Doubleday & Co., 1976), p. 744.
11. Porter McKeever, *Adlai Stevenson: His Life and Legacy* (New York: William Morrow, 1989), pp. 212–223.
12. Anthony Lewis, "The Civil Rights Plank," *The New York Times,* July 13, 1960, p. 20.
13. Martin, *It Seems Like Only Yesterday,* p. 143. Also see Martin, *Adlai Stevenson of Illinois,* p. 646 and 630.

paign, but despite their antagonism to each other, they agree almost entirely about the nature of their candidate's views.[14]

The liberal Martin declared that the even more liberal Arthur Schlesinger, Jr., considered Stevenson "far too conservative": "too pro-Southern and insufficiently committed to civil rights and labor, indeed, even anti-labor and anti-Truman."[15] One of Stevenson's "great fears," his own chief of staff reported, "was that the Democratic party would turn into the labor party."[16] Even the speechwriter most attuned to Stevenson's views, W. Willard Wertz, called an impromptu and "ill-tempered — and illiterate — reference to labor goons" during a speech a reflection of Stevenson's "sensitivity to the reaction of his [conservative] North Shore friends to the Labor Day Speech."[17]

When Stevenson wrote an article in 1955, he did not pledge to use government to protect people from the powerful. He proclaimed "my faith in democratic capitalism." Democrats, he asserted, should not have only an "antagonistic and critical" attitude toward "Big Business," and they should not speak of "economic royalists," as did Franklin Roosevelt. "At mid-twentieth century, mass manipulation is a greater danger to the individual than was economic exploitation in the nineteenth century."[18]

The hallmark of Stevenson's campaign was his genuine distaste for seeking the support of interest groups, especially the New Deal interest groups. In a letter to a friend, Archibald MacLeish, he declared, "I get so sick of the everlasting appeals to the cupidity and prejudices of every group which characterize our political campaigns."[19] He was quite explicit in an early speech to the American Legion:[20]

> Consider the groups who seek to identify their special interests with the general welfare.... I have resisted them before and I hope the Almighty will give me the strength to do so again and again. And I should tell you, my fellow Legionnaires, as I would tell all other organized groups, that I intend to resist pressures from veter-

14. One who was close to Stevenson's policy position, W. Willard Wirtz, annotated each speech for the archives, while one who favored a New Deal approach, John Bartlow Martin, interviewed participants and wrote Stevenson's definitive biography. All the campaign speeches with Wirtz's annotations are collected in the Stevenson archives at Princeton University under Wirtz's name. Martin's interviews are found in the Princeton archives in the separate collection of his John Bartlow Martin papers and are quoted at great length in his biography, *Adlai Stevenson of Illinois*. Martin also has 130 boxes of material in his large collection of papers at the Library of Congress that deal with Stevenson and his biography of him. Copies of his Princeton papers are included among them.
15. Martin, *It Seems Like Only Yesterday*, p. 148.
16. John Bartlow Martin interview with Carl McCowan, December 6, 1966, Martin Papers, Box 1, Folder 50, p. 27. John Bartlow Martin Papers, Princeton University.
17. Wirtz recollections, Evansville Speech, September 26, 1952, Box 3, Folder 5, and Wirtz memorandum, November 8, 1952, in Wirtz collection, Box 1, Folder 3, Stevenson Collection, Princeton University.
18. Adlai E. Stevenson, "My Faith in Democratic Capitalism," *Fortune*, October 1955, pp. 126-127 and 156-168.
19. Letter to Archibald MacLeish, August 11, 1952, in Walter Johnson, ed., *The Papers of Adlai Stevenson* (Boston: Little, Brown, 1974), vol. IV, p. 39.
20. In Walter Johnson, *The Papers of Adlai Stevenson*, vol. IV, p.51.

ans, too, if I think their demands are excessive or in conflict with the public interest.

Since the American Legion would never vote for Stevenson against Eisenhower, his speech seemed a tactically wise appeal to the broader electorate. Yet Stevenson often repeated the theme to key groups in the Democratic coalition that were vital to his effort. Stevenson clearly retained the old Progressive attitudes toward the Ellis Island immigrants. He was especially reluctant to speak to Jewish groups and expressed alarm that their campaign contributions might be too important to the party. He refused to attend the traditional Alfred E. Smith dinner in New York City that was sponsored by Cardinal Spellman. Stevenson also publicly refused to follow Roosevelt and Truman in sending an ambassador to the Vatican. Jake Arvey, the Democratic boss of Chicago, reported that Catholics "generally detested Stevenson ... picturing him as an intolerant Presbyterian."[21]

Stevenson certainly had the right to any views that he wanted, and the Democrats were well-advised to focus on reconciliation with the South in an election they were certain to lose. The apparent mystery is that Stevenson became an icon for the liberal intellectual wing of the Democratic Party. The basic reason is that they were not New Dealers and that they defined a cultural "liberal" differently than the South. For the intellectuals, the key questions were "civil liberties" (free speech and opposition to McCarthyism) and foreign policy. Stevenson was quite liberal on these issues, and the Southern politicians did not care much about them. The South focused on "civil rights" (rights for blacks), and Stevenson was conservative on them.

Two weeks after the 1948 election, the leading political columnist of the *New York Times*, Arthur Krock, wrote a piece that was prescient both in its contents and in its title: "Strength Displayed by the 'New' Democrats."[22] According to Krock, Stevenson represented important new forces in the party and was already being "surveyed" as a possible presidential nominee in 1952.

In 1960, Theodore H. White gave special attention to these "new forces in the party" and to Kennedy's need "to win the attention and support of the earnest citizen groups who play so large a role in Democratic politics."[23] The first to describe this group fully was James Q. Wilson, and, as he reports, Stevenson was their idol. Wilson emphasized their "outlook on politics, and [their] style of politics":[24]

> The amateur politician sees the political world more in terms of ideas and principles than in terms of persons. Politics is the determination of public policy, and public policy ought to be set deliberately rather than as the accidental by-product of a struggle for personal and party advantage....

---

21. Martin, *It Seems Like Only Yesterday*, p. 618. His actual religion was Unitarian. A number of others testified to Stevenson's anti-Catholicism.
22. Arthur Krock, "Strength Displayed by the 'New' Democrats," *The New York Times*, November 19, 1948, p. 2.
23. Theodore H. White, *The Making of the President, 1960* (New York: Atheneum Publishers, 1961), p. 34.
24. James Q. Wilson, *The Amateur Democrat: Club Politics in Three Cities* (Chicago: University of Chicago Press, 1962), pp. 2–3 and 18.

The amateur politician ... would in the ideal situation prefer to recruit candidates on the basis of their commitment to a set of policies. Voters would be mobilized by appeals to some set of principles or goals. The party would be held together and linked to the voter by a shared conception of the public interest. A politics of principle would necessarily attach little value to — and indeed would criticize — appeals to private, group, or sectional interest.

Wilson saw the base of the Democratic activists in "the chronic discontent among certain members of the educated, urban middle class." He quoted Richard Hofstadter at length to show the similarity of the modern activist and the Progressives of the beginning of the century who were part of "a well-educated, professional group with secure family positions," who had assimilated "Yankee-Protestant political traditions," and who took "middle class life for granted."[25]

Given Stevenson's theme of standing up for principle, it is not surprising that he was the man who, according to Wilson, "more than anyone, has served as the patron saint of the amateur politicians."[26] The activists did not, of course, think of themselves as a "special interest group," and Stevenson probably did not see them in these terms either. But, of course, when Stevenson refused to cater to the interests of the workers, farmers, blacks, Catholics, and "other interests," when he emphasized the dangers of manipulation by the mass media rather than economic exploitation, the principles to which he was committed obviously did serve some economic interests. Stevenson was appealing to the economic interests and the non-economic anxieties of the upper middle class in the "earnest citizen groups."

Certainly, those in the New Deal coalition who were being scorned saw the affluent activists as a well-defined group with its own interests and values. They responded coldly to Stevenson not because he was too intellectual or too honest, but because, knowingly or unknowingly, he was representing people who had specific economic interests and cultural values alien to their own. Whether he realized it or not, Stevenson was reaching toward the establishment of a new Democratic coalition based on the activists. The members of the old coalition were not happy.

THE TRANSITIONAL JOHN KENNEDY AND GEORGE McGOVERN

John Kennedy poses unique problems for the scholar. He was witty and charming in a way that still appeals to a modern generation, and he is eternally young because the last pictures of him were taken when he was 46 years old. He was a self-avowed representative of a new generation and emphasized the need for his generation to meet new challenges. It is literally impossible for us to believe that this "new generation" was Ronald Reagan's and that Kennedy would have been 88 years old in 2005.

---

25. Richard Hofstadter, *The Age of Reform, From Bryan to F.D.R.* (New York: Knopf, 1955), pp. 9, 138, and 168–169. Quoted in Wilson, *The Amateur Democrat*, pp. 8 and 25. The long quote on p. 8 shows the identity of approach that Wilson emphasized.
26. Wilson, *The Amateur Democrat*, p. 22.

The continuing attraction of Kennedy's words and style makes him even more difficult to discuss today than in the 1970s and 1980s, when his own generation was still in its prime and had fresh memories of him. In particular, a modern American can hardly avoid attributing values and views to Kennedy that a person of his style and personality would have today. That is a major mistake. Kennedy was quite cautious, perhaps even conservative, on cultural issues such as civil liberties and civil rights on which even conservative Supreme Court Justices today accept the liberal position of the time.

From our perspective the crucial question is the relationship of Kennedy and Stevenson on domestic policy. A number of the themes in Kennedy's acceptance speech at the 1960 Democratic convention were those of Stevenson. In part, he was trying to win the enthusiastic support of Stevenson activists, but he also was speaking for himself:[27]

> The old era is ending. The old ways will not do.... The New Deal and the Fair Deal were bold measures for their generation — but now this is a new generation.... The New Frontier of which I speak is not a set of promises — it is a set of challenges. It sums up not what I intend to offer to the American people but what I intend to ask of them.... There may be those who wish to hear more — more promises to this group or that ... more assurances of a golden future, where taxes are always low and the subsidies are always high.... The harsh facts ... are that we must prove all over again to a watching world [that we] can compete with the single-minded adversary of the Communist system.... Have we the nerve and the will?

Kennedy returned to the same theme in the most famous line of his inaugural speech: "Ask not what your country can do for you, but what you can do for your country."

In other realms Kennedy and Stevenson clearly were different. As individuals, they were highly suspicious and even scornful of each other because of real differences in personality. As many complained, Stevenson liked to talk in general and even philosophical terms about the nature of problems, but he often seemed to suggest that the problems were too complex or ambiguous to correct.[28] A newsman, Eric Severeid, wrote a tactfully critical letter to Stevenson in 1952 in which he called Stevenson "the moral and intellectual proctor, the gadfly called conscience."[29]

No one would describe Kennedy in these terms. Kennedy conveyed no sense whatsoever that he had any self-doubt or lack of certainty about anything. He obviously believed that he had the ability to deal with the enormous foreign policy problems facing his new generation. One sentence in his acceptance speech was remarkable for its implicit characterization of both the American commander in Europe in World War II and himself. "After Buchanan this nation needed Lincoln — after Taft, we needed Wilson — and after Hoover we needed Franklin Roosevelt."

---

27. Kennedy Acceptance Speech at the Democratic Convention, *The New York Times*, July 16, 1960, p. 7.
28. For the comments of the leader of the CIO trade union, Walter Reuther, see Wirtz. "The Labor Day Speech," Wirtz collection, Box 1, Speech Drafts and Notes, September 1, 1952 (Detroit Labor), Adlai Stevenson Papers, Princeton University.
29. Eric Severeid letter to Stevenson, October 2, 1952. Reproduced in Johnson, *The Papers of Adlai E. Stevenson*, vol. IV, pp. 133–134.

A second difference between Stevenson and Kennedy was that, while both were much more interested in foreign policy than domestic policy, their foreign policy positions were quite different. Kennedy was much more hard-line. In comparing himself to Lincoln, Wilson, and Roosevelt, Kennedy chose wartime Presidents, and the task that he set for his new generation was winning the new war against Communism. Those who think that he would have avoided Johnson's deepening engagement in Vietnam are taking a most improbable leap of faith. A more realistic question is whether he would have acted more boldly in threatening to send troops to overthrow the regime in Hanoi.[30]

A third difference was that Kennedy had very different political instincts from Stevenson. Kennedy's grandfather was an Irish-American mayor of Boston and his father was a high official in the Roosevelt Administration. Although many friends considered Kennedy a "good New Englander," "an English American," "a European ... more English than Irish,"[31] he instinctively was a traditional Irish politician in his belief in hard-ball politics and in his coalitional approach.

Despite Kennedy's disavowal of any intention to cater to "this or that group," he never felt any shame about being a politician or about taking political acts. Yet, as seen in the earlier discussion of his immigration policy, he was completely capable of catering to important interest groups on domestic policy before an election and then forgetting them afterwards until another election approached.

Nevertheless, on the issues of importance for understanding the future evolution of the Democratic Party, Kennedy was more similar to Stevenson than different. Lyndon Johnson at heart was even more of a New Dealer than Roosevelt, but Kennedy, like Stevenson, was a New Democrat, not a New Dealer on economic social welfare questions.

Biographers divide sharply on whether Kennedy had any significant liberal domestic accomplishments. Kennedy's actual economic policy in his less than three years in office was as conservative as Stevenson's and Jimmy Carter's — and less liberal than Richard Nixon's in office. Kennedy chose a Republican from Wall Street, Douglas Dillon, as his Secretary of Treasury, and his major legislative accomplishment was the enactment of an income tax cut that reduced the rates on the upper brackets much more than the lower ones. His aide, Arthur Schlesinger, Jr., reports that Kennedy was obsessed with the international balance of payments and a

---

30. China had intervened in Korea when US forces had crossed the 38th parallel to overthrow the North Korean government. The United States feared that such an intervention was also possible if it attacked North Vietnam. Kennedy would have had to threaten to use tactical nuclear weapons against Chinese forces and their supply bases. Especially after the Cuban missile crisis, this threat probably would have prevented Chinese intervention and produced a North Vietnamese retreat. But, of course, if the strategy failed, the results would have been catastrophic. In 1950, Truman had not had tactical nuclear weapons and did not want to take the risk, even if relatively small, of threatening a major retaliation. Neither Lyndon Johnson nor Richard Nixon wanted to take either this risk or that of using tactical nuclear weapons.

31. Robert Dallek, *An Unfinished Life: John F. Kennedy, 1917–1963* (Boston: Little Brown, 2003), p. 3.

sound dollar. In Schlesinger's words, "he used to tell his advisors that the two things which scared him most were nuclear war and the payments deficit."[32]

In fact, Kennedy had done little of a liberal nature by the time that he was assassinated, but in the summer of 1963 he introduced a number of liberal bills. Perhaps these were election proposals that would be forgotten or were expected to be defeated. Perhaps many of them would have been enacted. His supporters argue that he had promoted economic growth in his first term so that he would have resources for more liberal policies in his second term. Nevertheless, it seems wrong simply to list, as many do, Kennedy's policy proposals in 1963 and give Johnson only grudging credit for having passed measures that they believe Kennedy also surely would have passed. Johnson was an extraordinarily effective President and his landslide victory over Goldwater, which Kennedy would not have had, gave Johnson an unusual Congressional majority.

A key fact about Kennedy was that he was, indeed, an instinctive coalitional politician at a time that the Roosevelt coalition was coming apart. So long as Southern Democrats were simply interested in the autonomy that would let them maintain a one-party system, so long as Northern bosses did not need to represent the economic interests of workers, and so long as blacks voted Republican, the coalition was quite durable. When Franklin Roosevelt added the Midwestern populists and radical intellectuals to the coalition and started to represent the economic interests of workers, that too caused no immediate serious problems. The South had an interest in the economic policies of the New Deal.

But, of course, when blacks became Democrats and the Supreme Court began changing its view of segregation and voting rights, that was another matter. The central civil rights issue in the North was the unequal access to jobs that was produced by the reluctance of the trade unions, disproportionately Catholic in membership, to admit blacks. This tore at the heart of the Democratic urban coalition. Moreover, the radical college students of the New Deal period had moved into well-paying jobs, but stayed within the Democratic Party and remained fairly active. They became the modern Conscience Whigs, the Mugwumps, the Eastern Progressives, and the Amateur Democrats who saw politics in moralistic terms but who unconsciously promoted their own economic interests. The Ellis Island immigrants increasingly moved to the suburbs where the Catholics among them were increasingly attracted to moderate Republicanism. The Midwestern Progressives became extremely suspicious of Democrat policy toward Germany.

In such a situation, a coalitional politician who himself had moderately conservative domestic instincts and who defined politics as the art of the possible had a natural tendency to define the possible very narrowly and to do very little. Of course, the black revolution was just beginning in earnest in the summer of 1963. Lyndon Johnson's top political aide, George Reedy, wrote a memorandum that took for granted that a strong civil rights bill could not be passed, but he was increasingly stunned by the rapid increase in violence and the change in political situation it was producing. Kennedy would have had to respond in some manner, but his fiscal atti-

---

32. Schlesinger, *A Thousand Days*, pp. 654–655.

tudes would have prevented expensive social programs and a "war on poverty," especially if expenditures on Vietnam were to rise.

The great paradox of John Kennedy is that he actually made his major historical impact in the domestic realm not as the representative of the "a new generation," but as an inspiration for the children of this generation. Kennedy's "new generation born in this century" was the "greatest generation" — those born between 1905 and 1925 who fought in World War II. All the Presidents from 1961 to 1993 were born between 1908 and 1924 and were members of this generation. Kennedy was 27 years younger than Eisenhower, but those born during World War II and in the decade after the war were the children of Kennedy's generation. A person born in 1945 was 18 years old when John Kennedy was assassinated and one born in 1950 was 18 years old when the same fate befell Robert Kennedy. This was the generation inspired by Kennedy, but paradoxically was also the generation that rebelled against their parents in the 1960s when they were young and who said that no one over 30 years of age could be trusted. This then was the generation that idealized these very same parents as the "greatest generation" of World War II when it itself was approaching its sixties.

Although the Baby Boomers were the rebellious children of Kennedy's "new generation" and he was old enough to be their father, they responded to his words as if he were speaking to them. The Democrats among them repeatedly testified that they were inspired to enter politics by John Kennedy or his brother Robert.[33] Bill Clinton, the President who popularized the phrase "New Democrat," identified fully with Kennedy, A Congressman first elected in 1974, Timothy Wirth of Colorado, testified that this was true of most of the new members of Congress of his generation, "We were reflections of JFK as President, not FDR."[34] And, of course, the 1960s were also the period of the young Goldwater activists. They would scarcely admit it, even to themselves, but many of them may also have gained their example of a sense of mission and public responsibility from the politician they were trying to defeat.

Then, paradoxically, the Democrats of the generation of wartime and Baby Boom babies were mobilized into actual presidential politics by another candidate whose values differed both from Kennedy's and their own, George McGovern. In 1972 McGovern waged a puzzling campaign. A genuine hero as a B-24 bomber pilot in World War II, he almost never referred to that experience in his 1972 campaign nor explained why he thought that Vietnam did not meet the criteria for intervention when World War II did.[35] He also seemed a stereotyped strait-laced product of a Midwest small town, but he became identified with the outrageous personal behavior of elite college youth. It is a mystery why he did not choose to talk about his

---

33. David S. Broder, *Changing of the Guard: Power and Leadership in America* (New York: Simon & Schuster, 1980), pp. 51–62.
34. John A. Farrell, *Tip O'Neill and the Democratic Century* (Boston: Little Brown, 2001), p. 442.
35. For McGovern's wartime experience, see Stephen E. Ambrose, *The Wild Blue: The Men and Boys Who Flew the B-24s Over Germany* (New York: Simon & Schuster, 2001). Despite the title, the book is overwhelmingly about McGovern.

own experience and values in a way that easily could have appealed both to sup-porters and opponents of the Vietnam War.

In his views on domestic policy, McGovern actually was very close to the Lyndon Johnson whose war he detested. Even when McGovern sought the 1984 Democratic nomination, he remained "an unrepentant New Dealer who believed that the solutions once applied by Franklin D. Roosevelt remained the right solutions."[36] It probably would be more accurate to characterize McGovern as an unrepentant South Dakota populist, a group generally to the left of Roosevelt on economic policy.

Unlike Stevenson who explicitly repudiated Franklin Roosevelt's famous term "economic royalists," McGovern quoted Roosevelt directly in embracing it. During his campaign speeches in 1972, McGovern gave by far the most attention to the war, and the war played an even more prominent role in the campaign as a whole because the media focused on it in interviews and press conferences. Yet McGovern was relentless in attacking special privileges for the rich and Big Business, in rejecting a capital gains tax with lower rates than the income tax, and in condemning the usual "White House–Wall Street" connection.[37]

Still, in practice, McGovern, even more than Stevenson, was the candidate of the forces in the Democratic Party who rejected the New Deal. His supporters were over-whelmingly those who not only opposed the war but who rejected the cultural values of the past. In addition, they called themselves "the New Left" to distinguish themselves from the New Deal Left. They explicitly said they were different from the Old Left because of their distrust of an active role of government in economic affairs. A leading conservative of the time was reasonably accurate when he characterized them as part of the anarchist philosophical stream.[38] Members of McGovern's natural New Deal base detested those in his cultural base, and they abandoned McGovern in large numbers.

No doubt, large numbers of the political activists of the 1960s and 1970s would have moved into mainstream party politics, regardless of what happened in presi-dential politics. As early as 1962, James Q. Wilson wrote that "contemporary amateur politicians are critical of the naiveté of older reform efforts which sought to capture elective offices without first capturing the party organization."[39] Nevertheless, the McGovern presidential campaign gave the activists the opportunity to hone their skills in national-level party politics, to gain control of local Democratic Party orga-nizations, and to advance into high electoral politics in the 1970s far more rapidly than otherwise would have occurred.

The major breakthrough of the Democratic activists was to occur in the 1974 Congressional election, and they were so distinctive that they were called the Class

---

36. Richard Michael Marano, *Vote Your Conscience: The Last Campaign of George McGovern* (Westport, CT: Praeger, 2003), p. xi.
37. The generalizations of this paragraph are based on an examination of his speeches in 1971 and 1972 that are located in the George S. McGovern Papers, Princeton Univer-sity.
38. Gordon Tullock, ed., *Further Explorations in the Theory of Anarchy* (Blacksburg, VA: University Publications, 1974).
39. Wilson, *The Amateur Democrat*, p. 9.

of 1974. In 1970, the former member won in 85% of the districts, 94% of those in the Southern districts and 80% of those in other states.[40] The new members averaged 45 years of age and generally had been serving in the state legislature or another local position. A few members of the Class of 1970 were older radicals (e.g., Bella Abzug), and the handful of new black members had come out of the black activist movements and/non governmental organizations of the 1960s.

In 1974, by contrast, 75 Democrats were elected to Congress for the first time, and 31 of them had never held another elected post. They averaged 39 years of age. The district reports in the *Almanac of American Politics* often mentioned that the new members had been nominated not because of their support in the traditional party organization, but because that they had organized their own group of activists. Another 33 Democrats were elected in 1976 and 26 in 1978. The new Democratic members of 1976 and 1978 usually had more traditional career paths involving local elected positions, but they were only marginally older that the 1974 newcomers — 41 and 42 respectively.[41]

The Democratic Class of 1974 was to be famous for many reasons. As Speaker of the House Tip O'Neill discovered, the activist politics out of which they came neither prepared them for the Freshman member's traditional acceptance of party discipline and the norms of the Congress nor left them with the feeling that such party discipline or Congressional norms were even appropriate.

In addition, their policy views were far from those of the Democratic leadership. David Broder found that they were "cold-blooded in rejecting the New Deal policies of the past." One who was elected Senator, Gary Hart, told Broder that "We are not a bunch of little Hubert Humphreys." The group turned out to be, in Broder's words, "far more concerned abut middle-income taxpayers than many had expected."[42] Broder was fully aware that the new Representatives defined the term "middle" not as the statistical median, but as the income of the professional and managerial stratum. The new Republicans of the 1970s were not of a strikingly different type, except that they were not elected in large numbers until 1978 and 1980. They were the Goldwater activists of the 1960s and were much more ideological than their Democratic counterparts on economic matters. In this sphere, they too had an anarchist streak.

---

40. The South includes the Confederate states, Kentucky, Missouri, Oklahoma, and West Virginia.
41. The calculation of Congressional turnover is never exact because of changes that occur between regular elections, seats that remain open for some time, those held by persons who are (usually only nominally) independent, and so forth. I have calculated the average ages myself, but have adopted the overall figures of David Broder in his *Changing of the Guard*, pp. 34–35.
42. Broder, *Changing of the Guard*, p. 75.

JIMMY CARTER AND THE EVANGELICALS

Modern Americans take for granted that Christian fundamentalists are a core element in the Republican coalition. Yet, as has been seen, the original Southerners who voted for Republicans such as Eisenhower were largely from the middle class. They almost surely went to Establishment churches and/or had a more secular approach. The rural and small town white Southerners who were most likely to be fundamentalists were slower to shift to the Republican Party. From this perspective, it was not surprising that the first President with born-again religious views was a Democrat, Jimmy Carter. Like John Kennedy in 1960, Carter lost votes because of his religion in 1976, but, on balance, he almost surely gained more in key states. They likely provided his margin of victory.

Jimmy Carter was elected governor of Georgia in 1970 and, despite his inexperience, he still was offended when George McGovern did not pick him as his running mate at the 1972 convention. In October 1972 his chief political adviser, Hamilton Jordan, wrote a memorandum largely based on Carter's thinking that predicted the nomination of Ted Kennedy in 1976. Carter had hoped to be a conservative counterweight to McGovern on the 1972 ticket and clearly saw himself playing a similar role if Kennedy were nominated. But when Kennedy removed himself from consideration in 1974 shortly after Nixon resigned, Carter's calculations had to change.

Jimmy Carter came to treat his campaign for the 1976 nomination as a morality play. Neither Agnew nor Nixon had had to pay any legal price for their action, Agnew because of a plea agreement and Nixon because Gerald Ford pardoned him. Carter presented himself as a simple, honest outsider from Plains, Georgia who would reintroduce morality back into American politics. Many attribute Carter's victory to the popular response to the themes of his campaign, perhaps even to Ford's pardon of Nixon, but this surely is too simple.

Carter's strongest argument was that the Democrats needed to nominate a born-again Christian Southerner to win back those who had been lost to Wallace in 1968 and Nixon in 1972. Carter's religion was a central part of his public persona. He was always a Southern Baptist for whom religion was important, but in the late 1960s, his religious views evolved in a manner that often is labeled "born again." In 1976, Carter talked about his religious beliefs frequently with reporters, and he gave speeches about them, including before religious groups. His sister, Ruth Carter Stapleton, was a well-known evangelist, and she had a significant influence both on him and on the Evangelical community to whom she wrote widely about "his quality of deep personal commitment to Jesus Christ."[43]

Some who observed Carter closely were more skeptical. Carter's Catholic Secretary of Health, Education, and Welfare, Joseph Califano, wrote in his memoirs, "I thought 'there is some Elmer Gantry in this born-again President.'" Gantry was a fiery Evangelical preacher whose professed religious views were not sincere.[44] One

---

43. Peter G. Bourne, *Jimmy Carter: A Comprehensive Biography from Plains to Postpresidency* (New York: Scribners, 1997), pp. 166–173.

of the closest and shrewdest observers of the 1976 campaign, the reporter Jack Germond, expressed a similar view at the end of the crucial caucus in Iowa. Carter talked with a number of Catholic leaders and managed to convey the impression that he was for legislation to restrict abortion. As was the case on other sensitive issues, notably race, Carter claimed he was misinterpreted, but Germond saw it differently:[45]

> Jimmy Carter ... is, as those who have known him longest have been saying all along, an icy hard politician with a knack for recognizing and exploiting political targets of opportunity. His handling of the abortion issue late in the Iowa campaign is a case in point. Somehow he picked just that time to suggest that, although he opposed a constitutional amendment restricting the right to an abortion, he might not be opposed to a "national statute" on the same subject. Just how this could be done is not clear in light of the Supreme Court decision on abortion, and Carter did not burden Iowa Democrats with details. His own managers tended to roll their eyes to the heavens when anyone asked for particulars. But the point is that whatever the merits, Jimmy Carter ended up as the de facto antiabortion candidate Monday night.... All that soft Southern charm and preacher talk can be deceiving.

At least judging by the documents thus far available to the public, Carter and his aides, unlike those in the Kennedy campaign, did not discuss the political advantages of Carter's religious views, but these views undoubtedly had strong advantages as well as disadvantages. One of Carter's closest advisers, it may be recalled, says that Southern Evangelical Christians were "Carter's most bedrock constituency."[46]

The available papers in the archives indicate that the main concern of Carter's campaign was the need to reassure Catholics, Jews, and liberal secular voters. Stuart Eizenstat, head of Carter's issues office during the 1976 campaign, was in anguish after a Carter speech before a religious group in Indiana in June:[47]

> During my week in Washington at the Platform deliberations, I talked with a wide range of delegates from all over the country. The most commonly expressed problem that they felt you would have in their respective states was on the religious issue. In short, there is a common fear that you will attempt to impose your own religious beliefs on others through your office.... They expressed the feeling that [the West Lafayette] speech went beyond merely stating the need for a return to public morality and to the ethics from the Judeo-Christian faiths, and that you set up your

---

44. Joseph A. Califano, *Governing America: An Insider's Report from the White House and the Cabinet* (New York: Simon and Schuster, 1981). p. 407. Gantry was a character in the Sinclair Lewis novel of that name: *Elmer Gantry* (New York: Harcourt, Brace, and Co., 1927).
45. Jack W. Germond, "Lessons to Be Learned from Iowa's Caucuses," *The Washington Star*, January 21, 1976, p. A3. The question about Carter and race rose from his comments during the crucial Pennsylvania primary about the desirability of "ethnically pure" neighborhoods.
46. Bourne, *Jimmy Carter*, pp. 304–305 and 347.
47. Memorandum to Governor Carter from Stu Eizenstat, June 23, 1976, 1976 Presidential Campaign; Issues Office — Stuart Eizenstat, Box 25, Jimmy Carter Presidential Library. Eizenstat was mistaken about the locale of the speech, which was given on June 19 in West Lafayette, Indiana, not Indianapolis. The speech seems not to exist in the Carter archives.

own religious beliefs and the example of Jesus Christ and his life and works as the example that others should follow.... These people have pointed out that in effect you were using your position to promote those beliefs over others.

... With the greatest humbleness and sincerity, I would urge you in the strongest way to attempt to avoid setting up your own personal religious precepts as those which establish the basis of public morality.... No amount of stating that you believe in the separation of church and state can avoid the potentially damaging impact which many felt has already resulted from the Indianapolis [*sic*] address.

Carter's weakness among the "ethnics" was a continuing problem in the campaign. A month after the election, the person in charge of Carter's public opinion polling, Patrick Caddell, analyzed the survey data about his election. Caddell reported that Carter had a "nagging weakness ... with 'urban ethnics'" and that he did "somewhat below par with them."[48] Caddell understated the point, if the level of turnout is taken into account. He reported with alarm that Carter had received 800,000 fewer votes in New York than Kennedy had in 1960; 500,000 fewer votes in Pennsylvania, and about 150,000 each in Ohio and Illinois.[49] Ford won Illinois, and Carter won the other three, but quite narrowly. Since population had risen and turnout had increased among blacks, clearly many Catholics who had supported Kennedy in 1960 did not even come to the polls in 1976, and others voted for Gerald Ford.

The negative impact of Carter's religion upon ethnic voters easily could have disappeared after the election. In 1976 the Catholic Church was more agitated than the Evangelicals about the 1973 Supreme Court *Roe v. Wade* decision. The traditional Democratic coalition had brought together Catholics and Southern Evangelicals at a time when the South was much more anti-Catholic than in the 1970s. Carter easily could have worked to maintain and strengthen the Catholic-Evangelical coalition, and if he had, it is at least possible that the 1980s would have been different.

The institutional bases for such cooperation seemed in place. The Speaker of the House, Tip O'Neill, was an Irish-American, and he looked forward with great anticipation to working as Speaker with his first Democratic President. Carter appointed the leading Catholic on Lyndon Johnson's staff, the Italian-American Joseph Califano, as his Secretary of Health, Education, and Welfare and a Jewish-American, Michael Blumenthal, as his Secretary of Treasury. If Carter had developed a good working relationship with these three men and had compromised with them to a limited degree on issues important to them, they would continually have reassured members of their ethnic and religious groups about him.

This did not happen. The angry chapter in O'Neill's memoirs about the Carter years is filled with example after example of the President's unwillingness to work

---

48. Patrick H. Caddell, "Initial Working Paper on Political Strategy," December 10, 1976, Presidential Papers, Staff Offices — Press: Box 4, p. 10. Jimmy Carter Presidential Library. Carter's problem with the ethnics, especially the Catholics, was often mentioned in the press during the election.
49. Caddell, "Initial Working Paper on Political Strategy," p. 12. Actually, Caddell presented somewhat larger numbers, but he wrote when only the preliminary voting statistics were available. I have given the numbers from the final count.

with the Congress and with O'Neill personally. Carter appointed Hamilton Jordan as his chief of staff, and said that Jordan "is like a son to me." O'Neill became so disgusted with Jordan's arrogance and lack of attention that he openly began to call him "Hannibal Jerken."[50] An aide with whom O'Neill had reasonably good relations, Stuart Eizenstat, brushed off O'Neill's catastrophic health care project, the program in which the Speaker had the greatest emotional investment, with a curt memo that ended in capital letters "NOTE: CARTER IS COMMITTED TO A BALANCED BUDGET BY THE END OF HIS FIRST TERM."[51] Top personal aides simply do not engage in such repeated behavior unless their boss wants them to do so.

Jordan and Carter's press secretary, Jody Powell, savaged O'Neill, Califano, and Blumenthal in continuous leaks to the press. O'Neill in particular poured out his complaints to the press, but Califano was only slightly more discreet. Then in 1979 Carter fired Califano and Blumenthal in a humiliating manner.[52]

One reason for Carter's poor relationship with these men was personal. Carter was like Stevenson in being "an amateur Democrat" and seeing politics in terms of ideas and principles rather than the formation of coalitions. But while Stevenson, despite his rhetoric, had a political ability to work with establishment politicians of a variety of types and views, Carter made it clear to other politicians that he did, in fact, think that legislation through political give-and-take was dirty — and that they were dirty for engaging in it. In the words of Tip O'Neill, "I took it for granted that their anti-Washington talk was merely campaign rhetoric that would fade away after the election. But I was wrong. They really believed those things."[53]

A second possible factor was the long-time mutual suspicion between Southerners and Catholics. Carter seems to have gotten along well personally with his Polish Catholic National Security Adviser, Zbigniew Brzezinski, but he allowed the impression to be created that religion was a factor in his poor relations with his domestic lieutenants and with Tip O'Neill.[54] Carter himself always acted with politeness, but his closest aides behaved quite differently. Indeed, in 1978, Carter volunteered to the stunned editors of the *Washington Post* that Charles Kirbo, his best friend and chief legal adviser, did not like Califano at first because he was a liberal, a Catholic, an Italian, and a Northerner.[55]

Aside from personal factors, however, Carter's basic problem was that he would not choose between an alliance with leaders of the old Democratic coalition such as O'Neill and Califano and one with the activists from the "Amateur Democrats." A month after the 1976 election, Patrick Caddell, Carter's chief pollster, wrote him a long "working paper on political strategy" that emphasized that the old New Deal

---

50. O'Neill, *Man of the House*, p. 311.
51. Farrell, *Tip O'Neill and the Democratic Century*, p. 448.
52. For Carter's relationship with O'Neill and Califano, see Farrell, *Tip O'Neill and the Democratic Century*, pp. 440–462 (the Eizenstat memo is on p. 448), and Califano, *Governing America*, pp. 402–448. For the leaking, see Califano, *Governing America*, pp. 405 and 407.
53. O'Neill, *Man of the House*, pp. 312–313.
54. Farrell, *Tip O'Neill and the Democratic Century*, pp. 458–459.
55. For the Kirbo statement, see Joseph A. Califano, *Inside: A Public and Private Life* (New York: Public Affairs, 2004), p. 334. For the characterization of Kirbo as Carter's best friend, see O'Neill, *Man of the House*, p. 309.

coalition was rapidly dissolving. Caddell called upon Carter to court the middle-class, white collar voter.[56] Carter was to send his copy of the working paper to Vice President-Elect Walter "Fritz" Mondale, and he wrote on the cover: "Fritz. Excellent. See me re this. J."[57]

When Carter spoke with a distinguished English journalist in 1983, he looked back at his 1976 victory and saw it as embodying "a combination of approaches, some of which would be considered quite conservative and some of which would be considered progressive or liberal."

The conservative elements of the program as Carter described them to the British journalist were in his economic policy, and they clearly were those of "a modern New Democrat." "I think we ought to be fiscally conservative, reduce the deficit, pledge to deregulate the free enterprise system and to maximize competitions." These were the policies that were an anathema to O'Neill and Califano.

In the economic sphere Carter was, in fact, quite conservative as President. Since he faced severe economic problems, it is difficult to judge what he would done in better times, but his policy certainly was more conservative than Nixon's. His domestic spending rose much less than Nixon's if adjusted for inflation. Carter pushed through a major increase in the highly regressive Social Security Tax, and the AFL-CIO was extremely angry with him in January 1980. During the campaign he had promised a comprehensive government health program, but then, as has been seen, he brusquely rejected Tip O'Neill's dream of more limited catastrophic health insurance.[58]

To a modern reader, the surprise in Carter's self-description came in "the progressive realm." Carter said nothing about modern cultural issues, but focused on foreign policy: "a constant and strong defense ... I would say at a two or three per cent level above inflation ... resolve international disputes through negotiations and diplomacy ... a strong emphasis on ... human rights abroad ... be known as the champion of nuclear arms control." He became famous for his position on human rights and arms control.[59]

Carter's characterization of his foreign policy was quite accurate. He did increase military expenditures, but he did push through a treaty with Panama that gave it sovereignty over the Panama Canal and an agreement between Israel and Egypt that returned the Sinai Peninsula to Egypt. Both at the time and in retrospect, foreign policy specialists hailed these two agreements as great achievements, but neither gained him votes at home. Carter's human rights program was beneficial to the Solidarity movement in Poland, but, arguably, destabilized dictatorial regimes in

56. Caddell Memorandum of December 10, 1976. Discussed in Everett Carll Ladd, Jr., with Charles P. Hadley, *Transformations of the American Party System: Political Coalitions from the New Deal to the 1970s*, 2nd ed. (New York: W. W. Norton 1978), pp. 299–301.
57. Caddell, "Initial Working Paper on Political Strategy," p. 1.
58. Controlled for inflation, domestic spending rose 5.6% a year under Nixon and less than one percent a year in the first years of the Clinton Administration. Steven Rattner, "George Shultz Returns," *The New York Times Magazine*, October 5, 1980, p. 22.
59. "Carter Interview" with Henry Brandon, circa 1983, Henry Brandon Papers, Box 16, Folder 11, Library of Congress.

Iran and Nicaragua in ways that led to the oil crisis and seizure of American hostages in Iran and to the Sandinista regime in Nicaragua. These were short-term political disasters for Carter in the United States, and the Soviet foreign policy establishment was so angry at Carter's policy that it felt it had nothing to lose by intervening in Afghanistan.[60]

The problem was the "the progressive" and "liberal" approaches were not those wanted by "the middle class, white collar voter" of the North (really the relatively upper stratum voter). The non-economic issues of primary concern to them were domestic ones. In particular, abortion was becoming a litmus test for cultural liberals, and Carter was more conservative on the issue in 1976 than Gerald Ford. Carter had been absolutely clear in his campaign promises to end Ford's program of funding abortions under Medicaid, and he did secure the enactment of such legislation. He appointed liberal activists to middle-level posts in the Administration, but even in 1980 the National Organization of Women (NOW) ostentatiously refused to endorse him on the same day that it denounced Reagan as "medieval."[61]

In retrospect, Caddell's strategic advice to Carter in 1976 was probably not optimal at the time. In the long run, the Democratic nominating procedure may well have made his middle class suburban strategy inevitable, but the liberals never would have supported Carter against the only semi-viable alternative in the primary, Ted Kennedy, regardless of what Carter did. Moreover, as a Southern sitting President, Carter would have been difficult for anyone to challenge in the primary, and Kennedy eventually withdrew.

In November 1980, the basic problem with a suburban strategy was a demographic one. Throughout the 1970s observers had been looking at the aging of the Baby Boomers, especially as so many of them had moved into the professional and middle classes. A long line of politicians — John Kerry is only the most recent — have been disillusioned in their hopes to increase the turnout among those aged 20 to 35. In 1980, a person born in 1945 was only 35 years old, one born in 1950 was 30, one born in 1955 was 25, and one born in 1960 was 20. The Baby Boomers were still too young to have the voter turnout necessary to be decisive in the 1980 election, while those who were 20 years old in 1935 were still only 65 years of age and at the high point of their voter turnout.

---

60. Over the period from 1977 to 1982, I spent over eight months visiting Soviet foreign policy institutes. At the very time of the Soviet intervention in Afghanistan I was a guest for a month in the two major Soviet institutes on Asia. The book which emerged from this study was *The Struggle for the Third World: Soviet Debates and American Options* (Washington: Brookings Institution, 1986). Carter's problem in foreign policy was the same as in the domestic sphere. His Secretary of State, Cyrus Vance, and his National Security Adviser, Zbigniew Brzezinski, advised very different policies toward the Soviet Union. Carter would not make a decisive choice and hence had an inconsistent policy. The tragedy was that the American public generally "saw" only the softer policy of Vance, while the Soviet Union saw only the harsher and more provocative policy of Brzezinski.

61. Leslie Bennett, "NOW Rejects All 3 for President, Condemns Reagan as 'Medieval,'" *The New York Times*, October 6, 1980, p. A20.

As Carter looked forward to 1980, he could see that Ronald Reagan was very likely to be the Republican nominee. Reagan would frighten a fair number of professionals (he was to lose 6.6% of the vote to John Anderson from their midst), but be attractive to Southern Evangelicals and Catholic "urbans." It seemed clear that Carter's best personal strategy was to try to solidify his position among the Evangelicals and to court the Catholic urbans.

A cautious cultural policy that emphasized the similarities of the Evangelicals and the Catholic urban groups, but that remained to the left of Reagan (no difficulty there) seemed ideal. From this perspective, NOW's anger was quite helpful. In addition, a moderate New Deal policy, its limits explained by difficult economic times, also would have appealed to both groups. But, even more important, such a policy would have been highly pleasing to the Washington leaders of the urban Catholics. They would have made their satisfaction well known to the media.

THE DEMOCRATIC STRATEGIC CHOICES IN 1988

The high rate of inflation, the disasters of the Iranian hostage crisis, the Soviet invasion of Afghanistan, and the failed rescue effort in Iran left Jimmy Carter with no real chance in 1980. The Republicans had only to nominate a solid candidate. They, in fact, nominated a risky candidate in Ronald Reagan, and he had to reassure people that he was not dangerous. Even then, Reagan lost 6.6% of the vote to John Anderson, a moderate Republican who decided to run as an independent. Reagan himself received only 50.7% of the vote.

Once Reagan had a successful and relatively moderate first term, he was certain to be reelected so long as his health remained sound. For this reason the Democrats had no real strategic decision to make in 1984. They needed only to find a strong potential President who was willing to gamble on the slim odds that something untoward might happen to the President relatively late in the campaign. Walter Mondale, a distinguished Senator from Minnesota who had been Jimmy Carter's Vice President, was willing to play what was likely to be an unhappy role.[62]

Yet even in these circumstances Mondale was almost defeated in the 1984 primaries by Senator Gary Hart of Colorado. Mondale had a New Deal philosophy, while, as was discussed earlier, Gary Hart, the campaign manager of George McGovern, came from a new generation. Mondale was 56 years old and had been in elected office since 1960. Hart was 48 and was first elected to office in 1974 as Senator from Colorado. Hart ran on a suburban strategy that emphasized liberal cultural values rather than New Deal economic ones. Mondale would have lost the nomination to Hart if the delegates from the South had been excluded.

After Reagan was re-elected, however, the Democrats had real decisions to make. Reagan could not run for a third term, and the Republicans had competent

---

62. Steven M. Gillon, *The Democrats' Dilemma: Walter F. Mondale and the Liberal Tradition* (New York: Columbia University Press, 1992), p. 103.

candidates (e.g., Vice President George Bush and Senator Robert Dole) but no exciting ones. In the postwar period, the public had generally rotated the presidency between the two parties every eight years: 1945-1953 — Democratic, 1953-1961 — Republican, 1961-1969 — Democratic, 1969-1977 — Republican, 1977-1981 — Democratic, and 1981-89 — Republican. From this perspective, 1988 would seem to have been a natural Democratic year.

The Republicans had suffered no disaster that would make a Democratic victory almost inevitable in 1988, but we should not be misled by the mythology created by Reagan's supporters. Supposedly Reagan restored the confidence of Americans. Yet, although the public understood that Reagan had a more successful domestic and foreign policy than Carter, their answers to the basic questions about responsiveness of government on political science's major election poll, as has been seen, showed no improvement from 1980 to 1988.

In these circumstances the Democrats' choice of strategy and candidate might make a real difference, and three major options had strong support within the party: 1) A so-called Southern strategy, (2) A New Deal strategy, and (3) A Northern suburban strategy. But since Johnson and Carter had different Southern strategies and since the South did not have enough Electoral College votes for victory, the real choice was between the New Deal and suburban strategies.

1. The Ill-Defined Southern Strategy

The Southern Democratic leaders were extremely unhappy after the 1984 election. In 1976, Carter had defeated Ford by 54% to 45% in the former states of the Confederacy, and in 1980 he had only lost to Ronald Reagan in these states by 51% to 44%. But in 1984, Mondale had suffered a 62% to 37% loss in the Confederacy. Moreover, Mondale had received the votes of the South in the 1984 primaries because the South found the culturally-liberal Gary Hart even more unattractive. The Southern Democrats dreaded another such a choice in the future.

The contest to elect a new chairman of the Democratic National Committee in January 1985 deepened the despair of the Southerners. The Southern candidate, the moderate Terry Sanford, finished a weak third to the trade union candidate from Massachusetts. The spokesperson for the suburban strategy, a future Congresswoman from San Francisco, Nancy Pelosi, took second place. She had the relatively conservative economic position and decidedly liberal cultural policy that reflected the views of her constituency.

In 1985, a group of politicians from Southern and Border states led by Charles Robb of Virginia, Richard Gephardt of Missouri, and Sam Nunn of Georgia formed the Democratic Leadership Council (DLC) to oppose the liberal Democrats. The Southerners in the Democratic Leadership Council were joined by a number of Western politicians, notably from the Mountain states. Gephardt became the DLC's first chairman and originally saw it as a vehicle to promote his nomination in 1988.[63]

Although the Democratic Leadership Council advocated both a more conservative economic and cultural policy, it focused its criticism on the cultural "narrow special interests groups: the feminists, the activists of the civil rights movement, the environmentalists, and the National Education Association."[64] It also, however, had negative views about the trade unions. Jesse Jackson complained that the DLC's overt antagonism toward him was a cover for outright racism and/or a conservative economic policy. He charged that "DLC" really stood for "Democrats for the Leisure Class."[65]

The original policy position of the Democratic Leadership Council was deeply unrealistic. A simultaneous attack on cultural liberals and the trade unions was useful in fund-raising among conservatives — no doubt, a central motivating factor for the founders of the DLC — but a candidate with this position could never win a national majority in Democratic primaries. Indeed, Gephardt himself quickly decided he must move to the left and distance himself from the organization.

In addition, the South simply had too few Electoral College votes. A total of 270 Electoral College votes was needed for victory, but the states of the former Confederacy had only 138 and the three adjoining states that were most "Southern" (Kentucky, Oklahoma, and West Virginia) only 23 more. The DLC implicitly was focusing on the same "red state alliance" as the Republicans and proposing the same strategy to win them. The national Democratic Party, regardless of whom it nominated, was not likely to be more convincing than the Republicans in building such a coalition, at least with a conservative economic policy. A ticket that combined two men from Confederate states, Bill Clinton and Al Gore, won only four Confederate states in 1992 and again in 1996.

In fact, the results of the 1984 election suggested that the Democrats should not focus too much attention on the South. As Table 2 of the previous chapter indicates, Reagan won the former states of the Confederacy and the border states of Kentucky, Missouri, and Oklahoma by a 7.4 million vote margin. He won a combination of the Pacific Coast states and the Northern states from the Mississippi River through New England — essentially the "blue states" — by a nearly identical 7.5 million votes. The Pacific and Northern states east of the Mississippi had 294 Electoral College votes compared with 166 in the South and the three Border States.[66] Minnesota and Iowa — both west of the Mississippi — had a similar profile to the latter group, and they had an additional 18 Electoral College votes. The switch of some 4 million voters in the blue states would produce almost double the number of Electoral College votes as a similar movement of voters in the South.

63. The major book about the Democratic Leadership Council is Kenneth S. Baer, *Reinventing Democrats: The Politics of Liberalism from Reagan to Clinton* (Lawrence: University Press of Kansas, 2000), p. 41.

64. Baer, *Reinventing Democrats*, p. 41.

65. Jack W. Germond and Jules Witcover, *Mad as Hell: Revolt at the Ballot Box, 1992* (New York: Warner Books, 1993), p. 80. Bill Clinton remembers Jackson's characterization of the abbreviation as "Democratic Leisure Class." Bill Clinton, *My Life* (New York: Alfred A. Knopf, 2004), p. 365.

66. The "Pacific states" in this calculation include California, Hawaii, Nevada, Oregon, and Washington, but not Alaska, which votes as a Mountain state. The three border states of Delaware, Maryland, and West Virginia are included in the "Northern states east of the Mississippi."

Of course, this analysis did not answer the question of which Northern strategy the Democrats should adopt. The real question for the Democratic Leadership Council was whether it would emphasize its conservative economic approach or its conservative cultural position. The "silent majority" or the "Reagan Democrats" would applaud a candidate with the DLC's cultural policy, but would want more of a New Deal economic policy. The Northern suburbanites would like the DLC's economic policy, but not its cultural values.

The statistics of the 1984 election did, however, raise real questions about the type of nominee to choose. Jimmy Carter scarcely furnished a convincing example that a Southern candidate automatically appealed both to the North and South or, in 1980, even that he was guaranteed to carry the South. To be sure, the Democrats had lost with three Northerners from 1968 through 1984 (Hubert Humphrey, George McGovern, and Walter Mondale). Yet these three candidates came from the populist and rural states of Minnesota and South Dakota, and the three successful Democratic candidates from 1880 through 1944 had come from New York or New Jersey. A Democratic candidate from a large Eastern state with appeal to "ethnic" voters might well be ideal. The obvious candidate was the Italian-American Catholic from New York, Mario Cuomo, who was an excellent speaker and who had learned how to deal with issues such as abortion in a skillful manner.

2. The Competing Northern Strategies

There were various ways to describe the choice that the Democrats were making. As early as 1981, the sociologist Seymour Martin Lipset summarized the choice in language that was becoming increasingly popular among academics: "There are now two Lefts — the materialist and the postmaterialist — which are rooted in different classes."[67] The materialist left was interested in economic social welfare, and its primary base was found among lower and middle income voters. The postmaterialist left emphasized cultural liberalism, and it was based on the better educated and more affluent. Those who appealed to the materialist left were following what we call a New Deal strategy and those who appealed to the postmaterialist left were embracing what we call a suburban strategy.

During the 1980s the debate in the broader political world centered on a more practical question: why had Ronald Reagan done so well in the North? Why had he swept what came to be known as the blue states? Had he really appealed to "Reagan Democrats," that is, working class voters who were alienated by the cultural liberalism of the anti-Vietnam radicals and by Carter's abandonment of a New Deal economic policy at a time of wage stagnation? If so, a New Deal economic policy, coupled with a moderate cultural policy, seemed the best way to win them back.

---

67. Seymour Martin Lipset, "Party Coalitions and the 1980 Election," in Seymour Martin Lipset, ed., *Party Coalitions in the 1980s* (San Francisco: Institute for Contemporary Studies, 1981), p. 24. Lipset based his analysis of post-material or post-industrial society and values on Daniel Bell, *The Coming of Post-Industrial Society* (New York: Basic Books, 1973) and Ronald Inglehart, *The Silent Revolution: Changing Values and Political Styles Among Western Publics* (Princeton: Princeton University Press, 1977).

The "Reagan Democrats" were, of course, also the "George Wallace Democrats" of the past, and the Democrats already had had a debate on how to respond to Wallace. In 1970, two scholars, Richard Scammon and Benjamin Wattenberg, published a famous book on the subject, *The Real Majority*, that argued this position. They often reiterated their position in coming years and reaffirmed it forcefully in the introduction to a new edition of the book in 1992.[68] The proponents of a New Deal strategy thought that a "middle class tax cut" — perhaps a reduction in Social Security taxes — would be attractive to the Reagan Democrats. So too would be expenditures on social programs (e.g., health care) that did not seem focused on minorities. The old Northern Democratic Establishment and the trade unions wanted a return to the New Deal strategy, and their candidate in 1984 was Walter Mondale.

The suburban strategy was based on two arguments that were not really consistent. The first was that Reagan had won in the industrial states not so much because of the "Reagan Democrats," but because of "Anderson Republicans." This was Pat Caddell's position in 1976 even before Anderson's race for the presidency, but a decade later the demographic evolution of the United States had given it added weight. In the 1930s, 1.25 million babies a year had been born, 1.46 million a year in the 1941–1945 period, 1.82 million from 1946 to 1950, 1.99 million from 1951 to 1956, and a high of 2.13 million from 1956 to 1960. By 1990, a person born in 1960 was 30 years old, one born in 1950 was 40 years old, and one born in 1945 was 45. The latter two groups in particular were entering their years of high voter turnout.

The babies of World War II and the postwar period were much better educated and more affluent than their parents, and the proponents of a suburban strategy saw their defection from the Democratic Party as the main reason for Reagan's victory in the blue states. This defection was produced, it was argued, by the "class warfare" appeals of the Great Society. Those making this case pointed to the classic model of Anthony Downs and insisted that the Democrats must move toward the center of the economic spectrum — that is, to the right.

Bill Bradley of New Jersey was a strong proponent of the suburban strategy. He advocated a sharp reduction in the progressivity of the income tax in the 1980s and an emphasis upon economic growth (in practical terms, stock market growth) rather than redistributive policies. When Reagan proposed cuts in the upper rates of the income tax, Bradley was one of the Democrats who helped to enact even larger reductions than Reagan proposed. Not surprisingly, Bradley came from New Jersey, a state with a very high household income, and Bradley recognized in his memoirs that his program corresponded to the economic interests of his state.[69]

The second argument in favor of a suburban strategy insisted on the growing importance of postmaterialist values in modern society. Those postmaterialist values of political importance in the 1980s and 1990s were, it was said, equal opportunity

---

68. Richard M. Scammon and Ben J. Wattenberg, *The Real Majority* (New York: Coward McCann, 1970). The second edition was issued by Primus Publishers of New York in 1992.
69. Bill Bradley, *Time Present, Time Past: A Memoir* (New York: Alfred A. Knopf, 1996), pp. 93-96.

for women, women's free choice on abortion, environmentalism and, increasingly, gay rights. In the practical political sphere, the argument was simpler: John Anderson's 6.6% of the vote in 1980 showed that many in the Republican suburban base were not happy with Reagan's courtship of the religious right. Anderson did especially well among the wealthier districts, and their inhabitants seem to have become "swing voters."

A key role in this argument on the importance of cultural values was produced by the development of the so-called gender gap in 1980. In the past, women had usually voted as did their husbands, but women on the average voted somewhat more Republican than men. In 1980, however, Gallup found that 53% of men voted for Reagan, but only 49% of women did so. Obviously, the gender gap could be described as a Democratic loss of men to the Republicans and a problem that required more Democratic attention to male grievances.[70] Or, it could be described as a Republican loss of women that required a Republican response, and a continuing Democratic opportunity.

The media accepted the argument that the gender gap was really a "women's gap" produced by the new Republican alliance with the religious right, not a "men's gap" produced by misguided Democratic policies. However the gender gap should be seen, the nature of the Democratic nominating process made it virtually impossible for the party to respond otherwise than it did. The capture of the Democratic machinery by the activists of the 1960s and early 1970s and the party rule that half the delegates must be women ensured that nearly half the delegates at the Democratic Convention would be culturally liberal women. The front-loaded primary system gave little chance to a candidate other than a cultural liberal.

Nevertheless, the argument about postmaterialist values had an implication that undercut the first argument for the suburban strategy, but that never was advanced. Those such as Ronald Inglehart who did serious research on materialist and post-materialist values never claimed that postmaterialist values had become universal. Rather they argued that such values were much stronger among the young, the well-educated, and the affluent, especially the affluent professionals. The less affluent, by necessity, had to worry more about material concerns.

The implications of this analysis for the Democratic Party seemed quite clear cut. The Democrats should emphasize liberal cultural values to seek the support of the suburban voters. Of course, the party should adjust for the fact that the soccer moms and their husbands were not as radical as the more extreme activists on cultural issues, but even this still left them culturally quite liberal. But since the affluent and well-educated supposedly did not care about material values, the party could adopt a strong New Deal policy to seek the support of the poorer white voters, especially in the "red state" areas and socioeconomic groups.

---

70. In fact, a later study concluded that Democratic party identification among women remained steady and that the "gap" was produced by a shift of men away from the Democratic Party. See Nancy Burns, Kay Lehman Schlozman, and Sidney Verba, *The Private Roots of Public Action: Gender Equality and Political Participation* (Cambridge, MA: Harvard University Press, 2001), p. 111.

But, of course, this second argument about the crucial importance of values, especially for the well-educated, was really inconsistent with the argument that the well-educated in the blue states had voted for Reagan because of their dislike of the Great Society's "class warfare" appeals. Perhaps they would not vote for tax increases for themselves in order to create political cross-pressures upon the lower income.

In 1990, it seemed as if the contest for the Democratic nomination would be quite vigorous. But, perhaps because of George H.W. Bush's high approval ratings after the Iraq War, perhaps because of the difficulties that many candidates had in raising money, nearly all the viable candidates withdrew from the race. The one remaining strong candidate, Bill Clinton of Arkansas, adopted an extremely ambiguous position in the 1992 campaign, and hence when he defeated George Bush, he had to define his real strategy while occupying the Oval Office.

CHAPTER 9. THE RED STATE–BLUE STATE POLARIZATION AND THE ISSUE OF NATIONALISM

In the early 1990s, a red state–blue state polarization still seemed unlikely. Of course, the Baby Boom generation, both the anti-Vietnam activists and the Goldwater activists, had entered politics when politics had an ideological and confrontational nature. Nevertheless, the distinctive fact about the Baby Boom generation was that it was the first "white" generation, the first whose identities were not defined by the conflict between North and South and the antagonisms among the various European-American "races." The European-Americans for the first time were basically homogeneous in their national and ethnic identities. Moreover, the country was 79% urban, and this seemed to preclude an even division of voters based on modernist and traditional values.

In any case, there were no "red states" and "blue states" in America as late as the 1996 election. George H. W. Bush won six of the seven most populous Northern states in 1988, and Bill Clinton took 12 of George W. Bush's 2004 red states in 1992. Reagan had selected the elder Bush as Vice President in 1980 as a moderate figure to balance the ticket, and Bush's defeat in 1992 seemed to result largely from his age (68) and apparent loss of energy. Clinton was chairman of the conservative Democratic Leadership Council that was centering its attacks on the McGovern cultural liberals. This suggested that Clinton's cultural policy would not be far from that of Jimmy Carter.

Nevertheless, the relatively uninformed public as a whole often has an almost instinctive sense of what lies behind vague and ambiguous rhetoric.[1] As has been seen, the public, if not Walter Lippmann, understood in 1932 that Franklin Roosevelt was not in the conservative tradition of Cleveland and Wilson, but in the Bryan or really the La Follette tradition. Similarly, the public seemed to realize that Reagan's rhetoric did not mean a dangerous hard-line foreign policy toward the Soviet Union.

---

1. V. O. Key, Jr., *The Responsible Electorate: Rationality in Presidential Voting, 1936–1960* (Cambridge: Harvard University Press, 1966).

For this reason, scholars need to give much more attention to an event that has become almost a footnote to history — the success of Ross Perot in the 1992 election. Bush's foreign policy had been extremely successful, and Clinton was a good governor who was a highly skilled politician. The economy was beginning to improve. Bush was criticized for raising taxes, but Perot called for a 50-cents-a-gallon increase in the gasoline tax. As a person, Perot was a most bizarre candidate. Yet he received 19% of the vote, some 22%–23% of that of white males. Moreover, turnout rose precipitously: 91.5 million people voted in 1988 and 96.3 million in 1996, but 104.4 million in the intervening 1992 election.

Successful third parties have always tapped into some major popular grievance that the two major parties have neglected. Then the major parties typically respond in some way to deal with the grievance. The Democrats and Republicans cooperated to destroy the Populist parties of the 1880s and 1890s by instituting controls on democracy and, to a limited extent, upon the corporations. The Democrats under Woodrow Wilson co-opted Theodore Roosevelt's implicit anti-German line in 1912, and the Democrats under Franklin Roosevelt adopted the program of La Follette's Progressive Party of 1924. Ronald Reagan reassured the suburbanite Republicans who had voted for John Anderson in 1980 by adopting moderate policies in his first term.

The Republicans were not forced to change their cultural policy drastically in 1972 because the Democrats nominated an extreme cultural liberal and a would-be assassin paralyzed Wallace and drove him from the race. Eventually, however, the Republicans moved to the right on cultural issues. The only strong third party to which the major parties did not respond was the Know Nothings in the 1850s. The result was the collapse of the Whig Party and the cooptation of the Know Nothings' anti-Catholic theme by a new party, the Republicans.

The voting pattern of the 1996 election shows that, whatever the major grievance that Perot had exploited, neither Clinton nor his opponent, Robert Dole, had responded to it. Perot himself ran again in 1996 and won 8.4% of the vote — the fifth highest for a third party in the 20th century (behind Roosevelt in 1912, Perot himself in 1992, La Follette in 1924, and George Wallace in 1968). Despite a 1.7 million decline in the number of votes for Perot and an insignificant Republican 100,000 vote gain, Clinton received only 2.5 million more votes in 1996 than in 1992, when he won 43% of the votes. The Democrats had elected 63 fewer House members in 1994 than in 1990, and especially given these losses, Clinton's 8.2 million vote margin in 1996 normally would have produced a substantial gain in Democratic House seats. Instead, they won only 3 more seats than in 1994.

Standard surveys show that Perot's voters were highly alienated in 1992. The major political science study of the 1992 election found that 63% of all whites and 69% of blacks in 1964 thought that government was run for the benefit of all people instead of a few interests. In 1992 these figures had fallen to 20% and 19% respectively. In 1964, 77% of whites and 74% of blacks said that government could be trusted to do what was right almost always or most of the time; in 1992, these figures stood at 29% and 26% respectively.[2] Another poll in late March 1992 found that 73% agreed with the statement, "The entire political system is broken. It is run by insiders who do not listen to working people and are incapable of solving our problems."[3] Perot's supporters were more alienated than the population as a whole.

The Clinton Administration found it politically useful to say that Perot's support rested on his call for a balanced budget, but this is not credible. After all, Bush lost votes because he raised taxes. This chapter argues that the key concrete issue that gave Perot his huge vote was NAFTA (the North American Free Trade Association), especially the Mexican component of it. Perot skillfully used NAFTA to combine the grievances against the Bush Administration on economic issues with discontent about outsourcing and immigration that also produced the passage of the anti-immigrant Proposition 187 in California in 1994.

A decade later a flash of political lightning illuminated the 1992 election in an unexpected manner. Immediately after the terrorist attacks of September 11, 2001, George W. Bush adopted the slogan "United We Stand" to summarize the American response. Almost no one commented that this was Ross Perot's slogan and the title of his major book.[4] Turnout soared in the 2004 presidential election and, quite contrary to expectations, this benefited Bush rather than Kerry.

In some way Bush must have been tapping into the grievances of the Perot voter. If we are to understand the politics of the last 15 years, the meaning of the 2004 election, and the outlines of the future, we need to take "United We Stand" very seriously. It is the argument of this chapter that George Bush recaptured the religious right in the 2000 election. The secret of his success in 2000 was his use of Perot's nationalist issue.

H. ROSS PEROT AND NATIONALISM

In the 1992 election, Bill Clinton beat the incumbent, George H.W. Bush, by 5.6 percentage points and won by 370 to 168 votes in the Electoral College. Clinton defeated Bush outside the Confederacy by 331 Electoral College votes to 60, even more than Roosevelt's majority in 1940 and 1944. Nevertheless, Clinton only received 43.0% of the nation-wide popular vote. H. Ross Perot, perhaps the most improbable candidate in American history to receive widespread support in a presidential election, was supported by 19% of the voters. Theodore Roosevelt in 1912 was the only third party candidate in nearly 150 years to receive a higher percentage of the vote. Moreover, Perot did poorly among minorities and received fewer votes among women than among men. His total vote among white men was some 22 to 23 percent.

A large number of candidates run in every American presidential election, and many of them are quite strange in one way or the other. Yet, normally they receive the

---

2. Paul R. Abramson, John H. Aldrich, and David W. Rohde, *Change and Continuities in the 1992 Election* (Washington, D.C.: CQ Press, 1994), p. 122.
3. Martin Walker, *The President We Deserve. Bill Clinton, His Rise, Faults, and Comebacks* (New York: Crown Publishers, 1996), p. 140.
4. H. Ross Perot, *United We Stand: How We Can Take Back Our Country* (New York: Hyperion, 1992).

low number of votes that would be expected. Ross Perot was an implausible candidate who received a large number of votes after running a most implausible campaign. On February 20, 1992, Perot announced on the Larry King television show that he would become a candidate for President if people would organize to ensure that he was on the ballot in all states. Perot offered to finance his own campaign and was energetic in promoting his non-candidacy.

By the first week of May, Perot had the support of some 35% to 40% of the voters in the polls, enough for first place as Clinton and Bush split the rest of the vote. In the Oregon primary on May 19, Perot received a write-in vote of 10% to 15% in the primary of each of the parties. In the exit polls, 45% of the Democratic voters reported that they would vote for Perot in a three-way race and 42% for Clinton. Bush "defeated" Perot among Republicans by only 51% to 40% in such a hypothetical three-way race.[5]

The early Perot support was not as surprising as it seems. John Anderson's original poll support was in the mid twenty percent range in 1980, and the average voter knew little about Clinton at the end of the primary season. Sixteen percent of the electorate had a favorable view of him, 40% (probably mainly Republicans) an unfavorable view, and the rest were uncertain.

Normally, however, third party candidates fade rapidly as the major party candidates become better defined. Clinton skillfully used his rise from poverty in Hope, Arkansas, to symbolize the hope for a rebirth of America under his leadership. For reasons that still are not clear, Perot on July 16 suddenly announced the end of the candidacy he never had officially declared.

In retrospect, however, Perot's withdrawal as a non-candidate seems far more of a staged event than appeared at the time. His activists continued to work to get his name on the ballot in all 50 states, and they almost surely were being financed by money that Perot had given. They succeeded in mid-September. At the end of September, Perot's delegates met in convention in Dallas, and they nominated him for President. Perot accepted on October 1 and actually became a candidate for the first time. In the next three and a half weeks he spent $34 million in launching the most expensive television campaign in American history.[6] If Perot had not officially withdrawn, it would be difficult to notice any appreciable change in the campaign that he was running.

Public opinion polls put Perot's support at the 5% to 7% level in late September.[7] Nevertheless, Perot gradually regained his popularity in October and early November, and the last tracking poll before the election predicted he would receive 19% of the vote. This was precisely accurate.

---

5. R. W. Apple, Jr., "Perot's Strength Shown in Oregon," *The New York Times*, May 21, 1992, p. A1.
6. Kenneth D. Norden, "The Television Candidate: H. Ross Perot's 1992 and 1996 Presidential Races," in Ted G. Jelen, ed., *Ross for Boss: The Perot Phenomenon and Beyond* (Albany: State University of New York Press, 2001), p. 24.
7. Robin Toner, "Perot Re-Enters the Campaign, Saying Bush and Clinton Fail to Address Government 'Mess'," and R. W. Apple, Jr., "A Tremor Now, Not a Groundswell," both in *The New York Times*, October 2, 1992, p. A1.

A seemingly freak success often is less impressive when examined closely. The opposite is true in Perot's case. Voter turnout in 1988 had been 91.6 million in 1988 and 96.3 million in 1996. A simple extrapolation would lead to a prediction of a turnout in 1996 of approximately 93.9 million persons. In fact, 104.4 million persons cast a valid vote for President in 1992. If the turnout had been 93.9 million and Perot still received 19.7 million votes, he would have had 21.1% of the total rather than 18.8%. The analogous figure among white men would be correspondingly higher.

This large turnout was not the inevitable result of a three-way race. On the contrary, the other multi-party contests of the 20th century had relatively low turnout for their time. Table 1 compares the turnout in the multi-candidate election with that in the preceding and following election. Indeed, in every election except for 1968 and 1992, the turnout in the multi-party election was lower than that both of the previous and subsequent election. Indeed, special factors explain the relatively low turnout of 1920 and 1944: the initial impact of women's suffrage in 1920 and the soldiers at war in 1944. Perot himself clearly had a galvanizing effect on many habitual non-voters.

One reason that turnout normally arises after a major third party challenge is that a major party usually co-opts the main issue of the third party. Nixon was an exception in that he pushed racial integration in his first term and thus failed to attract large numbers of the Wallace voters, who stayed at home. Similarly, the extraordinarily low turnout in 1996 showed that Clinton had not persuaded voters that he had adopted Perot's policy, even though he sharply reduced the deficit both by raising the taxes on the rich and by instituting Perot's gasoline tax, although much more modestly.

Table 1: Turnout in Twentieth Century Multi-Candidate Presidential Elections

Year	Third and Fourth Candidates	Previous Election	Third Party	Next Election
1912	Theodore Roosevelt & Eugene Debs	65.7%	59.0%	61.8%
1924	Robert La Follette	49.3%	48.9%	56.9%
1948	Strom Thurmond & Henry Wallace	55.9%	53.4%	63.8%
1968	George Wallace	62.8%	61.5%	56.2%
1980	John Anderson	54.8%	54.7%	57.2%
1992	Ross Perot	54.6%	60.6%	52.6%
1996	Ross Perot	60.6%	52.6%	55.6%

Sources: Michael P. McDonald and Samuel L. Popkin, "The Myth of the Vanishing Voter," American Political Science Review, vol. 95, no. 4 (December 2001), pp. 963–974. The 1912 to 1948 figures are from Walter Dean Burnham, "The Turnout Problem," A James Reichley, ed., Elections American Style (Washington: Brookings Institution, 1987), pp. 113–114.

Naturally Clinton had an interest in interpreting Perot's large vote as a mandate for fiscal discipline and a balanced budget. No doubt, some of the upper income voters were natural Republicans who voted for Perot for this reason, but the polls in late September showed the limited size of this group.

When Perot was receiving 5% to 7% of the vote in late September, Stanley Greenberg reported that while Perot "was drawing the shake-up politics voters last spring ... now he's drawing support from voters who want to get spending under control. And that's a very different share of the electorate." And, of course, support for a reduction in spending is not the same as support for an increase in taxes.[8]

The rise in Perot's support back to the 19% level by early November resulted from the return of the "shake-up politics voters." Now they were coming from Clinton rather than from Bush. A CNN and USA Today poll gave Clinton 52% at the end of September, Bush 35%, and Perot 7%, and Greenberg was reporting a continuing decline in Perot's support in the week before Perot's reentry.[9] The final vote count was Clinton 43%, Bush 37%, and Perot 19%. The "shake-up politics voters" would have voted largely for Clinton if they had voted in a two-way race — but they would have been unlikely to vote at all.

Greenberg, Clinton's chief pollster in 1992, seems to describe the Perot voter quite accurately:[10]

> The Perot voters were independent, younger, mostly blue collar and noncollege-educated, financially squeezed in the 1980s and for most of the 1990s as well, who felt a deep sense of middle-class grievance. Their sensibilities were among the first to be shunned by the Clinton administration.... They were pro-America, suspicious of global forces, and pro-military, and thus likely thrown overboard by gays in the military, not to mention NAFTA.

Greenberg always uses the word "middle-class" in its literal meaning: those of median income, not those who are among the top quarter of Americans in income. Those with lower and middle levels of income saw the Republicans as less responsive to them on economic issues than the Democrats, but considered the Democrats unresponsive as well.[11] The Democrats' movement to the right on economic issues, designed to appeal to suburban voters, left lower- and middle-income voters with no perceived economic choice in either party. To the extent that the Democrats were seen as more responsive to the lower income strata, voters had a sense — and long had a mistaken sense — that the Democrats were responsive only to those of low income minorities at the expense of whites.[12]

The fact that Perot voters did not vote for him because of his 50-cents-a-gallon gas tax and his call for fiscal responsibility is dramatically shown in their subsequent failure to accept Clinton's first-term program of fiscal responsibility as an adoption of the Perot program. At the end of his presidency, only 41% of the Perot voters

---

8. Toner, "Perot Re-Enters the Campaign," p. A18.
9. Toner, "Perot Re-Enters the Campaign," p. A18.
10. Stanley B. Greenberg, *The Two Americas: Our Current Political Deadlock and How to Break It*, rev. ed. (New York: Thomas Dunne Books, 2005), pp. 89–90.
11. Voters' views are ably documented in Jeffrey M. Stonecash, *Class and Party in American Politics* (Boulder, Colo.: Westview Press, 2000), p. 52.
12. As early as 1970, Richard Scammon and Ben Wattenberg could write that "the national Democratic Party is perceived by the voter as being the champion of blacks over recent years." Richard M. Scammon and Ben J. Wattenberg, *The Real Majority* (New York: Coward McCann, 1970), p. 285.

approved of Clinton, compared with 58% for the nation as a whole.[13] The huge decline in turnout in 1996 to its lowest level in presidential elections in American history was a clear indication of their continued alienation from both major parties.

But why would the alienated vote for Perot? Perot often did talk about the rich paying their fair share of taxes, but his gasoline tax would affect everyone. Instead of promising anything like Clinton's health program or middle class tax cuts, he called for Americans to "do what you have to do" to end the deficit. Perot also did not embrace the cultural issues of the Christian right. Instead, his basic position was that "what people do in their private lives is their business." Abortion, he said, was "the woman's decision." His advice on premarital sex was, "Be careful. Be sure. If you're not sure, just hold off awhile." He said virtually nothing about religion, school prayer, and gun control.

Not surprisingly, as Lyman A. Kellstedt and John C. Green reported, only 15% of the Evangelicals supported Perot in 1992, and the great majority of them supported Bush.[14] Kellstedt and Green also emphasized, however, that only 12% of the seculars had voted for Perot. They saw 1992 as both the "year of the seculars" and the "year of the Evangelicals." They were peculiarly prescient in arguing that the election represented "the first rumblings of an electoral culture war." They saw the seculars and the Evangelicals as "the cultural cores" of the two parties.

Most of Perot's support came from the mainline Protestants and the Catholics, 25% of the former and 23% of the latter. His support among the white males of these groups was still higher. But while Perot's weak support among Evangelicals is understandable because of his cultural policy, that policy should have helped him among the seculars. Why had the seculars given him so much less support than the mainline Protestants?

In my opinion, the mainline Protestants, the Catholics, and the seculars all responded to the one theme with which Perot had been associated all his public life, the decline in national power and honor. Perot had been a successful entrepreneur who created a very profitable computer company (E.D.S) and sold it to General Motors in the mid-1980s for $1.7 billion. He was a very effective salesman, and he showed the same communication skills in politics as in business.

Yet even in the early 1970s Perot had come to public notice with a program to try to provide Christmas gifts for prisoners of war in Vietnam. Later in the decade he had organized a daring and successful rescue of several of his employees in Iran. Then in the mid-1970s he had become obsessed with those who were missing in action in the Vietnam War. Whatever the evidence (or lack of it), Perot seemed deeply convinced that many of them still were alive in Vietnam and that the US was refusing to try to liberate them because of cowardice. He focused much of his anger on George H. W. Bush, who had been head of the Central Intelligence Agency from 1975 to 1977 in the

---

13. Greenberg, *Two Americas*, p. 90.
14. Lyman A. Kellstedt, John C. Green, James L. Guth, and Corwin E. Smidt, "Religious Voting Blocs in the 1992 Election: The Year of the Evangelical?" in John C. Green, James L. Guth, Corwin E. Smith, and Lyman A. Kellstedt, eds., *Religion and the Culture Wars: Dispatches from the Front* (Lanham, Mary: Rowman & Littlefield, 1996), pp. 279 and 286.

immediate aftermath of the fall of Saigon and who then continued to have an interest in national security as Reagan's Vice President.

In the early 1990s, as Perot began to run for President, he turned his attention to the NAFTA trade treaty with Canada and Mexico. Proponents of NAFTA were correct in arguing that the treaty by itself did not have strong negative consequences in the United States. (These proponents did, of course, also exaggerate its benefits.) Not surprisingly, therefore, free trade with Canada did not become a significant political issue other than in the specific industries and regions directly affected by it.

The concern about NAFTA focused on Mexico because the treaty symbolized broad concerns about immigration, affirmative action for Hispanic immigrants, outsourcing, and the concomitant loss of jobs. These concerns deepened greatly during the recession of 1991 and still were intense in California in 1994 when whites passed Proposition 187 prohibiting services for illegal immigrants and their children, even access to public education.[15]

In a broader sense, NAFTA symbolized a set of major issues on which the Establishment, and most of all the seculars, had formed a consensus: globalization, outsourcing, immigration, free trade, and affirmative action. The major reason that Perot soared from 5% support when he rejoined the campaign in September to 19% in November was that Clinton formally endorsed NAFTA in early October.[16] The seculars did not join with many of the non-seculars on this issue since they were the strongest supporters of globalization. The non-secular instinctively saw the seculars as having an essentially religious attachment to globalization and environmentalism that amounted to the adoption of a kind of pantheism and an abandonment of attachment to a single God and single nation.

Since the 1840s, business always favored large-scale immigration because of its downward pressure on wage levels. Outsourcing was another factor that powerfully worked in the same direction. In the past, the multinational corporation often obtained raw materials abroad, and consumer-oriented corporations often established plants abroad to produce for the local foreign market. Both the workers and owners of such corporations benefited from such foreign activities and from tariffs.[17] As multi-national corporations began to produce components abroad, however, trade unions were forced to choose between jobs and wages. The wages of non-organized workers who competed against foreign workers were affected in like manner.

Perot was incensed not only by NAFTA, but also by Bush's war with Saddam Hussein over Kuwait. Perot became politically active once more in August 1990 precisely at the time when Bush began preparing for war. He often spoke against Bush's war policy, and everything about it seemed to anger him. "Just to show how corrupt

---

15. See Hugh Davis Graham, *Collision Course: The Strange Convergence of Affirmative Action and Immigration Policy in America* (New York: Oxford University Press, 2002), pp. 124-125.
16. Gwen Ifill, "Clinton to Endorse Free Trade Accord, *The New York Times*, October 4, 1992, p. A22.
17. Vladimir Lenin was so convinced of this fact that he insisted in his most famous work, *Imperialism*, that countries were driven to acquire more colonies and even had to go to war to achieve this goal and maintain social peace. Lenin was far from the only analyst to draw such a conclusion.

our system is, first off the reason we had to do this is because we told Saddam Hussein he could take the northern part of Kuwait and then got upset when he took the whole thing. We had to send the sons and daughters of working people off to fix that." In March 1992 he talked about the Emir of Kuwait whom the war put back in power as "this dude with seventy wives, who's got a minister for sex to find him a virgin every Thursday night."[18]

Perot especially detested the attitude of the upper strata who, he complained, did not send their sons and daughters into battle and would not support a war tax to pay for it. "We looked on this," Perot said, "as a Super Bowl. Believe me, war is not a Super Bowl.... War is great young people getting killed, getting pieces of their bodies blown away. War is the last resort, and if and when we do go to war, we must commit the nation and then commit the troops."

Perot also did not like the aftermath of the war:[19]

> When it was all over and everybody got all the publicity, I said, "Where is Sergeant York? Where are the battlefield heroes? Why are there no pictures of the wounded?" Isn't it bizarre that the only heroes from this war are generals and politicians? Think about it! Were there battlefield heroes? You bet there were.... We had our battlefield heroes. In any properly run government, they would have been the heroes in our war as they have always before. In any properly run government, a cross-section of America would have been on the battlefield. FDR's sons flew missions in World War II.

Perot did not mention it in this speech, but he must have had utter contempt for Bush's fear of removing Saddam Hussein when he had the chance after Hussein's army had been destroyed. In Perot's mind, the failure to remove Hussein must have seemed as cowardly as the failure to rescue the Missing-In-Action in Vietnam. The broader public too must have wondered about Bush's motivation. After all, the media universally described the United States as the only major power left in the world after the collapse of the Soviet Union and virtually omnipotent. Yet we were afraid to move against a defeated dictator

Perot had long been obsessed with Bush, but it is unclear what he would have done if the Democrats had nominated a critic of NAFTA in 1992. Bill Clinton, however, represented the epitome of everything that Perot detested. A Clinton letter to his Draft Board surfaced during the New Hampshire primary, and it contained a frank acknowledgement that he wanted to go to school in England to avoid the draft. The core of his foreign policy team consisted of doves from the Carter Administration or personal friends. Then in late September, the press began to report that

---

18. The first quote is from the speech of November 2, 1991, published in Ken Gross, *Ross Perot: The Man Behind the Myth* (New York: Random House, 1992), pp. 213. This was the major book published in 1992 in connection with the Perot campaign. Perot recommended the inclusion of this speech as best expressing his view. The second quotation, as well as the information about the timing of Perot's reentry, is from Gerald L. Posner, *Citizen Perot: His Life and Times* (New York: Random House, 1996), p. 245.
19. This statement and that from the previous paragraph are from the speech of November 2, 1991, in Gross, *Ross Perot*, pp. 212–214.

Clinton would endorse NAFTA. This was precisely the time that Perot re-entered the race.

BILL CLINTON AS AN AMBIGUOUS CANDIDATE

Every two years since the 1980 election, Paul Abramson, John Aldrich, and David Rohde have published the standard analysis of the previous election based on the results of the major scholarly survey long used by political scientists. In their 1991 volume, Abramson, Aldrich, and Rohde briefly discussed the forthcoming 1992 election. They listed 10 candidates and, like other observers, mentioned Bill Clinton as a long shot in 10th place.[20]

In fact, the likely candidates decided not to run, and most analysts believe that George Bush's high approval ratings after the Iraq War played a major role. Whatever the reason, and difficulties in fund-raising should not be discounted, Clinton's two main opponents in 1992 were California governor Jerry Brown and Massachusetts Senator Paul Tsongas, two seriously flawed candidates. Brown was known as a mystical near-hippy, while Tsongas had little experience to prepare him for the presidency and had had a serious operation for cancer. The 1991 book by Abramson, Aldrich, and Rohde understandably had not even mentioned Tsongas as a possible candidate.

The opposition to Clinton was so weak that even scandals about his woman-izing and draft-dodging that erupted during the New Hampshire period did not seri-ously harm him. Hence Clinton had great freedom in the campaign strategy he would use. Clinton and his supporters noted that the only Democrats elected President since 1960 were Lyndon Johnson from Confederate Texas and Jimmy Carter from Confederate Georgia. They argued that only a Southerner could win in 1992. To emphasize the point, Clinton took the unprecedented step of selecting a vice-presi-dential candidate from Confederate Tennessee, Al Gore, the first time the Demo-cratic Party ever had nominated a complete ticket from the Confederacy.

Nevertheless, the Confederate states had only 51% of the Electoral College votes needed for victory in the 1990s (59% if Kentucky and Oklahoma are included as part of the true South). Clinton and Gore were to win only 4 of the 11 Confederate states both in 1992 and 1996. Clinton's main task was to decide which strategy was most likely to win him the necessary Electoral College votes in the North. Since the Southern strategy of Jimmy Carter was not the same as that of Lyndon Johnson, Clinton could have followed a "Southern strategy" by choosing either Northern strategy.

Clinton's electoral strategy in 1991 and 1992 was clear cut: he would be as ambiguous as possible. He later became famous for "parsing" his words — being imprecise — in answering questions about his personal behavior, but he had long

---

20. Paul R. Abramson, John H. Aldrich, and David W. Rohde, *Change and Continuity in the 1988 Election*, rev. ed. (Washington: CQ Press, 1991), p. 345.

shown this ability in the political sphere. Like other great politicians, Clinton listened and responded to all visitors in a way that gave them the impression, often unwarranted, that he agreed with what they said.[21] His record as an Arkansas governor for ten years was moderately conservative, but, in the words of Earl Black and Merle Black, he "had spent his entire political career learning how to bob and weave liberal and conservative themes in order to create and maintain a successful biracial coalition."[22] Clinton ran as a "New Democrat," and that phrase was intended to mean anything the listener wanted.[23]

If Clinton were judged by his enthusiastic support for a comprehensive and expensive national health care program or for "middle class tax cuts," he would be seen as following in Lyndon Johnson's steps as President in the economic sphere. Those like the *Los Angles Times* reporter Robert Shogan remembered, however, that in September 1991 Clinton had emphatically rejected the idea of a national health plan, but in November 1991 had warmly embraced such a plan. In the November election, Shogan noted, Harris Wofford had unexpectedly won a special Senatorial election in Pennsylvania on the health issue, and John Kerrey was focusing on the issue in the battle for the Democratic nomination.[24] Clinton hired Wofford's chief political adviser, James Carville, as a major political adviser and adopted his advice on this issue. At the same time, Clinton remained fervent in supporting fiscal responsibility, and even the relatively unaware must have wondered with David Broder about the "fiscal legerdemain."

In March 1990, Clinton had accepted an offer to become chairman of the conservative Democratic Leadership Council (DLC) in hopes of using the post to gain financial support and win the nomination. If Clinton is judged by the operation of the DLC under his leadership, he was quite conservative. Clinton controlled the 1991 convention of the DLC, and Jesse Jackson was ostentatiously not invited even though he had often spoken to the organization before Clinton was chairman.[25]

The columnist David Broder was quite negative about the 1991 DLC Convention as a whole. Not only did it take a position on civil rights that was "a balancing act some of its own delegates called impossible," but the convention "did not look or feel like a Democratic gathering":[26]

---

21. This theme is especially emphasized in the memoirs of his chief lieutenant, Robert Rubin. Robert E. Rubin and Jacob Weisberg, *In an Uncertain World: Tough Choices from Wall Street to Washington* (New York: Random House, 2003). See, for example, pp. 133–134.
22. Earl Black and Merle Black, *The Rise of Southern Republicans* (Cambridge: Harvard University Press, 2002), p. 27.
23. In his memoirs, Clinton called Michael Dukakis a "New Democrat" with a program similar to Clinton's. This actually was an accurate analysis, but scarcely one that Clinton or his supporters made during the 1992 campaign. Clinton, *My Life*, p. 335.
24. Robert Shogan, *The Fate of the Union: America's Rocky Road to Political Stalemate* (Boulder, Colo.: Westview Press, 1998), pp. 69–70 and 74–75.
25. Dan Balz, "Democrats Face Minority Skepticism," *The Washington Post*, May 8, 1991, p. A7.
26. David S. Broder, "The DLC at Six," *The Washington Post*, May 12, 1991, p. C7.

You looked around the floor and saw few teachers or union members, few blacks and even fewer Hispanics. In their place, you had dozens of corporate lobbyists who pay the DLC's bills in return for access to its influential congressional members and governors. Many of the lobbyist-delegates acknowledge being Republicans; one was a top staffer for Spiro Agnew. But they were in there voting on resolutions, just as if they really cared about the Democrats' winning.

In the cultural realm, "New Democrat" was equally ambiguous. It could mean a rejection of the values of the McGovern activists or a more liberal cultural policy. In 1995, a *New York Times* article claimed that "President Clinton's campaign promise to 'end welfare as we know it' was the signature element of his contention that he was a 'new Democrat'." [27] Yet Clinton also flatly promised gay groups that gays would be fully accepted in the military. Each voter was invited to read his or her own preferences into the words and to point to this or that policy as "the signature element" of the program.

The same pattern was found in foreign policy. Thomas L. Friedman, the *New York Times* correspondent who covered the Clinton campaign, was very interested in foreign policy and was to become the newspaper's foreign relations columnist. Friedman reported late in the campaign that "the Clinton foreign policy ... is a blend of idealism and pragmatism, internationalism and protectionism, use of force and reliance on multinational institutions." [28] Friedman noted that critics claimed the policy was totally ambiguous, and he himself did not seriously argue against the point.

CLINTON AS A PRESIDENT WITH A SUBURBAN STRATEGY

After Bill Clinton defeated Bush in November 1992, the big question was whether the ambiguity in the definition of "New Democrat" was simply a campaign tactic or a reflection of genuine indecision and confusion in Clinton's own mind. The policy-making process in his first two years in office seemed to feature chaos greater than anything previously seen in Washington, and Clinton insiders contributed to this impression. [29] As a result, many found it difficult to see Clinton as a careful calculator. They believed that only after the Republican victory in the 1994 Congressional election did Clinton adopt a Northern suburban strategy under the influence of the consultant Dick Morris. [30]

---

27. David E. Rosenbaum, "Clinton in Awkward Role in the Debate on Welfare," *The New York Times*, September 21, 1995, p. B11.
28. Thomas L. Friedman, "Clinton's Foreign Policy Agenda Reaches Across Broad Spectrum," *The New York Times*, October 4, 1992, p. A1.
29. The sense of chaos is best conveyed in Bob Woodward's *The Agenda*. The problem with such books, however, is that the price for insider anecdotes immediately after an event is a willingness to accept the insider spin. The reader is always forced to judge how much the spin reflects the reality. Bob Woodward, *The Agenda: Inside the Clinton White House* (New York: Simon & Schuster, 1994), p. 125.

When closely examined a dozen years later, however, the evidence about the early Clinton Administration strongly suggests that the President was not groping chaotically for a political strategy. Instead, he deliberately seems to have encouraged a misleading chaos to obscure a suburban strategy already chosen that he knew would be highly frustrating to many supporters and voters.

Robert Rubin, who became the President's chief economic adviser and then his "prime minister," certainly saw a consistent strategy from the beginning. He began his autobiography by stating that "the Bill Clinton I watched [is] a misunderstood figure." Rubin did not believe the President was indecisive in his basic priorities. "Chaos was certainly not what I experienced," Rubin wrote in his memoirs.[31]

Rubin's judgment may simply be that of an ultimate winner who wrongly thought his victory was determined from the beginning. Yet the major loser on economic policy, Robert Reich, also had a clear sense of the President's early priorities, even if Reich retained hopes for the future. More important, the pattern of early events, including that reported in the media at the time, supports Rubin's judgment.

That Clinton would follow a relatively conservative economic policy was evident even before his inauguration. On December 10, 1992, scarcely a month after the election, Clinton introduced five members of his economic team at a press conference. They were the secretary and deputy secretary of treasury, the director and deputy director of the Office of Management and the Budget, and the head of a new Economic Council. The first four were what the New York Times called "super-hawks" on a balanced budget and deficit reduction. The fifth, Robert Rubin, also held these views, although more quietly.[32]

The press called the five persons announced on December 10 "the" economic team, obviously a reflection of briefings, but Clinton also had economic advisers with more liberal views. The next day, the major such advisers, Robert Reich and Laura Tyson, were named to minor posts, Secretary of Labor and Chairman of the Council of Economic Advisers respectively. Their appointments were announced along with those of the head of the Environmental Protection Agency and the Secretary of Health and Welfare, and three of the four were women. This was the point emphasized in the news coverage. No one could think they were key members of "the economic team."

---

30. Morris himself vigorously publicized his own role. See Dick Morris, *Behind the Oval Office: Getting Reelected Against All Odds*, 2nd ed. (Los Angeles: Renaissance Books, 1999). Nevertheless, Morris had been close to Clinton since 1977 — even though all his other clients were Republicans such as Trent Lott of Mississippi. A good sense of the relationship of Clinton and Morris in Arkansas can be gained from following the footnotes in David Maraniss, *First in His Class: A Biography of Bill Clinton* (New York: Simon & Schuster, 1995). See, for example, pp. 352 and 440.

31. Rubin and Weisberg, *In an Uncertain World*, pp. 6 and 143.

32. Thomas L. Friedman, "Clinton Team Takes Shape with Bentsen and 4 Others Named to Economic Posts," *The New York Times*, December 11. 1992, p. Al. In addition, Larry Summers, an extreme exponent of deregulation, was named undersecretary of treasury for foreign economic policy. He became the real Secretary of State on the major countries where economic reform was on the agenda: Russia, Eastern Europe, Latin America, East Asia, and the European Community. The character of the team is confirmed in Clinton's memoirs. Clinton, *My Life*, pp. 451–463.

Clinton held his first major meeting with economic advisers on January 7, 1993, again before his inauguration. The real question on the agenda was the position the key appointees would take at their Senate confirmation hearings over the next week. They argued for deficit reduction as their chief priority, but Rubin reports that Clinton showed his commitment to that priority even before they could make their case. The position was leaked to the press before they appeared in front of the Senate committee.[33]

It was clear by early January that Clinton would abandon the middle class tax cut. He proposed replacing it with a general 5% universal tax on energy, but Congress would only enact a 4.3 cents a gallon tax on gasoline. The Republicans charged that the energy tax was a middle class tax since everyone had to pay it, and Clinton conceded the point in his memoirs.[34] Although the President raised expenditures for all social goals, almost all the increases were so small that they were little more than symbolic.

The one major apparent exception to Clinton's early economic policy was his health program. He put his wife, Hillary, in charge of developing a program, a decision that supposedly showed his commitment to it. Hillary, however, developed a complex bureaucratic program that was easy to criticize. Secretary of the Treasury Lloyd Bentsen was told so little about the program that he could not estimate its costs and fit it within the budget. This strongly suggests that the program never was serious.[35]

Influential Senators such as Pat Moynihan and Robert Dole signaled their readiness to reach some compromise on a partial reform, but were ignored. Indeed, Dole in 1993 co-sponsored a more modest health program. He was told that he had to present his own universal program before the Administration would even negotiate with him. Originally, the Republicans thought it would be politically impossible to oppose health care reform, but they changed their mind as they saw how it was being handled.[36] A year after it was introduced, the health plan was declared dead.

The conventional explanation of the failure of the health plan centers on the complexity of the plan, the Clintons' political inexperience and incompetence (especially Hillary's), the skill of Republican advertisements against it, and the supposed public suspicion of national health care.[37] Robert Shogan is, however, quite convincing when he argues that Clinton never was willing to sacrifice his fiscal policy to pay for a comprehensive program, that he never invested any energy in passing it, and

---

33. Rubin, *In an Uncertain World*, pp. 95–96 and 118–119. Adam Clymer, "3 Congressmen Say Deficit May Delay Clinton's Tax Cut," *The New York Times*, January 11, 1993, p. A1; David E. Rosenbaum,, "Budget Nominee [Leon Panetta] Testifies Clinton May Set Aside Tax-Cutting Pledge," *The New York Times*, January 12, 1993, p. A1.
34. Clinton, *My Life*, p. 493.
35. Rubin, *In an Uncertain World*, p. 149.
36. Shogan, *The Fate of the Union*, p. 161.
37. For an early study that takes for granted Clinton's sincere dedication to the program, see Theda Skocpol, *Boomerang: Clinton's Health Security Effort and the Turn Against Government in U.S. Politics* (New York: W. W. Norton, 1996). For a recent such interpretation, see John F. Harris, *The Survivor: Bill Clinton in the White House* (New York:: Random House, 2005), pp. 110-119.

that he wanted it to fail.[38] The evidence suggests that Clinton put his wife in charge so that she could guarantee this result.

Clinton's cultural policy seemed as clearly defined at the beginning of his Administration as his economic policy. Given the extreme hostility of the Democratic Leadership Council to the cultural liberals, the most surprising fact about the Clinton Administration was how rapidly the President wholeheartedly embraced these very cultural groups.

Clinton had promised to have a cabinet that "looks like America," and in his memoirs he testified to his goal "of naming the most diverse administration in history."[39] His original 16 cabinet members included 4 women, 4 blacks, 2 Hispanics, and 1 Lebanese-American. The background of the sub-cabinet officers, but not the chief White House staff officials, had a similar character. The most radical prominent black, Lani Lanier, was nominated to be Assistant Attorney General for civil rights. Yet, the heads of departments did not include the usual diversity of a Democratic Administration among whites — not a single non-Hispanic Catholic-American and only one Jewish-American, the powerless Robert Reich.[40]

Even more dramatic was Clinton's decision to emphasize a new policy on gays in the military. As in the case of the budget, the policy was leaked to the press the week before the inauguration.[41] During the first week of the Administration, the press focused its major coverage on this issue, with reporters making it totally clear that the President wanted the military to accept gays fully and openly. The top generals, including the chairman of the Joint Chiefs of Staff, Colin Powell, were correctly said to be strongly opposed.

This issue, like that of health care, is often cited as evidence of chaos in the Administration, but the President told Robert Rubin that he recognized his position "was really going to hurt Democrats in the South for many years to come." When Rubin expressed doubt, Clinton answered. "'No, this is going to affect how people look at us for a long, long time.'"[42] It is difficult to believe that a Southern President who was leader of the Democratic Leadership Council understood this only after he had given such prominence to the issue.

In short, Clinton from the first days of the Administration showed very clearly that he would push for the relatively conservative economic policy and the very liberal cultural policy that constituted a wholehearted suburban strategy. When he agreed to welfare reform at the end of his first term, he was merely taking a decision that dramatized a general strategy already long in place. Welfare reform was the one cultural issue with significant budgetary implications and, not surprisingly, the budgetary consequences would benefit his suburban base. The appearance of chaos

---

38. Shogan, *The Fate of the Union*, pp. 157–162.
39. Clinton, *My Life*, p. 454.
40. Two Catholics were found in non-department cabinet posts, Madeleine Albright, as ambassador to the United Nations, and Leon Panetta, as director of the Office of Management and the Budget.
41. Eric Schmitt, "Clinton Aides Study Indirect End to Military Ban on Homosexuals," *The New York Times*, January 13, 1993, p. A1.
42. Rubin, *In An Uncertain World*, p. 154.

seems little more than a technique to forestall a recognition by the losers of a choice that was already made.

On the eve of the 1996 election, Clinton did make a series of well-publicized gestures to those who were culturally more conservative, but most had no concrete meaning.[43] Clinton in no way reversed his cultural policy with respect to the groups that had been so controversial — e.g., feminists, gay rights organizations, environmental activists, and the National Education Association. He did not reverse himself on gun control. No one thought that he was repudiating Hollywood or that he had become a born-again Christian in his personal behavior.

The Democratic Leadership Council shifted its position to correspond with the President's decisions. It no longer condemned the cultural activists. In early 1998, the DLC magazine, *The New Democrat*, carried a series of articles under the heading "The Myth of the Resurgent Left." None of the articles defined "liberals" as the McGovern cultural liberals or the cultural groups that most concerned the DLC in the 1980s. The left-wing issues now were only economic ones such as government spending, trade protectionism, and taxation, and the sole villain was the AFL-CIO for supporting them.[44]

An Al Gore speechwriter and DLC supporter, Kenneth Baer, asserts that a "profound change" had occurred in the Democratic Party:[45]

> A party that for the past thirty years had been seen as profligate "tax and spenders," reflective defenders of federal governmental programs, pacifist isolationists, and advocates of an active social liberalism now had a president who championed the reinvention of government, welfare reform, fiscal restraint, economic growth, free trade, mainstream values, and an internationalist foreign policy.

Mark Penn, who conducted Clinton's public opinion polling in 1996, made the same argument to the Cabinet immediately after the election, "The election signals the end of the old Democratic coalition of blacks, the elderly, and the downscale. It marks the emergence of a *new* Democratic coalition of women, Latinos, and especially suburban married couples."[46]

Many on the left agree with Baer and Penn, but phrase the point pejoratively. Even some who did not question the Administration's basic intentions in 1993 and 1994 became disillusioned. Theda Skocpol noted in 2000 that Clinton never returned to health care as an issue and that in 1999 neither he nor Al Gore ever repeated the 1991 and 1992 themes of the "forgotten middle class" or the "working poor."[47]

---

43. For part of this campaign, see the Introduction to paperback edition of Ben J. Wattenberg, *Values Matter Most* (Regnery Publishing, 1998), pp. ix–xiii.
44. "The Myth of the Resurgent Left," *The New Democrat*, vol. 10, no. 1 (January/February 1998), pp. 4–5.
45. Kenneth S. Baer, *Reinventing Democrats: The Politics of Liberalism from Reagan to* Clinton (Lawrence: University Press of Kansas, 2000), p. 2.
46. Robert B. Reich, *Locked in the Cabinet* (New York: Alfred A. Knopf, 1997), p. 330. Italics are in the original.
47. Theda Skocpol, *The Missing Middle: Working Families and the Future of American Social Policy* (New York: W. W. Norton, 2000), pp. 4–5, 7, and 141.

Stanley Greenberg, who was Clinton's chief pollster in 1992 and had been replaced by Penn in 1996, notes that "the middle class as actual voters and as a symbol was the central audience in the 1992 presidency." He is scathing about the actual policy that Clinton followed:[48]

> The Clinton Administration abandoned the middle class. This was partly sym-bolic, as middle-class grievances and wants were no longer the central passion of the project; this was partly real and material, as low-income populations took prior-ity and as middle-class incomes were low to rise; and it was partly about values, both real and symbolic.... The middle-class voters were driven from the project in 1994 by the deafening silence, taxes, stagnant incomes, no welfare reform, and the assault weapons ban. But even after all this, when Clinton climbed back to win in 1996, his second-term State of the Union addresses made almost no mention of the "missing middle."

ROBERT DOLE AND THE FAILURE OF REPUBLICAN GENERATION CHANGE

The 1996 election seems very anomalous. Ross Perot had received 19% of the vote in 1992, and Clinton clearly had not fully succeeded in removing the causes for grievance that Perot had tapped. The Democrats elected 63 fewer House members in 1994 than they had in 1990 and 9 fewer Senators. With the right kind of candidate, the Republicans seemed in an excellent position if they could win back the Perot voters and/or Baby Boomer suburban voters.

Instead, the Republicans named Robert Dole as their candidate after a nomi-nating process in which he had faced no credible competitor. Dole seemed the serious candidate with the least possible chance of mobilizing the Perot voters, the religious right, or the Baby Boomers. Dole did have an extremely impressive record. He had been in the Congress for 43 years, 27 of them in the Senate. From 1971 to 1973, he had served as chairman of the Republican Party, and three years later Gerald Ford had picked him as his vice-presidential candidate. That was 20 years before he ran for President in 1996. Dole had served as chairman of the Senate Finance Committee from 1981 to 1985 and then the Republican leader in the Senate from 1985 to 1996.

Yet, Dole was a most unlikely candidate for President in 1996. He had run in the Republican primaries in 1988 and had not been a successful campaigner. Born in 1923, he would be 74 years old in 1997, 5 years older than Reagan had been in 1981, and he did not have Reagan's special charisma. Dole was a member of John Kennedy's "new generation born in this century" — in practice, those born from 1908 to 1924 — who had occupied the presidency from 1961 to 1993. Like Dole, nearly all these presi-dents had been in the military in World War II, and they all had held important posts during the creation of the whites, the struggles over desegregation, and/or the political battles over the Vietnam War. Dole's generation had played a great his-torical role in American history.

---

48. Greenberg, *The Two Americas*, pp. 82–84.

Nevertheless, the defeat of George H. W. Bush in 1992 seemed to signify a public recognition that his generation had completed the role that Kennedy had defined. Kennedy's "new generation" was honored for its historic role, but, as with the election of Theodore Roosevelt, Taft, and Wilson in the early 20th century, the country showed that it believed that new problems loomed. It was ready to move into a new century with a new generation in charge. Yet, Dole was born a year before Bush. Clinton, by contrast, would be a 50-year-old Baby Boomer in 1996 and his running mate, Al Gore, would be 48 years old. It seemed highly improbable that the huge Baby-Boom generation would want to replace two of its own with a man five years older than Bush in 1992.

The 1996 campaign has generated few retrospective studies or memoirs. Those who did discuss the election at the time were struck most of all by the apparent incompetence of Dole's campaign. He came from rural Kansas, had not had a serious contest since 1974, and had done poorly in the 1988 presidential primaries. He appeared similar to Henry Clay and Martin Van Buren in the 1840s, men near the end of a career as consummate Congressional insiders who had little feel for a world that was changing and a national electorate much younger than themselves.

At the beginning of 1996, Dole had three serious opponents. One was Senator Philip Gramm of Texas, a person without any warmth in public who was passion-ately conservative on economic issues, but who had little interest in cultural issues. Gramm did, however, take extreme positions on cultural issues during the campaign to court the religious right. A second contender was a columnist, Pat Buchanan, who was a deeply committed member of the radical right on cultural and especially nationalist issues, but who was more imbued with New Deal economic values than the leading Democratic candidates. A third, Steve Forbes, was a millionaire through inheritance who had no real experience and who had a single issue, the flat tax, that was certain to be highly unpopular when examined closely. A fourth candidate, Lamar Alexander, was a credible moderate, but he had almost no funds.

Dole was long known as a conservative. It may be recalled that Ford selected him as a running mate in 1974 in part, and likely in large part, because he had shown an ability to defeat a Senatorial opponent in 1972 on the abortion issue. Nevertheless, in his work as a Senate leader Dole really was an old-time Republican moderate con-servative who was ready to reach the compromises necessary to enact legislation. In 1995 and 1996, the obvious differences between him as Senate majority leader and the new Republican speaker of the House, the radically conservative Newt Gingrich, strengthened his image as a moderate.

Dole's marriage also symbolized his moderate position.[49] In 1975, he had married a Federal Trade Commissioner who favored the Equal Rights Amendment and a women's right to choose abortion. His wife, Elizabeth, went on to serve as Sec-retary of Transportation from 1983 to 1987 in the Reagan Administration and Pres-ident of the Red Cross since 1991. Clearly Dole did not think that women must be traditional wives and mothers. Indeed, if he were elected, the first lady would have

---

49. See Chapter 6 for discussion of the possibility this was a factor in Ford's selection of him as the vice-presidential nominee.

had an even more successful career than Hillary Clinton and would be an excellent role model for working women.

Given the nature of his opponents in the primaries, it seemed virtually impossible for Dole to be defeated for the nomination, and he was far ahead in April and May 1995. Yet, he decided (wrongly, in the judgment of nearly all observers) that he had to move to the right on cultural issues to defeat Gramm and Buchanan in the primaries. He took an extreme position on abortion and gun control and returned a $1000 donation from a very respectable gay Republican group, the Log Cabin Republicans. He had always supported affirmative action, but now managed to suggest that he opposed it.[50]

Then at the convention, Dole ostentatiously moved to the center. Before the convention, Dole openly tried to modify the abortion plank in a more moderate direction, and the convention itself had a moderate tone, with abortion hardly mentioned.[51] However, in a process that lasted over a month, Dole failed in a humiliating manner to change the platform. As Ralph Reed, head of the Christian Coalition, boasted, a third of the delegates were associated with the religious right. Most of them may have been pledged to vote for Dole as a candidate, but they controlled the platform committee and had a free hand in the position they took. It was at this time that Reed made the earlier-quoted statement that Reagan had only given the religious right "warm fuzzies," but that it was better to have "genuine institutional strength or influence."[52]

The result was a political disaster for Dole. By seeking to soften the abortion plank, Dole reinforced the belief of the religious right that he was not sincerely committed to their cause. Yet, his failure to change the plank convinced others that he was not strong enough to control the religious right even on the platform where an odds-on nominee normally has a dominant role.

Not surprisingly, Dole failed to mobilize any significant base of support beyond traditional Republican voters and, as Table 2 indicates, large numbers of them did not come to the polls. The turnout was the lowest in any presidential election in history. Perot had not been effective in arguing against NAFTA in a debate with Gore and, in general, had not remained active in the intervening four years. He had lost much of his credibility. Perot's vote declined from 19.7 million in 1992 to 8.1 million in 1996, but Dole had less than 100,000 more votes than Bush. Clinton's vote total increased by only 2.5 million votes, and 8.1 million fewer votes were cast for President, despite the rise in population.

50. Jake H. Thompson, *Bob Dole: The Republicans' Man for All Seasons*, rev. ed. (New York: D. I. Fine Books, 1996), pp. 247-257.

51. Richard L. Berke, "Dole Ignoring His Advisers, Lashes Out at Abortion Foe," *The New York Times*, June 12, 1996, p. A1; Sam Howe Verhovek, "Abortion Barely Mentioned [at Convention], Its Opponents are Offended," *The New York Times*, August 15, 1996, p. A1.

52. For the defeat, see David E. Rosenbaum, "Dole Camp Accepts Uncompromising Abortion Plan," *The New York Times*, August 6, 1996, p. A12; for the Reed statement, Verhovek, "Abortion Barely Mentioned," *The New York Times*, August 15, 1996, pp. A 1 and A20.

Table 2: Total Votes in Presidential Elections, 1984-2000,
By Political Party

Year	Total Vote (Millions)	Republican Vote (Millions)	Republican %	Democrat Vote (Millions)	Democrat %	Perot/ Nader Vote (Millions)	Perot/ Nader %
1984	92,653	54,555	58.8%	38,577	40.6%	—	—
1988	91,595	48,886	53.4%	41,809	45.6%	—	—
1992	104,425	39,103	37.4%	44,909	43.0%	19,741	18.9%
1996	96,277	39,199	40.7%	47,402	49.2%	8,085	8.4%
2000	105,397	50,455	47.9%	50,992	48.4%	2,883	2.7%

Source: CQ's Guide to U.S. Elections, vol. 1, pp. 684-688.

It is, however, highly unlikely that any campaign strategy would have worked for Dole. He was too old, he was not a natural campaigner in an age of television, the economy and stock market were doing well, and Bill Clinton had corrected his major political and managerial shortcomings during his first two years in office. The most important question is why Dole was not seriously challenged in the Republican primary. Why did the Republicans not nominate their own Baby Boom candidate?

The obvious immediate answer to this question was that many potential candidates decided not to run because of difficulties in raising funds. Scholars study in detail "the invisible primary" — the campaign that takes place before the Iowa caucus, the pre-primary campaigning and maneuvering. The phrase is misleading, for most of this activity receives great media attention and is quite visible. The real "invisible pre-primary" is the effort to acquire the minimum $20 to $30 million that was said in the 1990s to be required before the Iowa caucuses.[53] The way in which fund-raisers decide whom to support is too little studied.

At the end of January 1996, only three candidates had crossed the $20 million threshold: Dole with $32.0 million, Senator Phil Gramm with $25.7 million, and Steve Forbes with $25.4. Dole had his old campaign finance network, and his role as Senate majority leader made it difficult for those with business interests to decline invitations to contribute. Gramm's economic views were popular with economic conservatives. Forbes had essentially raised his money from himself and did not qualify for any federal matching funds. He was not a serious candidate.[54]

---

53. Emmett H. Buell, "The Invisible Primary", in William G. Mayer, Jr., ed., *In Pursuit of the White House: How We Choose Our Presidential Nominees* (Chatham, N.J.: Chatham House, 1996), p. 12.
54. For the finances of the declared Republican candidates, see Emmett H. Buell, Jr., "Some Things are Predictable: Nominating Dole, Clinton, and Perot," in Harvey L. Schantz, ed., *Politics in an Era of Divided Government: Elections and Governance in the Second Clinton Administration* (New York: Routledge, 2001), p. 6. Buell has an excellent 17-page summary of the 1996 Republican nominating process on pp. 2–19 of this book.

The one Baby-Boomer among the plausible candidates, Governor William Weld of Massachusetts, was thought much too liberal to be nominated, and he could raise no money. Yet moderates who would have been very strong candidates in the old convention system also found it surprisingly difficult to raise money. Dole, it may be remembered, had raised $32.0 million by the end of January 1996 and Gramm $25.7 million. The moderate Lamar Alexander and Pete Wilson had raised $12.5 million and $6.4 million respectively, and virtually all of it had been spent.[55] Wilson had, in fact, dropped out of the race at the end of September 1995.

The California governor, Pete Wilson, is particularly interesting. He would be 63 years of age in 1996 and had served as Senator from the most populous state from 1983 to 1991 and its governor from 1991 to 1995. He had defeated Diane Feinstein in the 1990 gubernatorial race by a 49.2% to 45.8% margin and then the highly credible Kathleen Brown, daughter of the former governor, by a 55.2% to 40.6% margin in 1994. He alone had seized Ross Perot's issue and had tapped the anti-immigrant feeling in the state by sponsoring Proposition 187. The size of his victory against Brown indicated that he had found a winning argument.

Yet he could not raise funds.

There are a number of possible explanations for the lack of a credible challenger to Dole, but none seems proven or, by itself, highly probable. The usual explanation is that moderates almost always were pro-choice and that campaign contributors did not believe that that they could win primaries dominated by the religious right. A cynic might suggest — and, perhaps with reason — that the Republican Establishment had a prospective Baby Boom candidate in George H.W. Bush's son and that they actually preferred for the Republicans to lose in 1996 so that the Republican nomination would be open in 2000. Another possible explanation is the distribution of delegates to the Republican convention. The nine large industrial states in the North, Midwest, and West had 45% of the population in 1990 and 39% of the delegates to the 1996 Republican Convention. The Southern, Border, Mountain, and Prairie states had 43% of the population and 53% of the delegates.[56] Finally, business interests historically have always favored immigration, and this may have been a factor in Wilson not being able to raise money.

GEORGE W. BUSH AND THE 2000 ELECTION

The 2000 election was the first in which the terms "red state" and "blue state" came into general use. (The colors came from the color of the states given Bush and Gore respectively on television maps.) The reason is that it was the first election with such a clear delineation between the large urban states and the more rural Southern, Mountain, and Prairie states. Gore's 21 states were 85% urban, and Bush's

---

55. Buell, "Some Things are Predictable," p. 7.
56. The industrial states are California, Illinois, Maryland, Massachusetts, Michigan, New Jersey, New York, Ohio, and Pennsylvania. The Border states exclude Delaware and Maryland.

30 were 73% urban. The 13 states in which the candidates were separated by 5 per-centage points or less were 75% urban, 4 percentage points below the national average.

Many liberals think that a religious right takeover of the Republican Party explains the Republican strategy, but this is not accurate. As the biographers of Bush's chief political adviser, Karl Rove, remind us, even Democrats in Texas accepted that George W. Bush, like his father, was "a decent country club Repub-lican." In their words, the younger Bush "shunned the Christian Right and disdained the immigrant-bashers in his party." Bush had become a born-again Christian in 1986, but Rove was a non-believer. It was on economic issues, especially privati-zation, that Bush was deeply ideological. The religious right was cautious about him, but thought him superior to Gore and wanted him to win.[57]

The Republican Establishment politicians and financial contributors decided well before the first primaries to support George W. Bush. "W" not only had access to his father's network of financial contributors, but he also had made many contacts when his father used him in the 1988 and 1992 campaigns to handle political assign-ments. In addition, a very sophisticated calculation underlay the decision about the strategy to follow in what seemed a losing year for Republicans in 2000.

Swing voters generally are heavily influenced by the economic performance of the preceding few years, and the economy was very strong in Clinton's second term. A number of political scientists have developed models that attempt to use economic indicators to predict the actual vote. These models predicted that Gore would receive from 53% to 55% of the popular vote or, in one case, 60%.[58] Al Gore was, of course, not an incumbent President, but he was a Vice President with unusually deep involvement in policy-making.

The predictions of the political science models often are inaccurate in fairly close elections, and they fail to take into account the stock market. In fact, the NASDAQ index declined by 32% between March 2000 and the day of the election, and many new investors in technology stocks on the NASDAQ likely were swing voters. In essence, however, Bush was nominated before the market bubble burst, and professional politicians had to make their decision several years earlier. The pattern of party votes over recent elections was no more promising than the eco-nomic news. As was seen in Table 2, Ronald Reagan won 55.5 million votes in 1984, Bush 48.9 million in 1988 and 39.1 million in 1992, and Robert Dole 39.2 million in 1996. Bush would win only 50.5 million votes in 2000, 4 million votes less than Reagan in 1984 and only 1.5 million more than his father in 1988. The Democrats had

---

57. Lou Dubose, Jan Reid, and Carl M. Cannon, *Boy Genius: Karl Rove, The Brains Behind the Remarkable Political Triumph of George W. Bush* (New York: Public Affairs, 2002), pp. 84–87.
58. For a book published before the election, see James E. Campbell and James C. Garand, *Before the Vote: Forecasting American National Elections* (Thousand Oaks, Calif.: Sage Publi-cations, 2000). For a retrospective analysis of the mistakes in the models, see Helmut Norpoth, "Bush v. Gore: The Recount of the Economic Voting," in Herbert F. Weis-berg and Clyde Wilcox, eds., *Models of Voting in Presidential Elections: The U.S. 2000 Election* (Stanford, Calif.: Stanford University Press, 2004), pp. 49–64. The summary of the models and their predictions is found on p. 51.

steadily increased their vote: 38.6 million in 1984, 41.8 million in 1988, 44.9 million in 1992, 47.4 million in 1996, and 51.0 million in 2000.

In May 2000, *after* Bush's nomination was assured, a high-level Republican Commission recommended a fundamental change in the Republican nominating procedure. Chaired by one former Republican chairman (William Brock) and including three more former chairmen, the Brock Commission's report implicitly was based on the assumption that the party would need to change its nominating procedure after a third straight loss.

The nature of the recommendation of the Brock Commission was also highly interesting. It proposed that the primaries be divided into four groups of states.[59] The 12 or 13 least populous states would hold their primary in March, with equal numbers of more populous states holding their primaries in April, May, and June. The Brock Commission did not explicitly make the point, but the 13 least populous states that would vote in March had 11.5 million people in 2000, while the most populous states that would vote in June had 173.8 million, 62% of the national total.

From 1988 through 2000, the front-loaded system had produced three nominees from Texas and one from Kansas. So long as the finance laws were changed to ensure that the candidates would have money available in June, the populous urban states would have the decisive role in the Brock proposal. The Commission clearly believed that the red-state strategy led to an unacceptably large loss of Northern suburban voters. It was implicitly saying that the Republicans had to nominate candidates more responsive to those states' inhabitants. The way to do this was to give these voters the key role in the primaries.

The problem that Bush faced was how to win in this unpromising situation. Any serious presidential political strategy begins with an analysis of the Electoral College. In 2000, any serious Democratic candidate such as Al Gore was virtually assured states with 180 Electoral College votes. As a result, the Democrats only needed another 90 votes. Minnesota was a traditional Democratic state, and Pennsylvania and the old industrial states of Illinois, Michigan, and Ohio had benefited greatly from Clinton's economic prosperity. These four states had 72 Electoral College votes. Gore was from Tennessee, and he normally would be a favorite to win Tennessee, Arkansas, and West Virginia at a minimum. They had 22 votes. These three groups of states had 274 Electoral College votes, enough to win, and Gore might well win other states — e.g., Iowa, New Mexico, Oregon, and Wisconsin that he actually did win.

Bill Clinton had embraced and formalized the suburban strategy, but he never really had the suburban style. It was symptomatic that he and Hillary had never owned their own home in Arkansas or elsewhere. At heart he still seemed the boy from Hope, Arkansas, and blacks called him "the first black President" — a phrase that included a suspicion about his roots, but that at a minimum recognized his ability to communicate naturally with blacks and adopt their style.

---

59. Advisory Commission on the Presidential Nominating Process, *Nominating Future Presidents* (Washington: Republican National Committee, 2000).

Gore, although officially from Tennessee, was the son of a Tennessee Senator and had lived all his life in the Washington area. He had attended elite private schools from the elementary level upward, and his basic approach seemed almost a parody of the modernist secular suburbanite. Not surprisingly, Gore made his reputation as a fervent proponent of environmentalism, arms control, and globalization. He even boasted of being the father of Internet legislation. This provoked jokes because he imprecisely called himself the father of the Internet itself, but the truth behind the claim was politically more important. Gore was eagerly associating himself with the very symbol of modernity, the very technological innovation that brought pornography, sex chat rooms, and similar phenomena into the home.

In 1988, Gore had been the favorite conservative candidate of the Democratic Leadership Council, and throughout the late 1980s and the early 1990s he had the most conservative economic views of the various serious Democratic candidates. He continued to play a conservative role within the Administration. Then in 2000, Gore decided against selecting a running mate with more New Deal views (e.g., Richard Gephardt or Jay Rockefeller), but chose Joseph Lieberman, the most conservative Democratic Senator from a coastal state and a man with very close ties to Connecticut's insurance industry. Members of the inattentive public may have known little about this, but they certainly knew that Ralph Nader was charging that Gore was so conservative that a third party was needed.

At the end of the campaign, Gore emphasized Social Security as a populist issue, but the Democrats had joined with Republicans to lower Social Security payments by "postponing the age of retirement." Gore pledged a more comprehensive health care program, but he also emphasized fiscal responsibility. There was little reason to think he would be more successful than Clinton in passing a health care program unless he would accept compromises of the type imbedded in Bush's program. Quite aside from his cultural position, Gore did not have an economic policy that might overcome the Republican cultural advantage in competing for the lower and middle-income whites.

If the Republicans nominated a moderate Northern governor, they might win some of the northern states that seemed likely to vote for Gore, but they were likely to lose other states, especially in the South. Bush and the Republicans decided to concede most of the industrial Northern states and to try to win the less industrialized ones. In particular, the Southern, Prairie, and Mountain states had a total of 239 Electoral College votes, while Indiana and Ohio had 33 more, enough to win without any other states. Indiana had been a strongly Republican state for some time.

Ohio was a swing state that had voted for the winner in every election in the 20th century except the wartime election of 1944, and it would be crucial. Although Ohio had a population that was 77.4% urban, this was several percentage points below the national level. More important, many who lived in the southeastern quadrant of the state were migrants from the South, especially from West Virginia. Jimmy Carter had done very well in the rural areas and small towns of Ohio that were south of the "accent line," and a Republican counterpart of Carter was also likely to do well there.

These were the states that the Republicans targeted. Bush's red state strategy rested largely on his support of conservative cultural issues. As a governor, he had not spoken much about religion, but in late 1999, he began emphasizing the theme, as had Carter. In debates in Iowa he responded to a question about his favorite philosopher or theory by saying "Christ, because he changed my heart." He then expanded his answer. "When you turn your heart and your life over to Christ, when you accept Christ as the savior, it changes your heart. It changes your life, and that's what happened to me."[60] This was not really an answer about Christ's philosophy, but Bush was making a political point.

Bush's personal life seemed to confirm his claim. He had been a heavy drinker, but foreswore alcohol in 1986, the day after his 40th birthday. At this time, he had become a born-again Christian. He adopted the positions on contemporary cultural issues that would be expected of a born-again Christian. He even listed Antonin Scalia and Clarence Thomas as his favorite Supreme Court Justices. But he tried to signal in various ways that he would not be intolerant.

Other aspects of Bush's personality had great appeal in the red areas. His family background and his education at Yale were similar to Gore's, but the younger Bush, unlike his father, was a true Texan. He had had a company in the oil business, had bought a ranch, and wore the appropriate clothes. He then became president of the Texas Rangers major league baseball team. Bush was elected governor of Texas in 1994, defeating a popular governor, Ann Richards, by 334,000 votes, a 54% to 46% margin. Then in 1998 he was re-elected by 1,386,000 votes, a 68% to 31% margin.

Bush had never even visited Europe or Asia, and his only interest in a foreign country seemed to be Mexico. He became the butt of jokes for not knowing the names of foreign leaders, but politically this was a major plus for him among those on the cultural right and also among those who had been attracted to Ross Perot. He spoke fluent Spanish and, for a Republican, did unusually well among Hispanic voters.

In the economic sphere, Bush emphasized the need for tax reductions, but he pledged to be a "compassionate conservative" on economic issues. Indeed, he was to fulfill his pledge of a prescription drug program, and his tax program prominently included tax reduction for families with children. He continually emphasized that he was an heir of Ronald Reagan, but, of course, Reagan had combined tax cuts with a heavy spending program and had accepted a large deficit as "supply-side economics."

As all remember, Gore won the election by 550,000 popular votes, but lost it by 5 (really 4) Electoral College votes.[61] Gore could have won with a shift of 4,000 votes in New Hampshire, and he likely would have had victories in West Virginia or Missouri if he had picked Governor Jay Rockefeller or Representative Dick Gephardt as his running mate. Florida was, of course, was too evenly divided for the victor to be determined reliably, and the selection of its popular Senator, Bob Graham, as his running mate would have carried that state.[62]

---

60. Dubose, Reid, and Cannon, *Boy Genius*, pp. 55–56.
61. One Gore elector from the District of Columbia abstained to protest the lack of Congressional representation for the district, but she said she would not have done so if her vote mattered.

Many were to think that Bush owed his victory in 2004 to the religious right, but, in large part, the Evangelicals who abandoned Dole in 1996 returned to the polls to support Bush in 2000. As indicated in Table 2 above, the Democrats had a steady increase in total number of votes from 1984 onwards, partly as the result of growth in population, partly of a larger percentage of the total vote. By contrast, the Republican vote was much lower in the 1990s than the 1980s. Even though George W. Bush received fewer votes than Gore, he won far more votes than Dole in 1996.

As can be calculated from Table 3, Bush gained only 18.5% more votes than Dole in the Pacific states, 24.8% in the Mid-Atlantic, and 27.0% in New England in 2000. His gain was 29.5% in the Prairie and Mountain states, 30.2% in the South outside of Florida, and 31.6% in the Midwest. Since the South includes a large number of black voters, Bush's percentage gain was spectacular among the white voters of the red Southern states. It surely was particularly strong among the lower and middle-income whites, and they are the most Evangelical group.

Gore was, of course, criticized severely for losing an election he was thought certain to win. This criticism of Gore personally seems excessive. Gore was not a relaxed or charismatic candidate, but that fact was known when expectations were high. His policy positions or tactics often were criticized in retrospect, but most of the critics focused on relatively minor tactical questions, and they did not agree on their nature. This suggests that, if Gore made fundamental errors, they were the product of the suburban strategy and the nominating process, not of personal misjudgments.

BUSH'S FIRST TERM AND THE EMBRACE OF NATIONALISM

Political scientists looking at presidential strategy naturally focus on presidential elections, and this book has been little different. In reality, however, a major distinction should be made between the strategy of a challenger and that of an incumbent President. A challenger to an incumbent normally is explicit only in criticizing the record of the incumbent, while an incumbent essentially must run on a record. When there are two challengers in an election such as 2000, they normally are both quite ambiguous about what they will do.

---

62. Paradoxically, all political observers, surely reflecting Gore campaign briefings, attributed Lieberman's selection to the desire to expand the Jewish vote in Florida, and Lieberman spent almost the entire campaign on the east coast of Florida. Gore seemed totally unaware that the West coast of Florida was a major retirement area of Midwesterners and that Lieberman was certain to lose large numbers of German-American voters in their seventies and eighties. They remembered the 1940s and the conflict between the Jewish-Americans and German-Americans over policy to Germany. It is quite possible that Lieberman cost Gore more votes in Florida than he gained him, maybe considerably more votes.

Table 3: Democratic, Republican and Third Party Vote for President, By Region, 1992-2004

Region	Year	Total	Republican		Democratic		Perot-Nader	
South	1992	29,732	12,591	42.3%	12,337	41.5%	4,655	15.7%
	1996	28,314	12,967	45.8%	13,098	46.3%	2,037	7.2%
	2000	31,617	17,172	54.3%	13,731	43.4%	442	1.4%
	2004	37,647	21,423	56.9%	15,942	42.3%	—	—
South (Minus Florida)	1992	24,418	10,417	42.7%	10,265	42.0%	3,602	14.8%
	1996	23,010	10,722	46.6%	10,551	45.9%	1,553	6.7%
	2000	25,654	14,259	55.6%	10,819	42.2%	355	1.4%
	2004	30,037	17,458	58.1%	12,358	41.1%		
Mid-Atlantic	1992	17,733	6,325	35.7%	8,427	47.5%	2,866	16.2%
	1996	16,135	5,637	34.9%	8,889	55.1%	1,345	8.3%
	2000	17,472	6,937	39.7%	9,875	56.5%	515	2.9%
	2004	19,755	8,644	43.8%	10,901	55.2%	—	—
New England	1992	6,351	2,012	31.7%	2,820	44.4%	1,479	23.3%
	1996	5,703	1,769	31.0%	3,237	56.8%	576	10.1%
	2000	6,086	2,251	37.0%	3,417	56.1%	343	5.6%
	2004	6,652	2,717	40.8%	3,842	57.8%	—	—
Midwest	1992	25,196	9,167	36.4%	10,860	43.1%	5,037	20.0%
	1996	22,619	8,929	39.5%	11,206	49.5%	2,198	9.7%
	2000	24,589	11,740	47.7%	12,006	48.8%	613	2.5%
	2004	28,275	14,032	49.6%	14,017	49.6%	—	—
Prairie and Mountain	1992	10,158	4,034	39.7%	3,549	34.9%	2,461	24.2%
	1996	9,502	4,577	48.2%	3,874	40.8%	883	9.3%
	2000	10,276	5,827	56.7%	3,928	38.2%	349	3.4%
	2004	12,391	7,337	59.2%	4,895	39.5%		
Pacific	1992	15,255	4,974	32.6%	6,915	45.3%	3,245	21.3%
	1996	14,010	5,321	38.0%	7,098	50.7%	1,047	7.5%
	2000	15,355	6,528	42.5%	8,034	52.3%	621	4.0%
	2004	17,544	7,876	44.9%	9,430	53.8%		
Total	1992	104,425	39,103	37.4%	44,909	43.0%	19,742	18.9%
	1996	96,277	39,199	40.7%	47,402	49.2%	8,085	8.4%
	2000	105,397	50,455	47.9%	50,992	48.4%	2,883	2.7%
	2004	122,265	62,028	50.7%	59,029	48.3%	—	—

The 2004 figures were calculated from Curtis B. Gans, 'Turnout Exceeds Optimistic Predictions,' January 14, 2005.

The techniques of obfuscation are many and quite familiar. Challengers usually must position themselves in one way to appeal to the party base in the primaries and then take a more centrist position in the general election. Like Clinton with the term "New Democrats" and Bush with the notion of "compassionate conservative," they usually describe their position ambiguously or inconsistently. At a minimum, they promise a combination of programs that cost far more than the tax revenue they say they will seek.

Given this usual campaign strategy, voters usually are left to guess the real position of challengers except on a relatively few symbolic issues. Small wonder that the largest number of voters are guided by party identification and that swing voters usually vote "retrospectively" on recent economic performance or on the personalities of the candidates.

For this reason, presidential strategy is only revealed — and in some cases only developed — in the first term of a new President. A first term President wants to be re-elected and knows that voters will judge him or her on the basis of an actual record in office. Important concrete policy decisions and the way in which they are handled in conjunction with other issues are really part of a conscious re-election strategy — or at least this is true when the President is politically sophisticated and deserves re-election. Some think that Presidents should not focus their attention on the next election, but this is the primary way in which the responsiveness of government to a majority coalition is ensured.

To a large extent, the strategy that Bush originally wanted to follow in office will always remain unknown because of the surprise terrorist attack on September 11. When he won in 2000, he still faced the same problems that frightened the Brock Commission. Assuming that both candidates would be viable in 2004, the Democrats would have 173 Electoral College votes virtually assured them. Another 49 votes in Michigan, Pennsylvania, and Washington seemed likely if the election were close. The Democrats would need only another 48 Electoral College votes.

The election would be decided in the old Midwest, and most of this area was too urbanized and liberal to be naturally attracted to the cultural themes Bush used in the 2000 election. If the Democrats nominated a ticket that included in some order Dick Gephardt, the German-American Protestant from Missouri who favored a New Deal strategy, and a Northern Catholic attractive in the suburbs, that should be a very strong ticket in the Midwest. After all, neither Al Gore nor Joseph Lieberman added anything geographically to the ticket, and Gore personally was a very weak candidate. Nevertheless, Gore still had won by 550,000 votes.

The question of what Bush would have done without the terrorist attack of September 11, 2001, remains shrouded in mystery. Bush often talked about emulating Reagan. Reagan in reality followed a Keynesian policy, first raising interest rates to end Carter's inflation and then fueling growth with tax cuts, military spending, and a large deficit. The Clinton market bubble had already burst and the country was entering a recession when Bush came into power. Hence Bush could move directly to the stage of stimulation. He introduced a large tax cut, much of it oriented to investment, and he stimulated consumption through a sharp reduction in short term interest rates. The latter permitted the refinancing of mortgages and stimulated a boom in housing prices. These two developments combined to increase the population's purchasing power. In essence, Bush's economic policy was similar to Reagan's.

Reagan's other passion was foreign policy, and he pursued a very assertive, nationalist policy in his rhetoric — but not in actual practice. When over 200 marines were killed in a terrorist attack in Beirut, Lebanon, he responded by withdrawing troops from the country. While he talked about an evil empire, he energetically followed a policy of holding summit meetings with Mikhail Gorbachev and succeeded in humanizing him for the American public.

Of course, the Republicans had consistently followed such a course in the postwar period. In one way or another, they had emphasized the themes of patriotism and nationalism while actually following a policy of détente when in office. Nationalism was central in Goldwater's campaign, and even Nixon, who embraced détente with the Soviet Union and China, told his chief of staff, H. R. Haldeman, that "the real issues of the [1972] election are the ones like patriotism, morality, religion — not the material interests." He intended, he said, to "make patriotism and morality the issue and get above the material things."[63] Yet the Republicans had always supported détente in practice: Eisenhower, Nixon, Ford, Reagan, and George H. W. Bush.

George H. W. Bush never did associate himself with the patriotic appeals of Reagan, except when he wrapped himself in the flag while running against the second-generation American, Michael Dukakis, in 1988. Bush's lack of a patriotic theme as President was one aspect of his self-acknowledged problem with "the vision thing." While in office, a large part of his public persona was that of a man on a first-name basis with foreign leaders who talked with them frequently on the phone. He refused to remove Saddam Hussein from office in the Iraq War and explained this by limitations imposed by the coalition. Other Bush foreign policies also seemed to symbolize American weakness. For example, the Administration did not react strongly to Chinese suppression of students in Tiananmen Square in mid-1989, but visibly condoned it only a few months afterwards.[64]

Bush's son, by contrast, eagerly created a public image of having the opposite approach to foreign relations. He made it clear that he did not know the names of most leaders, let alone their first names, that he had little interest in foreign relations and that he would not guide his policy by the wishes of foreign leaders. From the beginning, he showed a special interest in Iraq and in Saddam Hussein. When he talked with Condoleezza Rice before he took office, he responded to her question by saying that he agreed with his father's decision to remain in southern Iraq. Yet Rice must have had a reason for asking, and his answer referred to the limitations of the United Nations resolution.[65] His top security advisers — Dick Cheney, Donald Rumsfeld, and Paul Wolfowitz — were hard-line conservatives who had been unhappy about the course of the first Iraq war, and the younger Bush was to support them strongly against others in the Administration.

Even before September 11, Bush identified himself with national independence from foreigners and the United Nations. He strongly embraced Reagan's Strategic Defense Initiative and was scornful of the limitations imposed by treaties such as the Anti-Ballistic Missile Treaty and the Kyoto Treaty on global warning. It is not clear what he would have done in the Middle East, but he certainly responded to September 11 by likening the attack to Pearl Harbor and indicating the United States was now in a war against terrorism not unlike World War II.

Very quickly Bush focused attention on Saddam Hussein as a threat because of his supposed weapons of mass destruction and his links with terrorism. Bush created

---

63. These and other such quotations are found in Robert Mason, *Richard Nixon and the Quest for a New Majority* (Chapel Hill: The University of North Carolina Press, 2004), pp. 63–65 and 180–186.
64. Steven Erlanger, "Top Aides to Bush Are Visiting China to Mend Relations," *The New York Times*, December 10, 1989, p. A1.
65. Bob Woodward, *Bush At War* (New York: Simon & Schuster, 2002), pp. 328–329.

a strong impression within higher British circles and among American conservative intellectuals with close contacts to the Administration that he intended to go to war with Iraq. Since he defined the problem as Hussein's unwillingness to dismantle his weapons of mass destruction and his links with terrorists, war with Iraq at this time clearly had to mean entry of troops into Baghdad and the overthrow of the Iraqi ruler. "Regime change" was the euphemism used.

There are many mysteries about the war with Iraq. Hussein could have demonstrated that he had no weapons of mass destruction, but inexplicably failed to do so. This made it a reasonable assumption at the time that he must be hiding something.[66] Yet there was no evidence that socialist Iraq had any meaningful connection with fundamentalist Muslim terrorists, let alone al Qaeda. Any Administration claims or hints to the contrary on this point were simply a device to increase support for the war.

The greatest mystery, however, revolves around a fact that is never mentioned: the President's quick adoption of Ross Perot's slogan "United We Stand" to symbolize the country's response to the September 11 attack. This could have been a spontaneous thought after the attack, but that seems unlikely. George W. Bush almost surely had long thought about the reasons for his father's defeat, and any such reasons had to include Perot's success in winning 19% of the vote. No doubt, "W" had a genuinely different attitude toward foreigners than his father, but he also was making a deliberate effort to emphasize and perhaps exaggerate those differences in public. As the crisis built in intensity, Bush did not consult publicly with his father or his father's top advisers. Rather the latter wrote op-ed articles warning of the dangers. The son was unusually blunt in indicating that he would not let large-scale foreign opposition sway him. He seemed almost to welcome such opposition.

It is difficult to avoid the conclusion that Bush came to power in 2001 determined to fight the 2004 election with a foreign policy image that was the opposite of that of his father. That is, he intended to win the normal Republican base and add the large number of Perot voters to it. Whether prior to September 11 he anticipated war with Saddam Hussein over the issue of weapons of mass destruction in order to reverse his father's policy toward the Iraqi dictator remains an open question, but the possibility is a real one.

Whether Bush thought that he might move away from the cultural issues of the previous quarter of a century and largely replace them with the cultural issue of nationalism also remains an open question. Reagan had followed the policy of giving the religious right little more than "warm fuzzies." Leaving aside a crusade against fundamentalist Islam, Bush was not that different. The 2004 Republican Convention featured leading proponents of women's choice such as former New York Mayor Rudy Giuliani and California Governor Arnold Schwarzenegger. Then Schwarzenegger, with his German accent, was to accompany Bush in the crucial last

---

66. It is, of course, most fortunate that Hussein had no weapons of mass destruction. Since the United States did not know where any such weapons were located and was not able to control the looting of conventional weapons along with all other valuables throughout Iraq, any weapons of mass destruction that did exist presumably would have fallen into the hands of terrorists.

weekend in German-American Ohio. The message to suburban women seemed to be, "Believe what we signal, not what we say. Don't worry about Court appointments undermining *Roe v. Wade.*"

Many believed the signals. Kerry declined 17 points among white women in Connecticut and New York and 22 points among white women in New Jersey.[67] When Bush nominated Harriet Miers to the Supreme Court after naming John Roberts as Chief Justice, the right exploded in a way that indicated they, too, were worried that Bush's signals in 2004 indicated his real intentions towards the Court. Perhaps his real attitude to the religious right was not very different from that of his father or Ronald Reagan.

THE 2004 ELECTION

The 2004 election will probably be seen in retrospect as transitional in character. The era of Democratic abandonment of the middle class on economic interests and of Republican emphasis of issues such as abortion seems unlikely to continue for a long time. Bush was a wartime President whose performance at the 9/11 crisis had been brilliant. The economy was doing well, and the President had enacted a prescription drug insurance program and tax cuts for the middle income. As a result, whites older than 60 gave Bush a 58% to 41% victory, a 17-point difference compared with 6 points in 2000.[68] Those who made between $30,000 and $50,000 a year voted for Clinton by a single point, but Bush won them by 13 points in 2000 and 17 points in 2004.[69]

The Democratic candidate in 2004 was, of course, extremely weak, and he conducted a very unfocussed campaign. Yet Bush won only 50.7% to 48.3% and 286 Electoral College votes to 252. If 60,000 voters had switched from Bush to John Kerry in Ohio — and the nomination of Dick Gephardt might have achieved this — Kerry would have won in the Electoral College despite a 3-million-vote loss.

The results cannot be comforting either to the Republicans or the Democrats as they look to 2008 and beyond. Indeed, the Democrats have even more reason to worry about coming elections if the red state–blue state alignment stays in place and continues to produce narrow margins. In 2004, Bush won 31 states to Kerry's 20. The permanent loss of many small states could once more deprive the Democrats of an Electoral College vote when they have a popular vote plurality. The probability seems great that someone will adopt a program that breaks with the old patterns or that major new developments in the economic and political environment will transform the terms of debate.

As these words are written, we still are too close to the election to have memoirs, archive material, or even journalistic books based partly on interviews.

---

67. Greenberg, *The Two Americas*, p. 332.
68. Greenberg, *The Two Americas*, p. 329.
69. Noam Scheiber, "Spent Force," *The New Republic*, October 10, 2005, p. 6. The figures were calculated by Ruy Teixeira from exit poll data. I am grateful to Noam Scheiber and Ruy Teixeira for this information.

Comprehensive public opinion poll data are only becoming available and scholars have not had time to publish thorough analyses. The exit polls had serious sample problems that made their demographic data highly suspect.[70] A really sound analysis of the election is not possible in the fall of 2005 on the basis of publicly available data, and we will content ourselves with making a few basic points. Some of the most important considerations will be discussed in the conclusion.

First, the most spectacular feature of the election was a massive rise in turnout. As shown in Tables 2 and 3 above, 96.3 million valid votes for President were cast in 1996 and 105.4 million in 2000. Pollsters were very uncertain about the turnout in 2004, but they unanimously predicted that a large turnout of 110 to 115 million voters would guarantee Kerry's victory. Instead, 122.3 valid ballots were cast for President, and Bush won by 3 million votes.

Some like to attribute the high turnout in 2004 to the efforts expended on turning out voters, and the Republican victory to the superiority of their turnout model.[71] No doubt, this factor had an impact, but organizational efforts were concentrated in the battleground states. The turnout in these states was, in fact, somewhat higher than the average, but even this difference could be attributed to the barrage of information about the closeness of the outcome in these states and memories of the 2000 result in Florida. As Stanley Greenberg emphasizes, states in which no one had any illusion that the election would be competitive and in which no one spent major effort on increasing voter turnout also saw a major increase in turnout.[72]

It is very difficult not to draw a connection between the 1992 and 2004 elections. Perot's campaign had produced an unusually high turnout, and neither party had co-opted Perot's themes in 1996 and 2000. As a result, the turnout rate in both elections was well below that of 1992. George W. Bush had adopted Perot's slogan and reversed the policy of his father both toward Saddam Hussein and toward American allies. Turnout had soared above the 1992 rate. It would be remarkable if there were not some cause-and-effect relationship.

Second, the media strongly emphasized the role of the religious right and the religious organizations in Bush's victory, but this emphasis seems quite misplaced. Once again, the problem was created by the exit polls, which gave voters a very limited choice of options in specifying the reason they voted. The media then over-generalized a vague answer, "values." Persons as far apart as Karl Rove and Democratic pollster Stanley Greenberg agreed on this point. Rove argued that the exit polls had erred in splitting the war against terrorism and the Iraq War and that a combination of the two showed their importance. Greenberg said the high turnout was "driven by many motivators — 9/11, Iraq, George Bush, the 2000 tie and the prospect of another, and the par-

---

70. If one believes the exit polls, Kerry received 11 percentage points less support than Gore in cities with over 500,000 people, but 3 percentage points more than Gore in rural areas and 10 percentage points more in cities and towns from 10,000 to 50,000 population. It seems an unlikely combination. "How Americans Voted: A Political Portrait 2000," *The New York Times*, November 7, 2004, section IV, p. 4.
71. Michael Barone, "Introduction," *The Almanac of American Politics, 2006* (Washington, DC: National Journal Group, 2005), pp. 21-23.
72. Greenberg, *The Two Americas*, pp. 326–327.

tisan and cultural battle that enflamed passions."[73] Greenberg did not explicitly say that this was the order of reasons, but the text made this clear.

In particular, Greenberg emphasized the "crash in the East." (See Table 3 for the details.) Kerry's total was down 10 percentage points in New Jersey, 8 points in Rhode Island, 7 in New York, 7 in Connecticut, and 6 in Delaware. Bush made his biggest gains in the blue East Coast states where Evangelicalism is weak — and against a Massachusetts candidate instead of one from Tennessee and in an election when Ralph Nader was drawing few votes from the Democrat.[74] No doubt, turnout increased among all voters, but the Evangelicals essentially returned to the polls to support Bush in 2000.

Third, the difference between the old party ideologies on economic issues and their real economic policies is undercutting the impact of the ideology. Greenberg as a Democratic pollster who wants work in 2008 has to be careful in what he says, and naturally his overarching statements have to treat this point gingerly. When he emphasizes the huge Democratic losses among retirees, Catholics, and those without a college education, when he says that "the flip of downscale America gave this election to Bush," he adds that they were culturally conservative and responded to Bush's cultural appeals. Nevertheless, a careful reader sees quite clearly that Greenberg does not think that only values matter. On the contrary.

A careful reader has no difficulty in discovering where Kerry rejected Greenberg's advice. Greenberg has a natural belief about the disastrous effects of these decisions. "These are special times," he writes, "when twenty-five years of accumulating inequality, now years of stagnant incomes, and new insecurities in education, health care, and retirement demand a bold politics." When he writes that "bottom line: the culture war was not pushed back by the class war," he clearly means that an emphasis on economic issues of importance to the middle income would have had a very positive outcome for the Democrats.

In short, Greenberg is saying that downscale America voted for its values because it was given no choice on its economic interests. As a Democratic pollster, he cannot say that Bush's prescription drug program and promotion of consumption actually did serve the short-term and medium-term interests of downscale America better than the Democratic program. I work under no such restraints, and it seems clear from the results that the middle-income whites thought Bush better served their economic interests than Kerry. However, the complex relationship between economic and cultural values — in particular, the reinforcement of cultural antagonism both by the middle-income voters' perception of economic arrogance and by the Democratic failure to use economic measures to put poor cultural conservatives under cross pressure — are matters that should never be forgotten. The Democrats must stop conceding the red areas to the Republicans if they are to win, and this is not done simply by adopting the red areas' cultural values. This is an argument to which we will return in the next chapter.

---

73. Greenberg, *The Two Americas*, p. 326.
74. Greenberg, *The Two Americas*, pp. 337–338.

CHAPTER 10. CONCLUSION

Two centuries of mist and legend have greatly obscured our understanding of American political evolution. The North American colonies were deeply divided by severe religious and ethnic divisions, many stemming from the civil wars in Britain. By the time of the American Revolution, the intensity of the conflict among the English in America had faded, but not the suspicions and prejudices. In September 1774, John Adams, a Puritan from New England, wrote that the delegates to the First Continental Congress in Philadelphia were "fifty gentlemen meeting together, all Strangers, [who] are not acquainted with Each other's Language, Ideas, Views, Designs ... [and who are] therefore, jealous of each other — fearfull, timid, skittish."[1] One of the most powerful men in New York had directly hinted to Adams on the latter's trip to Philadelphia that New Englanders were "Goths and Vandalls." As late as 1784, George Washington referred to the non-English in western Virginia as "foreign emigrants, who can have no particular predilection for us" and who might become "as unconnected with us, indeed more so, than we are with South America." [2] New waves of immigrants in the 19th and early 20th century included large numbers of Catholics and Jews from many countries, and it took two centuries to create a basic unity among the European-Americans.

One technique used to reduce such cleavages among European-Americans was to pretend that the cleavages did not exist, and this makes scholarly work on the subject quite difficult. Scholars have found it hard to say that the American Revolution was not the result of the intense nationalism of a people with a strong national identity, but more an attempt to create such an identity. Those who embrace the Confederate Flag in recent times have had no idea that it was the symbol of a rejection of American national identity.

---

1. John Adams to Abigail Adams, September 25, 1774, in Paul H. Smith, ed., *Letters of Delegates to Congress, 1774–1789* (Washington: Library of Congress, 1976), vol. 1, p. 99.
2. The references to these various statements are found on pp. 60, along with a fuller discussion of them.

Similarly, both those who want an American government with strong economic power and those who want the Supreme Court to follow the original intent of the Founders do not want to acknowledge that the Founders really wanted a confederation in the domestic sphere in 1787. It was not, however, really a confederation of states, but of the two great sections, slaveholding and non-slaveholding. The main function of the Constitution was to reassure the South about its continued ability to treat its slaves as it wished. The insistence of Justice Clarence Thomas that we follow the Founders' original intent is deeply ironic.

This book has argued that the checks and balances were not abstract institutional arrangements. Rather, the checks and balances were a brilliant set of institutions because of the unwritten rule that the slaveholding and non-slaveholding sections would have an equal number of states and thus a guaranteed veto. These checks and balances included equal representation for states (and, therefore, sections) in the Senate and in the presidential runoff in the House. The veto was strengthened by giving the Senate the responsibility to confirm important presidential appointees and to ratify treaties and by giving the Vice President, who was expected to come from the other section than the President, a tie-breaking vote in the Senate.

Even after the Civil War, the Northern and Southern political elite reestablished the basic principle of the Constitutional Convention: the South should have the autonomy to treat its blacks in a highly repressive manner. Incredibly, this agreement lasted for three-quarters of a century. But precisely because the South no longer had an equal number of states (indeed, the abrogation of this rule in 1850 was a major cause of the Civil War[3]), it was necessary to enforce the agreement with Congressional rules, an unnatural party alignment, and a reversal of the increase in the power of the central government by the 14th and 15th amendments.

When the North abrogated its agreement about the autonomy of the South between the 1940s and the 1970s, this transformed the basic institutional character of the United States, the basic political assumptions and culture of the American system, and the party alignments that had been in place for 150 years. A key factor in this development was a fading of the old antagonisms between Anglicans and Puritans, between Protestants and non-Protestant immigrants, and between North and South — that is, by the development of a common sense of "white" identity and community among warring European-Americans. The old party alignments were especially vulnerable since they were based on the assumption of a solid Democratic South and inevitably were destabilized by the introduction of party competition in the section.

Yet, since most of the old understandings were too sensitive to discuss, the political strata, practitioners and intellectuals alike, did not have a clear idea of the nature and consequences of the changes being introduced. In particular, the Baby Boomers, who had the key role in creating the red state–blue state alignment, first

---

3. Barry R. Weingast, "Political Stability and Civil War: Institutions, Commitments, and American Democracy," in Robert H. Bates, ed., *Analytic Narratives* (Princeton: Princeton University Press, 1998), pp. 150-153 and 157-158.

entered serious party competition in the 1970s and had a deep suspicion of the older generations of politicians because of the Vietnam War. They never really had the opportunity to learn the unspoken language of the past and the assumptions that lay behind it. Incredibly, James Madison, the defender of a brilliant solution to a political problem that he and other Founders hoped would fade with the passage of time, was lionized as a great philosopher of the eternal principles of government precisely at the time when the political problem that haunted him disappeared.

Naturally, politicians who now have to grope to replace political arrangements that have been in place for over 150 years have made mistakes. Inevitably, the need to operate in a totally different political environment has created enormous insecurity. Politicians reasonably enough have responded by isolating themselves as much as possible from outside political forces, especially those coming from people of lower and middle income. This meant a retreat from the drive to introduce majoritarian constitutional democracy that featured the New Deal period. It meant an acceptance of the definition of democracy of the Progressives of the early 20th century, a definition that emphasized power for the upper-middle class — the top quarter of the population in socioeconomic status.

The new party alignments and programs did, of course, alienate voters of middle socioeconomic status. Largely deprived of a choice on economic issues, these voters had no option but to select candidates on the bases of their position on cultural issues. Not surprisingly, they rejected with special force the cultural values embraced by their old party as it abandoned them on economic issues.

So long as consumption continues to grow, the party alignments are more or less stable. Nevertheless, the 19% of the vote Ross Perot received in the mild economic downturn of the early 1990s suggests that another economic correction, let alone a more serious downturn, would severely challenge the red state–blue state alignment. Or perhaps in an economic downturn a party whose President adopted Ross Perot's slogan "United We Stand" and his nationalist stance would move to adopt Perot's explicit rejection of free trade and his implicit negative attitude to immigration. Such a change in Republican cultural policy would simultaneously challenge the core economic and cultural issue of the Democratic suburban strategy. It would be interesting to see how the Democrats would respond.

POTENTIAL POLITICAL PROBLEMS

Any political observer should regularly recall the ancient wisdom: "this too shall pass." Party alignments and party programs always are attempts to reconcile the irreconcilable, and to a large extent they survive their inevitable contradictions only through sleight of hand. This technique can work for some time, sometimes even for a few decades, but then the tensions overwhelm the efforts to control them. Sometimes relatively minor changes in programs, symbols, and/or illusions suffice for a while. At other times, a major party realignment or change in institutions seems required.

In addition, completely unexpected events can sometimes overwhelm the fragile political arrangements that politicians have created. Who in January 1950 anticipated the Korean War six months later? Who at the beginning of the 1960s saw the turmoil of the Vietnam Era, and who a decade later foresaw the two major oil crises of the 1970s and their consequences? No one in the early 1980s expected the collapse of the Communist system in the Soviet Union and Eastern Europe, let alone the unification of Germany. Even a madman in 1990 would not have predicted that Ross Perot would receive 19% of the vote in 1992. Then, the destruction of the World Trade Towers on September 11, 2001, interjected powerful new elements into the political equation.

As these words are written in late 2005, the tensions in the red state–blue state alignment are quite visible and major potential shocks to the system are apparent to informed observers. The nature of an unexpected shock is, by definition, impossible to predict, but it is certain that one of some type will occur. However, when the President in October 2005 speculated that the military—really martial law—might have to be used in a serious flu epidemic, he may have been talking about a very low probability event, but it was a useful reminder that low probability events with drastic consequences are possible. At a minimum, the political stratum should be giving thought to potential problems so that it can deal with them and lessen their severity.

1. Tensions in the Blue State–Red State Alignment

Even should no unexpected shocks occur in the near and medium term to destabilize the red state–blue state alignment, the coalitions clearly have major internal strains. The Republicans still receive a majority of votes from those in the top quartile of the population by income, but a far higher percentage in the South than in the North. Yet, middle and lower income whites dominate the red areas that are the core base of the Republican Party. As has been seen, the exit polls showed that Clinton lost those whites making between $30,000 and $50,000 by a single point in 1996, while Bush won them by 13 points in 2000 and 17 points in 2004.[4] Bush followed an economic policy responsive to the immediate economic interests of those at almost all economic levels — highest, middle, and lower-middle — but his policy relies on a budgetary deficit that most economists think is quite unsustainable over the long or maybe even the near term. If policy has to be changed and choices have to be made, someone in the coalition will be unhappy. Indeed, even today, as has been seen, the long-term conservative George Will is one of many on the right who are already unhappy about "the grand spending party."

The cultural divisions in the Republican coalition are as large as the economic ones or larger. The members of the mainline Protestant churches, who still are overwhelmingly Republican, have far more liberal cultural values on the average than members of the more fundamentalist churches. The two groups may be able to coexist so long as both agree on gay marriages and so long as nothing forces the Court to reconsider *Roe v. Wade*. Yet, the strength of the conservative reaction to Pres-

---

4.   Noam Scheiber, "Spent Force," *The New Republic*, October 10, 2005, p. 6.

ident Bush's nomination of Harriet Miers to the Supreme Court shows the fragility of the alliance, and the confirmation hearing of Samuel Alito put more pressure on it. This may be particularly so since the major conservative columnists who opposed Miers are not Evangelicals and may have been reacting negatively to the fact that she is one.

The Democratic coalition is no less conflicted. Its Hispanics, blacks, and lower and middle-income supporters are very uneasy with the party's liberal social policy. All these people have a sense that members of the secular educated core of the Democratic party have different values ("secular humanism") than themselves. The whites in lower- and middle-income groups also believe that the educated population has deep prejudices and stereotypes about them and their religious beliefs. In this, the lower and middle-income whites are certainly right.

The prejudices and stereotypes about lower- and middle-class whites were reflected in a joke the most popular late-night talk show host, Jay Leno, told in 2005 — a joke that he never would have dared to tell about blacks, Hispanics, or even European ethnic groups. Leno began by mentioning the decision of a winery to have a NASCAR wine. NASCAR racing is the favorite sport of lower-income and middle-income whites in the South, and Leno quipped, "There are two types of NASCAR wine, the red neck and the white trash."[5] Neither he nor the educated members of his audience had the slightest awareness that this really was "N-word" language.

The Democratic cleavages on economic issues are even more obvious. As the party of the New Deal, the party long attracted strong support from the white working class, and official Democratic ideology on health care and Social Security still earns the party many votes from these groups. When voters are asked to place presidential candidates on thermometer scales on public opinion polls, they still are influenced by ideology, and they always place the Democratic candidate on the left half of the spectrum on all issues. Nevertheless the voting behavior of middle-class whites and retirees in 2004 shows that these groups responded to Bush's prescription drug program, not just to rhetoric.

Even so, the Democrats' suburban strategy has won it an unprecedented percentage of the voters in the North with a household income of $75,000 and above, the upper 25.1% of the population.[6] The Democrats do advocate raising taxes on those making over $200,000 a year, the top 2.3% of the population, but they assiduously protect those making between over $75,000 and $200,000 — the group that Mark Penn, Clinton's pollster in 1996, calls the middle class.

In 1992, Stan Greenberg was Clinton's pollster and in 2004 he was the chief pollster for MoveOn, the best-funded Democratic soft-money group, financed by George Soros. Greenberg's 2004 book, as has been seen, was scathing about Clinton's abandonment of the middle class after his promises in the 1992 campaign. If read very carefully, his chapter on the 2004 elections reports that he strongly urged Kerry to court the middle class, but that Kerry completely rejected this advice.[7] This book

5. *The Tonight Show*, NBC, June 8, 2005.
6. Calculated from *Statistical Abstract of the United States: 2004–2005* (Washington, D.C.: U.S. Government Printing Office, 2004), p. 443.

agrees with Greenberg's advice, and it has even suggested something that a Democratic pollster could never say, namely that the Democrats really have shifted back to a Grover Cleveland policy that once more puts them marginally to the right of the Republicans on the economic spectrum.

The Democrats face a major problem in a serious economic downturn. If the Republicans do not return to the right or if a serious economic downturn requires a choice between a Hoover and Roosevelt policy in the early 1930s, then the Democrats will have to decide whether or not to abandon their suburban strategy. Whatever the Republicans do, the failure of the Democrats to follow Roosevelt to the left (which would probably be accompanied by similar cries of betrayal and "class warfare" by their upper-income voters) would raise the potential specter of a major new left-wing third party that haunted Roosevelt.

2. A Perfect Storm?

The US economy and the stock market rose persistently, even spectacularly, from World War II to the present, but both are subject to cyclical corrections. The most recent bull market began in October 1992 when the Dow Jones Industrial Average stood at 7179 and the NASDAQ at 1108. In mid-December 2005, the Dow Jones average had risen 50% to the 10,800 level and the NASDAQ had doubled to 2,500. After three years of a bull market, it would be normal to expect a temporary correction of some 25% over the next few years. Judging by earlier experience, this might or might not forecast an impending recession. Depending on its timing, it might or might not have an impact on the 2008 election.

Some, however, see a series of economic problems that are interrelated and that might interact with each other to produce a much more pronounced economic downturn. David Ignatius, a columnist for the *Washington Post*, has speculated in the past about "a perfect storm." The most dangerous potential scenarios arise from the policies of the Clinton and Bush Administrations to expand consumption more rapidly than Gross Domestic Product. Gross Domestic Product rose 69% from 1990 to 2000 in current dollars, but personal consumption rose 76%, while these figures from 2000 to 2003 were 11.9% and 15.1% respectively.[8] In September 2005, Federal Reserve Chairman Alan Greenspan expressed deep concern that loans on home equity equaled 7% of personal disposable income in 2004, compared with 1% in 1994 and 3% in 2000.[9] Not all personal disposal income is consumed, but much of it is, especially if most house remodeling is not considered a capital expenditure but expanded consumption.

The Clinton Administration always sought to promote growth through a reduction of the deficit and a lowering of interest rates. When the stock market began to overheat and Federal Reserve Chairman Alan Greenspan warned about a

7. Stanley B. Greenberg, *The Two Americas: Our Current Political Deadlock and How to Break It*, rev. ed. (New York: Thomas Dunne Books, 2005), pp. 315–316, 320, 322–323, 329, and 336.
8. *Statistical Abstract of the United States*, 2004/2005, p. 425.
9. Greg Ip, "Greenspan Warns of Reliance on Housing Loans," *The Wall Street Journal*, September 27, 2005, p. A1.

"bubble" and "irrational exuberance" in December 1996, the Dow Jones average was at 6400 and the NASDAQ index was at 1300.[10] The Administration rejected his warning. It did not use monetary policy and higher margin requirements to control the excessive rise in the market, but encouraged a further boom by talking about a new type of economy with a permanent new acceleration of technology-based productivity.[11] The market continued to rise until the Dow Jones Industrial Average hit a high of 11,750 in January 2000 and the NASDAQ one of 5153 in March of that year.

Not surprisingly, technology stocks enjoyed spectacular success, and the talk about a new economy led many to think that it was safe to use some of their stock market gains to finance an increase in consumption. The rapid rise in the stock market also attracted strong foreign investment. Instead of taking steps to keep the foreign trade account under control, the Administration let it rise and thereby augment the level of consumption. As the dollar became progressively stronger, foreigners received both stock market and foreign currency gains and had an incentive to increase their investment. This contributed to a bubble both in the dollar and in the market.

The Bush Administration was then faced with an unusually sharp decline in the market, eventually 78% in the NASDAQ index and 39% in the Dow Jones industrial average. The Administration maintained consumption through reducing interest rates almost to zero. This allowed mortgage refinancing and an increase in disposal income. It also sharply lowered the monthly payments for new home buyers and produced a rise in housing prices. The resulting boom — some would say, a bubble — in housing prices increased the home equity for existing homeowners and allowed them to take out large loans against this home equity. The Bush Administration also permitted a sharp further rise in the foreign trade deficit, again contributing to a rise in consumption.

Of course, market economies ultimately are balancing and self-correcting mechanisms. The rise in home equity loans partially offset a decline in retiree income from interest in savings accounts or money market funds. Conversely, a rise in interest rates means increased income for those with their money in such locales. An end to the housing boom might lead to more investment in the stock market. A gradual decline in the value of the dollar would make American goods easier to sell abroad. People expect mildly bad times at periodic intervals and adjust to them, even though with complaints.

The most dangerous scenarios arise from the fact that the country simultaneously faces a number of potential economic problems that conceivably could

---

10. Floyd Norris, "Greenspan Asks a Question and Global Markets Wobble," *The New York Times*, December 7, 1996, p. A1.

11. Conventionally this policy is attributed to Greenspan, and he soon fell into line and adopted the argument about a new economy. However, the role of the Federal Reserve Board is to protect the President from responsibility for major economic decisions that he takes. No chairman of the Federal Reserve Board can follow a policy not favored (or at least permitted) by the Administration in power at the time, and Greenspan's policy in the 1900s and the 2000s was that of Clinton and Bush respectively.

interact with each other to produce a deepening downward spiral. These problems include excessive levels of consumption, an overpriced dollar and a growing trade deficit that requires a large continuing inflow of foreign investment, an inflated housing market, a structure of housing loans that will be dangerous if interest rates rise, a huge expansion in the number of unregulated hedge funds, a large government deficit at a time of an economic boom, a precipitous rise in oil prices, and a rising level of inflation that seems to require a continuing rise in interest rates.

Both overly optimistic and overly alarmist forecasts are a perennial part of economic analysis, and many of the problems discussed in the preceding paragraphs surely are overdrawn. The most worrisome aspect of the current set of problems is the possibility of a domino effect. Any serious economic difficulty produced by the various domestic problems would normally lead to a reduction of interest rates. Yet, if the market begins to fall, foreigners may decide to withdraw funds from the U.S. stock market rather than invest. The natural consequence would be a decline in the dollar that not only contributes to inflation, but also adds a currency loss to a market loss for foreign investors. If this makes it difficult to cut interest rates, an effective anti-recession program could become highly complicated. Obviously any such scenario, not even the most frightening one, would have very serious domestic political consequences.

3. The Dangers of Nationalism

A third potential set of problems that might impinge on the party system and alignments are those associated with what was called "nationalism" in the previous chapter. One aspect of the problem involves foreign policy directly.

Paradoxically, the major domestic political difficulties associated with foreign policy were produced by the most unexpected success in the 1980s: the reunification of Germany. As has been seen, the two parties positioned themselves in a very stabilizing manner on foreign policy during the Cold War. The ethnic base of the two parties pushed each of them in a different direction in their policy toward the Soviet Union and Germany, but each party then balanced its core policy with a countervailing ideological posture. The reunification of Germany ended the major ethnic influence on foreign policy, however, and left both parties with their ideology alone.

In addition, the end of the Cold War produced a sense in the United States that its democratic ideology was all-powerful and that everything was possible in the foreign policy sphere. The cost of this excessive optimism — some may say arrogance — may be extremely high if it leads some Middle Eastern oil producing country, most likely Iran, to cut back on its oil exports and/or to transfer its financial reserves from dollar investments to a basket of foreign currencies. In general, however, the purely foreign policy problem is self-correcting in the medium and long term. Even if the Iraq War eventually turns out reasonably well, it has created such major problems for the United States for such a long period that any administration of either party is likely to be much more cautious in the future.

The most dangerous and even explosive potential issues associated with nationalism are those of immigration and outsourcing. This is the issue on which the political elite of both parties have been the most unresponsive to public concerns. The public clearly wants immigration to be reduced and illegal immigrant immigrants deported, and this feeling was especially strong during the mild recession of the early 1990s. That was reflected in the support for Proposition 187 in California, and severe economic problems might produce a stronger political movement.

Nevertheless, leaders as diverse as President Bush and Senators John McCain and Ted Kennedy have introduced guest worker bills that effectively legalize illegal immigrants and that admit other immigrants beyond those who come through regular channels. Allegedly the millions of guest workers would be required to go home in a set number of years, but no one believes that the effort necessary to deport them would be made. In the interim, they would increase the downward pressure on wages. As a result, immigration and outsourcing are easy and intense symbols of general unresponsiveness of government for those in the middle and lower income brackets. They are also a cultural issue that symbolizes economic grievances and can be a powerful, emotional explanation for economic suffering.

This book has repeatedly emphasized the success of Ross Perot and his nationalist theme in 1992. It does not see the 2004 election as one in which the public was absorbed by the issues of abortion and gay marriages, but as one whose real character was foreshadowed by George Bush's adoption of Ross Perot's slogan, "United We Stand." Bush's major appeals were of a nationalist and patriotic character: the war against terrorism and Islamic fundamentalism, the Iraq War, a confrontational attitude towards foreign governments. The anti-immigrant feelings were deflected onto Muslims and European countries such as France, and no real pressure built up against Hispanics and Asian-Americans. The continuing difficulties in the Iraq War and the indictment of Vice President Dick Cheney's chief of staff, Scooter Libby, forced the President to re-emphasize the abortion issue, but others in the future surely will return to Perot once again.

The immigration issue is quite worrisome in historical perspective. As has been seen, immigrants have not come to the United States in an even flow, but in four major waves, each featuring new ethnic and religious groups little represented in the country in the past: 1755–1775, 1835–1860, 1895–1914, and 1975 to the present. The first wave, dominated by Protestant Scots, Irish, and Germans, was followed by the American Revolution. The second wave, which featured the first major influx of Catholics, was followed by the Civil War, and the third, overwhelmingly of non-Protestants from eastern and southern Europe, led to the disastrous ethnic policy of Woodrow Wilson during and immediately after World War I.

The fourth and current wave of immigration comes from Asia and Latin America. It is enormous in size and must continue if the retirement of the Baby Boomers is to be financed on the level that has been promised. The question is whether the fourth wave will produce a political reaction in difficult times that will have far-reaching consequences. Ross Perot's great success in the 1992 election during the relatively early stages of the wave of immigration suggests that the danger is not a hypothetical one. Throughout American history, one of the major parties has quickly addressed the grievance that led to a large vote by a third party. This did not happen after the 1992 election. Clinton spent most of his effort in 1993 in gaining approval for NAFTA and most of his effort in 1994 in securing American entry into GATT.

If anything, the leaders of both parties have become even more dedicated to free trade, immigration, and outsourcing since 1992. The Midwestern, German-American states clearly were going to be the major battleground states in 2004, and the obvious candidate to balance Kerry in geographic, ethnic, and policy terms was Representative Richard Gephardt, a Midwestern German-American. Gephardt was not chosen, almost surely because the party activists and financial contributors did not like his questioning of outsourcing and free trade. Then in 2005, President Bush spent great political capital to secure the passage of a free trade zone with Central America, and he proposed a guest worker program.

The foreign trade deficit has increased not only consumption but also kept the prices of outsourced industrial components abnormally low. This not only increased the downward pressure on manufacturing employment and wages, but also the profitability of technology firms and fueled the stock market bubble. So long as consumption was kept high by low prices of imported goods and by the availability of money from stock sales and housing equity loans, this kept the political force about immigrants and outsourcing at acceptable levels. But if economic conditions worsen, the emotions could rise rapidly.

There is another reason to fear a popular reaction in the sphere of foreign economic and immigration policy. As has been seen, Arthur Schlesinger, Sr.'s theory of 30-year cycles in American history corresponds fairly closely to the pattern of events for well over a century. The height of Reconstruction occurred in 1870, Theodore Roosevelt came to power in 1901, Franklin Roosevelt in 1932, and Lyndon Johnson in 1963. The conservative Grover Cleveland dominated the 1880s, Warren Harding and Calvin Coolidge the 1920s, Joseph McCarthy and Dwight Eisenhower the 1950s, and Ronald Reagan the 1980s. If this theory of cycles is accurate, then the 1990s should have been another period of transformation.

Much of the liberal disappointment that Clinton did not "fulfill his potential" explicitly or implicitly judged him by the expectations of the Schlesinger cycle. In retrospect, however, Clinton did embrace and preside over a political revolution that is now taken for granted: the revolution of globalization, integration of the United States into the world economy, and massive immigration from outside Europe. If Schlesinger's thesis is still relevant, the second Bush term should be the high point of the conservative cycle, and the counterrevolution should center on the issue that had featured the transforming part of the cycle. Bush is most unlikely to reverse himself on globalization and immigration, but in difficult times it certainly is easy to imagine that those issues would be raised by contenders in the 2008 primaries or by a third party.

THE RELATION OF CULTURAL AND ECONOMIC ISSUES

Many Americans have come to assume that the red state–blue state alignment in presidential elections is likely to be long lasting in character. To some extent this assumption simply reflects the perennial and natural tendency of most political observers to think that the status quo will continue indefinitely into the future. This may, in fact, be the wisest assumption from a practical point of view. Politicians who are thinking of running for the presidency in 2008 have a relatively short time horizon — not simply the next presidential election, but also the "pre-primary" in which campaign funds must be raised and impressions must be formed. Since drastic changes in the status quo are unpredictable, potential candidates can do little more than assume the present configuration of forces.

Others, however, genuinely believe that cultural values have become the decisive factor in politics. If so, the traditional-modernist divide in American politics is not likely to disappear and the problem of candidates will simply be to decide what position to adopt on current cultural issues, which cultural issues have become counterproductive (e.g., gun control for the Democrats), and what new cultural issue might more effectively appeal to existing values.

Nevertheless, it is difficult to imagine that the basic division of 2000 and 2004 will continue into the indefinite future. If nothing else, the very narrow margin of victory in the Electoral College seems likely to produce change. Only five of 25 presidential elections were narrowly decided in the 20th century (1916, 1948, 1960, 1968, and 1976), and politicians of both parties would like to end the uncertainty of the 2000 and 2004 elections. If either party seems destined to lose all the battleground states in some election, the other will be highly tempted to try a new approach to produce the relatively small change in votes that would be required for victory. In addition, another distorted result such as occurred in 2000 would create strong pressure for a popular election of the President. Either development would provide a different basis for alignment.

More basically, however, the current assumption that economic issues are irrelevant in politics contradicts the most persistent theme in political philosophy and analysis for thousands of years. As such, the assumption seems dubious on its face, and it really seems like an overreaction to the exaggeration of the economic factor in Marxism. Marx had treated all culture, religion, values, and politics as a "superstructure" that was determined by the economic "base." In response, the anti-Marxists among the French intellectuals treated culture as the determining factor in history, and their work became highly influential in American humanities and social studies, especially as Marxism fell into disrepute in the 1980s.

In reality, an examination of the evolution of American politics for over 200 years only confirms what sophisticated analysts both at home and abroad have long understood: the relationship of economic and cultural factors in politics is extremely complicated, and the two types of factors are almost always intertwined. As may be remembered, Frederick Jackson Turner, the great historian of the Western movement in the United States from colonial times to 1900, argued that in early

American history there was "such a connection of the [ethnic] stock, the geographic conditions, the economic interests, and the conceptions of right and wrong, that all have played upon each other to the same end."[12] This remained true in the 20th century. Any simple dichotomy between economics and values, let alone the belief that only economics matters or that only values matter, will not bear serious scrutiny.

In the United States, the lack of power of the federal government in the economic sphere prior to the New Deal did, in fact, mean that national political issues had to be largely non-economic in character. From the 1790s onwards, ethnic and religious issues were not only important in all political campaigns, but formed the very base of the two political parties. Even the battle of the two parties on the tariff after the 1820s lost much of its economic meaning because of the prolonged Democratic alliance between the South and New York and the Whig-Republican alliance between New England and the Midwest, alliances within each party between sections with different economic interests on the tariff.

Yet, it is obvious that the cultural issues in American politics did not stand alone. When Jefferson used foreign policy toward England and France as the defining issue on which he formed the first party system, he was playing on fears of Great Britain that dated from the American Revolution, but he was not making a simple foreign policy argument. Jefferson was using the cultural issue of foreign policy to mobilize the resentments of the Scots, Irish, Germans, and Dutch in Pennsylvania and New York about Hamilton's supporters among the ethnic English coastal economic elite. The latter were the country's export-import traders. They were the focus of antagonism for a number of contradictory economic reasons: e.g., consumer prices in the stores, prices paid to farmers for agricultural products, and the fear of artisans about competition from cheap English manufactured products. Both the economic and ethnic resentments were peculiarly strong because they reinforced each other.

Similarly, the antagonism in the mid 19th century of the Protestant Scots, Irish, and Germans towards the Irish Catholics and German Catholics partly had an historical source: the Catholic–Protestant conflict in Ireland and Germany that had gone back centuries. But the antagonisms also reflected the cultural and economic resentments of rural and small town America toward the large cities that the immigrants literally were building. The Irish immigrants were also coming to small towns across America to construct railroads, and they generally drove down wages in construction work. And behind the specific angers lay the tensions about rapid industrialization and marketization and the Panic of 1837. The Know Nothings were powerful precisely because these various factors were so interrelated, and the Panic of 1857 was a significant factor in Lincoln's victory in 1860.

After the Civil War, the impact of the Panic of 1873 and 1893 created a high level of economic pain in the countryside that was expressed in anti-immigrant feelings and support for cultural issues such as Prohibition. As the immigrants and their children gradually assimilated into American life, they began to protest their wages

---

12. Frederick Jackson Turner, *The Significance of Sections in American History* (New York: Henry Holt and Company, 1932), pp. 48–49.

and their working conditions in strikes and to vote increasingly for the Socialist Party. This, in conjunction with the Panic of 1893 and a new wave of immigration, led to new anxieties. Presidents at the end of the century avoided a Know Nothing Party both by taking an anti-immigrant line and also by embracing nationalism: McKinley in the Spanish–American War, Theodore Roosevelt in Latin America, and Theodore Roosevelt and Woodrow Wilson in World War I.

When Franklin Roosevelt brought economic issues to the fore, this immediately destroyed the oldest cultural issue in America, Prohibition. Yet, cultural factors continued to be important in voting behavior. The first major scholarly study of presidential voting behavior focused precisely on cross-cutting economic and religious-ethnic factors. Scholars studying Erie County, Ohio, divided a random sample of 3000 adults into five socioeconomic groups and found that 71% of those in the highest group expected to vote for the Republican candidate and 35% of those in the lowest group. The three intermediate groups voted 68%, 56%, and 46% respectively.[13] The Protestants voted 61% Republican and the Catholics 23%.[14] Obviously well-to-do Catholics and low-income Protestants were under cross-pressure, and Table 1 below shows the results.

Table 1: Party Preference in Erie County, Ohio, May 1940, by Socio-Economic Status and Religion

Religion	Socio-Economic Status							
	Highest		Above Average		Below Average		Lowest	
	Rep	Dem	Rep	Dem	Rep	Dem	Rep	Dem
Protestant	76%	24%	66%	34%	54%	46%	43%	57%
Catholic	29%	71%	25%	75%	23%	77%	14%	86%

Source: *Paul F. Lazarsfeld, Bernard Berelson, and Hazel Gaudet, The People's Choice: How the Voter Makes Up His Mind in a Presidential Campaign, (New York: Duell, Sloan, and Pearce, 1944), pp. 3, 19, and 22.*

The dual impact of economic and ethnic factors does not have to be clear cut. Indeed, non-economic issues themselves also interact with each other, sometimes directly and sometimes indirectly in strange and symbolic ways. The relationship between foreign policy and ethnicity in the 1790s was typical. In the middle of the 19th century, the Free Soil movement, the Prohibition movement, the anti-Papal movement, the Know Nothing Party, and the anti-Slave Power movement all seemed to attract and mobilize the same type of people and somehow all seemed to be tapping similar grievances and anxieties, whatever their ultimate cause.

Northern aversion to slavery and even its expansion into the territories seemed the least of the real resentments and grievances. The free soil argument was not just an anti-slavery issue. It also appealed to farmers who want "free soil" in all senses of the term (including the free distribution of government land to new settlers) and to

---

13. The authors excluded Independents from this calculation, and hence the Democratic result was the difference between the Republican vote and 100%.
14. The source is the same as in Table 1.

those who were anxious about the acquisition of large numbers of Catholic, Spanish-speaking, and Democratic-voting Mexicans (and Indians) in Mexico.

Similarly, after World War II, anti-Communism was a cultural issue that was used to denounce those who supported a harsh policy toward Germany. In the last quarter of the century, abortion was not literally a gender issue, for men and women had similar attitudes towards it. Abortion was, however, a powerful symbol of the woman's right to choose her way of life, as well as a number of other issues.

The relationship of economic grievances to various cultural issues has not been stable over American history. Differences in level of income did not have such a dramatic impact on voting prior to 1933, and they declined in importance in the 1970s. As has been seen, the relationship of income and level of support for Democrats among middle- and upper-income Northern whites in the 2004 election actually was the reverse from that in the New Deal period, especially in the North.

The question, of course, is why the relative importance of the economic factor rises and falls in comparison with key cultural factors. This question does not simply involve changes that occur within a country such as the United States, but also the comparative question about why, say, cultural issues are less important in Great Britain than in the United States.

If one observes that a cultural issue or issues seem all important, there are, at the simplest level, three possible explanations: (1) Cultural issues are, in fact, the most important, especially at the particular time or in the particular country; (2) Voters in a two-party system always must choose between lesser evils, and at a particular time and place, the two parties are giving them no choice on economic issues. Hence rational people must vote on the basis of cultural differences even if they resent being forced to do so; (3) The cultural issue may, in fact, symbolize some economic grievance that has not been raised explicitly. "Scapegoat" is a concept that goes back to *The Old Testament*. The explanation is an empirical one at a particular place and time and may vary. This book, however, has strongly suggested that the second and third explanations are central in the last few decades in the United States.

OPTIONS FOR THE FUTURE

A discussion of political alternatives in the United States always is difficult. The politicians who define presidential strategy have a short-term perspective. In their initial campaign for the presidency, they usually take an ambiguous position both in order to forestall opposition and to have flexibility in reacting to any unanticipated developments. In the language of chess, they follow the preferred strategy: domination of the center of the board so that they can take advantage of any opportunity.

So long as a majority of voters do not move from general alienation to specific anger and economic conditions do not weaken markedly, both parties are positioned more or less comfortably on economic issues today. The Democrats have an ideology that is directed to the middle income and an economic policy that is responsive to those in the top quarter of the population by income. The Republicans have an economic policy that is very responsive to the upper income and reasonably responsive to those of middle and lower income. It is an attractive policy if the deficits are sustainable.

A number of social and political thinkers would go further and say that the present economic policy of the Republicans and Democrats is highly desirable because of the rising percentage of the population who own stocks or mutual funds and their own homes. If people own enough real estate and stocks, then the average rise in wage level is not as important for them as capital appreciation in the value of their home and stock portfolio. They can achieve wage increases by acquiring new skills and added experience, and at crucial points they can draw money from their home and stocks. Even retirees may find a rise in the price of their house and stocks more important than their Social Security checks. Michael Barone argued in 2003 that for this reason "the saliency of the Social Security issue among the elderly will continue to decline."[15]

If people see their economic well-being associated with the performance of the stock and real estate markets, then they have a strong interest in government policies that improve that performance. If this is the case, the age-old conflict between labor and capital largely disappears. In 2002 those with stocks are said to have supported the Republicans by a 56% to 42% margin, while those without stocks supported the Democrats 52% to 45%. Nevertheless, an increase in stock ownership should not benefit the Republicans in the long run, but should simply make both the Democrats and the Republicans more responsive to the interests of stock-owners. That, of course, is the essence of the Democratic or blue-state suburban strategy.

But by the same token, this argument has corollaries that often are not recognized. The educated population largely understands that Social Security payments to retirees and especially the retiree consumption based on it must come out of current production, not some magical trust fund. As a result, Social Security faces a major problem as the number of retirees rises as a percentage of the employed. Consumption by retirees that is financed by the sale of stocks or reduction of house equity is not fundamentally different. Those in society who are not working are consuming goods and services produced by those are working.

The obvious solution to this problem is to maintain a large labor force by postponing retirement and by continuing to admit enough adult immigrants so that the percentage of retirees in society can be kept reasonably low. Wages should, of course, be kept low enough to finance retirees' consumption. This, indeed, has happened in the last two decades. The problem with this solution is that the level of immigration has been quite unpopular precisely at the time that the small cohort of Depression babies has been reaching retirement age. Soon the number of new retirees will begin soaring, and the number of immigrants needed to finance the current level of consumption would also have to rise.

The second problem, of course, is that widespread stock ownership by unsophisticated investors may create a truly major political problem if the stock market crashes. The population did accept a 78% decline in the NASDAQ and a 39% decline

---

15. Michael Barone, "Introduction, *The Almanac of American Politics: 2004* (Washington, D.C.: National Journal Group, 2003), p. 32.

in the Dow Jones Industrial Average after 2000, but much of the anxiety about the economy in recent years surely has reflected the fact that the stock markets have not surpassed their 2000 highs. Indeed, the NASDAQ technology stocks purchased by so many of the unsophisticated have remained more than 50% below their high. If a second major stock market decline occurs from more or less current levels, the disillusionment may be quite serious and the political consequences quite severe.

As we think about the near and medium term, we should reflect once more on several important facts discussed through this book. First, the present polarization of politics really is inexcusable. Political scientists for decades wrote about the American political culture of accommodation and consensus. This was always the major justification for a broad two-party system and for the system of checks and balances. This book has emphasized the need that lasted for 175 years to ensure the autonomy of the two great sections, but especially the autonomy of the white South. Now the conflict between the North and South is over. Now the warring European-American "races" are whites. Now the blacks who began migrating to the cities from the foreign country that was the rural South some 60 years ago are well along the path to acceptance. They are where the Irish were in about 1910 or the Italians, Jews, and Poles in 1950 — a long way from an ideal position, but also a long way from the original prejudices and discrimination. The non-European immigration of recent decades might create a serious political reaction among whites, but this issue has largely been kept off the political agenda.

The present cultural polarization in politics is not the result of a polarization within society, but is an artifact of the political system. The nominating process gives too much power to the ideological activists of both parties, persons who are basically well to do. The disastrous campaign finance laws direct money away from the political parties and to the more ideological groups, and politicians become beholden to them both for financial contributions and for support in the primaries, even more so below the presidential level.

The lead front-page story of the conservative *Washington Times* several days after Harriet Miers was withdrawn as a nominee to the Supreme Court was entitled, "Bush's Base Ill at Ease in Dissent." Yet, the correspondent described a very different situation in the middle of the story and implicitly raised the real meaning of the word "base."[16]

> Conservatives in the Bush-Miers camp last week were sniping at other conservatives claiming that private polls showed Evangelical leaders ..., who supported Miss Miers' choice, were in touch with grass-roots social conservative opinion outside the Beltway while many of the president's critics on the right were out of touch with the conservative base.

The conservative activist Phyllis Schafly, who opposed Miers' nomination, essentially supported this interpretation while dismissing it: "There is certainly a segment of the religious right that trusts the President.... However, they are not the

16. Ralph Z. Hallow, "Bush's Base Ill at Ease in Dissent," *The Sunday Times*, October 30, 2005, pp. A1 and A4.

majority of grass-roots conservatives you find in organizations like the Eagle Forum and Concerned Women for America." Mrs. Schafly does not even seem to realize what she is saying. It simply is not democratic for a handful of activists to have such enormous power when their so-called base, the broader members of the religious right, takes the opposite position. It is a general problem and in both parties.

Second, the level of alienation among a broader population remains quite high, even higher than at the end of the 1970s with its economic troubles and oil crises, with the fall of Saigon and the enormous difficulties produced by the overthrow of the Shah of Iran. Table 2 was presented in the Introduction. It is worth repeating.

Table 2: Sense of Political Effectiveness, United States, 1956–2000

Level of Effectiveness	1956	1960	1980	1984	1988	1992	1996	2000
High	64%	64%	39%	52%	38%	40%	28%	35%
Low	15%	15%	30%	23%	32%	34%	47%	40%

Source: Paul R. Abramson, John H. Aldrich, and David W. Rohde, *Change and Continuity in the 2000 Election* (Washington, D.C.: CQ Press, 2001), p. 87–88.

Third, although there are many reasons for a popular feeling that government is not responsive, one should not underestimate the role played by the basic economic situation in which people find themselves. The red states, the red areas, the red people, are not the economically more prosperous. The average US household income is around $43,000 a year, and the average Social Security payment is $922. The "suburban middle class" to which the parties respond are in the top quarter of the population — that is, those making above $75,000 and receiving Social Security payments closer to $1600 a month.[17]

This book has often quoted Stan Greenberg, Clinton's chief pollster in 1992 and then the leading pollster for George Soros in MoveOn in 2004. Part of a consultant's job is to supply a positive spin for the party that he or she represents, and many statements in Greenberg's book, *The Two Americas*, correspond to that expectation. But precisely for that reason, many of Greenberg's statements quoted in Chapter 9 deserve to be repeated and given the most serious thought.

Greenberg writes that "these are special times, when twenty-five years of accumulating inequality, now years of stagnant incomes, and new insecurities in education, health care, and retirement demand a bold politics." He emphasizes the huge Democratic losses among retirees, Catholics, and those without a college education in 2004 and concludes, "The flip of downscale America gave this election to Bush." While Greenberg writes that these groups, when forced to choose on cultural issues, chose the traditional values emphasized by the Republicans, Greenberg faults the Democrats for not giving them another choice. "Bottom line: the culture war was not pushed back by the class war."

Greenberg describes the Clinton Administration in terms that he clearly also means to apply to Al Gore and John Kerry:[18]

---

17. *Statistical Abstract*, 2004/2005, p. 350.
18. Greenberg, *The Two Americas*, pp. 82–84.

The Clinton Administration abandoned the middle class. This was partly symbolic, as middle-class grievances and wants were no longer the central passion of the project; this was partly real and material, as low-income populations took priority and as middle-class incomes were slow to rise; and it was partly about values, both real and symbolic. . . . The middle-class voters were driven from the project in 1994 by the deafening silence, taxes, stagnant incomes, no welfare reform, and the assault weapons ban. But even after all this, when Clinton climbed back to win in 1996, his second-term State of the Union addresses made almost no mention of the "missing middle."

Fourth, the readers of this book, who likely are in the top quarter of the population in income or are expecting to rise toward that level, should never forget the remarkable success of Ross Perot in 1992. One final citation from Stan Greenberg from Chapter 9 is worth repeating:[19]

The Perot voters were independent, younger, mostly blue collar and noncollege-educated, financially squeezed in the 1980s and for most of the 1990s as well, who felt a deep sense of middle-class grievance. Their sensibilities were among the first to be shunned by the Clinton administration.... They were pro-America, suspicious of global forces, and pro-military, and thus likely thrown overboard by gays in the military, not to mention NAFTA.

Perot greatly increased the turnout in winning 22% to 23% of the white male vote, and this in the aftermath of a very mild economic recession. When George W. Bush adopted Perot's slogan "United We Stand" and his nationalistic posture, he not only won a solid victory in 2004 but also produced an increase in turnout unprecedented in recent decades. If the level of popular resentment and sense of grievance rise further in very difficult times, it is unclear who might mobilize it.

In the fall of 2005, as the Iraq War continued to go badly and as Vice President Cheney's hawkish chief of staff was indicted for perjury, the President returned to abortion as his major cultural issue. He chose a Supreme Court nominee who was certain to provoke a major battle with the Democrats in the Senate and quite possibly a constitutional crisis over the Senate filibuster. In the future, however, other Republican conservatives are very unlikely to forget the lessons of the 1992 and 2004 elections.

Today we have a very paradoxical situation. A nominating process and campaign finance legislation introduced in the name of democracy produce political parties that are dominated by well-to-do activists with intense ideological attitudes. This is not surprising. The scholarly literature suggests that the well-educated are deeply concerned with "postmaterialist" (that is, cultural) values. Yet, as has been seen, this literature also suggests that lower- and middle-income voters give higher priority to materialist values. The assumption of the media that lower- and middle-income voters are driven solely by cultural values, and retrograde values at that, is most dubious. Moreover, the real strategies both of the Democratic and Republican parties actually are based on the assumption that it is the better-educated and affluent who are very focused on materialist values.

---

19. Greenberg, *The Two Americas*, pp. 89–90.

The great majority of the readers of this book, whether Democrats or Republicans, are likely to be of the better educated, more affluent stratum that produces party activists. They need to reflect deeply on the paradox of the previous paragraph. They need to reflect deeply on the relative priority of their various interests and values. They should be deeply disturbed by the polarization of politics along cultural lines and especially the rise in the importance of the nationalist issue at a time of potential serious economic problems.

Even without drastic measures, the United States changes its Constitution not by constitutional amendments, but by constitutional reinterpretation. This is how the Constitution was transformed in the 1880s and 1890s and in the 1930s. If the educated American population does not deal directly with the economic resentments of the middle-income over a long period but deflects them onto fundamental constitutional issues, it should not be surprised if the Constitution is transformed in ways that they do not approve.

The broad upper stratum of any society (and the top quarter of society is a broad upper stratum) also needs to worry about political stability. Americans now take stability for granted, but this is part of the arrogance of the time reflected in many misjudgments — for example, on the ease of the reconstruction of Iraq. President Bush is not a threat to the political system. Yet, the fact that he has been cavalier toward civil rights in a war of terror, has indicated the possible desirability of instituting martial law in a flu epidemic, and has insisted that a filibuster is illegitimate when the nature of the Constitution is at stake are not good precedents for the future. It also is not a good precedent that the political party that has long been identified with the middle income ideologically can follow a policy that one of its top pollsters can label as an abandonment of the middle class. And, of course, when a large proportion of the population remains convinced for decades that the political system is not responsive to it, that too is not a healthy situation.

A student of comparative politics is aware that the most explosive political situations occur when cultural and economic grievances overlap. This was a central conclusion of the generation that was absorbed with why Hitler was supported in Germany. The reverse side of this conclusion was that cross-cutting interests and values—"group memberships" in the language of the time[20] — were very stabilizing.

The conclusion has been reconfirmed after World War II. Marxism was popular in the Third World because the perception of exploitation by the economic elite was combined with anger at the Westernized "superstructure" or culture of that economic elite. The Shiites throughout the Middle East do not simply differ with the Sunnis in religious views, but are generally poor and resent the wealth of the Sunnis. By the same token, the French-speaking peasants of Quebec were angry that the use of English as the language of work benefited those speaking English. The Pashtuni speakers of Afghanistan had the same resentment toward the Farsi-speaking elite of Kabul. The Catholics were the poor of Northern Ireland and the blacks were the poor

---

20. The classic statement was David Truman, *The Governmental Process: Political Interests and Public Opinion* (New York: Knopf, 1951).

of the Southern states. They thought they were locked into their economic position by discrimination based on religion and skin color, respectively.

The first step for members of the upper stratum in the United States is to strive to overcome some of their overt prejudices toward lower- and middle-income whites and the less often expressed prejudices about the equivalent non-whites. The analysis of Kevin Phillips, a Nixon political aide, has been cited extensively in chapter 6. It is well to remember another statement that he made at the time:[21]

> The emerging Republican majority of the Nineteen-Seventies is centered in the South, the West and in the "Middle-American" urban-suburban districts. Whatever limousine-liberalism says, this is not reactionary country. On the contrary, it has been the seat of every popular, progressive upheaval in American politics.... Politics able to resurrect the vitality and commitment of Middle America — from sharecroppers and truckers to the alienated lower middle class — will do far more for the entire nation than the environmental manipulation, social boondoggling, community agitation and incendiary promises of the Nineteen-Sixties.

The early 1970s were, of course, also a time of polarizing rhetoric, and Phillips might want to revise the language of the end of the last sentence, but he is right about the "red" people of the "red" areas. Lower and middle income whites are not simply red necks who think only about abortion. When they were angry, the "red" voters supported George Wallace and Ross Perot, (neither of whom talked about religion or abortion) but, as Phillips argued 35 years ago, they would respond to an economic policy that took their interests into account. Senator Barack Obama's stirring words at the Democratic Convention about the people of the red areas were right.

Two changes seem vital. First, we must learn to treat lower-income and middle-income whites with respect and to recognize that they are part of a diverse America. Neither Jay Leno nor his audience recognized how close his joke about the red neck and the white trash NASCAR wine was to "N-word" language. It is that kind of disrespect, often shown toward Evangelical religion as well, that produces such a strong cultural counter-reaction.

Second, we must return to the insights of the political scientists of the mid-20th century about political stability. Cultural and economic grievances now reinforce each other. Instead the political strata should arrange that they be cross-cutting: for instance the Democrats might support with some caution the cultural values of the affluent suburbanites and with some caution the economic interests of the middle-income. The Republicans might reverse the pattern. Members of a wise Establishment think about reinforcing the norms and sense of community in a society, not tearing them apart. It is extraordinarily short sighted for those of us in the affluent stratum to fight to cut income tax rates to 32% instead of letting them rise to, say, 36% or 37% and then say to the middle-income, "let them eat cake." A tolerant and accommodating political culture that has been the great strength of America should be cherished and protected.

---

21. Kevin P. Phillips, *The Emerging Republican Majority* (Garden City, N. Y.: Doubleday & Co., 1970), Preface to the Anchor Books edition, pp. 23–24.

Putting the people of the red area under the cross-pressure of an attractive economic policy by one party and an attractive cultural policy by another would give both parties a chance to compete in those areas. Given the unfair advantage that the Senatorial electors give the small states in the Electoral College, a more even division of the red states between the parties is necessary to avoid another distorted Electoral College victory like the one in 2000. But, most important of all, the cross-pressure would reduce the sense of grievance and alienation and the fervor of the emotions. Despite prejudiced stereotypes about the red areas, such an approach would be quite successful.

Ultimately, however, the United States will have to face up to the question of political institutions. The United States at the beginning of the 21st century occupies a very peculiar position among the political systems of the world. Normally nation-states are semi-democratic at best in the early periods of their existence, and even such democracy is usually intermittent. When the population is poorly educated, it is dangerous to have democracy. Such a *demos* may support a demagogue in a democracy. But when the population is highly educated, it is dangerous not to have democracy. Over the decades or even the centuries, countries gradually move in the direction of a stable majoritarian democracy, but with many interruptions and retreats. The evolution of the United States to fuller democracy in 1937 and then still further in the 1950s and 1960s was typical in that respect.

The great advantage of constitutional democracy in which people have true universal suffrage in competitive elections is that it gives everyone symbolic recognition and provides incentives to politicians to be responsive to everyone. That is the first secret for stability in a well-educated society. The percentage of Americans 25 years of age and older with high school diplomas rose from 33% in 1950 to 83% in 2000, and those with college degrees from 6% to 25%, thereby creating an extremely strong base for majoritarian democracy.[22]

Yet, the limitations on majority democracy at the national level have become greater over the last three decades. The role of the broader population in the nominating process has declined; House district elections have become more non-competitive; the institutionalization of the filibuster in the Senate as a regular instrument of legislation has given a veto on legislation to 21 states with 11% of the vote; the red state–blue state alignment has magnified the bias in the Electoral College and given still greater power to the minority who live in rural areas and small towns; the Democrats have given eight big industrial states with 42.3% of the population 38.8% of the delegates to their convention, while the Republicans have given them 26.7% of the delegates to their convention..

This is not the place for a discussion of institutional reform, but clearly the end of the North–South conflict ends any positive role for the Electoral College. The winner-take-all rule artificially limits the campaign to a few battleground states —

---

22. U.S. Bureau of Census, *U.S. Census of Population, 1950* (Washington: US Government Printing Office, 1953), Vol. II, Part 1, p. 96; *Statistical Abstract of the United States* (Washington: US Government Printing Office, 2000), 120th ed. 2000, pp. 12, 14, 51, 251, and 469.

ultimately, in 2004, to 12 states with 23.3% of the country's population, 20.9% of its blacks, and 16.4% of its Hispanics.[23] The campaigns of both parties and the media almost officially were telling the voters in 39 states during the last two months of the 2004 campaign that their votes did not matter. Especially when the parties are following red state–blue state strategies, the election of the President depends on the random outcome in a small number of narrowly-divided states. The winner-take-all rule, together with the non-competitive district elections, encourages polarization in the red states and blue states. A national popular election would transform the dynamics of the election, and a simple runoff between the two top candidates would solve virtually any problems usually associated with a national election.

It is even more important to reduce the power of the affluent activists in the political system. The one indispensable reform is a national primary held late in the summer, again with a runoff if no one receives a majority on the first round. Certain types of government subsidy of successful candidates is desirable, but the time has long passed to abolish campaign finance restrictions that force people to give donations to organizations for whom the candidates are not held responsible and that contribute to a polarizing campaign. Specific funding for a national primary is crucial.

Major political reform will not occur, however, until a presidential candidate at a time of crisis decides that it is in his or her interest to fight for it. In the interim, the political strata should concentrate on ending the red state–blue state strategies. The logic of the political situation puts the main onus on the Democrats to take the first steps. They perhaps only need to remember history. In the New Deal period from 1932 through 1968, they won 7 of 10 elections, and two of their three losses were to Eisenhower and the third was a narrow one in the Vietnam election of 1968. In next 36 years, the Democrats won 3 of 9 elections, only once winning as much as 50.3% of the vote. The strategy that contributes to political stability and the end of polarization should also be profitable from an electoral point of view.

---

23. These were Florida, Iowa, Michigan, Minnesota, Nevada, New Hampshire, New Mexico, Ohio, Oregon, Pennsylvania, Washington, and Wisconsin.

ALSO BY JERRY F. HOUGH

The Logic of Economic Reform in Russia. Brookings Institution, 2001

Growing Pains: Russian Democracy and the Elections of 1993. Timothy J. Colton and Jerry F. Hough (eds). Brookings Institution, 1998

Democratization and Revolution in the USSR, 1985–1991. Brookings Institution, 1997

The 1996 Russian Presidential Election. Jerry F. Hough, Evelyn Davidheiser, and Susan Goodrich Lehmann. Brookings Institution, 1996

Opening Up the Soviet Economy. Brookings Institution, 1988

Russia and the West: Gorbachev and the Politics of Reform. Simon & Schuster, 1988

The Struggle for the Third World: Soviet Debates & American Options. Brookings Institution, 1986

Soviet Leadership in Transition. Brookings Institution, 1980

How the Soviet Union Is Governed. by Jerry F. Hough and Merle Fainsod, Harvard University Press, 1979

The Soviet Union and Social Science Theory. Harvard University Press, 1977

The Soviet Prefects: the Local Party Organs in Industrial Decision-Making. Harvard University Press, 1969

BIBLIOGRAPHY

ARCHIVES AND PAPERS COLLECTIONS

Clemson University: Special Collection, Clemson University Libraries, Clemson, S.C.
    James F. Byrnes Collection
    Strom Thurmond Collection
Dirksen Congressional Research Library, Dirksen Congressional Center, Pekin, Illinois.
    Everett Dirksen Papers
Duke University: Rare Book, Manuscript, and Special Collection Library, Durham, N.C.
    David Eugene Price Papers
Franklin D. Roosevelt Presidential Library, Hyde Park, New York.
    R. Walton Moore Papers
George C. Marshall Research Library, Lexington, Virginia.
    George C. Marshall Papers
Georgetown University Library, Special Collections Division, Washington, D.C.
    Eugene McCarthy National File
Harry S. Truman Presidential Library, Independence, Missouri.
    Clark Clifford Papers
    Harry S. Truman Senatorial Papers
Indiana University, Libby Library, Bloomington, Indiana.
    Claude G. Bowers Papers
Jimmy Carter Presidential Library, Atlanta, Georgia.
    Jimmy Carter 1976 Presidential Campaign Papers
    Jimmy Carter Presidential Papers

Library of Congress, Manuscript Division, Washington D.C.

      Charles E. Bohlen Papers

      Henry Brandon Papers

      Raymond Clapper Papers

      William E. Dodd Papers

      James A. Farley Papers

      Felix Frankfurter Papers

      Breckinridge Long Papers

      Robert A. Taft Papers

Lyndon Baines Johnson Presidential Library, Austin, Texas.

      George Reedy Senatorial Files

Marquette University, Dept. of Special Collections and University Archives, Milwaukee, Wisconsin.

      Joseph McCarthy Papers

Princeton University: Seeley G. Mudd Manuscript Library, Princeton, New Jersey.

      James Forrestal Papers

      George F. Kennan Papers

      George Bartlow Martin Papers

      George S. McGovern Papers

      Adlai E. Stevenson Papers

      W. Willard Wirtz Papers in Adlai E. Stevenson Collection

Richard Nixon Library and Birthplace, Yorba Linda, California.

      Richard Nixon 1946 Campaign Collection

      Richard Nixon 1950 Senate Campaign Collection

University of Alabama, The W. S. Hoole Special Collections Library, Tuscaloosa, Alabama.

      John Sparkman Papers

University of Arizona: Special Collections, University of Arizona Library, Tucson, Arizona.

      Lewis W. Douglas Papers

University of Delaware: University of Delaware Library, Newark, Delaware.

      George S. Messersmith Papers

University of Tennessee, Special Collections Library, Knoxville, Tennessee.

      Estes Kefauver Papers

Western Historical Association Manuscript Collection, Columbia, Missouri.

      Champ Clark Papers

PUBLISHED PRIMARY SOURCES

Abbot, W. W., and Dorothy Twohig, eds., *The Papers of George Washington. Confederation Series* (Charlottesville: University Press of Virginia, 1992).

Advisory Commission of the Presidential Nominating Process, *Nominating Future Presidents* (Washington, D.C.: Republican National Committee, 2000).

Butcher, Harry C., *My Three Years with Eisenhower: The Personal Diary of Captain Harry C. Butcher* (New York: Simon and Schuster, 1946).

Butterfield, L. N., ed., *Diary and Autobiography of John Adams* (Cambridge: Harvard University, 1962).

Israel, Fred L., ed., *The War Diary of Breckinridge Long: Selections from the Years, 1939–1944* (Lincoln: University of Nebraska Press, 1966).

Johnson, Walter, ed., *The Papers of Adlai Stevenson* (Boston: Little, Brown, 1972-1979).

Kennedy, John F., *The Strategy of Peace*, edited by Allen Nevins (New York: Harper, 1960).

Kennedy, John F., *Let the Lady Hold Up Her Head: Reflections on American Immigration Policy* (Washington, D.C.: American Jewish Congress, 1957).

Link, Arthur S., ed., *The Papers of Woodrow Wilson* (Princeton: Princeton University Press, 1980).

Merrill, Dennis, ed., *Documentary History of the Truman Presidency* (University Publications of America, 1995).

Mundt, Karl E., "From South Dakota to South Carolina — An Invitation and a Challenge," *Congressional Record — House*, June 4, 1956, pp. 9442–9448.

Oberg, Barbara B., ed., *The Papers of Thomas Jefferson* (Princeton: Princeton University Press, 2002).

Perot, H. Ross, *United We Stand: How We Can Take Back Our Country* (New York: Hyperion, 1992).

Public Papers of the Presidents of the United States: Harry S. Truman, 1953 (Washington, D.C.: US Government Printing Office, 1961).

Rutland, Robert A., *The Papers of James Madison* (Chicago: University of Chicago Press, 1975).

Smith, Paul H., ed., *Letters of Delegates to Congress, 1774–1789* (Washington, D.C.: Library of Congress, 1976-2000).

Taylor, Robert J., ed., *Papers of John Adams* (Cambridge: Harvard University Press, 1977).

Twohig, Dorothy, ed., *The Papers of George Washington. Retirement Series* (Charlottesville: University Press of Virginia, 1999).

Wainwright, Nicholas B., ed., Sidney G. Fisher, *A Philadelphia Perspective: The Diary of Sidney G. Fischer Covering the Years 1834–1871* (Philadelphia: Historical Society of Pennsylvania, 1967).

MEMOIRS

Acheson, Dean, *Present at the Creation: My Years in the State Department* (New York: Norton, 1969).

Ball, George W., *The Past Has Another Pattern: Memoirs* (New York: W. W. Norton, 1982).

Biddle, Francis, *In Brief Authority* (Garden City. N.Y.: Doubleday and Co. 1962).

Bohlen, Charles E., *Witness to History, 1929–1969* (New York: W. W. Norton, 1973).

Bradley, Bill, *Time Present, Time Past: A Memoir* (New York, Alfred A. Knopf, 1996).

Brownell, Herbert, *Advising Ike: The Memoirs of Attorney General Herbert Brownell* (Lawrence: University Press of Kansas, 1993).

Califano, Joseph A., Jr., *Governing America: An Insider's Report from the White House and the Cabinet* (New York: Simon and Schuster, 1981).

Califano, Joseph A., Jr., *Inside: A Public and Private Life* (New York: Public Affairs, 2004).

Clinton, Bill, *My Life* (New York: Alfred A. Knopf, 2004).

Creel, George, *How We Advertised America* (New York: Harper and Brothers, 1920).

Dent, Harry S., *The Prodigal South Returns to Power* (New York: Wiley, 1978).

Ford, Gerald R., *A Time to Heal: The Autobiography of Gerald R. Ford* (New York: Harper and Row, 1979).

Haldeman, H. R., *The Ends of Power* (New York: Times Book, 1978).

Hartmann, Robert T., *Palace Politics: An Inside Account of the Ford Years* (New York: McGraw Hill, 1980).

Kennan, George F., Memoirs (Boston: Little, Brown, 1967).

Kimbrell, Fuller, *From the Farm House to the State House: The Life and Times of Fuller Kimbrell* (Tuscaloosa, Ala.: Word Way Press, 2001).

Mangione, Jerre, *Mount Allegro: A Memoir of Italian American Life* (Boston: Houghton Mifflin, 1943).

Martin, John Bartlow, *It Seems Like Only Yesterday: Memoirs of Writing, Presidential Politics, and the Diplomatic Life* (New York: William Morrow, 1986).

Morris, Dick, *Behind the Oval Office: Getting Reelected Against All Odds*, 2nd ed. (Los Angeles: Renaissance Books, 1999).

O'Neill, Tip, *Man of the House: The Life and Political Memoirs of Speaker Tip O'Neill* (New York: Random House, 1987).

Reagan, Ronald, *An American Life* (New York: Simon and Schuster, 1990).

Regan, Donald T., *For the Record: From Wall Street to Washington* (San Diego: Harcourt Brace Jovanovich, 1988).

Reich, Robert B., *Locked in the Cabinet* (New York: Alfred A. Knopf, 1997).

Rubin, Robert E., and Jacob Weisberg, *In an Uncertain World: Tough Choices from Wall Street to Washington* (New York: Random House, 2003).

Safire, William, *Before the Fall: An Inside View of the Pre-Watergate White House* (Garden City, N.Y.: Doubleday, 1975).

Stockman, David A., *The Triumph of Politics: How the Reagan Revolution Failed* (New York: Harper & Row, 1986).

Tumulty, Joseph P., *Woodrow Wilson as I Know Him* (Garden City, N.Y.: Doubleday, Page, and Co., 1921).

White, F. Clifton, *Politics as a Noble Calling: The Memoirs of F. Clifton White* (Ottawa, Ill.: Jameson Books, 1994).

White, F. Clifton, *Suite 3505: The Story of the Draft Goldwater Movement* (New Rochelle, N.Y.: Arlington House, 1967).

White, William F., *A Man Called White: The Autobiography of William White* (New York: Viking Press, 1948).

STATISTICAL SOURCES

2005 County and City Extra: Annual Metro, City, and County Data Book (Lanham, Md: Bernan Press, 2005).

Barone, Michael, with different co-editors, *The Almanac of American Politics*, various years (Washington, D.C.: National Journal Group, 1971 to present).

Historical Statistics of the United States, Colonial Times to 1970 (Washington, D.C.: US Government Printing Office, 1975).

Pierce, Phyllis S., ed., *The Dow Jones Averages, 1885–1995* (Chicago: Irwin Professional Press, 1996).

Population in the United States in 1860: Compiled from the Original Returns of the Eighth Census (Washington, D.C.: US Government Printing Office, 1864).

Rusk, Jerrold, *A Statistical History of the American Electorate* (Washington, D.C.: CQ Press, 2001).

Scammon, Richard et al, *Who Votes?*, 24 vols. (Washington, D.C.: CQ Press, 1953 to present).

Sixteenth Census of the United States: 1940—— Population (Washington, D.C.: US Government Printing Office, 1943).

Statistical Abstract of the United States, 2004–2005 (Washington, D.C.: U.S. Government Printing Office, 2004).

The Congressional Quarterly's Guide to U.S. Elections, 4th ed. (Washington, D.C., CQ Press, 2001).

Thirteenth Census of the United States Taken in the Year 1910: Abstract of the Census (Washington, D.C.: US Government Printing Office, 1913).

Twelfth Census of the United States Taken in the Year 1900, Population, Part I (Washington, D.C.: Census Bureau, 1901).

U.S. Census of Population, 1950 (Washington, D.C.: US Government Printing Office, 1953).

SECONDARY SOURCES: BOOKS

Abramson, Paul R., John H. Aldrich, and David W. Rohde, *Change and Continuity in the 1980 Elections* (Washington, D.C.: CQ Press, 1982).

Abramson, Paul R., John H. Aldrich, and David W. Rohde, *Change and Continuity in the 1980 Elections*, rev. ed. (Washington, D.C.: CQ Press, 1983).

Abramson, Paul R., John H. Aldrich, and David W. Rohde, *Change and Continuities in the 1992 Election* (Washington, D.C.: CQ Press, 1994).

Abramson, Paul R., John H. Aldrich, and David W. Rohde, *Change and Continuity in the 1988 Election*, rev. ed. (Washington, D.C.: CQ Press, 1991).

Abramson, Paul R., John H. Aldrich, and David W. Rohde, *Change and Continuity in the 2000 Election* (Washington, D.C.: CQ Press, 2002).

Alexander, Thomas B., *Sectional Stress and Party Strength: A Study of Roll-Call Voting Patterns in the United States House of Representatives, 1836–1860* (Nashville, Tenn.: Vanderbilt University Press, 1967).

Allen, Theodore W., *The Invention of the White Race* (London: Verso, 1994).

Alsop, Joseph, and Turner Catledge, *The 168 Days* (Garden City, N.Y.: Doubleday, Doran, 1938).

Ambrose, Stephen E., *The Wild Blue: The Men and Boys Who Flew the B-24s Over Germany* (New York: Simon & Schuster, 2001).

Anderson, Benedict, *Imagined Communities: Reflections on the Origin and Spread of Nationalism*, rev. ed. (London: Verso, 1991).

Anderson, J. W., *Eisenhower, Brownell, and the Congress: The Tangled Origins of the Civil Rights Bill of 1956-1957* (Tuscaloosa: University of Alabama Press, 1964).

Anderson, Margo J., *The American Census: A Social History* (New Haven: Yale University Press, 1988).

Anderson, Stuart, *Race and Rapprochement: Anglo-Saxonism and Anglo-American Relations, 1895–1904* (Rutherford, N.J.: Fairleigh Dickinson University, 1981).

Babson, Roger, *Cox — The Man* (New York: Bretano's, 1920).

Baer, Kenneth S., *Reinventing Democrats: The Politics of Liberalism from Reagan to Clinton* (Lawrence: University Press of Kansas, 2000).

Bailyn, Bernard, and Philip D. Morgan, eds., *Strangers within the Realm: Cultural Margins of the First British Empire* (Chapel Hill: University of North Carolina Press, 1991). .

Bailyn, Bernard, *Voyagers to the West: A Passage in the Peopling of America on the Eve of the Revolution* (New York: Knopf, 1986).

Baldwin, Alice M., *The New England Clergy and the American Revolution* (Durham, N.C.: Duke University Press, 1928).

Barber, James D., ed. *Choosing the President* (Englewood Cliffs, N.J.: Prentice-Hall, 1974).

Barzun, Jacques, *Race: A Study in Modern Superstition* (New York: Harcourt, Brace, and Co., 1937).

Bass, Jack, and Marilyn W. Thompson, *Strom: The Complicated Personal and Political Life of Strom Thurmond* (New York: Public Affairs, 2005).

Bates, Robert H., *Analytic Narratives* (Princeton: Princeton University Press, 1998).

Beard, Charles A., *American Foreign Policy in the Making, 1932–1940: A Study in Responsibilities* (New Haven: Yale University Press, 1946).

Becker, Carl Lotus, *Beginnings of the American People* (Boston: Houghton Mifflin Co., 1915).

Bell, Daniel, *The Coming of Post-Industrial Society: A Venture in Social Forecasting* (New York: Basic Books, 1973).

Benedict, Ruth, *Race, Science, and Politics* (New York: Modern Age Books, 1940).

Bernard, William, *American Immigration Policy — A Reappraisal* (New York: Harper and Brothers, 1950).

Bernstein, Irving, *Guns or Butter? The Presidency of Lyndon Johnson* (New York: Oxford University Press, 1996).

Black, Earl and Merle, *The Rise of Southern Republicans* (Cambridge: Harvard University Press, 2002).

Blum, John Morton, *From the Morgenthau Diaries* (Boston: Houghton-Mifflin, 1967).

Bogardus, Emory S., *Immigration and Race Attitudes* (Boston: D.C. Heath, 1928).

Bourne, Peter G., *Jimmy Carter: A Comprehensive Biography from Plains to Postpresidency* (New York: Scribers, 1997).

Brauer, Carl M., *John F. Kennedy and the Second Reconstruction* (New York: Columbia University Press, 1977).

Bridenbaugh, Carl, *Mitre and Sceptre: Transatlantic Faiths, Ideas, Personalities, and Politics, 1689–1775* (New York: Oxford University Press, 1962).

Bringa, Tone, *Being Muslim the Bosnian Way: Identity and Community in a Central Bosnian Village* (Princeton: Princeton University Press, 1995).

Broder, David S., *Changing of the Guard: Power and Leadership in America* (New York: Simon and Schuster, 1980).

Bruce, Steve, *The Rise and Fall of the New Christian Right: Conservative Protestant Politics in America, 1978-1988* (New York: Oxford University Press, 1988).

Burns, James MacGregor, *The Deadlock of Democracy: Four-Party Politics in America* (Englewood Cliffs, N.J.: Prentice Hall, Inc., 1963).

Burns, Nancy, Kay Lehman Schlozman, and Sidney Verba, *The Private Roots of Public Action* (Cambridge: Harvard University Press, 2001).

Campbell, James E., and James C. Garand, *Before the Vote: Forecasting American National Elections* (Thousand Oaks, Calif.: Sage Publications, 2000).

Cannon, Lou, *Reagan* (New York: Putnam, 1982).

Casey, Steven, *Cautious Crusade: Franklin D. Roosevelt, American Public Opinion, and the War Against Nazi Germany* (New York: Oxford University Press, 2001).

Cebula, James E., *James M. Cox: Journalist and Politician* (New York: Garland Publishing, 1985).

Cecelski, David S., and Timothy B. Tyron, *Democracy Betrayed: The Wilmington Race Riot of 1898 and Its Legacy* (Chapel Hill: University of North Carolina Press, 1998).

Cell, John W., *The Highest Stage of White Supremacy: The Origins of Segregation in South Africa and the American South* (Cambridge: Cambridge University Press, 1982).

Charles, Joseph, *The Origins of the American Party System: Three Essays* (Williamsburg, Va.: Institute of Early American History and Culture, 1956).

Claude, Richard, *The Supreme Court and the Electoral Process* (Baltimore: Johns Hopkins University Press, 1970).

Clymer, Adam, *Edward M. Kennedy: A Biography* (New York: William Morrow & Co., 1999).

Coben, Stanley, *A. Mitchell Palmer: Politician* (New York: Columbia University Press, 1963).

Cook, Blanche Wiesen, *Eleanor Roosevelt* (New York: Viking Press, 1999).

Cooper, John Milton, Jr., ed., *Causes and Consequences of World War I* (New York: Quadrangle Books, 1972).

Corrado, Anthony, *Creative Campaigning: PACs and the Presidential Selection Process* (Boulder, Colo.: Westview Press, 1992).

Dallek, Robert, *An Unfinished Life: John F. Kennedy, 1917–1963* (Boston: Little Brown, 2003).

Daniels, Roger, *Guarding the Golden Door: American Immigration Policy and Immigration Since 1882* (New York: Hill and Wang, 2004).

Daniels, Roger, *Prisoners Without Trial: Japanese-Americans in World War II*, rev. ed. (New York: Hill and Wang, 2004).

Davis, David Brion, *The Slave Power and the Paranoid Style* (Baton Rouge: Louisiana State University Press, 1969).

De Santis, Vincent P., *Republicans Face the Southern Question: The New Departure Years, 1877–1897* (Baltimore: Johns Hopkins University Press, 1959).

DeConde, Alexander, *The Quasi-War: The Politics and Diplomacy of the Undeclared War with France, 1797–1801* (New York: Charles Scribner's Sons, 1966).

Degler, Carl N., *Neither Black Nor White: Slavery and Race Relations in Brazil and the United States* (New York: Macmillan, 1971).

Di Palma, Giuseppe, *To Craft Democracies: An Essay on Democratic Transitions* (Berkeley: University of California Press, 1990).

DiClerico, Robert E., and James W. Davis, eds., *Choosing Our Choices: Debating the Presidential Nominating Process* (Lanham, Mary.: Rowman and Littlefield, 2000).

Dietrich, John, *The Morgenthau Plan: Soviet Influence on American Postwar Policy* (New York: Algora Publishing, 2002).

Divine, Robert A., *American Immigration Policy, 1924–1952* (New Haven: Yale University Press, 1957).

Dollard, John, *Caste and Class in a Southern Town* (New Haven: Yale University Press, 1937).

Dollard, John, Neal E. Miller, Leonard W. Doob, O. H. Mowrer, and Robert R. Sears, *Frustrations and Aggression* (New Haven: Yale Univ. Press, 1939).

Dominguez, Virginia R., *White by Definition: Social Classification in Creole Louisiana* (New Brunswick, N.J.: Rutgers University Press, 1986).

Donald, David Herbert, *An Excess of Democracy: The American Civil War and the Social Process* (Oxford: Clarendon, 1960).

Donald, David Herbert, *Lincoln Reconsidered: Essays on the Civil War Era*, 3rd ed. (New York: Vintage, 2001).

Downs, Anthony, *An Economic Theory of Democracy* (New York: Harper, 1957).

Dubose, Lou, Jan Reid, and Carl M. Cannon, *Boy Genius: Karl Rove, The Brains Behind the Remarkable Political Triumph of George W. Bush* (New York: Public Affairs, 2002).

Dyer, Richard, *White* (London: Routledge, 1997).

Dyer, Thomas G., *Theodore Roosevelt and the Idea of Race* (Baton Rouge: Louisiana University Press, 1980).

Edwards, George C., III, *Why the Electoral College is Bad for America* (New Haven: Yale University Press, 2004).

Farrell, John A., *Tip O'Neill and the Democratic Century* (Boston: Little, Brown, 2001).

Finan, Christopher M., *Alfred E. Smith: The Happy Warrior* (New York: Hill & Wang, 2002).

Fiorina, Morris P., *Culture War? The Myth of a Polarized America* (New York: Pearman Longman, 2005).

Fischer, David Hackett, *Albion's Seed: Four British Folkways in America* (New York: Oxford University Press, 1989).

Fitzpatrick, John C., *George Washington Himself: A Common Sense Biography* (Indianapolis: Bobbs Merrill Company, 1933).

Foner, Nancy, and George M. Fredrickson, eds., *Not Just Black and White: Historical and Contemporary Perspectives on Immigration, Race, and Ethnicity in the United States* (New York: Russell Sage Foundation, 2004).

Fredrickson, George M., *White Supremacy: A Comparative Study in American and South African History* (New York: Oxford University Press, 1981).

Freidel, Frank, *F. D. R. and the South* (Baton Rouge: Louisiana State University Press, 1965).

Fromm, Erich, *Escape From Freedom* (New York: Farrar & Rinehart, 1941).

Garrow, David J., *Protest at Selma: Martin Luther King, Jr., and the Voting Rights Act of 1965* (New Haven: Yale University Press, 1978).

Gellinek, Christian, *Those Damn 'Dutch': The Beginnings of German Immigration in North America During the Thirty Years War* (Frankfurt: Campus Verlag, 1996).

Gellman, Irwin F., *The Contender, Richard Nixon: The Congress Years, 1946–52* (New York: Free Press, 1999).

Gellner, Ernest, *Nationalism* (New York: New York University Press, 1997).

Gellner, Ernest, *Thought and Change* (Chicago: University of Chicago Press, 1964).

Germond, Jack W., and Jules Witcover, *Mad as Hell: Revolt at the Ballot Box, 1992* (New York: Warner Books, 1993).

Gienapp, William E., *The Origins of the Republican Party, 1852–1856* (New York: Oxford University Press, 1987).

Gillon, Steven M., *The Democrats' Dilemma: Walter F. Mondale and the Liberal Tradition* (New York: Columbia University Press, 1992).

Glazer, Nathan, and Daniel Patrick Moynihan, *Beyond the Melting Pot: The Negroes, Puerto Ricans, Jews, Italians, and Irish of New York City* (Cambridge: MIT Press, 1963).

Glazer, Nathan, and Daniel Patrick Moynihan, *Beyond the Melting Pot: The Negroes, Puerto Ricans, Jews, Italians, and Irish of New York City*, 2nd ed. (Cambridge: MIT Press, 1970).

Golden, Harry, *Only in America* (Cleveland: World Pub. Co., 1958).

Goldin, Claudia D., *Understanding the Gender Gap: An Economic History of American Women* (New York: Oxford University Press, 1990).

Goldstein, Michael L., *Guide to the 2004 Presidential Election* (Washington, D.C.: CQ Press, 2003).

Graebner, Norman A., *Empire on the Pacific: A Study in American Continental Expansion* (New York: Ronald Press Co., 1955).

Graham, Hugh Davis, *Collision Course: The Strange Convergence of Affirmative Action and Immigration Policy in America* (New York: Oxford University Press, 2002).

Graham, Hugh Davis, *The Civil Rights Era: Origins and Development of National Policy, 1960–1972* (New York: Oxford University Press, 1990).

Green, Fletcher M., *Constitutional Developments in the South Atlantic States, 1776–1880* (New York: W. W. Norton, 1966).

Green, Fletcher M., *Democracy in the Old South, and Other Essays* (Nashville, Tenn.: Vanderbilt University Press, 1969).

Green, John C., James L. Guth, Corwin E. Smith, and Lyman A. Kellstedt, eds., *Religion and the Culture Wars: Dispatches from the Front* (Lanham, Mary: Rowman & Littlefield, 1996).

Greenberg, Stanley B., *The Two Americas: Our Current Political Deadlock and How to Break It*, Rev. ed. (New York: Thomas Dunne Books, 2005).

Greenhaw, Wayne, *Elephants in the Cornfield: Ronald Reagan and the New Republican South* (New York: Macmillan, 1982).

Grofman, Bernard, *Political Gerrymandering and the Courts* (New York: Agathon, 1990).

Grofman, Bernard, *Race and Redistricting in the 1990s* (New York: Agathon, 1998).

Gross, Ken, *Ross Perot: The Man Behind the Myth* (New York: Random House, 1992).

Guinsburg, Thomas N., *The Pursuit of Isolationism in the United States Senate from Versailles to Pearl Harbor* (New York: Garland Publisher, 1982).

Gusfield, Joseph R., *Symbolic Crusade: Status Politics and the American Temperance Movement* (Urbana: University of Illinois Press, 1963).

Guterl, Matthew, *The Color of Race in America, 1900–1940* (Cambridge: Harvard University Press, 2001).

Guth, James L., and John C. Green, ed., *The Bible and the Ballot Box: Religion and Politics in the 1988 Election* (Boulder, Colo.: Westview Press, 1991).

Hale, Grace Elizabeth, *Making Whiteness: The Culture of Segregation in the South, 1890–1940* (New York: Pantheon Press, 1998).

Harris, John F., *The Survivor: Bill Clinton in the White House* (New York: Random House, 2005).

Hasen, Richard L., *The Supreme Court and Election Law: Judging Equality from Baker v. Carr to Bush v. Gore* (New York: New York University Press, 2003).

Hayward, Steven F., *The Age of Reagan: The Fall of the Old Liberal Order, 1964–1980* (Roseville, Calif: Forum, 2001).

Higham, John, *Strangers in the Land: Patterns of American Nativism, 1870-1925* (New Brunswick, N.J.: Rutgers University Press, 1955).

Hine, Darlene Clark, *Black Victory: The Rise and Fall of the White Primary in Texas*, new ed. (Columbia, Mour.: University of Missouri Press, 2003).

Hirshson, Stanley P., *Farewell to the Bloody Shirt: Northern Republicans and the Southern Negro, 1873–1893* (Bloomington: Indiana University Press, 1962).

Hofstadter, Richard, *The Age of Reform, From Bryan to F.D.R* (New York: Alfred A. Knopf, 1960).

Hofstra, Warren R., ed., *George Washington and the Virginia Backcountry* (Madison, Wisc.: Madison House, 1998).

Holt, Michael F., *The Rise and Fall of the Whig Party: Jacksonian Politics and the Onset of the Civil War* (New York: Oxford University Press, 1999).

Horsman, Reginald, *Race and Manifest Destiny: The Origins of American Racial Anglo-Saxonism* (Cambridge: Harvard University Press, 1981).

Hough, Jerry F., *The Logic of Economic Reform in Russia* (Washington, D.C.: Brookings Institution, 2001).

Hough, Jerry F., *The Struggle for the Third World: Soviet Debates and American Options* (Washington, D.C.: Brookings Institution, 1986).

Hunter, James Davison, *Evangelicalism: The Coming Generation* (Chicago: University of Chicago Press, 1987).

Hutchinson, Edward P., *Legislative History of American Immigration Policy, 1798-1965* (Philadelphia: University of Pennsylvania Press, 1981).

Ignatiev, Noel, *How the Irish Became White* (New York: Routledge, 1995).

Inglehart, Ronald, *The Silent Revolution: Changing Values and Political Styles Among Western Publics* (Princeton: Princeton University Press, 1977).

Jacobson, Matthew F., *Special Sorrows: The Diasporic Imagination of Irish, Polish, and Jewish Immigrants in the United States* (Cambridge: Harvard University Press, 1995).

Jacobson, Matthew F., *Whiteness of a Different Color: European Immigrants and the Alchemy of Race* (Cambridge: Harvard University Press, 1998).

Jelen, Ted G., ed., *Ross for Boss: The Perot Phenomenon and Beyond* (Albany: State University of New York Press, 2001).

Jensen, Richard J., *The Winning of the Midwest: Social and Political Conflict, 1888-1896* (Chicago: University of Chicago Press, 1971).

Katznelson, Ira, *When Affirmative Action was White: An Untold History of Racial Inequality in Twentieth-Century America* (New York: W. W. Norton, 2005).

Kelley, Robert L., *The Cultural Pattern in American Politics: The First Century* (New York: Alfred A. Knopf, 1979).

Kennedy, David M., *Over Here: The First World War and American Society* (New York: Oxford University Press, 1980).

Kennedy, Paul M., *The Rise of the Anglo-German Antagonism, 1860-1914* (London: Allen & Unwin, 1980).

Key, V. O. Jr., *The Responsible Electorate: Rationality in Presidential Voting, 1936-1960* (Cambridge: Harvard University Press, 1966).

Key, V. O., Jr., *Southern Politics in State and Nation* (New York: Alfred A. Knopf, 1949).

Keyssar, Alexander, *The Right to Vote: The Contested History of Democracy in the United States* (New York: Basic Books, 2000).

King, Desmond S., *Making Americans: Immigration, Race, and the Origins of the Diverse Democracy* (Cambridge: Harvard University Press, 2000).

Kleppner, Paul, *The Third Electoral System, 1853-1892: Parties, Voters, and Political Cultures* (Chapel Hill: University of North Carolina Press, 1979).

Kotlowski, Dean J., *Nixon's Civil Rights: Politics, Principle, and Policy* (Cambridge: Harvard University Press, 2001).

Kousser, J. Morgan, *The Shaping of Southern Politics: Suffrage Restriction and the Establishment of the One-Party South, 1880-1910* (New Haven: Yale University Press, 1974).

Ladd, Everett Carll, Jr., with Charles D. Hadley, *Transformations of the American Party System: Political Coalitions from the New Deal to the 1970s* (New York: W. W. Norton & Company, Inc., 1975).

Langer, William L., and S. Everett Gleason, *The Undeclared War, 1940-1941* (New York: Harper, 1953).

Lasswell, Harold, *Psychopathology and Politics* (Chicago: University of Chicago Press, 1930).

Lawson, Steven F., *Black Ballots: Voting Rights in the South, 1944–1969* (New York: Columbia University Press, 1976).

Lazarsfeld, Paul F., Bernard Berelson, and Hazel Gaudel, *The People's Choice: How the Voter Makes Up His Mind in a Presidential Campaign* (New York: Duell, Sloan, and Pearce, 1944).

Leffler, Melvyn P., *The Elusive Quest: America's Pursuit of European Stability and French Security, 1919-1933* (Chapel Hill: University of North Carolina Press, 1979).

Leuchtenburg, William E., *The Supreme Court Reborn: The Constitutional Revolution in the Age of Roosevelt* (New York: Oxford University Press, 1995).

Lewis, Sinclair, *Elmer Gantry* (New York: Harcourt, Brace, and Co., 1927).

Lieberman, Robert, *Shifting the Color Line: Race and the American Welfare State* (Cambridge: Harvard University Press, 1998).

Link, Arthur S., *Wilson: Confusions and Crises, 1915–1916* (Princeton: Princeton University Press, 1954).

Link, Arthur S., *Woodrow Wilson and the Progressive Era 1910-1917* (New York: Harper, 1954).

Lippmann, Walter, *Interpretations, 1931–1932* (New York: Macmillan Co., 1932).

Lipset, Seymour Martin, ed., *Party Coalitions in the 1980s* (San Francisco: Institute for Contemporary Studies, 1981).

Lipset, Seymour Martin, and Earl Raab, *Politics of Unreason: Right-Wing Extremism in America, 1790-1977*, 2nd ed., (Chicago: University of Chicago Press, 1978).

Lowell, A. Lawrence, *The Government of England*, new ed. (New York, Macmillan, 1912).

Lubell, Samuel, *The Future of American Politics* (New York: Harper, 1952).

Luebke, Frederick C., *Bonds of Loyalty: German-Americans and World War I* (DeKalb, Ill.: Northern Illinois Press, 1974).

MacDougall, Hugh A., *Racial Myth in English History: Trojans, Teutons, and Anglo-Saxons* (Hanover, N. H.: University Press of New England, 1982).

Maraniss, David, *First in His Class: A Biography of Bill Clinton* (New York: Simon & Schuster, 1995).

Marano, Richard Michael, *Vote Your Conscience: The Last Campaign of George McGovern* (Westport, Conn.: Praeger, 2003).

Martin, John Bartlow, *Adlai Stevenson of Illinois: The Life of Adlai E. Stevenson* (Garden City, N.Y.: Doubleday & Co., 1976).

Marx, Anthony W., *Making Race and Nation: A Comparison of South Africa, the United States, and Brazil* (Cambridge: Cambridge University Press, 1998).

Mason, Robert, *Richard Nixon and the Quest for a New Majority* (Chapel Hill: University of North Carolina, 2004).

Massicotte, Louis, Andrei Blais, and Antoine Yoshinaka, *Establishing the Rules of the Game: Election Laws in Democracies* (Toronto: University of Toronto Press, 2004).

May, Ernest R., *The World War and American Isolation, 1914-1917* (Cambridge: Harvard University Press, 1959).

Mayer, William G.,Jr., *In Pursuit of the White House: How We Choose Our Presidential Nominees* (New York: Chatham House, 1996).

Mayhew, David R., *Placing Parties in American Politics: Organization, Electoral Settings, and Government Activity in the Twentieth Century* (Princeton: Princeton University Press, 1986).

McClelland, J. S., *The Crowd and the Mob: From Plato to Canetti* (London: Unwin Hyman, 1989).

McGerr, Michael E., *The Decline of Popular Politics: The American North, 1865–1928* (New York: Oxford University Press, 1986).

McGerr, Michael, *A Fierce Discontent: The Rise and Fall of the Progressive Movement in America, 1870–1920* (New York: Free Press, 2003).

McKeever, Porter, *Adlai Stevenson: His Life and Legacy* (New York: William Morrow, 1989).

Merritt, Richard L., *Symbols of American Community, 1735–1775* (New Haven: Yale University Press, 1966).

Mershon, Sherie, and Steven Schlossman, *Foxholes & Color Lines: Desegregating the U.S. Armed Forces* (Baltimore: Johns Hopkins University Press, 1998).

Merton, Robert F., *Social Theory and Social Structure: Toward The Codification of Theory and Research* (Glencoe, Ill.: Free Press, 1949).

Merzer, Martin, *The Miami Herald Report: Democracy Held Hostage* (New York: St. Martin's Press, 2001).

Miller, John C., *Crisis in Freedom: The Alien and Sedition Acts* (Boston: Little, Brown, 1951).

Miller, Richard L., *Truman: The Rise to Power* (New York: McGraw-Hill, 1986).

Miller, Russell, *Bunny: The Real Story of Playboy* (New York: Holt, Rinehart, and Winston, 1984).

Miller, William J., *Henry Cabot Lodge: A Biography* (New York: James H. Heineman, 1967).

Montagu, Ashley, *Man's Most Dangerous Myth: The Fallacy of Race* (New York: Columbia University Press, 1942).

Myrdal, Gunner, *An American Dilemma: The Negro Problem and Modern Democracy* (New York: Harper & Brothers, 1944).

Noble, Charles, *Liberalism at Work: The Rise and Fall of OSHA* (Philadelphia: Temple University Press, 1986).

Nobles, Melissa, *Shades of Citizenship: Race and the Census in Modern Politics* (Stanford: Stanford University Press, 2000).

Notter, Harley, *The Origins of the Foreign Policy of Woodrow Wilson* (Baltimore: Johns Hopkins University Press, 1937).

O'Grady, Joseph P., ed., *The Immigrants' Influence on Wilson's Peace Policies* (Lexington: University of Kentucky Press, 1967).

O'Toole, Patricia, *When Trumpets Call: Theodore Roosevelt After the White House* (New York: Simon & Schuster, 2005).

Olson, Mancur, Jr., *The Logic of Collective Action: Public Goods and the Theory of Groups* (Cambridge: Harvard University Press, 1965).

Park, Robert E., and Herbert A. Miller, *Old World Traits Transplanted* (New York: Harper and Brothers, 1921).

Perman, Michael, *Struggle for Mastery: Disenfranchisement in the South, 1888–1908* (Chapel Hill: University of North Carolina Press, 2001).

Peterson, H. C., and Gilbert C. Fite, *Opponents of War, 1917–1918* (Madison: University of Wisconsin Press, 1957).

Phillips, Kevin P., *Post-Conservative America: People, Politics, and Ideology in a Time of Crisis* (New York: Random House, 1982).

Phillips, Kevin P., *The Emerging Republican Majority* (New Rochelle, N.Y.: Arlington House, 1969).

Piven, Frances Fox, and Richard A. Cloward, *Why Americans Still Don't Vote and Why Politicians Want it That Way* (Boston: Beacon, 2000).

Polsby, Nelson W., *Consequences of Party Reform* (New York: Oxford University Press, 1983).

Posner, Gerald, *Citizen Perot: His Life and Times* (New York: Random House, 1996).

Pruessen, Ronald W., *John Foster Dulles: The Road to Power* (New York: Free Press, 1982).

Rabinowitz, Howard N., ed, *Race, Ethnicity, and Urbanization: Selected Essays* (Columbia: University of Missouri Press, 1994).

Rae, Nicol, *The Decline and Fall of the Liberal Republicans: From 1952 to the Present* (New York: Oxford University Press, 1989).

Reichley, A. James, ed., *Elections American Style* (Washington, D.C.: Brookings Institution, 1987).

Reichley, James, *Conservatives in an Age of Change: The Nixon and Ford Administrations* (Washington, D.C.: Brookings Institution, 1981).

Reichmann, Eberhard, LaVern J. Rippley, and Jorg Nagler, eds., *Emigration and Settlement Patterns of German Communities in North America* (Indianapolis: Max Kade German-American Center, 1995).

Reimers, David M., *Still the Open Door: The Third World Comes to America* (New York: Columbia University Press, 1985).

Roosevelt, Mrs. Franklin, *It's Up to the Women* (New York: Frederick A. Stokes, 1933).

Rosenfeld, Richard N., *American Aurora* (New York: St. Martin's Press, 1997).

Safire, William, *Safire's New Political Dictionary: The Definitive Guide to the New Language of Politics* (New York: Random House, 1993).

Saveth, Edward N, *American Historians and European Immigrants, 1875–1925* (New York: Columbia University Press, 1948).

Scammon, Richard M., and Ben J. Wattenberg, *The Real Majority* (New York: Coward McCann, 1970). The second edition was issued by Primus Publishers of New York in 1992.

Schantz, Harvey L., *Politics in an Era of Divided Government: Elections and Governance in the Second Clinton Administration* (New York: Routledge, 2001).

Schapsmeier, Edward L. and Frederic H., *Gerald R. Ford's Date with Destiny: A Political Biography* (New York: Peter Lang, 1989).

Schattschneider, E. E., *Party Government* (New York: Farrar & Rinehart, 1942).

Schattschneider, E. E., *The Semisovereign People: A Realist's View of Democracy in America* (New York: Holt, Rinehart, and Winston, 1960).

Scheiber, Harry N., *The Wilson Administration and Civil Liberties, 1917–1921* (Ithaca, N.Y.: Cornell University Press, 1960).

Schenk, Hans G., *The Mind of the European Romantics: An Essay in Cultural History* (London: Constable, 1966).

Schlesinger, Arthur Jr., *The Age of Jackson* (Boston: Little, Brown, 1945).

Schlesinger, Arthur, Jr., *A Thousand Days: John F. Kennedy in the White House* (Boston: Houghton Mifflin, 1965).

Schlesinger, Arthur, Jr., ed., *History of American Presidential Elections, 1789–1968* (New York: Chelsea House Publishers, 1971).

Shanks, Cheryl, *Immigration and the Politics of American Sovereignty, 1890-1990* (Ann Arbor: University of Michigan Press, 2001).

Shirley, Craig, *Reagan's Revolution: The Untold Story of the Campaign That Started It All* (Nashville, Tenn.: Nelson Current, 2005).

Shogan, Robert, *The Fate of the Union: America's Rocky Road to Political Stalemate* (Boulder, Colo.: Westview Press, 1998).

Silbey, Joel H., ed., *National Development and Sectional Crisis, 1815–1860* (New York: Random House, 1970).

Siney, Marion C., *The Allied Blockade of Germany, 1914–1916* (Ann Arbor: University of Michigan Press, 1957).

Skocpol, Theda, *Boomerang: Clinton's Health Security Effort and the Turn Against Government in U.S. Politics* (New York: W. W. Norton, 1996).

Skocpol, Theda, *The Missing Middle: Working Families and the Future of American Social Policy* (New York: W. W. Norton, 2000).

Skrentny, John David, *The Ironies of Affirmative Action: Politics, Culture, and Justice in America* (Chicago: University of Chicago Press, 1996).

Smith, James M., *Freedom's Fetters: The Alien and Sedition Laws and American Civil Liberties* (Ithaca, N.Y.: Cornell University Press, 1956).

Stagg, J. C. A., *Mr. Madison's War of 1812: Politics, Diplomacy, and Warfare in the Early American Republic, 1783–1830* (Princeton: Princeton University Press, 1983).

Stave, Bruce M., and Sondra Astor Stave, ed., *Urban Bosses, Machines, and Progressive Reformers* (Lexington, Mass.: Heath, 1971).

Stiglitz, Joseph E., *Globalization and Its Discontents* (New York: W. W. Norton, 2002).

Stonecash, Jeffrey M., *Class and Party in American Politics* (Boulder, Colo.: Westview, 2000).

Taylor, Gary, *Buying Whiteness: Race, Culture, and Identity from Columbus to Hip-Hop* (New York: Palgrave Macmillan, 2005).

Teixeira, Ruy A., *The Disappearing American Voter* (Washington, D.C.: The Brookings Institution, 1992).

Thompson, Jake H., *Bob Dole: The Republicans' Man for All Seasons*, updated ed. (New York: Donald I Fine, Inc., 1996).

Tichenor, Daniel J., *Dividing Lines: The Politics of Immigration Control in America* (Princeton: Princeton University Press, 2002).

Tilly, Charles, ed., *The Formation of Nation States in Western Europe* (Princeton: Princeton University Press, 1975).

Truman, David B., *The Governmental Process: Political Interests and Public Opinion* (New York: Alfred A. Knopf, 1951).

Tugwell, Rexford G., *The Democratic Roosevelt: A Biography of Franklin D. Roosevelt* (Garden City, N.Y.: Doubleday, 1957).

Tullock, Gordon, ed., *Further Explorations in the Theory of Anarchy* (Blacksburg, Va.: University Publications, 1974).

Turner, Frederick Jackson, *The Significance of Sections in American History* (New York: Henry Holt and Company, 1932).

Ueda, Reed, *Postwar Immigrant America: A Social History* (Boston: Bedford Books, 1994).

Wald, Kenneth D., *Religion and Politics in the United States*, 4th ed. (Lanham, Mary: Rowman and Littlefield Publishers, 2003).

Walker, Martin, *The President We Deserve. Bill Clinton, His Rise, Faults, and Comebacks* (New York: Crown Publishers, 1996).

Wang, Xi, *The Trial of Democracy: Black Suffrage and Northern Republicans, 1860–1910* (Athens: University of Georgia Press, 1997).

Ware, Vron, and Les Back, *Out of Whiteness: Color, Politics, and Culture* (Chicago: University of Chicago Press, 2002).

Wattenberg, Ben J., *Values Matter Most: How Democrats or Republicans or a Third Party Can Win and Renew the American Way of Life* (New York: Free Press, 1995).

Weisberg, Herbert, and Clyde Wilcox, *Models of Voting in Presidential Elections: The U.S. 2000 Election* (Stanford: Stanford University Press, 2004).

Weiss, Nancy J., *Farewell to the Party of Lincoln: Black Politics in the Age of FDR* (Princeton: Princeton University Press, 1983).

White, Theodore H., *The Making of the President, 1960* (New York: Atheneum Publishers, 1961).

Wilentz, Sean, *The Rise of American Democracy: Jefferson to Lincoln* (New York: W. W. Norton, 2005).

Williams, T. Harry, *Huey Long* (New York: Alfred A. Knopf, 1969).

Williamson, Chilton, *American Suffrage: From Property to Democracy, 1760–1860* (Princeton: Princeton University Press, 1960).

Williamson, Joel, *New People: Miscegenation and Mulattoes in the United States* (New York: Free Press, 1980).

Williamson, Joel, *The Crucible of Race: Black/White Relations in the American South Since Emancipation* (New York: Oxford University Press, 1984).

Wills, Garry, *Nixon Agonistes: The Crisis of the Self-Made Man* (Boston: Houghton Mifflin, 1969).

Wilson, Hugh R., Jr., *A Career Diplomat, The Third Chapter: The Third Reich* (New York: Vantage Press, 1961).

Wilson, James Q., *The Amateur Democrat: Club Politics in Three Cities* (Chicago: The University of Chicago Press, 1962).

Wilson, Woodrow, *A History of the American People* (New York: Harper & Brothers, 1902).

Wolfinger, Raymond E., and Steven J. Rosenstone, *Who Votes?* (New Haven: Yale University Press, 1980).

Woodward, Bob, *Bush At War* (New York: Simon & Schuster, 2002).

Woodward, Bob, *The Agenda: Inside the Clinton White House* (New York: Simon & Schuster, 1994).

Woodward, C. Vann, *Origins of the New South 1877–1913* (Baton Rouge: Louisiana State University Press, 1951).

Woodward, C. Vann, *The Strange Career of Jim Crow*, 3rd rev ed. (New York: Oxford University Press, 1974).

Wyman, Mark, *DP: Europe's Displaced Persons, 1945–1951* (Philadelphia: Balch Institute Press, 1988).

UNPUBLISHED DOCTORAL DISSERTATIONS

Freeman, Don M., "Religion and Southern Politics: A Study of the Political Behavior of Southern White Protestants," (PhD dissertation, University of North Carolina, 1964).

Jolly, Seth, "A Europe of Regions: Regional Integration, Sub-National Mobilization, and the Optimal Size of Nations," (PhD dissertation, Duke University, 2006).

Koed, Betty K., "The Politics of Reform: Policymakers and Immigration Act of 1965," (PhD dissertation, University of California at Santa Barbara, 1999).

Tingley, Donald F., "The Rise of Racialistic Thinking in the United States in the Nineteenth Century" (PhD dissertation, University of Illinois, 1952).

Wagner, Stephen Thomas, "The Lingering Death of the National Quota System: Immigration Policy 1952-1965" (PhD dissertation, Harvard University, 1986).

ARTICLES

Abramowitz, Alan I., "It's Abortion, Stupid: Policy Voting in the 1992 Presidential Election," *The Journal of Politics*, vol. 57, no. 1 (February 1995), pp. 176–186.

App, Austin J., "The Germans," in Joseph P. O'Grady, ed. *The Immigrants' Influence on Wilson's Peace Policies* (Lexington: University of Kentucky Press, 1967), pp. 30-55.

Barone, Michael, "Introduction," *The Almanac of American Politics, 2006* (Washington, D.C.: National Journal, 2005), pp. 21–36.

Buell, Emmett H. Jr., "The Invisible Primary", in William G. Mayer, Jr., ed. *In Pursuit of the White House: How We Choose Our Presidential Nominees* (New York: Chatham House, 1996), pp. 1-43.

Buell, Emmett H., Jr., "Some Things are Predictable: Nominating Dole, Clinton, and Perot," in Harvey L. Schantz, ed., *Politics in an Era of Divided Government: Elections and Governance in the Second Clinton Administration* (New York: Routledge, 2001), pp. 1-39.

Burner, David, "Election of 1924," in Arthur M. Schlesinger, Jr., ed., *History of American Presidential Elections* (New York: Chelsea House, 1971), vol. 3, pp. 2459-2581.

Burnham, Walter Dean, "The Turnout Problem," in A. James Reichley, ed., *Elections American Style* (Washington, D.C.: Brookings Institution, 1987), pp. 97-133.

Ceaser, James W. "Improving the Nominating Process," in A. James Reichley, ed., *Elections American Style* (Washington, D.C.: Brookings Institution, 1987), pp. 29-51.

Cooper, John Milton, Jr., "World War I: European Origins and American Intervention," *The Virginia Quarterly Review*, vol. 56, no. 1 (Winter 1980), pp. 1-18.

Cooper, John Milton, Jr., "World War in American Historical Writing," in John Milton Cooper, Jr., ed., *Causes and Consequences of World War I* (New York: Quadrangle Books, 1972), pp. 3-44.

Davis, James W., "The Case Against the Current Primary Centered System," in Robert E. DiClerico and James W. Davis, eds., *Choosing Our Choices: Debating the Presidential Nominating Process* (Lanham, Mary.: Rowman and Littlefield, 2000), pp. 27-50.

DiClerico, Robert E., "Evolution of the Presidential Nominating Process," in Robert E. DiClerico and James W. Davis, eds., *Choosing Our Choices: Debating the Presidential Nominating Process* (Lanham, Mary.: Rowman and Littlefield, 2000), pp.3-25.

Espiritu, Yen Le, "Asian-American Panethnicity: Contemporary National and Transnational Possibilities," in Nancy Foner and George M. Frederickson, eds., *Not*

Just Black and White: Historical and Contemporary Perspective on Immigration, Race, and Ethnicity in the United States (New York: Russell Sage Foundation, 2004), pp. 217–234.

Fogleman, Aaron S., "Immigration, German Immigration, and 18th-Century America," in Eberhard Reichmann, LaVern J. Rippley, and Jorg Nagler, eds., *Emigration and Settlement Patterns of German Communities in North America* (Indianapolis: Max Kade German-American Center, 1995), pp. 3-22.

Green, John C., James L. Guth, and Cleveland R. Fraser, "Apostles and Apostates: Religion and Politics Among Party Activists," in James L. Guth and John C. Green, eds., *The Bible and the Ballot Box: Religion and Politics in the 1988 Election* (Boulder, Colo.: Westview Press, 1991), pp. 113-136.

Hattan, Victoria, "Ethnicity: An American Genealogy," in Nancy Foner and George M. Frederickson, eds. *Not Just Black and White: Historical and Contemporary Perspective on Immigration, Race, and Ethnicity in the United States* (New York: Russell Sage Foundation, 2004), pp. 42-60. .

Harris, Carl V., "Right Fork or Left Fork: The Section–Party Alignment of Southern Democrats in Congress, 1873–1897," *The Journal of Southern History*, vol. XLII, no. 4 (November 1976), pp. 471–508.

Hofstra, Warren R., "A Parcel of Barbarian's and an Uncooth Set of People:' Settlers and Settlements of the Shenandoah Valley," in Warren R. Hofstra, ed., *George Washington and the Virginia Backcountry* (Madison, Wisc.: Madison House, 1998), pp. 87-114.

Itzigson, John, "The Formation of Latino and Latina Panethnic Identity," in Nancy Foner and George M. Frederickson, eds., *Not Just Black and White: Historical and Contemporary Perspective on Immigration, Race, and Ethnicity in the United States* (New York: Russell Sage Foundation, 2004), pp. 197–216.

Kellstedt, Lyman A., John C. Green, James L. Guth, and Corwin E. Smidt, "Religious Voting Blocs in the 1992 Election: The Year of the Evangelical?," in John C. Green, James L. Guth, Corwin E. Smith, and Lyman A. Kellstedt, eds., *Religion and the Culture Wars: Dispatches from the Front* (Lanham, Mary.: Rowman & Littlefield, 1996), pp. 267-290.

Ladd, Everett Carll, "The Brittle Mandate: Electoral Dealignment and the 1980 Presidential Election," *Political Science Quarterly*, vol. 96, no. 2 (Spring 1981), pp. 1-25.

Lipset, Seymour Martin, "Party Coalitions and the 1980 Election," in Seymour Martin Lipset, ed., *Party Coalitions in the 1980s* (San Francisco: Institute for Contemporary Studies, 1981), pp. 15-46.

Lipset, Seymour Martin, and Earl Raab, "The Election and the Evangelicals," *Commentary*, vol. 71, no. 3 (March 1981), pp. 25-31.

McCoy, Donald R., "Election of 1920," in Arthur M. Schlesinger, Jr., ed., *History of American Presidential Elections* (New York: Chelsea House, 1971), vol. 3, pp. 2349-2456.

McDonald, Forrest, and Ellen Shapiro McDonald, "The Ethnic Origins of the American People, 1980," *William and Mary Quarterly*, vol. XXXVII, no. 2 (April 1980), pp. 177-199.

McDonald, Michael, and Samuel L. Popkin, "The Myth of the Vanishing Voter," *American Political Science Review*, vol. 95, no. 4 (December 2001), pp. 963–974.

"New Day a'coming in the South," *Time*, May 31, 1971, pp. 14–20.

Nichols, Roy F., "The Kansas–Nebraska Act: A Century of Historiography," in Joel H. Silbey, ed., *National Development and Sectional Crisis, 1815–1860* (New York: Random House, 1970), pp. 195-218.

Norden, Kenneth D., "The Television Candidate: H. Ross Perot's 1992 and 1996 Presidential Races," in Ted G. Jelen, ed., *Ross for Boss: The Perot Phenomenon and Beyond* (Albany: State University of New York Press, 2001), pp. 15-34.

Norpoth, Helmut, "Bush v. Gore: The Recount of the Economic Voting," in Herbert F. Weisberg and Clyde Wilcox, eds., *Models of Voting in Presidential Elections: The U.S. 2000 Election* (Stanford: Stanford University Press, 2004), pp. 49–64.

O'Grady, Joseph P., "The Irish," in Joseph P. O'Grady, ed., *The Immigrants' Influence on Wilson's Peace Policies* (Lexington: University of Kentucky Press, 1967), pp. 56-84.

Olson, Mancur, "The Logic of Collective Action in Soviet-Type Societies," *Journal of Soviet Nationalities*, vol. 1, no. 2 (1990), pp. 8-33.

Prewitt, Kenneth, "The Census Counts, the Census Classifies," in Nancy Foner and George M. Fredrickson, eds., *Not Just Black and White: Historical and Contemporary Perspectives on Immigration, Race, and Ethnicity in the United States* (New York: Russell Sage Foundation, 2004), pp. 145-164.

Ranney, Austin, "Changing the Rules of the Nominating Game," in James D. Barber, ed., *Choosing the President* (Englewood Cliffs, N.J.: Prentice-Hall, 1974), pp. 71-93.

Roeber, A. G., "'The Origin of Whatever is Not English Among Us': The Dutch-Speaking and the German-Speaking People of Colonial British America," in Bernard Bailyn and Philip D. Morgan, eds., *Strangers within the Realm: Cultural Margins of the First British Empire* (Chapel Hill: University of North Carolina Press, 1991), pp. 220-283.

Scheiber, Noam, "Spent Force," *The New Republic*, October 10, 2005, p. 6.

Stevenson, Adlai, "My Faith in Democratic Capitalism," *Fortune*, October 1955, pp. 126-127, 156-168.

The 'Catholic Vote'— A Kennedy Staff Analysis," *U.S. News & World Report*, vol. XLIX, no. 5 (August 1, 1960), pp. 68-72.

Tilly, Charles, "Reflections on the History of European State Making," in Charles Tilly, ed., *The Formation of Nation States in Western Europe* (Princeton: Princeton University Press, 1975), pp. 3-83.

Weingast, Barry R., "Political Stability and Civil War: Institutions, Commitment and American Democracy," in Robert Bates, ed., *Analytic Narratives* (Princeton: Princeton University Press, 1999), pp. 148-193.

Wilson, James Q., "Reagan and the Republican Revival," *Commentary*, vol. 70, no. 4 (October 1980), pp. 25-32.

INDEX

P

Q

R

Printed in the United States
60088LVS00004B/64-90